D0098840

WITHDRAWN

WORN, SOILED, OBSOLETE

B BRYANT LO Dea

Dearborn, Mary V.
Queen of Bohemia : the
life of Louise Bryant /
FRSN 1030407355

FRESNO COUNTY FREE LIBRARY

Branches throughout the County to Serve You
You may return Library Materials to any Branch Library

PLEASE NOTE DATE DUE

Overdue charges will be assessed, ask at your
branch library. LOST or DAMAGED library materials
must be paid for

DEMCO

Queen of Bohemia

BY MARY V. DEARBORN

Pocahontas's Daughters: Gender and Ethnicity in American Culture

Love in the Promised Land: John Dewey and Anzia Yezierska

The Happiest Man Alive: A Biography of Henry Miller

Queen of Bohemia: The Life of Louise Bryant

Queen of
Bohemia

The Life of LOUISE BRYANT

Mary V. Dearborn

Houghton Mifflin Company   BOSTON   NEW YORK   1996

Copyright © 1996 by Mary V. Dearborn
All rights reserved

For information about permission to reproduce selections from this book,
write to Permissions, Houghton Mifflin Company, 215 Park Avenue South,
New York, New York 10003.

For information about this and other Houghton Mifflin multimedia trade
and reference products, visit The Bookstore at Houghton Mifflin on the
World Wide Web at http://www.hmco.com/trade/.

Library of Congress Cataloging-in-Publication Data
Dearborn, Mary V.
    Queen of Bohemia : the life of Louise Bryant / Mary V. Dearborn
        p.   cm.
    Includes bibliographical references and index.
    ISBN: 0-395-68396-3
    1. Bryant, Louise 1885–1936. 2. Women communists — United States — Biography.
3. Women journalists — United States — Biography. 4. Women revolutionaries — United
States — Biography. 5. Bohemianism — United States — History — 20th century. I. Title.
HX84.B73D43   1996
070'.92 — dc20   95-37607
[B]   CIP

Printed in the United States of America

MP 10 9 8 7 6 5 4 3 2 1

Book design by Melodie Wertelet

CREDITS

Permission to print the following is gratefully acknowledged:
    For quotations from the correspondence of Louise Bryant to Frank Walsh (Francis P. Walsh
Papers): Rare Books and Manuscripts Division, The New York Public Library, Astor, Lenox and
Tilden Foundations.
    For quotations from the correspondence between Louise Bryant and Claude McKay (James
Weldon Johnson Collection): Yale Collection of American Literature, Beinecke Rare Book and
Manuscript Library, Yale University.
    For quotations from the correspondence of Louise Bryant and John Reed, as well as other un-
published material: Houghton Library, Harvard University.
    For quotations from the correspondence between Louise Bryant and John and Marguerite
Storrs (John Henry Bradley Storrs papers, 1847-1987); from the correspondence between Louise
Bryant and Andrew Dasburg (Andrew Dasburg and Grace Mott Johnson papers, 1859-1969); from
the correspondence of Marsden Hartley (Marsden Hartley papers, 1900-1967, owned and microfilmed by the Beinecke Library, Yale University): Archives of American Art.
    For quotations from the correspondence of Virginia Gardner, as well as other unpublished ma-
terial: Virginia Gardner papers, Tamiment Institute Library, New York University.
    For quotations from correspondence between Louise Bryant and Andrew Dasburg (Andrew
Dasburg papers); quotations from correspondence between Louise Bryant and Granville Hicks
and unpublished material by Louise Bryant (Granville Hicks papers): Syracuse University Library,
Department of Special Collections.
    For quotations from correspondence between Louise Bryant and Upton Sinclair (Upton Sin-
clair Collection): Lilly Library, Indiana University, Bloomington, Indiana.

For Eric

Contents

List of Illustrations

The artist John Storrs. He and his wife, Marguerite, were Louise's closest friends during her years with Bullitt. *(John Storrs Papers, Archives of American Art, Smithsonian Institution)*

Lincoln Steffens, once a mentor of Jack Reed, became a close friend of Louise and Bill during the 1920s. *(The Bettmann Archives)*

Louise as a rich man's wife *(UPI/Bettmann)*

Louise acted as a mentor and patron of the young writer Claude McKay, even as she grew seriously ill. *(The Beinecke Rare Book and Manuscript Library, Yale University)*

The artist Gwen Le Gallienne, whom Bullitt named in his 1930 divorce suit against Louise *(UPI/Bettmann)*

A mannish-looking Louise, circa 1930. She was suffering the ravages of Dercum's disease and the ailments that accompanied it. *(By permission of the Houghton Library, Harvard University)*

Bullitt with Anne in 1933, after the divorce. Louise claimed she never saw her daughter again. *(UPI/Bettmann)*

Anne Bullitt in 1934, age ten *(UPI/Bettmann)*

Queen of Bohemia

Prelude: Paris, 1933

She is living in a seventh-floor studio adjoining a nunnery in the rue d'Assas, a studio she herself describes as "absurd." The rent is paid directly to the concierge by her wealthy third husband, William C. Bullitt — he does not trust her with the money. Bullitt is at this moment traveling by train across Europe to take up his new post as ambassador to the Soviet Union. She cannot afford electricity, so candles light the small room, casting dark shadows on the exotic trappings she has gathered from all over the world: icons, silk fans, bronze statuettes, Japanese boxes, and chunks of wet clay covered by Turkish towels.

Louise Bryant — she has kept her name, a name that was not really hers to begin with, through three marriages — is forty-seven, though she claims to be thirty-nine. Once a beautiful young woman, and well aware of the stock in trade her youth and beauty represented, she began shaving years off her age at the age of twenty, when she passed for eighteen. In later years the ploy has backfired, for she cannot possibly be under forty, but she has been caught up by her earlier lies. Her eyes are still beautiful — sometimes a deep violet-blue, at other times a luminous blue-gray. Her hair, dyed, is glossy and black. Her clothes are exotic; she still treasures the sables and embroidered boots she bought for a song in Russia with John Reed in 1918. On one hand she wears a brilliant star sapphire, a gift from Bullitt, that has been in and out of the pawnshop. From a distance she is striking, indeed beautiful. But up close her features look coarsened and dulled; her body is lumpish in some places, emaciated in others.

This particular morning she reaches for a bottle of *vin ordinaire* and a train schedule. She has a rare and incurable disease (the source of her strange body shape) that has led her to drink on an almost daily basis for the last four years. Her physical troubles aside, she has found solace in drink, after a brutal divorce from Bullitt in 1930 in which she was denied custody of her daughter, Anne, born in 1924. She has barely seen Anne in the last five years. A good deal of her time is given over to trying to discover news of her daughter: writing to ex-nannies, neighbors of Bullitt's at his country estate in Massachusetts, State Department officials, anyone who can help.

A new meaning has come into her life recently, however, and with it hope that she might receive some news of Anne on a regular basis. In one corner of her studio stand several large trunks, trunks Bullitt shipped to her in great disarray after much pleading on her part and, finally, intervention by old labor lawyer friends. They contain all her personal papers — letters from luminaries like Upton Sinclair, Jane Addams, Clarence Darrow, Emma Goldman, and equally prized letters from old friends Sara Bard Field and Clara Wold and ex-lovers Andrew Dasburg and Frank Walsh. But she has finally accepted, tiredly, the judgment of others that what is of "real" value in the trunks are the papers of her second husband, the revolutionary journalist John Reed.

Some people from Harvard, Reed's alma mater, have been making discreet inquiries about these papers; it seems a biography is in the works. Louise herself has tried such a project several times; she is fearful that her husband's life and work will be distorted by those who would claim him for their own ends. But the people from Harvard seem professional and well-meaning, and she still nourishes hopes that she will be able to collaborate on the project. They have offered to send a young man — they are all men — to work with her in sorting the papers; they have promised her regular news of her daughter. They are solicitous to a fault. What troubles her is their absolute indifference to her side of the story. She has written to them rather pointedly that having been married to Reed she knew him quite well and ought at least to be interviewed. But they seem interested only in the papers.

(What she doesn't know is that the Harvard men are reduced to almost farcical consternation in their attempts to win over the widow and obtain the papers. They make elaborately nasty jokes at her expense — suggesting, for example, that an emissary be sent to Paris bearing opium, which it is rumored she takes — but underlying the nastiness is a desperate determination to get the material at all costs. They are afraid she will burn it.)

On this February day, like most others, she does little writing. From time to time she undertakes a play, or a poem or two. She had been one of the most widely respected journalists of her day, covering the Russian Revolution side by side with John Reed, and after his death going on to become the Hearst chain's top international correspondent. When she married Bullitt in 1924, she gave up her position but continued to write, though not as a working reporter. She still gets fired up about issues — on a recent visit to the United States she went to Washington to cover the Bonus Marchers — but more often than not her illness and her alcoholism make it impossible for her to follow through. But she still considers herself an artist — she sculpts, draws — and is recognized in Paris circles as such.

On this February day, she avoids the typewriter and the damp clay and instead writes several feverish letters in a barely legible hand, to the Harvard men and to old friends in the U.S. She needs advice, support, money. Noting the time, she gathers up her things and rushes down the seven flights of stairs to the street, admonishing herself to be careful. Accident-prone since childhood, she has stumbled many times lately, sometimes in a drunken and confused state, often with dire results.

But as she makes her way through the Paris streets she is reminded that she is still in the land of the living. Waiters at the cafés she passes greet her; patrons sitting at the tables out front hail her. She is known for holding late-night parties at her studio, often wild parties to which the police are called. Years before, she'd been in love with an artist named Gwen Le Gallienne; indeed, his wife's "perversity" was a deciding factor in Bullitt's divorce case in 1930. Though the affair with Gwen ended badly, Louise is well liked by the Paris lesbian community, and women like the writers Natalie Barney and Janet Flanner keep an eye out for her, making sure she has enough money, eats now and then, and stays out of the company of the shady characters she seems to attract. (She has a penchant for Algerian soldiers, one of whom stole money from her.)

Recently — incredibly — she has taken up flying, taking solo flights at the field at Le Bourget, where Lindbergh had landed six years before, and she likes to affect the costume of an aviatrix, complete with goggles slung around her neck and a scarf trailing behind her.

She is hobbling now, having suffered a foot injury jumping out of a second-story hotel room in one of her increasingly frequent bouts of paranoia. The politically ambitious Bullitt is a deeply suspicious man, and in the course of the divorce employed detectives and elaborate ruses to entrap Louise; no doubt he also has his ways of keeping tabs on her in Paris, out of concern for her well-being, or for his own reputation, or both. However legitimately born, Louise's fears have grown more florid and ornate as the years pass. The eagerness of the Harvard men to lay their hands on Reed's papers only feeds her sense of desperation. She must live long enough properly to serve the memory of what she and John Reed had achieved together.

These fears hound her as she hails a taxi. Her train schedule tells her very little; she can only guess at the time Bullitt's train will pass through Paris. It will only slow down, at that; it is not scheduled to stop. But she hopes for a glimpse of Anne as the train pulls through.

At the Gare Montparnasse, she takes surreptitious sips from a flask in her bag as she waits in the cold. She imagines herself elsewhere: as a little girl growing up on the Nevada desert, with only an old man and a Chinese servant for company; as the unconventional wife of a dentist in thoroughly conventional Portland, Oregon; in the studio she shared with John Reed in Washington Square in the bohemian days before the Russian Revolution, writing and loving with equal fervor; on the beach and at the theater with Eugene O'Neill in Provincetown; marching on the White House in support of woman suffrage and hunger-striking in jail; returning to Portland triumphantly on a speaking tour, flourishing a red cape that dared Portlanders to imagine her beliefs; living it up with expatriate Americans in Paris in the twenties. Mostly, she remembers being at Reed's side as he lay dying of typhus in a Moscow hospital; it is a scene she has relived and replayed, with embellishments, over the years. She is not bitter, only tired, and sometimes she thinks that was all her life was for: being there at her hero husband's death. She knows that is not true. Her life has had shape and meaning, though it is hard for her to see now. And she has not given in, she has never given in — there is Anne, after all, due through in just minutes, if she has calculated right.

She has made mistakes, unwise choices, but she has never compromised. She has carried on, and surely there has been some meaning in that.

The train thunders by, slowing imperceptibly, and she is left standing alone on the platform.

Louise Bryant came out of nowhere and reinvented herself, becoming one of the leading journalists of her day and the dedicated chronicler of the convulsive aftermath of the First World War: her life was an achievement, but one that many of her peers found suspect. "She had no right to have brains and be so pretty," sniffed one contemporary observer. From the moment when Louise stepped off the train in New York City in 1916, after a long struggle to free herself from her working-class background and a subsequent struggle to escape the claims of a bourgeois, middle-class existence as the wife of an Oregon dentist, she demanded the right to enter history on her own terms. Women were striving to find a place in history that transcended becoming muses to their men, but when they wanted more they were considered suspect, automatically hubristic. Louise was often written off as a journalist whose success was entirely due to her association with the better-known John Reed, dismissed as an archetypal girlfriend in radical legend. Later, when she married Bill Bullitt, she was believed by many to have cast off her beliefs and principles by becoming the wife of a rich man. Her talents and achievements — including her ability to create her life for herself in spite of being associated with such outsize personalities — are too often overlooked. A talented, self-possessed, attractive woman seemed threatening both to men and to those women who knew full well how difficult her task was. When illness overtook Louise and she began her long decline, there were observers who felt vindicated and expressed their satisfaction in the cruelest possible terms, though, to be sure, there were others who understood the tragedy of her plight and admired her bravery.

With her talent, energy, and remarkable personality, Louise was an explosion on the early twentieth-century scene. A great irony is at work here: in spite of, or even because of, her great contemporary impact, her presence has barely been recorded. Recovering her story is to realize just how surely she did enter history and to understand in turn just how much gender politics figures in the making of history. The nuances of

Louise's story — the choices she made, the risks she took, the battles she fought and the battles she chose not to fight — show us vividly that women earn a place in the historical record not only through their achievements but through the lives they create for themselves. Louise Bryant's life sheds dramatic light on the avenues open to women and the choices available to them, the resources they must bring to their endeavors, and the extraordinary difficulties faced by even very talented women in gaining recognition. Recovering her story discovers a true twentieth-century heroine and the circumstances that made her, a heroine who has, ironically, been overlooked by traditional history and nearly lost to legend.

PART I

Frontiers without Vistas

1

Child of the West

B orn in San Francisco on December 5, 1885, Anna Louise Mohan did not thrive. She was a pretty baby, with deep blue eyes, a shock of brown hair, and high coloring that was taken in those days to mean heart trouble. She later described herself as having "curious and sudden illnesses." Something of the sort was to plague her throughout her brief life.

The sights of this little girl — who would call herself Louise Bryant — were set high. Indeed, nothing characterizes her early life more acutely than her determination to put her past behind her and invent herself as an actor on a larger stage. As a matter of course, she routinely altered details about her background and upbringing. It is no less true for being a cliché that certain individuals set out to make their lives works of art, and Louise Bryant was one of them, making of an imperfect and (for her time) relatively mundane early life a seamless if mysterious whole. Very much a child of the West, Louise (she was never called Anna) took to self-invention with alacrity. One's background counted for a lot or it counted not at all; events like the San Francisco fire of 1906, which destroyed all official records, only made it easier for westerners to fabricate their histories. So, according to Louise, her antecedents included not only Aaron Burr but Oscar Wilde, whose scandalous behavior was splashed across the newspapers in her girlhood. Her father, who was to disappear from her life when she was four, became, variously, an extravagantly successful miner, a lawyer who died in Colorado, or a politician. Irish only on her father's side, Louise nonetheless identified herself always as Irish.

But for pride, her parents might have approved such self-invention. They were vigorous and determined characters, possessed of a pioneer spirit and a fervent wish that their children might succeed. Not much is known of Louisa, Louise's mother. She may have been German (Louise at one point spoke of her Germanic ways), though other accounts say she was French and Spanish. How she made her way to the West Coast is not known. At her marriage to John Reed, Louise Bryant would declare that her mother was from Louisiana, but this was probably fanciful, perhaps based on an obvious family fondness for the name Louise. Indeed, Louise's grandmother, a Flick, was named Louise. While nothing is known of Louise Flick's first marriage, her second husband, James Say, was a colorful western rancher and miner who was to play a major role in his granddaughter's life. Of Irish stock, Say was born in England but emigrated in the 1850s, settling first in Virginia and then in New York, making his way to Churchill County, Nevada, in the 1860s.

James Say arrived "with stock and goods" in the fall of 1866 at White Plains, Nevada, where he made a living ranching but devoted most of his energy and dreams to finding mineral deposits in the arid wastes that were his property. These were the Nevada Territory's boom years, the era of the great Comstock Lode, which threw off hundreds of millions of dollars in silver and gold, luring enterprising easterners to the region in droves. Say threw in his lot with other hopeful miners from time to time, working the Badger mine and other properties. He had a successful station at Humboldt Lake, at the end of the lengthy desert over which all California-bound settlers had to pass. The second of his three wives was the young widow Louise Flick, Louise Bryant's grandmother; after her death, Say raised her daughter, Louise's mother, as his own.

Some time in the 1880s, Louise Bryant's mother made her way to San Francisco, where she met and married Hugh Mohan. With some alterations, Mohan was a colorful enough figure to enter Louise Bryant's pantheon of celebrated ancestors; emotionally, he became her lodestar. Born in Minersville, Pennsylvania, on April 9, 1848, Mohan was the son of Michael Mohan and Anna Ford Mohan, Irish immigrants from the county of Fermanagh. By the age of twelve, Hugh was living with the family of Charles and Arretta Mohan; most likely he was orphaned and relatives took him in. These Mohans were prosperous innkeepers, but as one of eleven children Hugh had to make his own way. With what seems to have been characteristic energy, he did, though he worked for a time as well in the coal mines and as a machinist. With a year or two of college at St. Bonaventure University, a New York Catholic institution, he returned to Pennsylvania and moved about the state working in journalism and local Democratic politics. Active in labor causes and well known as a stump speaker (he was dubbed the "Young Irish Orator"), Mohan was carried to Washington with the congressional Democratic tidal wave of 1874, where he held various government positions and continued to agitate in the pages of periodicals like the *Irish World.* He served as secretary to two senators, one of whom, P. D. Wigginton of Oregon, became a patron. When the Republican candidate Rutherford B. Hayes won the presidency in 1876 — despite the fact that Congress remained Democratic — Mohan saw the writing on the wall and followed Wigginton to California and again won a reputation as a rousing speaker and something of a wit.

The only real city on the West Coast thus far, San Francisco was likely to attract an ambitious young man with an eastern political background. It had a full complement of newspapers and a highly developed political life, similar to that of the cities of the East. Yet Mohan was unable to find a firm foothold there. He wrote for all three of San Francisco's dailies and periodically sought government work. Dependent as he was on the vagaries of the political climate, Mohan understandably moved from job to job; still, his career conveys a sense of restlessness and promise unfulfilled. He drifted about the state, attracted to the state capital at Sacramento. There he compiled, with two other political types, a series of portraits of "representative men" called *Pen Pictures,* for which he wrote a charming, even puckish, introduction.

Mohan was thirty-two when he married Louisa Flick on May 3, 1880. A daughter, Barbara, was born in 1880, and a son, Louis Parnell (given the masculinized family Christian name and the middle name of the Irish patriot and statesman), in 1882. The family made its home at 2943 Howard Street, close to the civic center and newspaper offices (and bordering on the city's notorious Tenderloin district), but even then Mohan was rarely present. Having taken a job gathering statistics for the Bureau of Labor, he traveled around the West for months on end.

After Louise's birth in 1885, the Mohans relocated to Reno, Nevada, and Mohan found work on newspapers in Virginia City and Carson City. The move also brought Louisa Mohan closer to her stepfather, James Say — a man considerably more successful than her husband. With the tapping out of the Comstock Lode and other mines in the 1880s, Nevada had entered what was to be a twenty-year depression a few years before, and jobs were hard to find. Except for this, conditions were little changed from the hilarious and often hair-raising adventures in frontier Nevada that Mark Twain had described in his 1872 *Roughing It*. Civilization encroached and then retreated; gunfights were still common, and prostitutes, cowboys, and miners thronged the saloons of Reno. It was a small city (the population in 1880 was only one thousand), but along with nearby Virginia City and Carson City it was the only significant outpost in the vast territory of Nevada. Known as "the tough little town on the Truckee River," Reno could not have been more different from San Francisco, which appeared eminently respectable by comparison. The Mohans saw that there was a living to be made in Nevada — albeit with difficulty — but little else to strive for. It was a place you left behind, not a final destination.

Hugh Mohan seems to have caught on to this fairly quickly, and turned increasingly to drink. Louise knew about his problem, later developing an almost prudish abstemiousness that she credited to her father's drinking. How bad it was she may not have known. One day her father simply disappeared and did not return. Her mother divorced him in Reno in August 1889, and the judge found that Mohan was "of drunken and improvident habits, and of wandering and migratory disposition."

Louise, however, always maintained that her father died when she was four. She told several different versions of his death, but the common thread was her intolerable bewilderment and her mother's great grief. "Coming from one of those broken homes where one of the parents is dead and the other grief-stricken beyond all recovery," she wrote toward the end of her life, "I found myself a very lonely child sitting for hours in a corner listening to my mother play the piano." A tireless reinventor of her own life, Louise may well have invented her father's death. But it is equally possible that Barbara, Louis, and Louise were simply told their father had died while on the road. That their mother put up with Mohan's wandering ways for as long as she did suggests that his charm was considerable, and she may well have mourned his absence from her life. More practically, she found herself an unmarried woman with three children in a frontier community and may have chosen to present herself as a widow rather than a divorcée. Whatever the combination of circumstances, Louise Bryant at a very early age felt a gaping hole in her universe.

"I *had* a father!" Louise shrieked when presented with a stepfather, Sheridan Bryant, the man who was to raise the Mohan children and whose name she was given. "He was a kind man. But I had all the resentment of having lost my own father and wanted no substitute." The comparatively placid Sheridan Bryant introduced stability and security into his new family's life. Originally a brakeman, Bryant had recently been promoted to freight train conductor on the Southern Pacific. Settling the family in an eight-room frame house in Wadsworth, a large town thirty-five miles outside of Reno, Bryant applied for a position on the "Truckee swing," a kind of traveling switch engine that delivered freight between Reno and Truckee, California. The idea behind the Truckee swing was to save the big trains bound for San Francisco and Sacramento from having to make numerous small stops along the way; Bryant's sole object was to get a route that allowed him to return to his family every night.

If this was a comedown for Louise Bryant's mother, it was a tradeoff she was willing to make. Mohan had been a cut above, a journalist with political connections and aspirations. Yet the rough-and-tumble of late-nineteenth-century politics and, more significantly, his own temperament and habits had been his undoing, and his ex-wife was willing to sacrifice upward mobility for stability. The railroad was known as an industry that took care of its own, and the Bryants had only to work and save to ensure a better future for the family. Louisa Bryant viewed education as the way for her children to move upward; stability and security were what she valued now. It speaks to her ambition and resourcefulness that she sent to college four of the five children she would bear.

But stability was not what Louise sought. Like her father's, hers would be a restless life. Her physical ailments persisted: she was thought "nervous," a perception that she found early on would serve her well, bringing her the attention she craved but did not receive from her distracted mother. It was a considerable relief for the Bryants when

Louise's stepgrandfather, James Say, offered to take her to his mining station for an extended visit. The child was brought into the kitchen and told the decision was hers to make. "After a long deliberation," Louise later wrote, she said, "Well, sir, I think I'd like to come."

After a long train ride and an eight-mile carriage ride from the station, Louise and her stepgrandfather arrived at the Mines, a settlement on the desert near Carson Sink. The years that passed there — three or four — suited Louise's temperament thoroughly, and any nervousness disappeared. She was given a white horse and learned to ride, daily traveling the eight miles to the station, where newspapers from England were thrown off the train for her grandfather, chasing coyotes along the way. Various dogs and cats roamed around the settlement (there was a mill and a machine shop, as well as the cattle barns and mine itself), and Louise made them her pets. She would always find animals the least complicated of beings, and easiest to love.

While other girls of her station were going to school and taking dancing and music lessons, Louise grew up on the plains, without friends her own age. This is perhaps why, later in life, she bridled at criticism, as so many on the left did, that she was too "bourgeois." Her experience at the Mines was unconventional in a way an easterner could never understand, and it marked her life indelibly.

"It was a strange and curious bringing up," Louise later wrote. Say might suddenly announce a business trip and bring Louise along to places like Reno, where they would stay at the Riverside Hotel and Louise would marvel at the open gambling and prostitution. Their travels seemed so long she often felt they had journeyed to another country. At the Mines her only companions, besides the animals, were the Chinese servants. She became closest to Yeegee, a Chinese man who served as Say's secretary, overseer, and right-hand man. Yeegee taught her snippets of German and Chinese — languages came easily to her — and she became his special pet. He sent her into paroxysms of laughter by imitating a stock Chinaman who spoke Pidgin English. When she was ill (the nerves might have vanished, but she had the usual childhood diseases) a little bell at her bedside would summon Yeegee, who brought her hot drinks, and said "Allee right, lil missie," humoring her.

Somewhat bitterly, Louise later recalled that while she wrote her mother at least once a week, her mother wrote her only once or twice a year, though the letters began "My dear little girl." Louise and Say visited her rarely, and Louise felt her mother resented her for looking too much like her father. Her stepgrandfather remained somewhat distant from her, but Louise idolized him, all the more so because he spoke highly of her father. Never forget, he used to tell her, that you are your father's daughter, "and whatever the family may say about your father, I always liked him better than any of them." She also learned from him, she said, never to cry in public, to go to her room all alone at night and stay there, and to avoid superstition and prejudice.

The idyll of Louise's childhood had to end. When she was twelve her mother wrote to Say asking that her daughter return, in order to receive a proper education. Naturally bright, Louise read proficiently and knew her numbers, but she needed the refinements her mother thought necessary for a young lady's education. One can only guess at the scorn her life with Say had given Louise for convention and civilization, and how much she resented having to rejoin her family. Ever after, she would choose adventure over security, rebellion over conformity. And she never forgot she was her father's daughter.

In the interim, the Bryant family fortunes had turned. Sheridan and Louisa had two sons, Floyd Sherman, born in 1894, and William Philip, born in 1896. The Mohan children had taken their stepfather's name, and the entire family were now practicing Episcopalians rather than Catholics. The Bryants' life was very closely bound up with the railroad, and shortly after Louise's return, when the Southern Pacific moved the western terminal of its Salt Lake division to the tiny town of Sparks, just outside Reno, the family moved from Wadsworth. Like other Wadsworth railroad families, they were given a boxcar and "transported bodily" to Sparks, where they received a house lot in the Reserve, an area designated for about seventy Southern Pacific families. Four miles west of Reno, the town prized its respectability; the gambling, prostitution, and liberal divorce laws that were winning Reno notoriety stopped at the city line.

However much she may have enjoyed her restless and adventurous childhood at the Mines, Louise settled into family life and school in Sparks without any outward difficulty. Indeed, with puberty she became transformed. The next decade would be marked by what appeared to be acceptance of conventions. Now a member of a household clinging to bourgeois respectability, Louise played along, still interested in leading a more exciting life but finding little in school and Sparks society that conflicted with her parents' desires. Her sister, Barbara, five years older, married a railroad man named Hansen; they set up house together in a boxcar. While neighbors marveled at the wonders Barbara worked on her inauspicious surroundings, Louise instinctively felt that such a life was not for her. Yet few alternatives presented themselves to her. It would be unheard of for her not to marry, yet she knew she had talent and she wanted something more. The conservative western society she moved in simply presented her with no clear choices. She turned her attention to art and writing, while at the same time becoming an enthusiastic, if sometimes rebellious, young coed.

She transferred from Wadsworth High School to University High School in Reno in 1903. The University High School existed, as its name suggests, in part to prepare students for the newly created University of Nevada, then called Nevada State University, and Louise's courses in her last two years there were credited toward university matriculation, which she undertook in 1905. The extracurricular activities of the university were available to her, and she was a staff member of the semiweekly *Student Record;* secretary of the school's liveliest social and debating organization, the Crescent Club; and a staff member of the yearbook, the *Artemisia.* She played forward on the women's basketball team (they were all packed and ready to go to a meet in San Jose when the great earthquake hit nearby San Francisco and the trip was called off). Her contributions to the school's publications were largely drawings, often copied from magazine covers or other illustrations, and she thought seriously of becoming a commercial artist. She contributed to the literary magazine, the *Chuckawalla.* A surviving piece, "The Way of a Flirt," has as its interesting premise the argument that flirts are more complex than most people give them credit for, but is otherwise undistinguished.

Louise wrote from experience; by all accounts, she was a first-class flirt. She acquired the nickname Dolly, which seemed to fit. Startlingly attractive, her beauty marred only by slightly crooked teeth, she had an intense and lively presence that captivated men and impressed women. She danced beautifully and took up skating; the frozen Manzanita Lake on campus was a good place to meet boys. But a friend stressed that while Louise might have appeared gay and flirtatious, she was never silly, and at the same time made it very clear that she did not intend to settle down.

In reminiscences dictated near the end of her life, Louise mentions nothing about her high school and college years in Nevada, but she describes what she calls a breakdown she suffered when told of her stepgrandfather's death in June 1906. During her recovery, her mother offered her an allowance — perhaps part of her inheritance from Say — to go wherever she felt might make her feel better. The university's placement office had posted a listing for a teacher in a mostly Mexican town called Jolon in southeastern California. Louise knew that teaching was the most likely professional option for her — a lot more attainable than becoming an artist — and thought the job sounded appealing. The experience lived up to her expectations. Jolon was an isolated town forty miles from the nearest railroad, and she boarded at a cattle ranch. She remembered that she wore khaki shirts, rode horseback and danced with the Mexicans, learned Spanish in a month, and got so sunburned no one in Nevada would recognize her. In short, it was like returning to the Mines. Little was required of her as a teacher beyond minding the youngest children, which was just as well, for she felt no real vocation for teaching — though she would turn to it as a way out several more times in the coming years.

In her Nevada years the only antidotes to her restlessness were similar changes in scenery. She was no stranger to picking up and moving when things were unsatisfactory. At the age of twenty in 1906, she felt, however, that for all her travels she was going nowhere. She resolved to begin all over again in a new place where she could create herself anew, make another try at shaping her life in a way that gave her direction and allowed her talents to flower.

2

Surfacing

*L*ouise's early years were marked by the vicissitudes of necessity and daily life more than any clear sense of self-direction. She picked up and moved to Eugene, Oregon, in the summer of 1906. Her sister's husband was with Southern Pacific, as was her oldest brother, Louis, and when Southern Pacific told them their jobs were moving elsewhere, they went — Barbara and her husband to Roseburg, about fifty miles south of Eugene, and Louis to Eugene proper. When Louise was up there for a summer visit, she asked around at the University of Oregon and found she could transfer her University of Nevada credits toward a degree. Nothing held her in Nevada; Oregon represented a chance to begin again. She entered the university on September 27, declaring a major in history, and boarded with a family called the Watsons in a respectable neighborhood near the college.

Louise quickly made a name for herself on the Eugene campus. "She was a young woman who knew where she was going. She didn't fiddle around. She was not only a beautiful woman, but a deep-thinking woman," said classmate Jacob Proebstel. Indeed, she seems to have shed the shallow, flirty facade that she had adopted in Reno, throwing herself into college activities in a more concerted fashion.

This is not to say she had developed any great purposefulness. But she was open to experience, and especially romantic experience, more than she had been in Nevada. She was now old enough to marry;

indeed, at twenty, some might even have felt she was destined for spinsterhood. Louise was aware of this and, when she registered for classes, changed her birthdate, lopping off two years, so that she now passed for eighteen. She did so lightheartedly, without a thought for the future or the consequences, but it was a move more highly charged and pregnant than she thought.

She quickly surrounded herself with girlfriends and male admirers. As she had at the University of Nevada, she aroused both admiration and envy among her classmates. She had turned into a remarkable beauty, her most striking feature perhaps her eyes; she was especially vain about her long lashes. She had a short upper lip and a rosebud of a mouth. She dressed to dramatic effect. She always wore three sets of petticoats, for example, rotating them so that the most recently washed and starched one was on the top, giving her what a friend called a "floaty" look. More than a few of her fellow students were jealous of Louise, one classmate remembered, and because she kept her own counsel others called her "our mystery girl."

In the spring Louise and five of her friends formed a small sorority, Zeta Iota Phi, a chapter of the national Chi Omega, with Louise as president. Lacking a charter and therefore official recognition by the university, the girls rented a small house and set up housekeeping. Classes were not taken very seriously. College at that time and place was quite different from the usual four-year plan common to eastern institutions. Few students matriculated full-time but instead "dropped in" for a semester or a course. In such a climate, social life flourished, and the students spent weekends climbing nearby Spencer's Butte, on day outings to Judson's Point or to swim at Millrace, or picking wild strawberries in the hills around Eugene. Willamette Valley, often shrouded in fog and surrounded by majestic forested hills, could not have been more different from the brown plains of the Nevada desert.

But Louise was interested in her studies for perhaps the first time. She came under the influence of one memorable English professor, a dyed-in-the-wool freethinker named Herbert Crombie Howe. He had already aroused suspicion among the administration by teaching such "modern" authors as Ibsen, Shaw, Wells, Tolstoy, London, and Zola to "mixed" classes, but when he gave a talk on the humanity of Christ (seemingly innocuous, but not in a community that was suspicious of anything but literal readings of the Bible) an uproar ensued that nearly got him fired. Louise and her friends defended him vociferously in the pages of the college newspaper, and eventually the administration backed down. But for many students, Professor Howe's classes were entrées to a world of new ideas, to a life beyond the frontier — to new frontiers, as it were.

And Louise also experienced social protest for the first time — in the novels and plays she read, and then, perhaps more meaningfully, in the students' defense of their professor. Whether the incident suited her intellectually, there is no doubt it suited her temperament. It came at a time when Louise was getting something of a reputation on campus: she was "fast." Her high coloring made many suspect she used rouge, then quite scandalous. Her association with a young man named Carl Washburne did not improve matters in this regard. The son of a prominent Eugene family, Washburne was Louise's frequent escort, but he was thought to be "not a marrying man," or in another version, to want to "marry money." Whatever the case, it was clear that he and Louise were not courting with any view to marriage, which left open the question of what they were actually doing together.

Rouged cheeks, a flashy boyfriend — not much in the way of rebellion, perhaps. Her rebellion may have been more personal than it was overtly political. Few, in fact, remembered Louise as very outspoken on political or social issues. She wrote her senior thesis on the Modoc Indian Wars, but Indian history was the pet subject of Dr. Schaeffer, her American history professor. One classmate remembers a passionate discussion about the exclusion of Jews from fraternities and sororities, and Louise's relative indifference. But one telling incident reveals how deeply rooted was her rebellious and independent nature.

The University of Oregon was a state-run school, and the citizens of the state were mostly small farmers, hardworking and conservative in their views, who kept a close eye on the new college at Eugene. In 1907 a university professor published a relatively obscure article about some bones he had found, bones that indicated the three-toed horse was the ancestor of the camel. By inference, of course, he had found empirical evidence of evolution — then a radical, indeed dangerous, concept. The university was faced with a major public relations crisis, as the largely Baptist farmer population threatened to see that legislative support for the school was cut. In response, the university mounted an impressive publicity campaign, sending students around the state to board with farmers and speak at grange halls, ready to answer questions in a careful, respectful fashion. As part of the same effort, the students who remained on campus, Louise among them, were warned that they were under particularly close scrutiny. Luella Clay Carson, the dean of women students, "cautioned all students to be careful that [their] behavior on and off campus be such that no offense could be taken," wrote one female student.

Louise bridled, not over anything so lofty as the evolution issue, but over the threat to her independence such strictures implied — and, quite possibly, over the hypocritical cowardice they revealed. "Louise Bryant interpreted [the dean's warning] as a violation of her civil liberties," the same student remembered, "and she openly flaunted drinking, smoking, and 'flashy' dressing in local cafés and neighboring towns."

No action was taken, but the word was out: Louise Bryant was absolutely not to be reined in.

Louise took off the spring semester in 1908. Some classmates attributed her departure to ill treatment at the hands of Carl Washburne. "It was why she ran off," said one observer. Another reason might have been her health. She had had an episode in class in which she fainted in her chair; some classmates remembered the incident as a heart attack, and the ever-vigilant sorority sisters speculated that her red cheeks might be attributable not to rouge but to heart trouble. Then again, the reason may have been simply economic, for she left the university to take a job. Her brothers Floyd and Bill had shouldered the largest burden in putting her through school, presumably supplemented with contributions from her mother and stepfather and perhaps her other siblings.

She briefly taught school on Stuart Island, a tiny outcropping in the San Juan Islands in Puget Sound. Ten families lived on the island — most of them salmon fishermen — and twelve or fourteen students, many of whom rowed over from neighboring islands, attended classes in the one-room schoolhouse. She lasted there only two months. Looking to begin a career as an illustrator or reporter, she then went to San Francisco. She met with all the news editors, she reported to a former classmate, but the newspapers had all fallen on hard times and were not hiring. She was doing some free-lancing, she said, but she doubted whether she was a dedicated enough artist to stick it out: "I'm sure if I had to live on what I get by drawing pictures and writing dabs of poetry I'd be like the regular storybook artist and live in a garret and die slowly of hunger."

That fall she returned to the university and received her B.A. in January 1909. More serious rumors sprang up around her. Some, of course, concerned Carl Washburne, though he was now for the most part out of the picture. She was involved with another man, Harry Mix; rumors circulated that they were secretly married. The most scandalous report — like most rumors, unconfirmable — held that she was involved with a leading Eugene businessman, a member of the city council; it was said to be an "open secret."

No doubt the reality was far more mundane. Most of Louise's friends had graduated and moved away; many of the women were married. As one cynic had predicted, Carl Washburne *did* marry money — an event that must have at once saddened and embittered Louise, perhaps shaking her certainty that she was marked for better things. Whoever Harry Mix was, he does not seem to have been a viable contender for marriage. Most likely, Louise spent the fall of 1908 quietly, working on her thesis about the Modoc Indians.

In her college years she had experimented in a small way with making herself a legend — her classmates would always remember her (quite apart from John Reed and her later adventures) as a figure of extraordinary romance — and her success heartened her. But in a practical sense she was left with very little. Few of her college friendships would survive. Her degree was almost worthless: it made her more employable as a teacher, perhaps, but she was through with teaching. It meant nothing to newspaper editors, who hired women reporters, if at all, to cover society events. It helped her artistic ambitions not at all. At twenty-three — passing for twenty-one — her future was not at all clear.

She rebounded with characteristic resiliency, surfacing in Portland in the spring of 1909. Aside from San Francisco, Portland was the largest city she had lived in — nearly 150,000 people were living in the Oregon city in 1905. It was beautifully situated, sprawling over the banks of the wide Willamette River, with the snow-capped peaks of Mount Hood, Mount St. Helens, and Mount Adams in the distance. Still very much a frontier city, Portland had its seamy side, its harbor area crowded with sailors, lumberjacks, miners, cowboys, and prostitutes; a small, unassimilated Chinese community flourished. Officially, however, Portland was straitlaced and foursquare, governed by sober and industrious men who valued hard work, church, and family. As the city grew, its civic-minded citizens did not neglect the arts: there was a museum and a symphony, even a growing theater scene. It was, in the most American sense of the word, civilized, and initially must have held great promise for Louise.

For the time being, it was the best she could do, and she determined to make a go of it. Desperate to find a way to make some money of her own, she scoured the want ads in the daily *Oregonian* — which held, not surprisingly, little promise for her. She was resourceful, however: when the Povey Glass Company advertised for a person who could make a stained glass window, Louise applied for the job. A friend asked her what she knew about stained glass, and Louise said she could learn whatever she needed to know in the public library. She convinced whoever was hiring and designed a stained glass window for a church in Jefferson, Oregon, just outside of Salem.

Her luck persisted. At the University of Oregon she had made the acquaintance of a remarkable Norwegian-American family of four girls. Clara Wold, who became a librarian in Portland, was her closest friend. Emma, Jean, and Cora would become teachers; Emma, who had been an instructor at the University of Oregon when Louise was there, would become an important suffragist and a key figure in Louise's life. Clara invited Louise to share her apartment at 415 Yamhill in downtown Portland, and Louise moved in. When a studio became available in the same building, she took it. The rent was cheap, and the young women enjoyed an almost dormitorylike existence.

Before long, she found work, probably part-time and definitely not very demanding. Failing to find a place on *The Oregonian,* she got a position on the recently founded and decidedly more frivolous *Spectator* — the publisher, Hugh Hume, was a great ladies' man, which may have helped — contributing line drawings that she signed, in an artistic squiggle, Holli. Her skillful drawings appeared frequently, and she showed herself a talented commercial artist. She would eventually rise to become society editor, which at least enabled her to develop her reportorial and writing skills, even if her beat was ladies' lunches and teas.

She had the independence she had long craved, and a thriving social life as well. She hung about the *Spectator* offices at the chamber of commerce building on the corner of Fourth and Stark. Her closest companion was the drama editor for *The Oregonian,* a one-armed young woman named Cas Baer. Through Cas, Louise became involved with the little theater, designing sets and taking small parts. The Wold girls knew almost everyone interesting in Portland. Along with Cas Baer, they were conscious of social issues, especially the burgeoning woman suffrage movement, and Louise felt she had found, for the time being, a place where she could thrive. She sought out exotic furnishings for her studio, her first real home; she had close female friends; the Oregon climate and the lovely setting of Portland appealed to her; she had solid, if not completely satisfying, work.

And she met a man, one who was, unlike Carl Washburne, very definitely the marrying kind. She caught the attention of Paul Trullinger, a handsome bachelor, blond and blue-eyed, with a neat mustache and a patrician nose. Born in 1880, Trullinger came from an old pioneer family; his grandfather, John, was the first to establish an electric light plant west of the Rockies. Less conventional than his staid family, Paul had originally wanted to be an artist — his uncle, John H. Trullinger, was a well-known painter of the impressionist school — but his father convinced him to become a dentist. After a brief courtship, Paul and Louise were married on November 13, 1909, in Oregon City, though they kept it a secret for a month, perhaps fearing his family might not approve.

They took up residence in Paul's decidedly unconventional home — a rented houseboat in a small colony run by the Oregon Yacht Club on the east bank of the Willamette, on the southern edge of the city. Fifty or sixty boats were moored there, in the shadow of a huge stand of oaks on the bank. Existence itself was interesting, as acquiring the necessities of living took patience and hard work, drawing the small community together. Groceries were bought from a boat that called at the moorage, a boat fondly nicknamed the Bumboat after a character from the Gilbert and Sullivan song "Little Buttercup." Most of the residents held conventional jobs in the city, but life on the houseboats had a bohemian flavor that lifted Louise's spirits.

By all accounts the couple were very much in love. Paul was a lifelong Democrat (in a family of Republicans), and decidedly in favor of woman suffrage. He accepted Louise's iconoclasm, telling a friend with some pride that "she was not the sort of woman to be confined to a kitchen with pots and pans." He still painted as a hobby, and collected art, jewelry, and interesting furniture. He had a successful practice with a partner, John Chance, but dentistry to him was very much just a job.

An early joint letter from Paul and Louise to the Trullinger family attests to the quality of the affection between them. They were writing after a romantic getaway to a ranch the Trullingers were building in Astoria, a beautiful spot at the juncture of the Columbia River and the Pacific. They had loved the new fireplace, Louise wrote; it had been just cold enough to enjoy it. They had stuffed themselves with hotcakes. Louise affectionately chided Paul for having locked the keys in the cabin; Paul added a postscript saying the ranch was going to be a "humdinger." The tone bears the marks of the slightly silly self-centeredness of a couple newly in love.

Thus far, Louise had sought independence while remaining essentially within the bounds of respectability. But no sooner was she safely married (to a husband who respected her independent nature) than she began a strenuous campaign not to become a conventional housewife. She sought out any signs of life in conservative Portland, fighting bourgeois complacency wherever she found it. She kept her small studio at 415 Yamhill, listing her name in the city directory as Louise Bryant. Later she rented a studio in the Murlark building, listing herself as Anna Moën, taking back her father's name and changing the spelling, not to make it sound less Irish — she was proud of that — but to make it sound somehow more elevated.

For if Louise was a freethinker, she could also be a bit of a social climber. This is not as contradictory as it seems at first consideration, especially given the nature of western society. Louise wanted to rise above her circumstances, to get ahead. As much as she wanted to be free of social convention, she recognized that it was easier to do so if you were thought to come from a "good" background. On one level, she could simply get away with a lot more. On another, she had determined at an early age to improve her lot, and if vaulting ahead in class would enable her to do that more easily, she had no problem with it.

It was the bourgeois respectability that went with such a change in station that rankled her. She had seen and experienced more than almost all of the people she and Paul associated with, and yet she was taken as an ordinary housewife. When Paul built her a new house in the northeast Rose City section of Portland — then a very fast-growing residential area we would today characterize as suburban — Louise's disquiet grew. She and Paul settled into domesticity, Louise unhappily. She didn't want children yet; instead, the couple raised Persian cats, who were annoyingly prone to giving birth on the marital bed.

As she had in Eugene, she began to develop a reputation. She posed for Paul's uncle in a picture hat and tightly corseted red velvet dress, but rumor had it she posed nude. There were those who said she was having an affair with Paul's brother Ross. She also had her share of admirers, though, and they were adamant about her charms. Adele Trullinger, Paul's aunt (and the only family member who really approved of her), thought Louise "very intelligent, wise, and interesting"; she remembered shopping trips that Louise made into great adventures. The daughter of one of Louise's former teachers remembered being invited for tea, where she found Louise dazzling: "She wore a long smoke-colored chiffon hostess dress and a bunch of fresh violets which matched her eyes. Her two large gray Persian cats matched the dress. I was only a child, but I went away with the impression that Louise was very different, very romantic."

A story her admirers liked to tell concerned an incident on the Morrison Bridge over the Willamette River. One wintry day Louise saw the driver of a beer wagon whipping his horses relentlessly, trying to get them to cross the icy bridge. Louise ran up to the driver and scolded him roundly, then took the reins of the horses and, murmuring to them gently, led them over the slippery bridge. "I thought, 'Oh, God, I wish I had done that,'" said one contemporary, voicing an opinion many shared — that Louise did things none of them would dare.

Louise and Paul's social life was active, and decidedly not stuffy. Paul and his officemates — two other doctors and Thomas Ross, a photographer — on the twelfth floor of the Selling building downtown combined their waiting rooms into a common area. On Friday afternoons they would invite their wives up and throw martini parties, often leading them to Paul's office to inhale ether. The group frequently went on outings to the Columbia Gorge Hotel, about sixty miles out of town on the Columbia River, a big and eccentric-looking lodge that witnessed several wild goings-on. Paul, like many of Portland's men, had claimed lands in wilderness areas on Mount Hood, between the coast and Bald Mountain, where they put up crude shacks. Sometimes by themselves, sometimes with their girlfriends or wives, they would leave the city for overnight camping parties. Evenings were spent around huge bonfires, and, away from the proper society of "pioneer" Portland, liquor flowed freely and inhibitions fell away. "We would have been called hippies [in the 1960s]," remembers one of Louise and Paul's friends.

But this was, again, hardly the stuff of serious rebellion; today, the Trullingers' doings sound downright collegiate, however much they may have scandalized proper Portland. Louise had achieved a professional success that was inconsequential by her own standards: reporting on social events, contributing little line drawings to a second-rate paper. Her manifestations of independence — maintaining her own studio, using her maiden name — spoke to a more serious streak in her rebelliousness. The rough-and-tumble of local politics, the kind Hugh Mohan had thrived on, had never moved her, but she heard with interest about wider political arenas, about issues that aroused her most passionate sense of justice. In short, midway into her marriage to a dentist, Louise Bryant the political person came into being.

The catalyst in Louise's awakening to political consciousness was a new friend, Sara Bard Field, then Sara Ehrgott. One of Portland's most iconoclastic figures, Sara was a preacher's wife when Louise first met her, but she soon developed a scandalous and very serious liaison with the legendary western scion, Colonel C. E. S. Wood. Indian fighter, explorer, lawyer, poet, Wood was a *bon vivant* and patron of the arts, the founder of the Portland Art Museum. The father of four, he was a notorious womanizer, though he settled down when he met Sara (he would marry her many years later, after his wife's death). A Democrat, he was, according to his son, a philosophical anarchist like Kropotkin or Jefferson, believing the best government governs least. In his law practice, he took on many unpopular causes, defending birth control activists, the IWW, and the anarchist Emma Goldman's right to free speech.

Sara believed she was responsible for Louise's awakening; she may have been right. Certainly she recognized Louise's discontent with the role of a dentist's wife. She later commented: "I opened the door to her ability. Louise hated housework. It seemed that Louise felt that she was condemned to wash windows, punch up pillows all day long. I said to her, 'Well, yes, if you are not very much in love and trying to make a lovely home, that is hard for a girl with your brains.' She was not in love with her husband . . . and she didn't feel she was accomplishing the work she could do."

Louise's interest in Sara was surely sparked by Sara's open affair with a leading citizen and married man, but it was Sara's interest in suffrage that cemented their friendship. The issue of suffrage electrified Louise. She saw that without full political citizenship there could be no advancement for the American woman; indeed, the arguments of suffrage opponents — that women were not capable of reason or fit for social responsibility, that the vote would destroy the family — simply outraged her. The suffrage issue — seemingly so simple, yet, as continued opposition to it indicated, in reality so complex — struck the most passionate chords in her independent soul. The struggle appealed to her as well — for it *was* a struggle, with hard-won individual victories and failures — and she threw herself into it with unmixed emotions.

In 1912 Sara invited Louise to join the College Equal Suffrage League, founded by Emma Wold under the tutelage of Oregon's leading suffragist, Abigail Scott Duniway. As the league's paid state organizer, Sara dedicated herself to her work, and Louise soon became as involved as her friend. In June *The Oregonian* reported on the suffrage float in a Flag Day parade: of the "eight pretty maidens" gracing it, one was Louise Bryant. Several leading suffragists, the report went on, would be leaving the next day for Astoria, where they would be addressing two open-air meetings and one of their own; among them were Sara Ehrgott and (more decorously) "Mrs. P. A. Trullinger." Sara and Louise quickly became well known for their effectiveness touring the state addressing hostile crowds. "Oregon was extremely primitive the minute you got away from the larger cities," remembered Sara many years later. "The people were backward in their thinking; [they] stood solidly in those parts against suffrage." The beauty and youth of the two women no doubt drew audiences. It is also fair to assume that Louise had inherited some of the rhetorical skills of her silver-tongued orator father. With pleasure, the suffragist workers watched as the tide gradually turned. The die was cast when the dominant Democratic party supported the measure, and woman's suffrage was passed into law in Oregon in the same year.

Here the paths of the two friends diverged, at least outwardly. Sara had established herself as a serious journalist in 1911, covering the trial of the McNamara brothers, union members who were accused of bombing a California newspaper office, for the *Oregon Daily Journal*. Louise continued on as society editor for the *Spectator*. Sara moved to Nevada to divorce her husband and stayed there for two years, agitating for woman suffrage; her career in the suffrage movement would take her to the national stage. Louise remained firmly committed to woman suffrage — it was perhaps the most firmly held political conviction of her life — but something kept her back from pursuing her convictions in a wider arena at this moment.

In short, Sara left, while Louise stayed. And stayed. She and Paul may have separated for a while — a city directory lists them at different residential addresses in 1914 — but later in that year they moved to a new and larger house at 11801 Southwest Riverwood Road, in an exclusive and bucolic riverside neighborhood. Materially comfortable, gainfully employed, pleasantly diverted (those Persian cats, those ether parties) Louise bided her time.

3

Enter Jack

*L*ouise had heard about John Reed long before they met. In fact, she later claimed that she had been reading a story of his in *Metropolitan Magazine* in 1913 on a streetcar, so mesmerized that she read on past her stop, and realized she had fallen in love with the person who'd written it.

John Reed was not exactly Portland's favorite son, though his family was old and eminently respectable, one of the most prominent in the city. Reed's grandfather, Henry D. Green, was an extremely successful frontier capitalist, building his fortune first on trading and later on the more permanent lode of city utilities. Cedar Hill, the five-acre estate he built at Portland's highest point, was known as "the pride of the city." Charlotte Green, like her husband a native of New York, did not pause after Henry's death in 1885, becoming the acknowledged social arbiter of Portland and cementing her reputation as its most vigorous hostess. Shortly after his death, the fourth child, Margaret, married local businessman Charles Jerome — C.J. — Reed. Himself successful — he supervised the western sales of a large eastern manufacturer of agricultural machinery — C.J. was extremely personable, welcomed by the Portland business and social community for his wit and good humor. But beneath C.J.'s ironic and joking demeanor lurked a discontent with the provincialism of Portland life. C.J. once wrote that in twenty-five years on the

West Coast he had never "become tolerant of the rawness and crudity of the West."

Son John — soon nicknamed Jack — was born on October 22, 1887, when the Reeds were living with Mrs. Green at Cedar Hill. Jack was raised in the lap of luxury, cared for by servants, driven about in carriages attended by uniformed footmen, his usual companion his younger brother Harry. At six, he developed a kidney condition that led to constant cosseting by his mother. "A great deal of my boyhood was illness and physical weakness," Reed later wrote, "and I was never really well until my sixteenth year." As a result, he developed a rich inner life, reading romances and determining to become a writer. He did not fare well at Portland Academy, where he chafed at the stuffy educational principles of the time and made few friends, later remembering himself as cowardly and shy.

By the age of sixteen he had come out of his shell a little, contributing enthusiastically to the school literary magazine and frequenting newspaper offices downtown. But his parents decided two years of college preparatory work in the East would fit him best for what they planned for him: a Harvard degree.

At Morristown Academy in New Jersey, Jack came into his own, emerging as the radiant personality that others would remember with admiration. He succeeded at everything he tried — at writing, at football, with women. He had C.J.'s easy joviality and a magnetic quality all his own. He got in trouble more than once with school authorities but never over anything very serious. More importantly, he began to look at the world around him with an increasingly critical eye. In short, he, too — and at about the same time as Louise Bryant — was developing a political consciousness.

In part Jack's new awareness was due to the responsibility his father had (after considerable misgivings) just taken on as U.S. marshal in charge of breaking up the Oregon land fraud ring. It had come to the attention of President Roosevelt's secretary of the interior that speculators, in the (recent) days before the West was bought up and settled, had illegally claimed ownership to hundreds of thousands of acres of valuable timberland. C. J. Reed worked with Francis J. Heney and Lincoln Steffens, two reformers who were the forerunners of the political group that would come to dominate the national scene, the Progressives, to uncover the network of fraud that had settled over the northwestern cities. The fraud touched almost every businessman in the area, and C. J. Reed, forced to identify friends and associates who were implicated in the fraud, was not a popular man. The considerable courage he brought to the undertaking was not lost on his son, who credited his father with being a pioneer of the Progressive Era, which he characterized as giving "expression to the new social conscience of the American middle class."

Brash, exuberant, filled with high ideals, Jack felt that bound for Harvard he was bound for glory. He was rudely brought up short soon after his arrival in Cambridge in the fall of 1906. First, he was simply a little fish in a big pond: his class alone was seven hundred strong. More subtle was the complex social stratification he found in the Harvard community. He was a westerner; he had not gone to one of the prestigious eastern prep schools; his edges were rough.

Characteristically, and tragicomically, he fought back. When snubbed or passed over for freshman club memberships, Jack called his classmates on it, winning himself a reputation for pushiness and gaucheness that would linger for years. He did things he would later be ashamed of: after agreeing to room with a Jewish boy named Carl Binger, he changed his mind, seeing Binger as a potential social liability. But his native tenacity and determination eventually made it possible for him to slip in through the cracks, writing for the *Lampoon* and the *Harvard Monthly*. Never fully accepted by the prep school boys, he made the most of his Harvard years, becoming president of the Cosmopolitan Club, manager of the Musical Club, captain of the water polo team (he loved swimming), and so on. He found friends in Bob Hallowell, an aspiring painter, and the intellectual Walter Lippmann, already something of a pundit and president of the newly formed Socialist Club, which Jack admired but did not join. He came under the influence of the legendary "Copey," Charles Townsend Copeland, an English teacher who took him under his wing and urged him to take his writing seriously.

These were heady times at Harvard; they would later be characterized by Reed himself, in fact, as "the Harvard renaissance." The Socialist Club was but one manifestation. Everywhere the air was thick with talk of radicalism and social change. Jack's classmates were part of a new generation of men and women who fought off the constraints of convention, struggling to transform both themselves and the world. Jack was caught up in this enthusiasm, and would no doubt have characterized himself as a radical — but he was preoccupied with his writing, and soaking in all experience. He may have seemed directionless — his father gave him a year abroad as a graduation gift, and Jack took it, sowing his oats liberally — but he was unwittingly laying the best groundwork for what was emerging as his profession: that of a journalist actively participating in social change.

It was Lincoln Steffens, his father's old acquaintance, to whom Jack turned when he got back from Europe and it was time to find work. Steffens's lavish description of Jack's arrival at his office in 1911 suggests something of the enormous potential everyone saw in him: "When Jack Reed came, big and growing, handsome outside and beautiful inside, when that boy came to New York, it seemed to me that I had never seen anything so near to pure joy. No ray of sunshine, no drop of foam, no young animal, bird or fish, and no star, was as happy as that boy was. If only we could keep him so, we might have a poet at last who would see and sing nothing but joy." When Steffens asked Jack what he wanted to do, Jack answered that he didn't know, except that he wanted to write. "Steffens looked at me with that lovely smile," Reed remembered, "and answered, 'You can do anything you want to.'"

For a time, it seemed he could. Steffens got him a job on the muckraking *American Magazine* and an apartment in his own building on Washington Square. Jack wrote with enormous energy, selling articles and short stories to *Collier's*, *The Saturday Evening Post*, *The Smart Set*, *The Forum*, and *The Century*. He came into his own as a journalist covering a silk workers' strike in Paterson, New Jersey, during which he was jailed for four days. With characteristic energy, he seized on the suggestion of friends — including his then lover, Mabel Dodge — to organize a pageant depicting the strike, with the workers playing themselves, to be staged in Madison Square Garden. It was a wonderful vision: art and politics would come together, and the pageant would bring home the plight of the striking workers to the press and the public. Though the pageant was a financial flop, everyone involved remembered the event — the IWW banners strung across the thronged hall, the red lights outside proclaiming revolutionary slogans in letters ten feet tall.

Professionally, Jack settled in at the *Metropolitan*, a monthly magazine given over mostly to writers like Rudyard Kipling and Joseph

Conrad. Financed by the millionaire Harry Payne Whitney, the magazine declared itself Socialist in 1912; increasingly, articles on political, social, and economic issues by writers like Lippmann and Steffens filled its pages. Though it would drift toward the right in the years to come, for the time being it was good to Jack. He drew what was then a very respectable salary of $500 a month.

In the creative hub that was Greenwich Village in the early teens, Jack thrived. Bohemian communities had sprung up across the country in the last half of the nineteenth century — most notably in San Francisco and Chicago — but with the new century Greenwich Village, with its winding streets, cheap rents, and intimate atmosphere, quickly became the place where like-minded people congregated. It was home to a loosely connected imaginative community, free-spirited souls who, under the pressures of a range of forces that included urbanization, fragmentation, and the findings of Darwinism, had come to believe that the old ways no longer sufficed, that the established order in politics was implicitly under question, that Victorian morality was outmoded, even useless.

These were people passionate in their beliefs, who translated their ideas into action. Issue after issue was debated nightly at places like the Hell Hole on Sixth Avenue and 4th Street, home to a dreaded gang called the Hudson Dusters and frequented by the young Eugene O'Neill; Luke O'Connor's fancifully named Working Girl's Home; and Polly Holladay's restaurant on MacDougal Street, the headquarters of the Liberal Club, which had splintered off from its decidedly stodgy uptown counterpart. As might be expected, love was inseparable from work, and work from play: the novelist Floyd Dell spoke of the Village as an arcadian place where "vagabond youths . . . ignored the codes invented by those who have settled down and have a property-stake in the world." In this atmosphere, "secrecy and hypocrisy were unnecessary."

Jack established his beachhead right at the heart of things, in his apartment at 42 Washington Square. (Resident revelers had twice climbed to the top of the arch at the opposite side of the square to declare the Village "the Republic of Washington Square.") He brought into his ménage Harvard classmates Eddy Hunt, for whom he secured an editorial job at the *American,* and the set designer Robert Edmond Jones. He worked and played at a feverish pitch, unsure yet whether he was a poet or revolutionary — or perhaps both. Indeed, one of his best efforts dates from this period, an extremely long and rollicking poem called "The Day in Bohemia, or Life Among the Artists." It evokes as well as any contemporary account the at once ebullient and ironical character of its author:

> Yet we are free who live in Washington Square,
> We dare to think as Uptown wouldn't dare,
> Blazing our nights with arguments uproarious;
> What care we for a dull world censorious
> When each is sure he'll fashion something glorious?

He published the poem privately and carried a stack of copies with him everywhere, selling them for a dollar. The poem spoke to the Village denizens, and Jack's reputation as a Village bard and spokesperson for the Village spirit grew.

Jack's legend developed a new dimension with his impassioned coverage of Pancho Villa and the Mexican Revolution in a series of articles for the *Metropolitan* in 1914. His identification with the rebel general was obvious; Villa reciprocated, nicknaming Reed "Chatito," for his pug nose. Following Villa's army, often coming under fire itself, Jack discovered, he later wrote, that "bullets are not very terrifying, that the fear of death is not such a great thing." His journalistic reports were laced with his own escapades to the extent that he appeared almost as heroic — or certainly as romantic — as Villa. The *Metropolitan* advertised his articles as "word pictures of war by an American Kipling," emphasizing Reed's youth and personal involvement in the cause.

But who was this character, this genius who seemed to rocket to the center of where things were happening, this young man who charmed rebel generals and hardened union men? Physically, he was prepossessing: large-boned and lanky, he appeared devastatingly handsome despite what some characterized as a "smashed-in" face. He was excited, restless, sometimes boyish in his enthusiasms despite his growing social convictions. He had a certain naiveté that served him to his advantage: in Paterson, for example, he led the striking workers at rallies in renditions of Harvard football songs (he had been a cheerleader at Harvard).

Despite his experience, he remained in many respects a wide-eyed innocent. Women were in abundance in his life, but they bewildered him as much as they drew him. There had been an engagement with a French girl — much to his parents' dismay — an affair with the wife of a friend, and, most significantly, a long and stormy involvement with the wealthy Mabel Dodge, the hostess of a salon on Fifth Avenue that drew the most innovative artists, radicals, and thinkers of the day. Mabel, described by a Reed biographer as "a woman who would later drive two psychoanalysts to distraction," demanded Jack's total attention, even as he threw himself into his journalism and radical work. It speaks to his boundless energy that he was able to give it.

It was *The Masses,* really, that brought Jack and Louise together. A magazine founded in 1911 by the Dutch anarchist Piet Vlag, *The Masses* was, from the start, dedicated to Socialist principles. It didn't come into its own, ironically, until it went bankrupt the next year, and the editorship, at no pay, passed into the hands of a new convert to Socialism, the enormously talented Max Eastman. Eastman assembled a remarkable array of contributors — among them William Carlos Williams, Randolph Bourne, Upton Sinclair, Sherwood Anderson, Maxim Gorky, and Bertrand Russell — and an editorial board that included John Reed and Louis Untermeyer.

Reed's enthusiasm for the venture was immense. The pages of *The Masses* were open to anything new: anarchism, Marxism, feminism, birth control, Freudianism, literary experimentalism, and free love. The editorial offices were chaotic in the extreme. All editorial decisions were made collectively, of course, which fed the chaos. Editor Hippolyte Havel, a decidedly eccentric anarchist, disrupted one meeting by shouting, "Bourgeois! Voting on poetry! You can't vote on poetry!" And one wag produced an enduring little rhyme that went to the heart of some of the real problems of the magazine:

They draw nude women for *The Masses*
Thick, fat, ungainly lasses —
How does that help the working classes?

The mood of prewar America, open to the "shock of the new" and ready to reject Puritanism in all its forms was such that *The Masses* survived — and thrived. (And Eastman, for his part, had a knack for finding wealthy, usually female, backers.) All across the country, rebels in the making, among them Louise Bryant, found solace and inspiration in its pages (as well as, perhaps, practical aid — the "back of the book" carried advertisements for marriage manuals and thinly disguised birth control aids, products hard to find in places like Portland).

Louise, in fact, was so enthusiastic in raising subscriptions in Oregon that Max Eastman came to recognize her name in New York. Colonel C. E. S. Wood was a frequent contributor, and that made her feel she had some kind of connection. She wasn't ready to submit her work to the magazine yet, though she was sending poems and stories to the anarchist Alexander Berkman's San Francisco–based *Blast*. In the meantime, she read each issue of *The Masses* avidly, watching for John Reed's name.

Their meeting was inevitable, less in a fateful sense than a logistical one. Dr. Trullinger and his wife, with his background and respectable profession and her charm, were accepted among Portland's elite. They were also unconventional enough that those Portlanders who were proud of John Reed — like Colonel Wood and the artist Carl Waters, who also sold *Masses* subscriptions — boasted of him to the young couple. In Portland, at least, Louise and Jack traveled in the same circles.

Louise may have been waiting for Jack for several years before meeting him. In a hastily written memoir, she follows her description of reading one of his stories with a sentence that speaks very simply to her desires: "I always wanted somebody who wouldn't care what hour you went to bed or what hour you got up, and who lived in the way Jack did." She wanted independence, then, and excitement, a relationship in which she would not feel constrained by convention. With unerring instinct, she chose the right man.

They met more than a year before they became lovers. It was the summer of 1914, and Jack had come home for a visit. How they met is not known, but Jack's activities must have placed him in her path. There were teas and luncheons held in his honor, a speech by Emma Goldman at the IWW hall, and a lecture before the University Club, where Jack delivered a ringing indictment of the class system instead of the travelogue on Mexico the audience had expected. These were the kind of occasions that Louise probably would have attended with her husband, and she seems to have caught his eye at the University Club in particular, where he detected mirth around her eyes. They were formally introduced at the home of the Graves sisters at Southeast 12th Street, a lovely dark Victorian house, where Jenny Frasier, a former teacher of Louise's, poured tea. There must have been subsequent, secret meetings, because when Jack was called away in July by a flurry of telegrams from Carl Hovey, his editor at the *Metropolitan,* ordered to cover the war breaking out in Europe, he told Louise he would be back for her in a year. They had pledged their love.

Louise waited in the wings. She later commented, of this period, "It is a very difficult thing to wait a year if you are young and very much in love." Jack had yet to extricate himself from his romance with Mabel Dodge. He spent six months traveling through Europe, once again pulling no punches in his dispatches home, denouncing both sides as cynical and profiteering, declaring ringingly in piece after piece, "This is not our war." In Paris, he had a brief affair with a married woman, which left him feeling free of Mabel; he cabled her with the news. Called home by the *Metropolitan,* he was abruptly sent back to cover the war on the eastern front — in Yugoslavia, Turkey, Serbia, and Russia. The last particularly drew him. Echoing Louise, he wrote, "Everyone [in Russia] acts just as he feels like acting, and says just what he wants to. There are no particular times for getting up or going to bed or eating dinner, and there is no conventional way of murdering a man or of making love." Back home in the fall, he wrote up his articles and published them as a book called *The War in Eastern Europe.* Before setting off again — he didn't know where, perhaps China — he made his Christmas visit to his mother in Portland.

Events proceeded as they had during Jack's visit to Portland the year before. He and Louise met at teas, luncheons, the homes of mutual friends like the Frasiers and local artist Lola Fenton. His talk of Socialism and the heady goings-on in Greenwich Village and the offices of *The Masses* inflamed her; there *was* a world elsewhere. With Reed she might see that world, experience it, change it.

Physically, their mutual attraction was tremendous. Louise was at her very best then: a contemporary photograph radiates youth, beauty, and an aura of mischief. Jack was a bear of a man — six feet tall, green-eyed, curly-haired — who exuded both confidence and vulnerability.

They had found ways to be alone. Meeting by chance one day on a snowy street, Jack told Louise that he had a cold. With a strong, self-acknowledged maternal streak, she brought him directly to her studio on Yamhill, lit the potbellied stove, and fixed him hot milk and honey. As the sides of the stove glowed red and they settled in on her divan, she showed him some of her poetry, which he, himself a striving poet, admired. They had silly moments, with Jack imitating the kisses of elephants, camels, and giraffes. But they also exchanged confidences; he told her about the love affair with Mabel, at long last over, and she told him about her fondness for and unhappiness with Paul. They both agreed that marriage was an abominable institution and that men and women should be able to love freely, according to their own personal vows.

By the time they showed up for a dinner party that evening at Carl and Helen Waters's — the enlightened Carl had planned to introduce them to each other — it was obvious to all present that they were very much in love. Dozens of Portlanders later claimed to have been instrumental in their romance. Sara Bard Field said she brought them together and that it was clear immediately that they loved each other "passionately," adding that she felt a lot of sympathy for Paul, but "he was just not the kind of man to hold a woman like Louise."

However much sympathy there was for Paul — and it was considerable, for he was by all accounts a likable man — Louise's friends rallied behind her. When Jack left, as planned, just after Christmas, they wondered what she would do. This time he had asked her to join him in New York and left her train fare. She needed to spend a little time with Paul, she said, in order to explain things to him — and also to raise a little cash for her new life.

"This evening when I came home," she wrote to him in a letter full of longing, "the streets were all slippery with ice and now when the first light of day is coming through my window the world seems quite frozen. This is all as it should be — silly old town — it had your glowing presence here for weeks without appreciating it — now a capricious old winter has turned it to ice as soon as you are gone."

She concluded, "Wonderful man — I know there isn't another soul anywhere so free and so exquisite and strong!" Her fire was quite out, but she couldn't write any more in any case: "I want you too much — all of a sudden — dear. Goodnight."

As Reed's train traveled across the country, he too wrote letters, telling his friends of his new love. The most ardent of these, however, had been written several days before, to his good friend Sally Robinson, wife of the illustrator Boardman Robinson, who had accompanied Jack to the eastern front:

This is to say, chiefly, that I have fallen in love again, and that I think I've found her at last. No surety about it, of course. She doesn't want it. She's two years younger than I [she was actually two years older], wild and brave and straight, and graceful and lovely to look at. A lover of all adventure of spirit and mind, a realist with the most silver scorn of changelessness and fixity. Refuses to be bound, or to bound . . . has done advertising, has made it a success, quit it at the top of the wave; worked on a daily newspaper for five years, made a great success, and quit it because she outgrew it and wanted better. [What *had* she told him?] And in this spiritual vacuum, this unfertilized soil, she has grown (how, I can't imagine) into an artist, a joyous, rampant individualist, a poet and revolutionary.

Louise left Portland on New Year's Eve. Paul, who evidently did not believe she was leaving him for good, and for another man, accompanied her to Union Depot, giving her a bunch of violets that she wore as she took leave of her friends. They were all there: the Wolds, Cas Baer, the Waterses, Brownell Frasier. To one woman present on the occasion — Marguerite Dosch, whose brother Roswell Dosch had a studio in Louise's building — the drama was not that Louise was going to join another man but that she was going "to make her way in the larger world." She was leaving Portland, this "silly old town," for the stage on which she always knew she should appear.

PART II

A Gypsy Compact

4

Love, Free and Not So Free

WHEN Louise's train pulled into Grand Central Station on January 4, Paul's violets long dead, Jack was there to meet her. Her first impression in New York City was the Woolworth Tower, "suspended between earth and sky," which, as the world's tallest building, seemed immense to a westerner; it inspired her to write a poem. But Jack spirited her off to his new apartment on Washington Square. He had taken a room for her at the other end of the street, at number 60, but she never even saw it. They simply could not be apart; moreover, they were determined to put their ideals into practice, living together without the bonds of marriage regardless of what people thought. As the *Masses* editor Max Eastman observed,

> Poetry to Reed was not only a matter of writing words but of living life. We were carrying realism so far in those days that it walked us right out of our books. We had a certain scorn of books. Jack Reed did especially. His comradeship with Louise Bryant was based on a joint determination to smash through the hulls of custom and tradition and all polite and proper forms of behavior, and touch at all times and all over the earth the raw current of life. It was a companionship in what philistines call adventure, a kind of gypsy compact. And that will to live, to be themselves in the world, and be real, and be honest, and taste the whole tang of it, was more to them than writing. It was more to them than any

particular practical undertaking, even a revolution. It was as though they had agreed to inscribe at least two audacious, deep, and real lives in the book of time and let the gods call it poetry.

Few of Louise and Jack's friends or neighbors would blink an eye at their unconventional living arrangement. Greenwich Village seemed like paradise to Louise. Unmarried couples lived together openly, and the air was thick with talk of new ideas and social change. Everybody seemed to support suffrage, and other, more radical feminisms abounded. Sara Bard Field, in New York after a successful cross-country automobile trip on behalf of suffrage, took Louise to a meeting of a remarkable women's group called Heterodoxy, a club that Mabel Dodge described as existing "for unorthodox women, women who did things openly." There she met such women as Crystal Eastman, Max's sister and a political activist, the anthropologist Elsie Clews Parsons, the journalist Mary Heaton Vorse, the feminist Charlotte Perkins Gilman, and the writers Zona Gale, Mary Austin, and Fannie Hurst.

Louise could not have imagined an environment more different from Portland. There had been only two men in her life whom she respected and loved as much as Reed: her father and her stepgrandfather, both long gone. As Louise later put it, "I began for the first time to lead a life that was not unhappy and lonely." There was "a common purse," she later commented, just as there had been at her grandfather's — in other words, any money that came into the household could be dipped into at any point, with no questions asked. This does not seem unusual in itself, but it suggests that Paul had kept her on a short leash indeed — even though she kept a separate studio — and she must have felt liberated in the communal life she suddenly found herself living with Jack. In short, she had found a place she had only vaguely imagined, containing elements of the best worlds she had ever known — her grandfather's ranch, the salon of C. E. S. Wood and Sara Bard Field, an allowance for solitude, and an active political life. The Village and life with Reed seemed to bring it all together.

She and Jack had adjoining workrooms, and Jack used to dictate all afternoon, then join her in her room for tea. "We had a habit of taking long walks after tea, to all different parts of New York, going over bridges, to the East Side, Harlem, anywhere," Louise later wrote. Neither cooked much; they took their meals in the Hotel Brevoort at the foot of Fifth Avenue, or at Three Steps Down on 8th Street.

In good time, Louise met Jack's friends. Some encounters were happier than others. Mabel Dodge, hearing rumors that Louise had replaced her in Jack's life, showed up at their Washington Square apartment early one evening on the pretext of retrieving her typewriter. Hardly a disinterested party, Mabel admitted that Louise was very pretty and observed that she was "clever with a certain Irish quickness, and very eager to get on." But Louise used Reed, Mabel thought, "like a stepping stone . . . through him she met a lot of people she never would have known otherwise." Mabel's was a reaction that would be shared by many, as Louise aroused curiously vehement responses among her female peers.

At *The Masses* offices, for instance, she got a decidedly suspicious reception. Dorothy Day commented that "the people on *The Masses* didn't like Louise. I think it was jealousy. She had no right to have brains and be so pretty. They were constantly minimizing her." To some, her taste in clothes — she favored costumes that made "statements," outrageous and seemingly extravagant — rendered her bourgeois and therefore suspect, a charge that conveniently overlooked Louise's frontier upbringing. To others her iconoclasm seemed affected. Such extreme reactions were owing not simply to envy but to Reed's status among the Villagers. He was the reigning king of Bohemia, and this upstart from out West had taken the throne beside him in the blink of an eye. Moreover, the prevailing sexism of the day — so endemic that even women as seemingly liberated as those the Village attracted could not escape it — made immediately dubious the motivations and methods of a woman who aspired to be more than a companion.

Louise put up a brave front, but she clung increasingly to her friend Sara, who was staying with the talented amateur actress Ida Rauh, married to *The Masses* editor Max Eastman but very much living an independent existence. Sara was less important as a tie to Portland (Louise wrote of Portland, not long after, as a "terrible" place: "Sometimes I have nightmares and wake up shivering, just imagining I have to go back") than as someone who functioned in both worlds and knew and liked Louise independently of Reed. Through Sara and Heterodoxy she made friends, among them Madeleine Doty, another journalist; Inez

Milholland, a radical activist married to the wealthy Eugen Boissevain, later Edna St. Vincent Millay's husband; and Stella Ballantine, active in the theater. To Louise's delight, Clara Wold soon made the pilgrimage from Portland to the Village, taking a studio in Patchin Place with her companion, the writer Norman Matson.

Louise was serious about pursuing a writing career, though she made few inroads in the popular press. She broke into *The Masses* four months after her arrival in New York, in April 1916, with an article about two exemplary Portland judges, one of whom had presided over Emma Goldman's trial for dispensing birth control literature in Portland the year before. Both judges were confronted by the hopelessness of the legal system in a time of economic insecurity and social upheaval, but one had resigned and the other had, "though he looks pretty tired sometimes," stayed on the job. "You honor the action of the judge who resigned," Louise addressed *The Masses* readers in closing, "as you must honor every sincere and noble action. But the man who stayed — didn't he do something better still? What do you think?" Her poetry, written in the flush of her love for Jack, would begin appearing in the same journal that summer. Moreover, she was beginning to be drawn to the passionate, participatory reportage Jack favored. At Three Steps Down she met the Irish labor leader Jim Larkin. Fired by his rhetoric and her own fervent identification with the Irish cause, she wrote a piece called "The Poet's Revolution." A ringing call to support the revolutionists of the Easter uprising, the piece proclaimed that theirs was a revolution led by poets and scholars, a "sublime protest of the 'dreamers' . . . that has given a depressed and bewildered world a new faith in mankind." It was a romantic view — her poet-revolutionary lover held a similar view of politics in these years — but it represented a deep belief, common enough in their circle in the prewar years, that art and revolution were coming together in new and transformative ways.

But Louise was often lonely, and surely knew her career was at best off to a shaky start. Jack was often away, and their separations were difficult. On a trip south to interview William Jennings Bryan, just over a month after Louise's arrival, Jack wrote to her from the train as evening fell: "[M]y little lover, I become more and more gloomy and mournful to think I'm not going to sleep over you in our scandalous and sinful voluptuous bed." Understandably, Louise often felt herself adrift during Jack's absences. She told one friend that she missed the long walks she and Jack loved to take; without him, she often got lost on the city streets. In what would become a pattern during Jack's absences, she sought out male companionship.

Each time this happened, it began simply enough. In the spring of 1916 she turned to the young sculptor and painter Andrew Dasburg. Dasburg, a strikingly handsome man, slightly lame, was married to the sculptor Grace Johnson, although their marriage was an open one — he had had an affair, most recently, with the ubiquitous Mabel Dodge. Louise simply showed up at his studio one day, a few doors down from her place with Jack on Washington Square, and asked him if she could see his work. He invited her in; she told him about her (still undissolved) marriage and her efforts at writing. A close friendship developed, but — perhaps because of what seems to have been an uncharacteristic naiveté on Andrew's part — nothing more, for the time, ensued.

That Louise turned to other men when Jack was away was one part insecurity and one part a desire to remain in control of her life. Jack had confessed early on that he was susceptible to frequent, inconsequential affairs; in fact, his infidelity would later come close to driving them apart. But Louise, ever a survivor, responded by exploring possibilities, lining up possible replacements for Reed. She may have worried that one of his liaisons would prove consequential — after all, theirs had. Psychologically, she likely had a deep-seated fear of abandonment. She had lost her beloved father and later her grandfather at a young age, and she had spent most of her childhood (albeit happily) without her mother. She also simply felt alone in the East and, for all her independence, worried at being cast adrift. What's more, her behavior seems to have been reflexive: she was a beautiful, seductive woman, and confronted with a talented and handsome man she reacted instinctively. That she always chose someone approaching Reed in stature, potential, and charm speaks to something more complex in her nature, a shadowy game plan for her life, the outlines of which were perhaps indistinct even to her.

The spring and summer of 1916, which Louise and Jack spent in Provincetown, was more than an idyll: it was a vision of what the future might be.

It was as if Greenwich Village had gone to Provincetown en masse. The tiny coastal hamlet, three miles long and two streets wide, had been discovered by New York's bohemians a few years before. Physically, it was not unlike Greenwich Village, with its small, winding roads, its cheap rents and lively restaurants and saloons. The setting was dramatic: nestled around a bay in the curl at the tip of Cape Cod, the town was surrounded by towering dunes and, beyond them, the crashing ocean. Once a whaling port, Provincetown was populated by Portuguese fishermen and the occasional Yankee. As Louise wrote to Sara Bard Field, "It is such a queer little fishing village — almost all Portuguese and they stare at us with awe and whisper, 'New Yorkers!'"

Louise and Jack were invited to visit by Mary Heaton Vorse, a writer who could be said to have founded Provincetown's artistic community. When they arrived they found Vorse engrossed in one of her many love affairs, and decided it was best to rent a place of their own. They found a pleasant house that was unusually large in the town of tiny cottages, at 592 Commercial Street, just across from the bay.

As Louise later wrote, "It was a strange year. Never were so many people in America who wrote or painted or acted ever thrown together in one place." As her comment indicates, it was a summer of art more than it was of politics — though for these visionaries the two were never clearly divided. Jack extended an open welcome to many of his Harvard friends: the painter Marsden Hartley, an imposing presence with china blue eyes under bristling brows; Robert Edmond Jones, Jack's old roommate and a talented artist; Charles Demuth, a painter who came and simply stayed. "Never any women," Louise commented dryly. Jack apparently found the arrangement congenial, but he rented a room over John Francis's General Store, where he could get some work done.

The flowering of the Provincetown Players was the great product of the summer of 1916. The founders of modern American drama, the Players were a visionary group whose goal was to transform theater in America. The guiding figure was a midwesterner, George Cram Cook; the two men whose energy and talent turned his vision into reality were Eugene O'Neill and Jack Reed. In the wings, as it were, was the seductive figure of Louise Bryant, Jack's lover and, as it would turn out, Eugene's as well.

Efforts to start a theater movement in Provincetown had begun the summer before, in strictly amateur fashion but with great seriousness of purpose. Cook — "Jig," as he was known to everyone — had a deep admiration for all things Greek and especially the Dionysian dimensions of Greek drama, in which he saw the social potential of communal theater. He had been moved by Reed's staging of the Paterson silk workers' strike to believe that art and politics could fuse in a dynamically radical way. American commercial theater, meanwhile, was at a decidedly low ebb. Broadway's idea of what would uplift and entertain the nation was such mediocre fare as *Peg o' My Heart* and *Twin Beds*. The Provincetowners bucked the prevailing trend that saw the playwright only as a kind of tradesman who wrote the words that a group of "professionals" would then turn into something commercially acceptable. In their view, the playwright was an artist who should direct the show and all aspects of its production, who would create an event that went beyond words on a page.

The group staged its first plays in the summer of 1915 at 621 Commercial Street, the home of Hutchins Hapgood, the journalist, and his writer wife, Neith Boyce. First on the bill was Boyce's *Constancy*, a comedy inspired, ironically enough, by the affair between John Reed and Mabel Dodge. It was staged on the porch, with the sea in the background and the audience in the living room. After this performance, the audience moved onto the porch, inspected Robert Edmond Jones's scenery, and sat there to watch *Suppressed Desires* by Cook and his wife, Susan Glaspell, a farce on the impact of Freudianism on advocates of free love.

The experiment was such a success that neighbors complained that they had been excluded, and the group moved its activities to the Lewis Wharf fish house, kindly lent them by Margaret Steele, who was renting it for the summer with her husband, Wilbur. Later in the season two more plays were produced on the wharf, one by Cook and one by Wilbur Steele. To Mary Heaton Vorse, the site was distinctly romantic: "The fishhouse was a hundred feet long and fifty feet wide. It had a dark, weathered look, and around the piles waves always lapped except at extreme low tide. There was a huge door on rollers at the side and another at the end which made it possible to use the bay as a backdrop. The planks were wide and one could look through the cracks at the water. The color of the big beams was rich with age." Performances were lit with lamps and lanterns with tin reflectors; the audience sat on hard wooden benches.

By the next summer, when Jack and Louise arrived, electric lights were installed, stationary benches built, and a name chosen: The Wharf

Theatre. The first bill reprised *Suppressed Desires* and introduced Neith Boyce's *Winter's Night* and Reed's *Freedom,* a farce turned out with his left hand about a poet who derives his inspiration from being in jail.

Louise and Jack were drawn by Cook's vision and the promise of communal work in the theater, and Louise began to write a play of her own. She later recalled that she spent almost the entire summer in a bathing suit, only occasionally changing into a white linen sundress. Jack was an enthusiastic swimmer, plunging daily into the bay. Max Eastman, living across the street with his wife, Ida Rauh, and their baby, described the goings-on at the home of Jack Reed and "his red-cheeked, freckled, grey-eyed Irish bride from Oregon": "Louise herself was no housekeeper," he later wrote, "and their place was almost barnlike in its physical aspect. A large assortment of interesting males was provided with abundant nutrition, however, and beds to sleep on."

The theater members, who had named their group the Provincetown Players, were looking for scripts for the second play in their second program when, in early July, Terry Carlin and Eugene O'Neill, both friends of Jack's from Greenwich Village, turned up in nearby Truro. Described by Malcolm Cowley as a "hobo philosopher and mystic who boasted of never having worked at all," Carlin was functioning that summer as the young playwright's sidekick and protector, having helped O'Neill over a drunken winter. He and Gene were out of money and went over to Provincetown to hit up Hutchins Hapgood for ten dollars. On their trip to return the money, Terry ran into Susan Glaspell on the street and she told him of the Players' need for scripts. Terry replied that he himself didn't write at all, "but Mr. O'Neill has a trunk full of plays." Susan told Terry to bring O'Neill by the Cooks' Commercial Street house that evening.

Too nervous either to read his own play or even to hear it read, O'Neill sat silently in the dining room as Frederick Burt, a professional actor, read *Bound East for Cardiff* in the living room, with Jack and Louise, the Cooks, and the self-styled "tramp poet" Harry Kemp, with his beautiful girlfriend Mary Pyne, in the audience. Cook was particularly enthusiastic, his vision of a rejuvenated Dionysian theater seemingly realized. O'Neill "was not left alone in the dining room when the reading had finished," Susan Glaspell later wrote simply. "Then we knew what we were for."

For the summer of 1916 also marked the beginning of the long and enormously successful career of Eugene O'Neill. Born in 1888 (he was three years younger than Louise, though no doubt he didn't know that) into the family of the matinee idol James O'Neill, Gene spent his early life trying to avoid his roots in the theater. Indifferently educated — he dropped out of Princeton after a year — he bummed his way around the world, prospecting for gold in Honduras, serving as a mule tender on a cattle boat out of South Africa, beachcombing in Argentina, and most notably, signing on as an able-bodied seaman on passenger ships. He did try acting briefly in his father's stock company, and worked as a reporter for a newspaper in his native New London, Connecticut, but in 1912 he found himself in a sanatorium with tuberculosis. During his enforced rest he tried his hand at writing plays, and in 1914 enrolled in a drama workshop at Harvard run by Professor George Pierce Baker, whose criticism dampened him somewhat.

He wound up in New York City, drinking too much, spending most of his time at the Hell Hole in the company of prostitutes and assorted no-accounts. He wrote listlessly, and as a writer in the Village he inevitably came to know Reed and his circle, coming to depend on them for handouts and, in Reed's case, readings of his work. He didn't think much of bohemian New York — he was at once too apathetic and too experienced for that scene — but he admired Jack Reed tremendously and was excited by the growing interest of the Players in the new, transformative modern theater movement.

Bound East for Cardiff, produced in July 1916, was a rousing success, not least because of the setting. Susan Glaspell later wrote, "The sea has been good to Eugene O'Neill. It was there for his opening. There was a fog, just as the script demanded, fog bell in the harbor. The tide was in, and it washed under us and around, spraying through the holes in the floor, giving us the rhythm and flavor of the sea." Jig Cook played the dying sailor, and "the old wharf shook with applause."

O'Neill's one-acter shared the bill with Wilbur Steele's *Not Smart* and a play by Louise Bryant called *The Game.* Also set at sea, *The Game* was distinguished by its staging. The sculptor William Zorach and his wife, Marguerite, designed a set that can only be described as high modernist. "We . . . turned an English morality play into a sort of Egyptian panto-mime," Zorach wrote. "The backdrop was an expensive and abstract

pattern of the sea, trees, the moon, and the moon path in the water. . . .
The costumes were slight and abstract and the movements were worked
out in a flat plane in pantomime."

The play boasted a remarkably overstated and formalized acting
style. Life and Death played dice for the lives of the Youth (a poet) and
the Girl (a dancer). Utterly, deliberately nonrealistic, the play received
more acclaim than it perhaps deserved. Designs from it became the logo
for the Players' programs, and it was the first play they performed when
they returned to New York.

For the time being, Louise put aside her journalistic ambitions and
worked tirelessly at the theater. She and O'Neill were in rehearsal for yet
another O'Neill production, *Thirst.* Gene played a mulatto sailor who
shares a raft with a dancer; Louise, as the dancer, desperately thirsty,
tries to seduce the sailor, mistakenly believing he has water. She was
required to pass out on stage, a scene she enjoyed and happily reprised
for anyone who asked.

"Life was all of a piece," Susan Glaspell wrote about that summer,
"work not separated from play, and we did together what none of us
could have done alone." For Jack, however, the idyll was punctuated by
"real" work; in June he traveled to Chicago to cover the Progressive party
convention, and throughout the summer he retreated to his rented
studio to turn out a series of articles for *Collier's* and some lucrative but
inconsequential stories for the *Metropolitan.*

In his absence, Louise found herself drawn into a flirtation with
Gene O'Neill. Intensely romantic, the young playwright tended to ide-
alize women, and before long he was deeply in love with Louise. His
Irishness appealed to her, as did his sheer need. He was struggling to
control his drinking, and Louise's maternal streak ran deep — in fact,
Max Eastman believed there was nothing between Gene and Louise
beyond her efforts to dry him out. But Louise's independent streak ran
equally deep. Instinctively she believed that she could have her erotic
and emotional needs met without sacrificing her autonomy. In fact,
those needs could not be met unless she felt herself spiritually, legally,
and emotionally free.

In short, she and Jack professed free love and were part of a community that practiced it. To her it may have seemed an eminently safe
arrangement — though if it did, she was underestimating Gene's single-
mindedness. He was more cautious, knowing his own nature and admir-

ing Jack as deeply as he did. Louise assuaged his guilt by saying that because of Jack's physical condition — he was having a recurrence of his childhood kidney trouble — they lived together as brother and sister.

Louise seems to have instigated the affair, passing O'Neill one of her recent poems, "Dark Eyes," tucked into a book:

> Dark eyes
> You stir my soul
> Ineffably.
> You scatter
> All my peace.
> Dark eyes,
> What shall I do?

She followed him about the tiny town. When he came out of the water after one of his marathon swims, Louise would be sitting on the shore waiting for him. He and Terry Carlin moved into a sailmaker's loft catercorner to Jack and Louise's house; despite the sign on the door that read GO TO HELL, Louise frequently knocked. And, of course, as Louise disingenuously put it in a letter written much later, "Gene and I were working day and night in the theater."

Before long, Gene succumbed. "When that girl touches me with the tip of her little finger," he told Terry Carlin, "it's like a flame." Word soon spread among the Players, many of whom were deeply resentful. One woman said bitterly about production of *The Game*, "Just because someone is sleeping with somebody is no reason we should do her play." Mabel Dodge, hearing the rumors, hurried up from New York, staying with the Hapgoods, determined to win Jack back. "When I saw Reed on the street, he steeled himself against me," she later wrote in her memoirs. "Though I wanted to be friends, he wouldn't. People said Louise was having an affair with 'Gene O'Neill . . . and I thought Reed would be glad to see me if things were like that between him and Louise — but he wasn't." Of course, things weren't "like that" between Jack and Louise; in fact, Mabel fundamentally misunderstood their relationship.

What did John Reed make of all this? By most accounts, the situation was amicable all around — indeed, it *had* to have been, with the three of them working and living so closely together. Jack respected Louise's freedom and genuinely believed in their vows of free love. However psychologically unlikely that may seem, Louise's account of the summer and Jack's complicated response bears it out. Hers is a bizarre story, written many years later in troubled times, but it is bizarre enough in its details to be, as such stories often are, plausible.

Reed had developed a strange relationship with a British radical named Fred Boyd. Boyd had been jailed during the Paterson strike, and subsequently recanted his association with the IWW. In keeping with his characteristic iconoclasm, Reed became Boyd's champion, eventually secured his release, and then gave him intermittent employment over the years. Boyd, not surprisingly, was devoted to Reed. One night in the summer of 1916, Boyd was drinking with friends when the subject of Louise's affair with Gene came up. He became enraged and determined that the only solution was to buy a gun and kill O'Neill. Lacking the money to buy a pistol, at around four in the morning he appeared drunkenly in the doorway of the bedroom Louise and Jack shared in the house on Commercial Street, demanding forty dollars.

"Jack asked him what he wanted it for," Louise wrote. "He said that he had to kill Eugene O'Neill because I was untrue to Jack and Gene was the culprit." In response, Jack leaned over and kissed Louise and told Boyd to go home and go to bed.

The next morning, Louise continued, Jack showed up at Gene's shack, and said, "Boyd was drunk last night and shooting his face off around town. If you hear any stories don't pay any attention to them. And I wish you and Terry Carlin would take all your meals with us for a while."

Louise did not venture comment on this odd response, and of course Jack's action served her purposes well. But why did he answer a charge that Gene was sleeping with Louise by offering the playwright a place in their household? By the standards of a later time, when sexual freedom seems more natural and less ideological, the answer would probably be masochism or willful denial. We assume that sexual jealousy comes into play in such a situation, but it need not: both Louise and Jack seemed to have felt free of any sense of the conventions of sexual ownership. In this light, Jack's response was simply a manifestation of his commitment to free love. He asked Gene to take meals with him and Louise, in part, of course, to diffuse the gossip that was likely to spread about the three of them. But more importantly, he was acutely aware that anyone who preached free love but could not accommodate it in his own life was a hypocrite. The Provincetowners might gossip about him being "cuck-olded," but cuckoldry was a concept quite literally medieval to Louise and Jack's thinking. For Jack, Louise's relationship with Gene simply did not — could not — matter. Furthermore, if he demanded that Louise keep their relationship exclusive, such a threat to her autonomy might well drive her away.

For his part, O'Neill came to see Louise, according to Agnes Boulton, who would become his second wife, as "a great woman, something out of the old Irish legends, betrayed by life . . . always the pivotal person, beautiful, passionate, and strange." She would be the model for Nina Leeds, the heroine of his 1928 play *Strange Interlude,* who gets everything she wants — but at a terrible price.

Her relationship with Jack endured, even thrived. O'Neill was always secondary, despite the heat of their relationship. Temperamentally, she and Jack were better suited: Gene was introverted, brooding, passive, while Jack was a man of action. Louise too wanted to act, to write, to leave her mark; Jack did not expect her to be a conventional companion or wife, while Gene was far more traditional in that respect. In fact, Gene promised, and presumably expected, exclusive devotion. This was absolutely anathema to Louise.

The letters Jack and Louise exchanged during his absences that summer speak to the rich sympathy between them — and the continuing physical passion. Louise wrote of waffle parties and rehearsals, of gathering cornflowers and marigolds for his arrival. She told him that Hippolyte Havel, their anarchist friend and housekeeper, called their place "a little dove cottage," adding, "He is quite inspired by us. He told me he always thought people had to quarrel just to stir themselves up to keep loving each other. 'But it's not so — why the wrong people get together is all — and dis is so lovely — you and Jackie!'" The antics of their two cats — Samuel Hooper-Hooper and Julius Ward Howe (named, by Jack's friend Bobby Rogers, in tribute to the writer of "The Battle Hymn of the Republic") — were duly reported, as well as the latest love affairs and scandals among the Players. (Clever cat names were popular that summer in Provincetown; the Cook cat was called Copycat, short for Carnal Copulation.)

In a scrawled letter to Sara Bard Field, Louise wrote of her relationship with Jack that "it has been so beautiful and so free! I don't know why Jack and I should ever quarrel. We don't *interfere* with each other at all — we just supplement each other — we feel like children who will never grow up." The only sticking point, she confided, was their not being married:

> Everybody in town seems to be discussing our most intimate affairs and saying 'Of course Jack won't marry her.' As if *marriage* — that most diabolical of all laws — could *purify anything*. Jack has always wanted to marry me *just* because of that gossip. Personally, I don't care at all. I hate marriage like you do but we want to go to China in February and we will have such a hard time to do it otherwise and I want sometime — so much — to have just one child. It is hard to know what to do.

If her love for Jack was her constant refrain, free love was her song. Her distrust of marriage seems to have been genuine. She was, after all, undergoing a divorce at the time, which was granted on July 7, 1916. Paul, who now realized she had deserted him, complained of cruel and inhuman treatment. In another letter to Field, she enclosed a poem called "My Rebels," writing "This and my daffodils are dedicated to Sara Bard Field, Emma Goldman, Margaret Sanger and the rest of my nice rebels." The poem began by asserting that she wished to have no business with "the monotony" of those "who sit and muse upon your virtue rare," and continued,

> I wish to stay with those brave souls who dare
> To break your Stone Age laws and in defiance
> Tear the swathings from your mummy church,
> Who have the valour and the strength to love;
> For in their mighty arms the whole world rests
> And breathes and grows and takes the sunshine in.

❀   ❀   ❀

And so the summer played itself out. In August, Louise was visited by her half brother William, the only family member with whom she was regularly in contact. The Provincetowners, O'Neill among them, drifted back to the city. Tired after the activity and emotional drama of the summer, Louise and Jack took a small cottage by themselves in the comparatively isolated Truro for the month of September; on impulse,

Jack bought it. The month was a time of rest. Jack's kidney had been bothering him all summer; one observer remembered him passing out on stage one evening at the Wharf. But the affair with O'Neill, however distant it might have seemed, had not played itself out, and Louise's faith in the ideals of free love would be shaken to its foundation in the months to come.

5

Playacting and a Separation

With the move back to Washington Square, Louise and Jack were once again consumed by activity. In late summer, the Provincetown Players had caught the attention of a reviewer for the *Boston Globe* who published a glowing account (together with a picture of Louise) that fueled the Players' enthusiasm. They met on September 4 at the Wharf Theatre and incorporated, with Louise acting as secretary, and turned out a document expressing their purpose: "To encourage the writing of American plays of real artistic, literary and dramatic — as opposed to Broadway — merit." They raised donations of $320, and Jig Cook set off to find a theater in Greenwich Village.

The right location was found, in a stable at 139 MacDougal Street, just next door to Polly Holladay's restaurant. Jack provided the motto that was carved into the theater door: "Here Pegasus was hitched." (The winged horse Pegasus is a symbol of immortality — the sure destination of the Players, they thought.) Great energy was required to convert the structure into a theater, and great sums of money were needed — the latter raised mostly by Jack, through an appeal to the New York Stage Society. Financial, legal, and logistical problems had to be worked out at the same time that the plays scheduled for the first bill went into rehearsal in early November. Spirits were high, though, and the Players delighted in firing off missives on their new letterhead, which featured a woodcut from the program for Louise's play.

On that bill were O'Neill's *Bound East for Cardiff,* Bryant's *The Game,* and a farce by Floyd Dell called *King Arthur's Socks.* Because the Players' mission called for the playwright to act as the director, Louise and Gene shared rehearsal space, Louise directing Jack in her play, proud that the Players had chosen it for their first bill.

On weekends, exhausted, they escaped the city to visit the Robinsons — Boardman, known as Mike, and Sally — who had a cottage in the small village of Croton-on-Hudson in Westchester County, an hour north of the city by train, on Mount Airy Hill, a part of town so frequented by radicals that it would be dubbed "Red Hill." Croton was a favorite Villager retreat — Max Eastman and Mabel Dodge had week-end cottages there — and Jack and Louise soon found themselves house-hunting. Louise, as much as she loved New York, was particularly vociferous on the need to have an escape from the city: Jack had, she said, grown too accustomed to wasting himself with Greenwich Villag-ers. At "quiet and peaceful and happy" Croton, she urged, they could "*work* out here, uninterrupted, and play in town. We can't put off real work year after year." By the end of October they had found a house, a cottage called Innisfree.

But they were now working — and playing — under a cloud. One of Jack's kidneys, the doctors determined, had to be removed. He was to undergo treatment at Johns Hopkins in Baltimore, which, under Dr. Hugh Hampton Young, had become one of the foremost urology cen-ters in the country. Jack, with his Harvard connections and his family's influence, received the best care. His admission to the hospital was scheduled for November 12. His operation (indeed, any operation in those days) was deemed gravely serious, and Jack wanted Louise to be his legal heir. To this end, they were married in the city clerk's office in Peekskill, New York, Louise giving her age as twenty-six to Jack's twenty-nine, and her occupation "story writer" to Jack's "journalist." Jack instructed his lawyer, Amos Pinchot, to deed the house to Louise for the same pragmatic reason.

"I had a lump in my throat as big as the Woolworth Tower when I left the station," Louise wrote after seeing Jack off on the train to Baltimore on November 12. She wrote him nearly every day, affectionate, newsy letters with much talk of the Players and getting the Croton house ready to move into. Jack's letters were equally affectionate and solicitous — filled with domestic details about bills and mortgage payments — and sometimes grumpy, when she didn't attend to details properly. But as his stay went on — the operation was scheduled for November 22, and in the meantime he underwent a series of very painful tests — his handwriting became ragged, his tone more plaintive.

It was a tortuous situation, the details of which are extremely hard to decipher. O'Neill had a room at 38 Washington Square and, of course, worked daily at the theater with Louise. But his presence was only part of the puzzle. Louise's domestic situation was getting more and more complicated. Marguerite and Bill Zorach, along with their little son, Tessim, had moved in with Jack and Louise for a time. Also living there was Nani Bailey, a friend who had recently opened a successful tea shop called the Samovar around the corner from the Hell Hole. Nani irritated Louise by throwing late-night parties. Added to the ménage was an elderly black woman named Caroline who served as cook, maid, and general factotum; presumably she roomed elsewhere.

The very evening Louise saw Jack off, she wrote that she was having dinner with "Nonnie" (as she always referred to her) and Gene. Thereafter, this pair — "the old faithfuls" — dominated her letters; at one point she even declared herself "*tired* of their faces and chatter." She complained of waking up and finding the studio filled with bottles and partygoers: Nani, Charles Demuth, even Marcel Duchamp. She reported on the Players' progress: Jack's *Freedom* went off well enough in his absence, but O'Neill's *Before Breakfast* was not as well received as his last effort. She had been rehearsing with the poet William Carlos Williams in Alfred Kreymborg's *Lima Beans,* a play the group didn't like but over which Jack had threatened to resign if they refused to produce it.

But another note threaded through her letters: Louise was intermittently gravely ill, with a gynecological trouble that ominously involved reproduction and, indirectly, sexual infidelity. "Do write me right away and tell me all about how your insides are doing," Jack wrote urgently the day after he entered the hospital. Louise reported that she had seen Harry Lorber, her doctor, and "he put on another poultice and he thinks that will be the end of it."

Lorber, a colorful Village figure who in his girth and dress resembled nothing so much as a southern sheriff, was the man to whom Villagers turned when periods were late or venereal diseases suspected; it was Lorber who was called when a peyote party at Mabel Dodge's got out of hand and Andrew Dasburg almost lost it. You paid Dr. Lorber what you could, when you could. He had Louise under close watch.

On December 7 Louise wrote Jack again: she had taken very ill up in Croton, and Lorber ordered her either to go to a hospital or have home care. Nani was unable to help her — she had a party under way — but her friend Beckie Edelson, a union leader, had installed Louise in the Morningside Drive apartment she shared with her lover, Charlie Plunkett. Louise needed constant enemas, douches, and ice bags. The abscess was gone, she reported, but her "insides" on her left were inflamed and infected. Lorber hoped at any cost to avoid an (unspecified) operation. And, she added, most curiously, "They think maybe I got it from your condition."

Jack, understandably, was dismayed and agitated. Sure that Louise was not telling him everything, he wrote that he wanted to speak to Dr. Lorber himself. He protested that he had asked the experts and that his kidney trouble could not possibly have anything to do with whatever was wrong with her. In his alarm at the prospect of her operation, he was unwittingly — or unconsciously — thoughtless: "But honey — it's awful to remove your ovaries, isn't it? Doesn't it make you incapable of having children and everything like that? I never heard of that being done to anybody but dogs, cats and horses." He went on, more sensitively, to say that he was eagerly waiting for any word.

Reed was especially anxious to hear whether her condition was in any way tubercular; he may well have suspected that whatever Louise had could have been contracted through sexual contact with O'Neill, an arrested TB victim. Even the specialists at Johns Hopkins (and among them was Carl Binger, Jack's old Harvard classmate) would likely have been puzzled by Louise's symptoms. Word around the Village was that Louise was suffering from a botched abortion and that the father was O'Neill.

The issues surrounding Louise's illness seem to have been surprisingly confused in the minds of all three of the players in this drama. Louise had told Gene in the preceding summer that she and Jack were not sleeping together because of his kidney. She may have meant that Jack was in too much pain to make love, but her later suggestion that she might have caught her condition from his ailment suggests rather that she was woefully, or willfully, naive about human sexuality. Jack worried too that contagion was possible, which suggests similar ignorance.

O'Neill may have simply relished the drama of the situation; in fact, one likely scenario is that Louise had an ovarian infection and led Gene to believe she had aborted his baby.

For there is no question that Louise and Gene had resumed their affair. In fact, Gene moved in with her right after Jack's departure. A letter from Louise to Amos Pinchot says only that he had a studio "on the same floor" and was so much a part of her life that she did not even bother to edit him out of her letters to her husband. Jack knew that the theater would have thrown them together in any case. But terms had shifted somewhat in that she deliberately misled Jack about where O'Neill was living. When Jack threatened to visit, she repeatedly told him not to surprise her: "[B]e *sure* to let me know when you are coming. Surprise parties won't do for me darling — not now."

In all likelihood, the real story was one of decisions, changes of mind, and anxiety over how the other person might feel. Louise had resolved to break off with Gene, probably during her month alone with Jack in Truro, and had told Jack of her decision. The news that she had resumed the affair would have been difficult to break under the circumstances — indeed, confessing to a man as ill as Jack would constitute cruel, even gratuitous honesty. She may have tried to tell him during a brief visit she made to Baltimore at the end of November but lost her nerve. Once again, of course, his ignorance served her purposes well. But she may also have felt, as she had earlier, that the affair was inconsequential, having no effect on her relationship with Jack. And, of course, her behavior was becoming instinctive: when alone and frightened (as well as, in this case, very ill) she turned to a lover who was close at hand.

Still, the letters between Jack and Louise maintained the note of affection and passion of their summer correspondence, particularly as they both grew stronger. Their marriage remained a secret — which Louise rather enjoyed. All his friends wanted to do something for Jack, she wrote: "Oh honey heart — everyone's been pouring out love over you all day long and it's nice to have the little secret about us when they do." Of course, she related, it was considered by those in the know as a "terrible *scandal*" that was bound to get out. "Everyone else seems stupid" when Jack was away, she wrote impatiently.

She was busy making preparations to move to the cottage in Croton, finalizing the financing, packing, and cleaning up the cottage to rid all traces of its former inhabitants, Ida Rauh and Max Eastman. She spent several days up there in November, staying with Mike and Sally Robinson until the place was habitable. Jack finally left the hospital in mid-December, with strict warnings about the need for full recuperation. With a weakened Jack in tow, Louise set up housekeeping in time for Christmas.

For such peripatetic and adventurous souls, Louise and Jack were intensely domestic, their surroundings very important to their well-being. The white clapboard house on Mt. Airy Road, with its black shutters and commodious grounds, brought them both immense satisfaction. The setting was quite grand: Croton overlooked the Hudson, and to the north they could see the Bear Mountain Bridge, to the south the Palisades and, even back then, the skyscrapers of Manhattan. The house itself was tiny — only four rooms — with very low ceilings, the bedroom little more than an attic. But it had three fireplaces, and the overgrown yard, even in the dead of winter, showed signs of once having been carefully tended. As the weather warmed, Jack and Louise bought seedlings and shrubs; Jack built what would grow into a dense box hedge separating the house from the road by settling tiny sprigs in the ground, watering them and monitoring their progress daily. There was a beech tree with a circular bench around it, and at some distance from the house was a shack that they would use as a studio or, when nights were very hot, a place to sleep. The little place seemed too modest to bear a title like Innisfree, and they soon dropped it.

However domestic were Jack and Louise's natures, neither had much to do with household chores. For a few weeks they had a trained nurse with them while they recuperated, and Caroline had been with them from the start. The house was heated by the fireplaces, and Caroline turned out delicious southern dishes in the rudimentary kitchen, equipped with only a kerosene stove and a tin oven. "We were soon feeling very strong," Louise wrote.

Consciously or not, they steered clear of the Village for the moment, perhaps aware that they needed time alone together to get their relationship back on track. They put aside their theatrical ambitions and turned their energies back to journalism. Throughout the months of Jack's sickness — and before — they had dreamed of going to China together to cover the revolutionary uprisings. Louise envisioned them working cooperatively and at each other's side — not at all in competition. She compared them to another working couple, Inez Hayes Gillmore and Bill Irwin, who apparently came home from Europe on separate steamers five days apart in order to scoop each other. "We won't *ever* do that anyway. That is just one thing that I love about our being together. You want to see me do my best and I want you to — *at any cost!*" In a letter to Jack written in November, she declared, "China is going to be a splendid thing for both of us!" Leftists around the world focused on China in 1916. Sun Yat-sen, the republican leader, had raised a rebellion against China's warlords, and, more than a year before the czarist regime in Russia was overthrown, China was the place where world revolution seemed to be fomenting.

Jack's doctors gave the trip the go-ahead in early January 1917. Jack was to write a series for the *Metropolitan*, which announced, "He will hold the mirror up to this mysterious and romantic country, and we shall see its teeming millions and the big forces at work there." With her background on the *Portland Spectator*, but without any "hard" journalism clips to show for herself, Louise got press credentials from the *New York Tribune*.

They were poised to leave when, in late January, Germany announced that it would sink all ships and submarines, belligerent and neutral, in a wide band surrounding the Allied countries in Europe. President Wilson was forced to sever diplomatic relations with Germany, and war was clearly imminent. Carl Hovey canceled Jack's trip, suggesting he might be needed in Europe, and Louise reluctantly gave up her plans as well.

The spring was professionally uneventful but emotionally stormy. Jack wrote a few things — most notably a profile of the American Federation of Labor president, Samuel Gompers — but Louise's career was on hold. Money was tight, and Jack was forced to pawn his father's gold watch and later to sell the Truro cottage. (Margaret Sanger took over the mortgage.) War was declared on April 6, to the dismay of Jack, Louise, and other antiwar organizers. The same month, Jack published the ringing piece in *The Masses* that asked repeatedly *whose* war this was — that of the American people, or that of warmongering capitalists bent on profit. The piece concluded, defiantly, "Whose war is this? Not mine." It was a refrain he would repeat on speaking platforms and before Senate committees, and it was a stance that alienated not only some of his friends and family but almost all of his potential employers.

Louise shared his convictions utterly. But when her half brother Floyd Sherman came through town in uniform, she defended him with as much conviction as Jack showed in his writing and speechmaking. Floyd was at the beginning of a successful business and government career. After graduating from the University of Nevada, he had received a Rhodes scholarship to study law at Oxford. He had undergone officers' training at the Presidio in San Francisco, and came to the Village in full officer's regalia. Louise greeted her brother warmly, without making any comments on his uniform, and took him out to dinner with a group of their friends. Over the meal, talk turned to the war and someone challenged Floyd's participation. Louise stood up and made a speech of her own: "You can think anything you want, but you are not to criticize my brother. He is doing what he believes in."

The O'Neill drama had not yet played itself out. Louise had met O'Neill's family in New London, and they had taken to her, considering her a restraining influence on their son's drinking and thus an honorary daughter. Gene's brother, James, turned to her in the spring of 1917, asking her help in getting Gene off the streets of New York. After Louise and Jack packed off to Croton, Gene had returned to his old habits — drinking at the Hell Hole, sleeping on the floors of acquaintances' apartments. His parents had taken a room at the St. George Hotel in Brooklyn Heights, but Gene would have nothing to do with them. Louise found Gene at the Hell Hole, unwashed, unshaven, and truculently drunk. Somehow she charmed him onto a bus and got him to the St. George, where he sobered up. A few days later he telephoned her in Croton. She came to see him and they had, she later reported, "a serious talk." Gene decided to go to Provincetown, where temptations were fewer and perhaps he could work. In the same intimate conversation, she agreed to visit him there.

What — or whether — she was telling Jack at this point is not clear. He was gone for a good part of May, organizing antiwar demonstrations in Washington. Louise traveled up to Provincetown to meet Gene that month. She later said that he was "thunderstruck" to see her, and she took a room not far away. She stayed for a week, until she received a telegram from Jack. It pulled at her heart: "Peach tree blooming," he cabled, "and wrens have taken their house." She took the next train out of Fall River to Grand Central, hastened up to Croton, and found that Jack had filled the house with little bunches of wild wood violets. The stage was set for a pastoral idyll, a chance to regroup and rethink their personal and professional goals, some time together to mend their troubled relationship.

An explosion intervened, an explosion that led to a desperate and miserable separation. Just what happened can only be pieced together through Louise and Jack's letters while they were apart; indeed, even during their separation new troubles surfaced that deepened the rift between them.

It seems that Jack had slept with another woman — more than one, in fact. There had been no deep attachments; he loved Louise, but it was difficult to resist the advances of the many young, pretty, and intelligent women whose paths he crossed. These dalliances meant little to him; perhaps he did not even confess them to Louise but rather she saw telltale signs and drew her own conclusions. Yet in the aftermath, the fact of these affairs came to cause Jack considerable torment, suggesting that the explosion had as much to do with a more general crisis in the state of their relationship as it had to do with their highly vaunted but, as it turned out, ambivalently held ideas of free love.

It was impossible for Louise to remain cool and detached under the circumstances. For all her independence, she was extremely dependent on Jack, both for a sense of her own identity and because she continued to feel rootless and insecure, as she had for much of her life. Jack was her mainstay. She felt, somewhat unreasonably, that *her* affair with O'Neill was quite different — Jack had known about (parts of) it and had implicitly sanctioned it. She justified it as well by her inward conviction that it would never shake her love for Jack: all he had to do was wire her that the fruit trees were blooming at their little cottage and she was at his side, Gene forgotten. But she could not be so sure about Jack; she knew all too well how charming he could be and the lengths to which women might go to attract him. Moreover, passing affairs, she felt, somewhat romantically, suggested that their sexual relationship was something less than the exalted state they had always proclaimed it.

She may also have been genuinely shaken by the hypocrisy she sensed in her own reaction. Could it be that her feelings about free love in actuality were not as mature as her philosophical belief in it? She was highly principled about such matters in the abstract, and her response to Jack's affairs threw her into a state of great confusion and emotional crisis. She went absolutely to pieces, lashing out at Jack in a lacerating series of scenes of recrimination and fury. Jack suddenly seemed to understand completely, and this crisis was to lead to a major stocktaking of his own. Their feelings began to move away from outrage over betrayals to a more major assessment of their marriage and their own personalities.

It was clear that Louise had to get away, and she felt that work might be the one thing that could save her. In fact, Jack's betrayal and the ensuing crisis galvanized her. She turned to friends for help. Mike Robinson suggested that she go to France to cover the war. Before she knew it Jack had secured her press credentials with John Wheeler of the newly formed Bell Syndicate. She lost a little of her nerve: it all seemed very sudden — almost a *fait accompli,* she said a little resentfully. It had happened "as the heart beats," she wrote.

While she prepared to sail, Jack moved to the Harvard Club. From Croton, Louise wrote to him in a dark mood. A trip to Europe was extremely dangerous at the time, not least because of the German U-boats. She was distinctly morbid, but whatever her feelings, she was determined not to shrink from the challenge. Suggesting how deeply felt were her worries — not only about her safety but her very future — she told Jack that if anything happened to her he should get in touch with her mother in Sparks, Nevada. She added, with her old defiance, "My people are in no way a part of me — please don't ever connect them with me, but I just feel they'd need to know — just as you'd write to a paper or recorder's office." She vowed to work hard in France, and added a note about Jack's infidelities, suggesting that they hoped to work things out with time and distance: "If this thing happens again *don't, don't* get despondent. Maybe I'll understand better when I get back."

She sailed on the *Espagne* on June 9, on a boat occupied mainly by ambulance service troops. As the boat pulled out, a group of ambulance men had their arms around her shoulders, shouting to Jack, "We'll take care of her!" "Which didn't help any," she later observed dryly, indicating how strained the parting was. She tried to keep her letters sprightly, describing the friends she met on the boat: Frances Joliffe, a newspaperwoman from the *San Francisco Bulletin* who took a great fancy to Louise; the Misses McClellan and Smith, interior decorators from Wanamaker's whom Louise found shallow; Mademoiselle Bell, a French teacher from, of all places, Portland; and the usual component of journalists. A couple named Jerry and Lucille Blum took her under their wing, insisting she share their stateroom; it seems Lucille was, like many of those on board, terrified of being torpedoed. These fears were not unfounded. Louise would very soon write about the journey for the *New York American* in a piece that shows her growing flair for description and the evolution of her personalized, participatory style. Opening by claiming the voyage was "the most exciting trip from New York any ship of this line has made," she plunged right in: "Attacked by a submarine eight days out, and with an American ambulance recruit going violently insane the second day at sea, the crowded cabins had little room for gloomy introspection." The mood was tense, with strangers telling each other their life stories, and the passengers' inactivity broken only by regular lifeboat drills. Most of the life preservers on board, she wrote tersely, had been eaten by rats. Her description of the submarine sighting and the ship's attack in response was vivid: "Bells jangled, the ship trembled with all the engines could bear, and we began to zigzag lurching heavily, to outwit the monster trying to hit us broadside on." She described how the periscope of the U-boat slowly slipped from view without having fired a torpedo, so pressed had it been to avoid the *Espagne*'s shots. The passengers had drawn together: "Almost everyone slept, or rather dozed in their chairs on deck that night and also the next night. Sunday morning we woke at dawn to see the shores of France in the distance."

This kind of tension, coupled with Louise's wracking worries about her relationship with Jack, made for a terrible strain, and her letters showed it. On her sixth night at sea, she wrote that she thought their separation was necessary, however painful. She recalled a moment early in their relationship, when he told her "that people seldom find the lovers they dream about. Oh my darling, I think they seldom *know* when they *do* find them — they let them slip away. My deepest belief is that . . . from now on we *will* know." She implied that the fault was not hers: "I always *knew* but you didn't. It seems to me that I loved you before I was born, before I can remember and no one else — ever. No one *could* love you as I do!"

Reed was suffering too. He was working for the *New York Mail* (German-owned, though he didn't know it) and had taken a room on 7 West 14th Street, telling no one of his whereabouts so he could get some work done — and, perhaps, remain free from temptation. From Croton he wrote Louise a defeated but reassuring letter:

> Dearest of honies . . . it isn't you who must learn, my honey, but me. In lots of ways we are very different, and we must both try to realize that — while loving each other. But of course on this last awful business, you were humanly right and I was wrong. I have always loved you my darling ever since I first met you — and I guess I always will. This is more than I've ever felt for anyone, honestly. I know the one thing I cannot bear any more is consciously to hurt you honey.

Louise landed in Bordeaux on June 18 and spent two days there. She used the time to write. On board ship she had met and extensively interviewed a Vanderbilt dowager who was president of the American Ambulance Corps, Louise thought, or at any rate who supported them handsomely on $32,000 a month. An ambulance driver she met in Bordeaux proved an even better source on the corps, and she dashed off an article that she sent to Jack, enclosing as well the piece about her voyage under the threat of torpedoes. Jack cobbled her stories together with excerpts from her letters, and then turned them over to Wheeler, who usually placed them in the *New York American*. Explaining the editorial work he did on the *Espagne* story, he wrote, "When I say I've 'finished a story,' don't imagine I am rewriting it; I'm using your words, only editing a little."

Louise was feeling her way journalistically and no doubt was grateful for Jack's help. She was stymied by her inability to get credentials from the Maison de la Presse, without which all her stories would be censored. She camped out in front of the American ambassador's office hoping to get him to use his influence, and eventually she prevailed. She teamed up with another transplanted Villager, Esther Andrews, a writer on a magazine called *Women's Wear* who had come to Paris looking for more meaningful assignments. Esther became an immediate friend (she had known Jack and Max Eastman in New York and had once in fact rented the little Croton house). Their aim was to get to the front, where they hoped to see the Bastille Day celebration. Louise finally prevailed. She reached the front lines in early July. The danger there was very real: once she narrowly missed German bombs by taking cover in an ammunition dump. When the American troops reached the front, she was the only reporter present, and the soldiers greeted her with delight. For the most part, however, she gathered material behind the lines, talking with the British and Australian troops, mostly ambulance men. She genuinely enjoyed their company, writing later: "When they used to come on leave to Paris, I used to go about with them, seeing the night life, and I lived absolutely and completely an army existence." Though Louise sent off several articles to Wheeler by way of Reed (none terribly consequential — a representative one reported the order that women correspondents wear uniforms), after a time she contented herself with listing story ideas in letters to Jack, stories she would write up on her return. She hung about the cafés and complained about the ubiquity of stringers from the wire services and homesick Americans who were afraid to return because of the U-boats. She herself was homesick, she wrote time and again — not for any particular place but for him: "I just want my honey. Wherever he is, is home."

And she made more friends, among them a couple who would remain close to her throughout her life. John Storrs was an American painter married to a French woman, Marguerite. The son of a wealthy Chicago architect and real estate developer, Storrs had lived abroad since his marriage in 1914, but the terms of his trust dictated that he spend six months of the year in America. The arrangement left Storrs feeling isolated and uprooted, and he privately asked Louise to persuade Marguerite to accompany him to New York from time to time. The Storrs were "faithful and humble" admirers of Jack, she wrote happily.

Indeed, everyone admired Reed and treated Louise with respect as his wife. Away from him, her feelings coalesced, and she tried to tell him that she had overcome any doubts about their life together:

O dearest, I *could* talk to you now. I *could* air every part of my heart and brain. I understand you and I understand myself better than you think. We would be happy — more deeply happy than we have ever been — this just *had* to happen — not this miserable mess but *something* to make us find each other. I love you with all my heart — I can never love anyone else. I want everything about you to be beautiful and fine. You are essentially so wonderful and so big. Artists you do not know at all love you over here. I will tell you all that when I see you — I hope to God it is soon.

But Jack was stumbling toward conclusions of his own, confused and lonely as he was. He wanted to understand better what role Louise's infidelities had played in the current crisis, and he sought out Dr. Lorber. It is impossible to know what Lorber told him, but evidently he had to reveal Louise and Gene's autumn affair, for Jack wrote Louise about his meeting, saying laconically, "Think about you and me a good deal, will you? It is not worth keeping going if you love someone else better," signing it simply "Yours, Jack."

Before he received her reply, Jack wrote a long and tortuous letter, one that indicates how the crisis had come to encompass far more than personal infidelities. He tried to be frank and forthright about his feelings and about his sexuality and succeeded only in showing how confused he was about both. He'd met a young girl who wanted to make love, he said, adding, inscrutably, "I didn't, and couldn't." Still, however, he was plagued by desires: "I think there's something terribly wrong about me — that I may be a little crazy, for I had a desire once, just the other day. I can't tell you how wretched that made me feel — how I have looked into myself and tried to know why these things happen." It seems that he was saying that he could not distinguish between a passing desire and infidelity — hardly an indication that he had anything figured out.

But he shifted focus in the same letter, seeking to understand the reason for his confusion. It was women, he concluded: "You see, my dearest lover, I was once a free person. I didn't depend on anything. I was as humanly independent as it was possible to be. Then along came women, and they set out deliberately, as they always do, to break that armor down, to make the artist a human being and dependent upon human beings. Well, they did it, and so now without a mate I am half a man, and sterile." He liked this reasoning, for it explained why he felt "under repression" so much of the time. While this state of mind is hardly borne out by his actions in these years, it is evidently an honest assessment of his psychic state: "I feel that I am always on the verge of something monstrous. This is not as bad as it seems, dear — it is just that no one I love has ever been able to let me express myself fully, freely, and trust that expression."

He returned to his infidelities, which he referred to as "four or five of these things that have worn you down." Again, he retreated into his abstract belief in independence and free love while overlooking how disastrously botched those beliefs had turned out thus far in their own marriage. He continued, "Still, my darling, *you've* got to make up your mind to trust me or our life together will be a farce. . . . It would be intolerable to both of us if you felt you had to direct and censor my thoughts, my actions — as you have in the past — as you did in your letter telling me not to drink."

If his request for trust was more reasonable than his blaming her for his repression, he became confused again when he tried to assess his sexuality and how they could deal with it in their relationship. He asked simply for acceptance: "In other words, you've got to realize that I'm defective (if that is it) or at any rate different, and though I won't do anything you ask me not to, you must accept a difference in my feelings and thoughts."

Few women would know how to respond to such an outpouring; Louise simply professed her love. She had recovered her equilibrium and felt sure enough that she could calm Jack and even allude to her affair with O'Neill in a way that would reassure him of her love and his worthiness of it. "Dearest," she began. "Now, honey . . . , I am feeling *very calm* as I write this. Nothing matters so much as my love for you — I don't know what you have said to Lorber or what he has said to you — I *don't* love anyone else. I'm *dead sure* of that I just love you." Cabling Jack that she would return in August, she gathered her notes, resolving to craft them into articles on her return.

Jack wrote her back, though he knew the letter probably would arrive after she sailed; they both felt a need now to speak with conviction: "I must write anyway from my full heart, to tell you how glad I am you are at last coming home. It will be wonderful, my own sweetest, to see you again and hold you in my arms. I do love you very much, no doubt about that. I love and need you. I don't mind saying that it has been a pretty terrible summer for me. And it is probably going to be hard still for a while, but when you are here I won't mind so much." The crisis had passed, it seems, through their very determination to let love carry the day. Yet many issues remained unresolved.

That summer, Jack was preoccupied with one of his most powerful writing efforts. "Almost Thirty" — Jack was twenty-nine — was not a piece of reportage or a political essay but an autobiographical narrative, a moving attempt at self-examination and self-expression. He speaks of love only at the end, first voicing some of his old confusions about his sexuality and his love affairs, but closing with a stirring declaration of his passion for Louise: "In thinking it over, I find little in my thirty years that I can hold to. I haven't any God and don't want one: faith is only another word for finding oneself. In my life as in most lives, I guess, love plays a tremendous part. I've had love affairs, passionate happiness, wretched maladjustments; hurt deeply and been deeply hurt. But at last I have found my friend and lover, thrilling and satisfying, closer to me than anyone has ever been. And now I don't care what comes."

For Louise's part, her attempt to establish herself as a professional journalist was a personal victory. She came away from the drama of her relationship with Jack in 1916 and 1917 with a clear sense that she must achieve something independent of him, forge her own career, and carve out her own life. Her feminism now extended well beyond suffrage and free love; she wanted to be a person in her own right. A daughter of the frontier, she had come from nowhere, had always had ambition, and was determined not to let traditional ties hold her — especially the tie of marriage, however newly sure she felt about the love between her and Jack. She was poised to come out of her husband's shadow and take flight, in a world where revolution and previously unheard of freedoms seemed tangible realities.

6

At the Barricades

*L*ouise's voyage home from France was far less of an ordeal than
her voyage out. On her first crossing, the threat of U-boats lay
ahead, as the *Espagne* approached European waters; going back,
the danger was over early, and the rest of the trip passed without any
such foreboding. More importantly, her emotional turmoil had eased,
though issues between her and Jack were very much unresolved — as,
for that matter, were those between her and Gene. But she felt sure, at
least, that she and Jack would manage somehow to continue on together. She had a new determination to create an independent life for
herself. On the other hand, the prospect of U.S. entry into the war and
dramatic changes on the international scene made her future uncertain.
She would go where the news was; that was all she was sure of.

Any uncertainties were swept aside when Jack met her ship at the
dock on August 13. There was a tremendous heat wave, she remembered
later, and a perspiring Jack was decked out in a white Shantung suit and
Panama hat. They were off to Russia, he announced, in just four days.
Revolution there looked imminent. Everything fell into place; for two
ambitious journalists, the course was clear.

They headquartered at the Hotel Brevoort, sending Caroline up to
close the Croton house. The days passed in a flurry of activity. In France,
Louise had made promises to John and Marguerite Storrs about what
she could do for them stateside. Addressing them as "dear people," she

wrote that she had showed Max Eastman John's etchings, which were met with great enthusiasm, and that she had left Marguerite's poems with *Seven Arts* editor Waldo Frank. Equally pressing, however, was the need to prepare for what might prove to be a long stay in Russia. She and Jack hoped to remain at least until late fall, and accordingly set out to find heavy winter clothing. In the middle of a heat wave, this was hard to do, and they had to set out "without even enough clothes to keep us warm," as Louise wrote the Storrses.

Jack had made some preparations for the trip before Louise's return. He had to be legally exempted from the draft to obtain a passport; though he preferred to take a moral stand against the war, he decided instead to take an easy physical exemption on the grounds of his kidney removal.

Finding the money for the journey was more difficult, as none of the mainstream magazines or newspapers would send him, citing his anti-war stance and Socialist tendencies. Max Eastman wanted to send him on behalf of *The Masses,* and enlisted the support of Eugen Boissevain, who eventually raised $2000 for Reed's expenses. Reed also agreed to act as correspondent for the Socialist *New York Call* and the cultural monthly *Seven Arts,* though they could not furnish him with funds.

Louise had an easier time of it, because she had not advertised her political views in print as much as Jack had. Women correspondents were still not fully trusted by the mainstream press; they were seldom appointed to file "pure" news stories. Quite typically, then, the Bell Syndicate, which had given Louise credentials for her Paris trip, appointed her to cover the revolution "from a woman's point of view." She was also appointed as correspondent for the *Metropolitan,* Jack's erstwhile venue, and for *Seven Arts* and *Every Week* (which would both go out of business very soon).

Jack and Louise assembled their passports and bought their tickets, but when they went to get their final visas the day before they were to sail, the clerk confiscated their passports. A Socialist peace conference — the Second International Congress of Socialists — was scheduled for August in Stockholm, and Jack had hoped to attend. The State Department was determined to throw any roadblock it could in the path of an American radical looking to go abroad.

Jack was downcast and deeply pessimistic about this unexpected reversal. He said to Louise, "I had so planned to write about Russia, I don't know what to do." Not so Louise. "I thought it over myself," she wrote later, "and decided a little vamping was necessary." Leaving Jack asleep in the hotel, she got up very early and went down to the same office. "I smiled at the clerk — nobody else was about — we sat down and talked. I let him hold my hand and we got very chummy." Then she coyly murmured, "Now, you're going to give me back those passports, aren't you?" He did, and she rushed back to the hotel, woke Jack, and told him to get ready to sail.

Having done her bit, on August 17, aboard the Danish steamer *United States*, Louise Bryant sailed with Jack Reed into the revolution.

Their timing could not have been better — a tribute in part to Jack's fantastic journalistic instinct, but even more so to the extraordinary enthusiasm both he and Louise brought to covering the Russian people's convulsive year, as well as the speed with which they grasped the complicated sequence of events in the months before the revolution.

The world war had been a series of disasters for the Russian empire. Its armies, compared to those of Germany and Austria, its chief opponents on the eastern front, were simply not strong enough. As early as the fall of 1915, Russia had lost a million men. By the end of 1916 the czar, traditionally revered by the Russian people as the "Little Father" of the nation, had become dismally unpopular. Order — the sine qua non of the czarist regime — was deteriorating dangerously. Mutinies were breaking out in the barracks and at the front, strikes and mass demonstrations were rife, workers were forming committees, or soviets, in urban factories. Faced with serious shortages — especially of food — and prices that were rising faster than wages, the people were acutely discontented. In March 1917, the large Petrograd Soviet of Workers' and Soldiers' Deputies, in concert with the Duma, Russia's parliamentary body, set up a provisional government. On March 15,* this body sent delegates to the czar, effectively forcing him to resign, thus ending Russia's thousand-year-old monarchy.

The new provisional government faced enormous obstacles, most crucially the decision of whether to pursue the war, which was quickly

* The Russians would not change over to the Gregorian calendar until February 1918, but dates are given here in the so-called New Style. The Old Style date of the czar's resignation would be March 2. Thus the so-called October Revolution is here dated, according to the New Style, in November.

spinning out of control for the outmatched, incompetently led Russian troops. When Foreign Minister Pavel Milyukov prevailed on his colleagues to make a fresh commitment to Russia's allies, Britain and France, he provoked the mass demonstrations of the April Days, and the first government of the new era was forced out. A new cabinet, with Aleksandr Kerensky as war minister, took over. Kerensky, a moderate Social Democrat, seemed at first to understand the mixed signals the people were sending amidst the increasing disorder. Thinking that some sign was needed to show that centuries of repression were giving way to real political change, the new government granted a general political amnesty that included advocates of revolution like Lenin and Trotsky.

But the new government was still out of touch with the people. The war had shattered Russia economically, and the people — soldiers, peasants, urban workers — were more concerned with the basics — food, shelter, and an end to the long state of siege — than with political gestures that most of them did not fully understand. Not surprisingly, then, the Kerensky government made two fatal mistakes.

First, and most disastrous, was the government's decision to press the war. They felt Russia's honor depended on its alliance with France and Britain, and they feared a substantial loss of Russian territory to the Germans. Persuasive reasons to fight — but not at a time when Russia's army was close to collapse and the people were desperate for peace. It would take the Bolsheviks — and especially Lenin — to grasp the necessity of leaving the war, and the opportunity this could give to a well-organized opposition.

Second, thinking it impossible to hold elections in wartime, they put off a promised election for an assembly to write a new constitution. Suspension of the elections guaranteed that Russia would continue without a popularly sanctioned government for an indefinite period. This gave the Bolsheviks, the left Social Revolutionists, and the other radical parties whose members were streaming back to Russia in the wake of the amnesty, a very big, very real issue to flog.

Just before Louise and Jack sailed, a sequence of events paved the way for the revolution. The Bolsheviks had been gaining strength in the spring, building up their representation in the soviets. Their ascendancy culminated in the July Days, a series of Bolshevik-led strikes and demonstrations that made revolution seem imminent. But the Bolsheviks decided their timing was wrong and drew back, and the party was banned by the provisional government, now with Kerensky as its prime minister. In the wake of the July Days, the conservatives in the government pressed their new advantage and threw their support behind General Lavr Kornilov, Kerensky's chief of staff. Kornilov attempted a putsch, which was quickly defeated. But it electrified the more radical elements in Moscow and Petrograd, revealing the existence of an opposition on the right and thus spurring those on the left to seek more radical solutions.

What Kerensky could not see, Louise and Jack, outsiders though they were, understood clearly. To the dramatic dance of events in Russia, they brought a profound sympathy for the Russians and the radical revolutionaries, born of their experience with American workers and radicals. Equally important in shaping their views was their journey through Russia en route to Petrograd and Moscow.

With them on the Danish steamer that took them to Europe were assorted Scandinavians, American salesmen hoping to do business in Russia, a group of young college men going to work for an American bank in Petrograd, and — what particularly moved Louise — about a hundred exiled Jews hoping to return to their homeland. "From my elevation on the first-class deck on the first night out I could hear returning exiles in the steerage singing revolutionary songs," Louise later wrote. "In the days that followed I spent most of my time down there."

They had expected delays and complications in abundance. In Halifax, Nova Scotia, the ship was stopped by British officers searching for contraband. A great number of the exiles, weeping and begging for mercy, were put off to be returned to the United States. The British were cautious enough that they delayed the steamer for a week, conducting exhaustive searches and background checks. Jack had a number of papers he didn't want the British to see — letters from American radicals to Russian socialists, as well as his invitation to the Stockholm peace conference. He and Louise hid the papers under the rug in their cabin, greeting the officers with a bottle of whiskey and expansive congeniality, which apparently did the trick, as the papers remained undiscovered.

The atmosphere on board, once they cleared Halifax, was strangely celebratory: the band played nonstop, and the first-class passengers dressed for every meal. Reed and Bryant may have been heading into the revolution, but the rest of the world seemed oblivious to it, so the two went along in their usual spirited way. Louise placed bets nightly on the ship's mileage that day; when she won three days in a row and the other bettors began to mutter darkly about inside information, she and Jack put a sign over the bar to the effect that her winnings were to be used for free drinks for all comers. Jack played some pranks that involved getting various husbands upset about their wives' whereabouts. The time passed.

At Christiania (now Oslo) in Norway their real troubles began. They were packed aboard a train for an eighteen-hour ride to Stockholm, where they had to wait a week for the necessary clearances and visas to proceed. In Stockholm, they went immediately to the International Socialist Bureau, where they learned the conference had been postponed. The bureau was teeming with radicals, Russians and others, all full of questions about events in Petrograd. Jack and Louise got some half-credited information that Riga, the second largest port after Petrograd on Russia's Baltic coast, had fallen to the Germans in early September. This rumor, eventually proven true, made Jack even more eager to get to the capital. He asked the delegate of the Russian Workmen and Soldiers' Council to speed up his visa; it was done, to his and Louise's delight, "by the power of the Soviet."

"After we left Stockholm my own curiosity grew every hour," Louise later wrote. "As our train rushed on through the vast, untouched forests of northern Sweden I could scarcely contain myself. Soon I should see how this greatest and youngest of all democracies was learning to walk — to stretch itself — to feel its strength — unshackled!" On the day they reached the border, all passengers were up at first light, most of them travel-weary after a month en route. There, at Haparanda, near the Arctic Circle, their baggage was searched again, and they were bundled onto a ferryboat that took them to Tornio, on the edge of Finland.

They were greeted there by their first glimpse of some radicalized units of the Russian army, an impressive sight, as Louise wrote: "great giants of men, mostly workers and peasants, in old, dirt-coloured uniforms from which every emblem of Tsardom had been carefully removed. Brass buttons with the Imperial insignias, gold and silver epaulettes, decorations, all were replaced by a simple arm-band or bit of red cloth." A returning exile among their party ran up to the soldiers excitedly, and, after a few words, anxiously asked, "Is Russia not free?

What begins now but happiness and peace?" The soldiers coldly replied, according to Louise, "Now begins work. Now begins *more fighting and more dying!*" They were grim words, adding to the travelers' sense of excitement a note of foreboding.

As they traveled south across Finland on a Russian train, word began to reach them of Kornilov's counterrevolutionary putsch. When some aristocrats on board ventured their support of Kornilov, Jack, as he noted in his account of his journey to Russia, started to "dimly perceive that the Russian Revolution had become a class-struggle, *the* class-struggle." Such perceptions formed themselves gradually in their minds as the train steamed toward Petrograd, with frequent stops by soldiers — privates, who snubbed the officers. After they went by Åbo, revolutionary soldiers cried "Bourgeoisie!" at the passing train. Some British officers warned Reed not to take his wife farther. "But she wants to go," he responded simply. "Nobody believed that our train would ever reach Petrograd," Louise wrote. "In case it was stopped I had made up my mind to walk, so I was extremely grateful for every mile that we covered." She may have exaggerated, but it was indeed frustrating to have come so far with the ever-present fear of not reaching her goal.

At Vyborg, the working-class district outside of Petrograd, doubts as to who was in control of Russia's capital became acute, driving almost all the passengers except Jack and Louise off the train. It was after midnight when they drew into Beelostrova, the Finland station. After another ominous interrogation, this time by Russian army officers, Jack and Louise were at last let loose in the revolution.

Enthusiastic about Russian culture as well as witnessing the political upheaval, Louise and Jack took in as much of the city as they could. From their enormous, opulent rooms at the Hotel Angleterre — they would soon move into an apartment to save money — they ventured forth, Louise picking up necessary color for her "woman's point of view" dispatches. (Before long she and Jack would stop even trying to get articles home, instead storing up material to be written later.) "Out on the streets I wandered aimlessly, noting the contents of the little shops now pitifully empty," Louise wrote. "It is curious the things that remain in a starving and besieged city. There was only food enough to last three days, there were no warm clothes at all and I passed window after window full of flowers, corsets, dog-collars and false hair!"

With Jack, she went to the theater and the ballet; at the latter they saw the great dancer Karsavina, and Louise was moved by the "marvelous audience; an audience in rags; an audience that had gone without bread to buy the cheap little tickets." She was most struck by the willful massiveness of the city Peter the Great had built. She wrote to the Storrses, commenting on the massive buildings and wide avenues and the "huge and hugely ugly" statues everywhere. As she later wrote, "Petrograd looks as if it were built by a giant who had no regard for human life."

Rumors were rife in the capital, and the scene was ominous in spite of the theater openings and flower displays in the shops. Jack would later write in *Ten Days That Shook the World:*

> Under dull gray skies, in the shortening days, the rain fell drenching, incessant. The mud underfoot was deep, slippery and clinging, tracked everywhere by heavy boots, and worse than usual because of the complete breakdown of the municipal administration. Bitter damp winds rushed in from the Gulf of Finland, and the chill fog rolled through the streets. At night for motives of economy as well as fear of Zeppelins, the street lights were few and far between; in private dwellings and apartment houses the electricity was turned off from six o'clock until midnight, with candles forty cents apiece and little kerosene to be had. It was dark from three in the afternoon to ten in the morning. Robberies and house breaking increased. In apartment houses the men took turns at all-night guard duty, armed with loaded rifles.

Jack had last seen the city two years before when he was covering the eastern front in the company of his Croton neighbor Mike Robinson. To Robinson he wrote now, "The old town has changed! Joy where there was gloom, and gloom where there was joy. We are in the middle of things, and believe me it is thrilling. There is so much dramatic to write about that I don't know where to begin."

It was unnecessary to find a place to begin; Jack and Louise were plunged into events. In the wake of Kornilov's attempted takeover, the country was polarized between the left and right. The peasants had begun to rise up, and the military deteriorated even further as peasants deserted in droves. On the eve of the revolution Jack and Louise sought an interview with Kerensky in Nicholas II's lavish paneled library in the Winter Palace, where he and his followers now headquartered. Kerensky "lay on a couch with his face buried in his arms, as if he had suddenly been taken ill, or was completely exhausted," wrote Louise. "We stood there for a minute or two and then went out. He did not notice us." At a subsequent meeting, they came away impressed with the man but dubious about his staying power: he showed, Jack observed, "no fixity of purpose — as the leader of the Russian Revolution should have."

The Bolsheviks, who had been in control of the Soviets since mid-September, were promising "Peace, Land, and Bread." They made their headquarters the Smolny Institute, built as a nunnery in 1748, and more lately the home of a finishing school for the daughters of nobility. Resolutions were hammered out in classrooms, and committee members held forth in the auditorium. "In the great white hall, once the ballroom, with its graceful columns and silver candelabra, delegates from Soviets all over Russia met in all-night sessions," wrote Louise. "Men came straight from the first line trenches, straight from the fields and the factories. Every race in Russia met there as brothers." Jack and Louise haunted the Smolny's corridors, taking their meals in the basement refectory, sharing cabbage soup and black bread with boisterous "comrades." Trotsky, the maverick left Socialist leader who would soon hitch his star to the Bolsheviks', had been released from jail after the Kornilov affair and had recently been made head of the Petrograd Soviet; he electrified audiences at the Smolny in speeches that lasted for hours. Louise described one such appearance: "Flashing out of that remarkable gathering was [Trotsky's] striking personality, like a Marat; vehement, serpent-like, he swayed the assembly as a strong wind stirs the long grass." On October 30 Jack and Louise won an audience with him in a small attic room at the institute. He spoke for over an hour, declaring that "We will complete the work scarcely begun in March."

The future of the revolution seemed to hang in the balance, but, in reality, its course was fixed with Lenin's secret reentry into the capital on October 23, disguised in a wig and false beard. The provisional government had recently, and reluctantly, bowed to popular pressure and begun making preparations for a Constituent Assembly. But they had already lost the initiative. The Bolsheviks walked out of the pre-Parliament scheduled in preparation for the Assembly, and Lenin insisted that the Bolsheviks remain intransigent, convincing the Bolshevik Central Committee to place armed insurrection on the agenda. When a rumor surfaced that Kerensky had decided to move the capital to Moscow in order to cede Petrograd to the Germans, the Bolsheviks, at Lenin's order, appointed a Military Revolutionary Committee (MRC) to watch over the garrison.

The actual revolution, on November 6 and 7, was by all accounts surprisingly easy. It was triggered by a government crackdown: Kerensky shut down the Bolshevik newspapers, a move that was perceived as an indicator of counterrevolution. The Bolsheviks, conferring at the Smolny, called out the troops and the workers' Red Guard, but found the government troops almost nonexistent. By nightfall on November 6, they held most of Petrograd, controlling the utilities and government buildings and, within hours, the railway stations, the bridges across the Neva, and the telephone system. On November 7, Trotsky's MRC proclaimed the overthrow of the provisional government.

That morning, after staying up nearly all night shuttling between the Winter Palace and the Smolny, Jack and Louise emerged from their apartment building only to be handed leaflets stating "Citizens! The provisional government is deposed. State power has passed into the organ of the Petrograd Soviet of Workers' and Soldiers' Deputies." When Jack asked a soldier guarding the doors of the State Bank whether he was on the side of the government, he replied with a triumphant grin, "No more Government! *Slava Bogu!* Glory to God!" In the aftermath of the revolution, when the decrees of the new era were announced at the second session of the Congress, they heard Lenin declare, to a roaring ovation, "We shall now proceed to construct the Socialist order!"

The siege of the cabinet at the Winter Palace ended in little bloodshed, but the capture of the Palace was highly charged symbolically. A Second Congress of Soviets ratified the Bolshevik coup, and local soviets across the country did the same, with serious fighting only in Moscow. When the Soviet government issued its first decrees, they were confirmations of the profound change that had occurred: Private property was abolished, and the land was given to the peasants who worked on it. The Bolsheviks announced that they would seek peace with Germany "without annexations or indemnities"; the unvoiced threat was that without peace world revolution would be imminent, a possibility that seemed very real both within and without Russia at the time. Banks were nationalized, and courts were abolished in favor of revolutionary tribunals and workers' militias. Equality between the sexes was decreed. Equal rights were for the first time bestowed on Jews and other previously subject peoples, and ownership of the means of production was vested in the workers.

These reforms, which had been considered unthinkable and certainly unachievable under the old regime, seemed to be happening with astonishing swiftness. To onlookers, including Louise and Jack, the revolution was real: "backward" Russia had outstripped the United States as a progressive country, in spite of its troubles, simply because that was what the people wanted.

The change in daily life was fantastic, marvelous because it had seemed so unimaginable. As Jack had perceived on his journey into Russia, the working class had awakened to its class role, just as Marx had said they would. Waiters refused tips and people helped each other in the streets. Everyone was addressed as "comrade" — *tovarisch* — or "citizen," a dramatic change in a previously stratified society like Russia.

Thrilling in themselves, these sweeping transformations convinced observers like Louise and Jack that there were lessons to be learned in Russia, and taught in turn to revolutionaries at home. The disorganized American left had been unable to reach the man in the street with its ideas, ideas that in Russia seemed to transform themselves into action spontaneously.

"The Bolsheviks took Petrograd and Jack and I were part of it all," Louise later wrote proudly in an unpublished memoir. They were constantly at the scene and behind the scenes, scribbling furiously, straining to understand what was being said and demanding on-the-spot translations in French or German when they couldn't get them in English.

Louise and Jack were by no means the only American journalists in Russia, and all of them worked mightily against considerable odds to file their stories. They needed endless passes — passes from the provisional government, passes from the Military Revolutionary Committee. They fought their way through cordons during the siege of the Winter Palace only to be accused by the Red Guards of looting during the aftermath. As seemingly well-heeled Americans, they were fair game for epithets and more serious challenges. As radicals themselves, they were subject to nagging self-doubts; the American left had not been able to make a revolution, after all. Albert Rhys Williams, a former minister turned war correspondent, remembered asking Reed repeatedly, "Do you think we'll ever make the grade? Or are we tagged for life? The humanitarians, the dilettantes?" He and Jack once exchanged insults, Williams calling Reed "Harvard Red! Football cheerleader!" Bessie Beatty, a *San Francisco Bulletin* correspondent, broke up the tiff, saying, "You're both acting like small boys. Call yourselves radicals? You're a couple of spoiled American brats. Why don't you learn discipline from the Russians?"

Yet all were working in great earnest, and there was little time for self-doubt or socializing. Acting assiduously on their best journalistic impulses, Louise and Jack sought out and focused their writing on the strong personalities who had shaped the revolution, those who seemed to be possessed of real vision rather than mere politicians. Naturally, as Lenin emerged as a commanding presence, he engaged their attention, though they were unable to interview him until the revolution's aftermath (when he took a distinct liking to both of them). Louise found him far less personable than Kerensky, but possessed of a stunning intellect. Lenin spoke fluent English, having taught himself the language while in jail, and he was able to communicate on a highly sophisticated level with the American journalists — as was Trotsky, himself a strong intellect and a spellbinding organizer, who had even spent some time in New York. Louise and Jack eventually interviewed both men repeatedly and heard them speak countless times, assembling their impressions for the portraits that would appear in their respective books about the revolution.

For it was becoming clear to them that their articles could be assembled into book-length works about Russia's recent history. Jack's, of course, was to be the epic *Ten Days That Shook the World,* Louise's the more modest but equally compelling *Six Red Months in Russia.* Though both reporters shared a fundamental sympathy for the Russian cause, and a sophisticated understanding of the nuances of revolutionary politics, the resemblances between their journalistic approaches stopped there. Jack wrote as one dedicated to history: he assiduously collected every document — broadsheet, leaflet, newspaper article — producing them verbatim in his book; similarly, he wrote down every word of every speech he could decipher, sometimes acquiring copies of them in Russian and translating them later, and inserted them virtually without comment in his narrative. As a result, his book is an invaluable piece of reportage, an immediate historical document that strives for absolute accuracy. But to the reader of today, the effect of much of the amassed detail is lost except as documentation, and the result is most impressive for the sheer energy that went into it. Reed projected it as the first volume of a life work on Russian history, and his devotion to the writing of history comes through on every page.

Louise's reportorial agenda was quite different, though she shared the same instinct for accuracy. She saw her mission as more conventionally journalistic; she was there not only to record events but to interpret and comment on them. If Jack's book gives us the "big picture," history as made by great men, it is Louise's book that one turns to for the texture of daily Russian life in the days of the revolution: the bread lines, the icy streets, the mood of the workers. In Petrograd, she wrote, "Weeks at a stretch the street cars would not run. People walked great stretches without a murmur and the life of the city went on as usual. It would have upset New York completely, especially if it happened as in Petrograd that while the street cars were stopped, lights and water also were turned off and it was almost impossible to get fuel to keep warm." Yet the Russians had a wonderful persistence, she continued, keeping the theaters open, for instance:

> The Nevsky after midnight was as amusing and interesting as Fifth Avenue in the afternoon. The cafés had nothing to serve but weak tea and sandwiches but they were always full. . . . Men and women wear what they please. At one table would be sitting a soldier with his fur hat pulled over his ear, across from him a Red Guard in rag-tags, next a Cossack in a gold and black uniform, earrings in his ears, silver chains around his neck, or a man from the Wild Division, recruited from one of the most savage tribes in the Caucasus, wearing his sombre, flowing cape.

The author of *Six Red Months* is free with her opinions, and very mindful of the need to reach her readers; phrases like "Americans must remember that revolution in Russia has had a long history" and "We must somehow make an honest effort to understand what is happening in Russia" recur throughout. If Jack's book is a galvanizing historical document for the left in the West, Louise's is a *useful* account, providing inspiration to liberal-minded individuals of all stripes, and educating those less than sympathetic to the goals of revolution. Hers, moreover, is a book with a strong sense of narrative, and it is a narrative shaped by the author as much as Jack's is by events. She inserted herself into the narrative when necessary, and the effect is a greater immediacy than Jack achieved with his more dispassionate account. For example, she describes a heated debate at the Smolny on the day the Winter Palace fell, a debate that culminated in the dissenting Menshevik (Social Democratic) and Socialist Revolutionists being ousted by the Bolsheviks, ordered to march through the firing lines and die with the provisional government:

> Of course we followed the bolting delegates. All the street cars were stopped and it was two miles to the Winter Palace. A huge motor truck was just leaving Smolny. We hailed it and climbed on board. . . . They warned us gaily that we'd probably all get killed, and they told me to take off a yellow hatband, as there might be sniping.
>
> Their mission was to distribute leaflets all over town, and especially along the Nevsky Prospect. The leaflets were piled high over the floor of the truck together with guns and ammunition. As we rattled along through the wide, dim-lit streets, they scattered the leaflets to eager crowds. People scrambled over the cobbles fighting for copies. We could only make out the headlines in the half-light.

Louise's is an engrossing, vivid account; interestingly, some of the leading historians of the revolution and biographers of Louise and Jack have relied more heavily on Louise's account than on her husband's in reconstructing the chaotic days of the revolution, however invaluable *Ten Days That Shook the World* may be for specific political developments. It is Louise, for example, who tells us of the incongruous elegance of the Smolny Institute and the fevered atmosphere within, of the dismay and confusion of the young guards when the Winter Palace fell, of the evacuation of art and treasures from the Hermitage and the Winter Palace to the safety of Moscow's Kremlin. Jack's revolution is magnificently recorded, Louise's is subtly brought to life.

As she gathered the material for her book, Louise discovered her vocation. In her four months (not six) in Russia, she came into her own as an autonomous reporter and writer, a woman with a clear professional identity and a genuine calling. It was a happy coincidence that her husband was covering the same events: it made the work mutually easier and more satisfying. Theirs took on all the happy characteristics of a working marriage: both had their own projects and at the same time were side by side. They both had stories to tell, equally compelling.

Louise was no longer in Jack's shadow. The great adventure had at last
made their marriage the union of equals she had wanted all along.

At Christmas, in the wake of the revolution, Louise gave Jack a poem
she had written, at once passionate and sober, tender and wry. It read,
in part,

> It is fine to be here in the North
> With you on Christmas
> In a land where they really believe
> In peace on earth
> And miracles
>
> . . . .
>
> What I want most to tell you
> Is that I love you
> And I want more than anything
> To have you stay strong and clear-visioned
> In all this world madness . . .
> You are the finest person I know
> On both sides of the world
> And it is a nice privilege to be your comrade.

They were, as Jack had written in "Almost Thirty," friends and lovers.
But to be comrades — that was an exalted state indeed.

7

The Comrades Return

Jack didn't seem to want to leave Russia. On December 1 both he and Rhys Williams took a job with the Bureau of International Revolutionary Propaganda at a salary of fifty rubles a month. They edited an illustrated weekly called *Die Russische Revolution in Bildern* (*The Russian Revolution in Pictures*) and wrote for revolutionary newspapers like *Die Fackel* (*The Torch*) that were to be smuggled into Germany and distributed to prisoner-of-war camps across Russia. Although he would not have seen his activity in these terms, he was temporarily abandoning journalism — or history writing — to serve the revolution. Though he took his work very seriously, he approached it with his customary exuberance. When he and Williams heard news of a brief strike among intellectuals, Jack proposed that they appoint themselves commissars. He would be commissar of art and amusement, telling Williams he would do "thousands of things. First of all, put joy into the people. Get up great pageants. Cover the city with flags and banners. And once or maybe twice a month have a gorgeous all-night festival with fireworks, orchestras, plays in all the squares, and everybody participating."

The context of Jack's efforts was the Bolshevik mandate to end the war. Acting on that, they were abandoning the Allies and negotiating a separate peace with Germany — if need be, at the cost of much Russian territory. The Russian Revolution, to be successful, must be a world revolution, and to that end the Bolshevik line was that peace gave them the opportunity to encourage the Germans — and other "captive" European nations — to overthrow their oppressors and join the Socialist cause. While foreign correspondents like Louise and Jack were ambivalent about the prospect of a separate peace (did the securing of a Socialist government justify the loss of self-determination for millions of Russians and non-Russians in the western parts of the old czarist empire?), the cause of world revolution, for Jack, prevailed.

Louise remained more or less aloof from active political work, continuing her coverage of the revolution's aftermath. Less directly involved in the political scene, she met a different group of people from those Jack associated with, people who presented her with different versions of events. Among other things, she learned that the Bolsheviks were not as monolithic as Jack sometimes made them seem.

As it happened, Louise's mandate to report events from a woman's point of view suited her purposes better than she might have imagined — and, of course, she saw such a view as excluding absolutely nothing. But this meant more to her than simply securing interviews with female revolutionary figures — though her portraits of the novelist and educator Aleksandra Kollontay and the revolutionary heroine Marie Spirodonova are incisive and insightful, models of intellectual reportage, the real strong points of her book. Even more so, she saw the question of feminism, or equality between the sexes, as an integral part of the revolution.

Such equality was born out of practical necessity as well as high principles. The revolutionary movement in Russia, for so many decades exiled, underground, and on the run, had naturally developed a more egalitarian order. Women were accorded equal responsibility and equal rights in the movement partly because of radical principles, but also because their male counterparts simply did not have the luxury of keeping sex roles separate and distinct. The Bolsheviks and other parties of the Russian revolutionary left not only gave lip service to feminism — as many radical movements in America did — but seemed to be able to deliver on it. Louise saw this at work in the lives of women like Lenin's wife, Nadezhda Krupskaya, who was a well-trained educator and a powerful Central Committee member. The first Bolshevik minister of education, serving in the cabinet with her husband, Krupskaya seemed to have a remarkable marriage, a true partnership that made a powerful statement both to the Russian people and to Louise. To the degree that she would ever feel any disenchantment with the revolution, it was over the Soviet treatment of these pioneering heroines in subsequent years. For Louise, as for any feminist, the personal was political, and the fact that women took an active role in building a new society in Russia was a point of crystallization for her as a political observer — and actor.

Two of the women she most admired, Spirodonova and Kollontay, were adamantly opposed to a separate peace, and were fighting Lenin every inch of the way on the issue. In her last interview with Spirodonova, Louise asked her about the negotiations at Brest-Litovsk. Spirodonova had no faith whatsoever in them, and was agitating to create what she called a "Socialist army" that would pursue the war in the name of Socialist Russia.

As Louise sharpened her own feminist perspective, she increasingly sought the opinions of these revolutionary heroines on the role of women in the new society. Spirodonova had a singular view: she pointed out that women had been equally represented among exiled revolutionaries and suggested that martyrdom came easily to women because it was instinctive rather than learned. On the other hand, she went on, men become politicians when they are elected to do so, not because they are especially suited to the work. Women couldn't do that: "I think women are more conscientious," she told Louise. "Men are used to overlooking their consciences — women are not."

Angelica Balabanov, future secretary of the Communist International, who was still in exile when Louise met with her in Stockholm on her journey over, had a perspective Louise characterized as "much the same." Balabanov said, "Women have to go through such a struggle before they are free in their own minds. . . . freedom is more precious to them than to men." In other words, women's different experiences made them fundamentally different from men.

"I wish I could believe it," Louise wrote simply in *Six Red Months in Russia*. "But I can never see any spiritual difference between men and women inside or outside of politics. They act and react very much alike; they certainly did in the Russian Revolution." Reflecting the deep pragmatism that was the underpinning of her feminism, she added, "It is one of the best arguments I know in favour of equal suffrage." Anticipating one of the debates that has come to characterize modern feminism, she refused to believe that women were essentially different from men — that biology is destiny. Such a belief had disastrous implications: while it might grant women many protections, it opened the way for unequal rights, which Louise could understand best in terms of suffrage, the lodestar of her politics.

Yet it was the revolutionary heroines' actions, which bore out her belief in the centrality of equality to the revolution's goals, that held Louise's greatest admiration. As the new Minister of Welfare, Kollontay, known by the people as "Little Comrade," was juggling the demands of her new bureaucratic duties after a long career of active revolutionary work that resulted in many jail terms. Kollontay, who, as Louise wrote, "works untiringly and, through persistence born of flaming intensity . . . accomplishes a tremendous amount," had to make budgetary cuts to ensure medical care and pensions for disabled soldiers; she had to arrest a rogue band of the striking bourgeoisie, which caused her a tremendous inner struggle; she rearranged the public school system and outlawed private institutions. The work she was doing for new mothers and children was remarkable: "On Kollontay's suggestion, the Bolshevik Government passed a measure providing free care for sixteen weeks for women before, during and after confinement. When they leave the home they can go back if they are not well, and they are required to work only four hours a day in the factories for the first month after returning. This applies to all women, whether married or single. The Bolshviki believe that this care of mothers is one of the first debts to the State."

Marie Spirodonova, whom Louise admitted to admiring even more than she did Kollontay, impressed Louise with her bravery. She was an unlikely heroine, just over thirty and standing barely five feet tall. She looked "as if she came from New England. Her puritanical plain black clothes with the chaste little white collar, and a certain air of refinement and severity about her seem to belong to that region more than to wild, turbulent Russia — yet she is a true daughter of Russia and the revolution." Her early history as a revolutionist impressed even her fellow Russians, used as they were to martyrs. She had murdered an unspeakably oppressive governor when she was nineteen. In her jail cell the Cossacks tried to extract the names of her colleagues, beating her, pulling out "bunches of her long, beautiful hair," and burning her with cigarettes. After serving eleven years of a life sentence in Siberia (where she "kept her mind clear" by learning languages), she took up revolutionary activity again, serving a number of peasant congresses, and was an active leader in the left Socialist Revolutionist party. Louise saw her in action at the Democratic Congress, where heated wrangling characterized a debate about how best to return land to the peasants. "A hush fell over the place when she walked on the stage," Louise wrote.

> She spoke for not more than three minutes, giving a short, concise, clear argument against coalition [one of the various strategies advanced]. She began:
>
> "*Krestian* — peasants — if you vote for coalition you give up all hope of your land!"
>
> The great palace shook with the roaring protests of the proletariat against coalition when she ceased. Millions of peasants trust her implicitly and move with her judgment almost invariably. She has the greatest political following of any woman in the world.

Her last remark may seem like an overstatement; it may even have seemed so to Louise as she made it. But she may have found that to her delight and amazement it might well have been true, that this tiny, understated woman might have "the greatest political following of any woman in the world." In Russia, under equality, such things were possible. It was not, then, Louise's mandate to write from a woman's point of view, or any identification she may have felt with these pioneering women, but the fact that they represented, even as they had helped to forge, a new, genuinely free future.

In short, in interviewing revolutionary heroines and covering the new order in Russia, Louise was not only coming into her own professionally but also reaching a new intellectual and emotional maturity. As a Socialist feminist *and* a dedicated advocate journalist, she wanted to convey news of the progress being made in the implementation of Socialist and feminist thought in Russia, hoping to influence American politics by the examples she provided. Her primary concern was not the ultimate success of the Soviet system, but that she had seen with her own eyes that the oppressed — women and workers — could have a better life after the revolution. So long as she believed the Bolsheviks were dedicated to these principles, she would defend any attempts to subvert their project. As a journalist, she could unite her desire to observe and write with her commitment to what she now saw was imperative to convey. She had found her subject, and it launched a dazzling career.

Her new professional maturity and sureness of purpose in turn translated into a certain authority that would characterize the articles that would become *Six Red Months in Russia*. In her introduction, for instance, she began modestly, claiming that she was only an observer, setting forth the facts so that the reader could judge for himself: "I am but a messenger who lays his notes before you, attempting to give you a picture of what I saw and what you would have seen if you had been with me." Immediately, however, she asserted:

> Socialism is here, whether we like it or not — just as woman suffrage is here — and it spreads with the years. In Russia the socialist state is an accomplished fact. We can never again call it an idle dream of long-haired philosophers. And if that growth has resembled the sudden up-shooting of a mushroom, if it must fall because it is premature, it is nevertheless real and must have tremendous effect on all that follows. Everything considered, there is just as much reason to believe the Soviet Republic will stand as that it will fall. The most significant fact is that it will not fall from *inside* pressure. Only *outside*, foreign hostile intervention can destroy it.

This is the language of authority born of conviction. In the months and year to come, the question of the "truth" about Russia and the "facts" about Russia would become a hotly debated question both on the left and, more ominously, in the larger arena, many sides purporting to know the truth. When Louise spoke of the fact that only intervention would topple the new Russia, she would seem to have been expressing an opinion rather than a truth. But the intensity of her conviction, borne out by the facts she presents in the rest of her reportage, carries the weight of truth. In short, she has earned the right of her conclusions, and the reader believes her.

The same authoritativeness marks the rest of her coverage, as she takes her readers through the incidents leading up to the fall of the Winter Palace, pausing for chapters to explain matters like the opposing political parties, or the status of free speech under the soviets. She is evenhanded in her determination to let the facts be known, even when they might wreak havoc with the overall picture she wants to present. So, for instance, knowing that misperceptions about the degree of force used in the revolution were rife in the American press, she writes, "If one expects to find nothing but bloodshed and one finds there is much else, that one can go about in a fur coat without the least hindrance, that theatres, the ballet, movies and other more or less frivolous institutions still flourish, it may subdue the tone of one's tale, but it is highly necessary to note the fact. It is silly to defend the revolution by claiming there has been *no* bloodshed and it is just as silly to insist that the streets are running blood." (While Jack would be equally eager to dispel rumors about excessive bloodshed in Russia, one cannot imagine him doing so in quite this fashion, running the risk of indirectly fueling the arguments of the opposition.)

On the condition of women, Louise was most eager to correct misrepresentations. There was much talk in the Western press of the so-called nationalization of women: rumor had it that in Russia women over the age of eighteen were declared public property. Such rumors were the work of some Odessa anarchists, and in no way reflected reality. Understandably, Louise was eager to describe the undisputed equality she saw women enjoying in the new Russia. "I was present at the meeting when the decrees of the Soviets regarding marriage were passed and have the correct data," she wrote smoothly, and proceeded to outline the new marriage laws, which provided for a far more egalitarian institution than the West had known, but no increase in "immorality." Indeed, "with the removal of all kinds of suppression immorality notably lessens. Russia can boast of less immorality than any country in the world."

On every issue — German propaganda, the decline of the church, the status of the Cossacks — she presented what she had seen and heard and confidently summed up the situation. For a relatively inexperienced reporter, thrust into the heart of a world event on a world-shaking scale, she not only held her own but produced a masterly piece of writing. She had come a long way from her days of reporting on fashions and ladies' teas for the Portland papers.

Moreover, while she and Jack shared a common Socialist vision, Louise was developing her own views on particular issues. Much of what made their new partnership work was that they never put themselves in the position of having to admit any differences. Their common priority was *not* to convert their Western audience but, first, to convince them to discourage an invasion of Russia and to give the new country a chance. They also wanted to show that Socialist Russia was an experiment to be watched for lessons that could be applied in America. She and Jack and other leftist journalists were accused of trying to import a foreign system, but they asked only that the West open its eyes to what was going on in this far part of the world and learn about what it had to offer. Both Jack and Louise were aware of ambiguities in Soviet policy and of the likelihood that there were things about the new state the West might never expect — and they were known to disagree on the nuances of such points. But they saw that it was important that they present a smooth, united front, dedicated to preventing intervention and educating the world about the successes of the revolution. The strategy did not work. The Allies intervened, and the truth about Russia became a political football. But Jack and Louise played their parts brilliantly. For Louise, Russia was an inspiration, affording her glimpses of new worlds of possibility for herself, for all women, and for the human race.

While events in Russia still commanded world headlines — the Bolsheviks, in the wake of a severe loss in the Constituent Assembly elections in November, consolidated their power, and the threat of civil war loomed — the story of the revolution was nearly played out by the new year. Jack began to think of going home when news reached Russia that *The Masses* had been suppressed and he and four other editors had been indicted for conspiracy to obstruct the draft. He felt it his duty to stand trial with his colleagues, and he and Louise scheduled their journey home for January 20. As the date approached, however, he decided he wanted to stay for the Third Congress of Soviets, slated for January 23.

Louise, however, resolved to return home with two journalist friends, Bessie Beatty and Madeleine Doty. Doty described the trip for *Good Housekeeping:* They left Petrograd in a blinding snowstorm, with temperatures far below zero, and boarded the last train to get to Finland, where the civil war between the White Russians and the Red Guards was already erupting in brushfires. From Finland they crossed an iced-over river into Sweden, bundled into fur coats aboard a sleigh, sitting three abreast to keep from freezing.

As a returning radical, Louise had anticipated trouble on her journey home, fearing especially that her papers and notes would be confiscated.

Russia's assistant foreign minister issued a statement she could carry with her indicating that she was acting as a courier to Stockholm for the People's Commissars of Foreign Affairs, thus assuring her safe travel through the war-torn regions of Russia. Even more useful was a letter from a Red Cross representative, Raymond Robins, to the Marine naval attaché in Christiania asking that Louise be given passage on a steamer to the U.S. on the grounds that "she and her husband have been helpful in the work we have been doing in Petrograd." Without it, she might well have been detained there for some time under suspicion that she was a Bolshevik sympathizer — as Jack would be just after her.

As it was, the journey to reach Christiania was eventful. When she crossed over the Finnish border into Sweden, Louise was alarmed to see a group of German officers on board. They seemed to have friends all along the way, which indicated to her how strong pro-German sentiment was in Sweden as well as in Finland, an especially ominous development since Germany had just initiated a major offensive against Russia. On her arrival in Stockholm, she sought out Bolshevik officials to get word to them of this German presence. She received little help from the conservative, pro-German Swedes from whom she tried to get directions to Bolshevik headquarters. "We have nothing to do with Bolsheviki!" screamed one hysterical Swede, over and over. "I have nothing to do with such scum!" answered another icily. When Louise finally found the office, with the help of the American foreign ministry, the Russian consul took her to a tea shop and asked to hear all the news from Russia and details of her journey. At the meeting, she was consumed by deep emotion and ambivalence about going home. "Seated at the table, we looked out across the wide street at the slow-moving barges going up and down the canals. Vast Russia lay behind. I was homesick for my own country, but I thought of the German advance and my heart ached. I wanted to go back and offer my life for the revolution": a dramatic statement, to be sure (from a lover of high drama), but Louise felt the power of her convictions, and no doubt she meant it.

With Beatty and Doty, she sailed on board the Norwegian ship *Bergensfjord*, arriving in New York on February 18. As the steamer was going through customs, reporters were allowed on board, and Louise found herself something of a celebrity. She refused to answer questions about the revolution, saying that she was writing a book, but what the reporters really wanted were details of Jack's dismissal as Russian consul to the U.S.

Louise, of course, hadn't even known of his appointment to the post. Jack had asked Trotsky for the courier status that Louise had, and Trotsky had in turn conferred the consul post on him. Though aware that acceptance might mean arrest for treason on his arrival in America, Jack thought the post would bring wanted publicity to the Bolshevik cause and accepted it. (He told Louise that on receiving his appointment from Trotsky at a revolutionary conference, he asked if it meant that he had the authority to perform marriages. If so, he said, he would use the words "Proletarians of the world, unite!" No one got the joke.) The situation was not so simple, however, and U.S. Ambassador David Francis, embarrassed by the move, convinced the Soviets to withdraw the appointment. Jack by this time had already reached Stockholm, bearing no Bolshevik credentials at all.

In the confusion over his status, the State Department issued word that Jack should not be given a visa to return, and he was forced to cool his heels for over a month in Christiania. He rented a room, where he began writing what would become *Ten Days That Shook the World*. His letters were censored, and Louise would not hear a word from him until April, almost three months after they parted.

Despite the clarity of purpose and intellectual maturity she had attained during her stay in Russia, Louise remained a headstrong and impulsive woman. Although her actions usually had an internal, idiosyncratic logic, at various points in her life they appear bizarre or inexplicable. Often they seem to have been borne out of what might best be described as panic at crucial junctures, when her course in life seemed less than sure, when abandonment threatened. In such moments, her instinctive action was to hedge her bets: she was, after all, first and last a survivor. At no period is this more evident than in the months after her return from Russia, while Jack was marooned in Norway.

An accomplished journalist with a book in progress, a woman newly secure in her marriage to a man she loved, Louise returned to the U.S. only to begin a determined campaign to win back her old lover, Eugene O'Neill.

Gene had fled Greenwich Village in horror in late March, after a disturbing incident involving the deliberate drug overdose of his friend Louis Holladay, the brother of the Villager hostess Polly. Gene was living with a young woman named Agnes Boulton in the familiar setting of Provincetown, where he was working on the play that would eventually be produced as the extremely successful *Beyond the Horizon*, a drama about two men in love with the same woman. According to another Provincetowner, Agnes, a dark, pretty writer of magazine stories, was deeply in love with Gene but refused to marry him, saying simply that Gene was still in love with "that girl."

Louise, staying at the old apartment on 8th Street while she was putting together her book, heard all the news — and the rumors — from mutual Village friends. It was said that Gene had been heartbroken when she left for Russia with Jack, and that had driven him into Agnes's arms. Many thought that the twenty-four-year-old Agnes bore a striking resemblance to Louise. Gene was reported to have pronounced his despair at his lost love all over the Village, on one occasion climbing on a chair and turning back the hands of a mantelpiece clock, shouting melodramatically, "Turn back the universe and give me yesterday!"

The sheer drama of this would have appealed to Louise's romantic side, and O'Neill's distress awakened her deepest maternal instincts, as well as her love of danger and risk-taking. She acted without any thought of the consequences, for almost definitely she did not want to endanger her marriage. But her seeming shortsightedness, in fact, may go far in explaining her actions. She was alone in New York, cut off from Jack, who was most likely in danger, and she had always had, since her father's disappearance, a sharp nose for any signs of abandonment. Jack might be lost to her — there was no telling what had happened to him, and for the longest time she didn't even know where he was — and Gene too might be forsaking her for another woman. In trying to replace the intimacy suddenly lost to her, she acted instinctively and self-protectively — and selfishly.

Louise wrote to Gene in Provincetown urging him to rejoin her in New York. Agnes had anticipated this: well-meaning friends had told her all about the legendary Louise, and of their physical resemblance. Harry Kemp's girlfriend, Mary Pyne, had said, "She will come back from Russia and want him back. She is much more clever than you, and they were very much in love. That is, if torture is love. I sometimes think Gene enjoys being tortured."

Agnes described Gene's reception of Louise's letter, which he handed her to read:

> Louise wrote that she must see him — and at once. She had left Jack Reed in Russia and crossed three thousand miles of frozen steppes to come back to him — her lover. Page after page of passionate declaration of their love — of hers, which would never change. She had forgiven him. What if he had picked up some girl in the Village and become involved? There was no use writing letters — she had to see him! It was all a misunderstanding and her fault for leaving him, for going to Russia with Jack.

The letter was a transparent ploy, Agnes concluded — she was especially scornful of the dramatic reference to the frozen steppes — but she was horrified by its effect on Gene. She knew as well the formidable quality of her rival. What *did* impress her in Louise's letter was "such assurance, such surety of her hold over this man."

According to Agnes, another, special delivery letter immediately followed, which Gene said he didn't want to read: "*She's crazy!*" he said. He did read it, though, and was immediately drawn into an exchange of letters with Louise. Agnes and Gene debated the terms of their meeting (she didn't want him to go to New York, for obvious reasons and also because he might be tempted to drink). Over and over, he and Louise discussed the terms of their separation, what had driven them apart. Louise acted as if she had gone to Russia fully intending to resume the affair on her return; she presented the case as if it were a *fait accompli,* Jack having agreed to a new arrangement in which she would live with Gene and see Jack on the side.

Louise and Gene continued writing even after Gene married Agnes on April 15. Louise wrote, according to Agnes, that she understood the marriage was "both escape and revenge. But she would forgive that. There were more, much more important things in the world now than marriage." Finally, Agnes suggested that Gene propose meeting Louise halfway between Provincetown and New York, in Fall River, Massachusetts.

When Gene presented her with Agnes's compromise, Louise realized that he had succumbed to the other woman's influence and that she had lost. She replied furiously, according to Agnes:

> Her reply was quick and impetuous — a vibrant assault upon and belittlement of me; and a denunciation of Gene for his weakness and lack of understanding. She made it clear that he had fallen greatly in stature in her eyes; and also that there were other and greater concerns on her mind than going to Fall River. She implied that as she was a clever journalist and writer there was a greater orbit in which she circled — of world happenings and important events — than that to which Gene in his Provincetown flight had relegated himself.

Whatever Louise implied — and surely part of Agnes's recollection was a projection based on her own insecurities and jealousy — it was clear that she was bitterly hurt, and was lashing out at Gene (and Agnes) in the most vituperative and condescending manner possible. In fact, the tone of the letter suggests just how abandoned Louise felt, and to what extent the fear of abandonment had motivated her actions throughout. Agnes recounts that Louise later fabricated stories about O'Neill showing up drunk on her doorstep after her return from Russia. Whether or not this is true, Louise may have enjoyed saying that she had rejected O'Neill and broken his heart — a story that had, after all, once been true. In later years she would dismiss O'Neill as a counterrevolutionary, painting him as an apolitical aesthete unfazed by the prospect of world revolution, which in 1918 looked possible indeed. But at the time she felt bereft, and with Jack still gone, more than ever alone.

Louise and Jack were writing regularly through this period, but none of their letters reached the other. Louise suspected he had either been caught in Finland or had gone back into Russia when the Germans renewed fighting in February, she wrote a friend. She wanted to go back for Jack, she said, but had to wait until she'd heard from him — and also, she confessed, because the situation in Russia really scared her: "It's a most awful situation up there — beside which anything I've ever seen is tame, and I've been on both fronts. It's a plain matter of 'King Hunger' with all the Imperialists on both sides getting poor Russia into a trap."

On March 15 Louise appealed to the State Department for information and was told only that Jack was in Christiania and that she should expect visits from investigating officials and try not to let them bother

1030407355

her. As their reply indicates, Jack was possibly in danger or at least under serious suspicion from his own government.

So too, by this point, was Louise — and not only as John Reed's wife. Since her return, she had plunged back into her chosen work of telling the public what she had seen in Russia and of the dangers that faced the revolutionaries. She was accepting speaking engagements, and her appearances attracted attention. She addressed a crowd of three hundred on March 15 at the Rand School in the Village ("which is known to be a center of communist activity," the State Department later commented, in one of its many internal memoranda about Bryant's activities), and another on March 21; at the latter, the Socialist *New York Call* reported, she "brought home the suffering which revolutionary Russia is enduring in such a . . . forcible manner that a committee of Bolshevik relief was immediately formed." Her activity naturally roused suspicion, but especially in the climate of 1918, when attacks on radicals, in the wake of the October Revolution, were escalating across the country.

By April, in the midst of this activity, Louise had completed her book and had sold her thirty-two stories to the *Philadelphia Ledger,* which in turn syndicated them to the Hearst chain's *New York American* and to more than a hundred newspapers across the U.S. and Canada; they were eventually translated into five languages. She was considered an authority on Russia and now a highly visible political persona. By virtue of the syndication, hers was quite literally a household name — for better or for worse. She must have had mixed emotions about the many people from the past — her family, her college friends, the Portlanders (including Dr. Paul), and old beaus — who would see her name and read of her exploits. Even Russia's detractors, fundamentally unsympathetic to radical causes, would have seen and devoured her articles, so eager was the country for any news of the earthshaking events in that part of the world.

Every evidence suggests that however lonely and dependent she may have felt emotionally in these months — and however bizarrely she was conducting her personal life — Louise had become a successful, and startlingly self-assured, writer and public figure. As early as April 1918 she was testing the waters to see if she could be issued a passport to Ireland. (Her passport had been canceled on her return from Russia.) Inspired by the Easter uprising of 1916, about which she had written for

The Masses, Louise was an avid follower of the Irish nationalist movement. In Ireland as in Russia, wartime distress was offering the best chance in years for revolutionary change, as British conscription efforts were met first with hostility and then with a widespread public embrace of nationalism.

Ireland's revolution was unfolding every day, and Louise wanted to be there. But her early inquiries were regarded with suspicion. One report, calling her "a writer of considerable ability," went on to call her "a dangerous and . . . undesirable character" who "has talked as an ardent pacifist." Louise made her official application for a passport in August, declaring England and then Ireland as her destinations. Later the *Ledger* withdrew its support for the trip, and her passport application would be summarily rejected in September. A State Department official commented that given the "well-known Bolshevik tendencies" of John Reed, "which are no doubt fully shared by his wife," he did not "believe it would be desirable to permit her to proceed to England, much less to Ireland." Louise would not make the Ireland trip for over a decade.

With little knowledge of any of his wife's activities, Jack was increasingly restless, writing angrily to the American minister in protest at being held in Norway. Even after his visa was finally issued in April, Edgar Sisson, the fervently anti-Bolshevik officer of the Committee on Public Information who had been responsible for Jack's enforced stay in Scandinavia, issued orders that on his arrival in the U.S. the State Department should confiscate all his papers.

Jack's ship, also the *Bergensfjord,* arrived in New York on April 28; Louise, who was there to meet him with a Croton lawyer friend, Dudley Malone, had a daylong wait as his papers were confiscated and he was stripped, searched, and held for questioning. Malone was also there in his capacity as the lawyer for *The Masses,* and Jack was arraigned the next day and released on $2000 bail.

"It is hard for us to get used to complacent America after the whirlpool of Revolution," Louise wrote to John and Marguerite Storrs on May 9. Indeed, Jack was to spend a frustrating summer, unable to write his book without the confiscated papers. He made a quick trip to Washington just after his return to see what he could do to get them released, but to no avail. He enlisted the help of an old journalist friend,

William Bullitt, now with the State Department. But though Bullitt applied his considerable energies to the matter, the government was determined to thwart John Reed in any way possible.

Unable to start his book — or to find any outlet for his writing, for that matter — Jack turned to lecturing, addressing his audiences as "*Tovarischi!*" and agitating for recognition of Russia. After a speech in Philadelphia at the end of May, he was arrested on charges of inciting to riot. In early July he was in Chicago for a mass trial of the IWW, the first of many government prosecutions intended to smash the radical union. However ominous, the event moved him greatly: the Wobblies had always been heroes to him. Still, he was frustrated by his inability to write and get published. Meanwhile, Louise's stories were appearing daily in the spring and early summer, as he said in a letter to Lincoln Steffens in June: "I started a big newspaper syndicate series, like Louise's, but the newspapers were afraid to touch them; some of them sent the stuff back after it was in type. Then Collier's took a story, put it in type, and sent it back. Oswald Villard [of *The Nation*] told me he would be suppressed if he published John Reed!" In the same letter, he bemoaned his inability to deliver his book to Macmillan in the absence of his papers: "I am . . . unable to write a word of the greatest story of my life, and one of the greatest in the world. I am blocked."

Stifled by suspicion and prejudice, Jack proposed to Louise that they spend the summer in Croton, in retreat. Louise's career was at a crossroads; Jack's under a very real threat. Instead of world revolution, they found themselves living in the hostile, paranoid climate of wartime America. In a telling move, Jack joined the Socialist party that summer; the Bolsheviks were looking outside Russia for international support, and there was power in the streets that the Socialist party seemed unable to pick up. Jack believed that poets must become active revolutionaries, and if it meant putting his writing on hold he was willing to do it. For Louise, however, the goals of revolution and professional success were not at all exclusive: she was furthering the cause *and* her own career with her writing.

While the paths they had been pursuing throughout the spring and early summer had been parallel, they had been independent. In Croton, they rediscovered common ground. They made some repairs to the old farmhouse and finished converting the outbuilding to a studio. They spent hours in the small yard, as their interest in gardening developed into an intense, mutually held passion. On the brink of professional success and considerable celebrity, Louise felt freer, more confident, no longer in Jack's shadow, and she thrived under his attention. O'Neill was behind her, dismissed now as unimportant, though the bitterness lingered. A bigger stage awaited.

8

New Developments at Home

*T*here were moments of intense harmony in the relationship between Louise and Jack, when not only were they in love but every one of their activities seemed to mesh, from gardening, writing, and politics to the more general pursuit of history. But they still insisted that theirs was an open marriage. Each was still committed to the *idea* — if not all the consequences — of free love. Their convictions were strengthened by their experiences in Russia and the vision of a new, free world in which all outmoded conventions were smashed.

Their convictions meshed more thoroughly than ever with their natures. Both were tremendously charismatic and attractive people, larger-than-life personalities who seized the attention of, and drew immediate ardor from, almost all members of the opposite sex with whom each had contact. And both were generous souls, with giving hearts, who found it hard to say no. Jack always tolerated old friends like Fred Boyd who turned into obnoxious hangers-on. And as he admitted in letters to Louise in France, when very young, friendless girls pursued him, he had to exert great efforts of will not to succumb to them.

And though Louise was largehearted — it was as much her maternal streak as a general adventurousness that drew her to the troubled Gene O'Neill — her impulses in seeking out other men generally seem to have been motivated by more complicated configurations. Now, her new independence — the result of her galvanizing experience in Russia as well as her professional success — and her emergence as a partner in a more equal marriage contributed to an inner strength, a renewed sense of purpose, and a deeper security in her relationship with Jack. Hereafter her extramarital involvements, and her responses to Jack's, would take on an entirely different coloration. Her approach to free love became, as it were, less constrained, less desperate — more free.

Of course, it is possible that they were both, against their own will, more ambivalent about free love than they professed — especially Louise, given her experiences to date. Hazel Hunkins, a suffragist friend from the early days in the Village, believed that, all else being equal, Louise would have preferred a monogamous relationship. Any involvements with men on Louise's part, Hunkins said, were "a reaction to Reed's behavior and naturally foreign to Louise." This seems an over-statement, however: Louise took up with O'Neill initially when Jack was completely faithful to her, for instance. Moreover, Louise's attraction to other men and theirs to her seems quite the opposite of "foreign": it was an intrinsic part of her personality and *modus operandi*. Perhaps she might have preferred a monogamous relationship, but it was simply not in her nature, nor was it in her husband's.

Hazel Hunkins, of course, believed she was defending her friend's honor; she was also reacting to advances Jack made to her in the spring of 1918, when he was in Washington trying to get his Russia notes released. At a party in her apartment, when she didn't know him very well, she said, "John Reed started to make love to me. Much as I admired the things he stood for, I disliked him for his promiscuity — and with a wife like Louise! He was a handsome, big, muscular man, *very* sexy." Jack's pass, though, was fairly routine behavior in bohemian circles.

So Louise and Jack, in spite of the growing bond between them, were acting in what were, to them, fairly familiar ways. They were people to whom others were attracted, and they found it difficult not to respond. But the extramarital involvements they enjoyed in the remaining years of their marriage did not have the unsettling effect their previous affairs had; it was as if they had at last mastered the conflicting emotions that went along with the territory of free love.

In no case is this more clear than in Louise's involvement with the painter Andrew Dasburg, which began in the summer of 1918. A familiar figure in Village circles — he taught at the Art Students' League —

Dasburg was a gentle, good-looking man. Max Eastman described him as "the handsome, limping painter, mighty-chested and with blue eyes like a cornflower." Though he was married to the talented sculptor Grace Johnson — known simply as Johnson — with whom he had a son, Dasburg lived separately from his wife in a truly open marriage. They shared custody of their child.

Andrew and Louise had met in 1916, in the early, insecure months of her relationship with Jack. In Jack's absence, she had made a rather bold advance that Andrew deflected with great sensitivity, perhaps intuiting that she was acting out of a quiet desperation rather than any real feeling for him. But their paths crossed often over the years. In 1917 Mabel Dodge offered him the use of her husband's studio in Croton, and Andrew accepted. His place in the city was a few doors down from the Reeds' original apartment on Washington Square. The virtual summer campus of the Art Students' League was at Woodstock in upstate New York, an arts colony sometimes called the other Provincetown, where Louise and Jack, on occasional visits to friends, often encountered Dasburg. Though Dasburg was a quiet man, what one might call introverted, he too had been swept up by the events of the Russian Revolution and was a great admirer of Reed.

Over the years, Andrew and Louise flirted. But Andrew admired Louise as well as Jack and was reluctant to press his case. On Louise's side, her involvement with Andrew did not fit the pattern of the messy, tumultuous relationships that rocked her emotionally and shook her marriage with Jack. And Andrew was hardly the dramatic, larger-than-life sort of man Louise usually preferred.

In August 1918, Louise went for a long weekend to Woodstock, where she and Andrew became lovers. Dasburg met her at the carriage that connected with the train for New York at West Hurley and walked together with her to his rustic cottage halfway up Overlook Mountain. When they arrived, Louise gave him a present, a beautifully carved Russian icon. They enjoyed the quiet, talking for hours, often about the war — "We all hated the war," Andrew said. Once or twice they visited Andrew's neighbors, the fellow artist Henry Lee McFee and his wife, Aileen. Andrew continued to teach his art classes, and Louise would walk down the mountain and meet him for lunch afterward.

According to Andrew's accounts, and judging from the tone of Louise's later letters to him, this visit, and subsequent ones like it, were tender idylls, undisturbed by jealousies or worries about their future together. "Our relationship was so perfectly normal," Dasburg said. "There was no secrecy about it. None that we felt." He added, however, with what seems to have been characteristic circumspection, "Of course, one doesn't invite the public in at such times."

With his calm and undemanding nature, Andrew would become a reassuring presence over the next few years. He seems to have evoked a relatively unusual calm in the otherwise volatile Louise. He described her as a simple, guileless creature, not given to intrigue or wiles. This observation suggests that there was another side to Louise, one that few saw.

But it is no doubt significant that Louise confined her relationship with Andrew to isolated, nonthreatening interludes such as these days in Woodstock in 1918. She needed more energy, more drama, men with outsized personalities. But the relationship lasted, and it was apparently characterized by an abiding love and mutual respect. The oasis of security Andrew provided seems to have mitigated the desperation and fear of abandonment that usually made Louise turn to other men, suggesting in turn how deep that desperation and that fear ran.

After the idyll in Woodstock — about which it seems Jack knew nothing — Louise returned to Croton to shut up the house for their return to the city in September. She had just finished reading page proofs for her book, scheduled to be out the following month, and Jack, whose papers were finally released from Washington, was settling down to finish *Ten Days That Shook the World.*

Because the quarters on West 8th Street had been only temporary, the first item on their agenda was finding an apartment. After a good deal of looking, Louise found something quite special: a ground-level floor-through in a small house in a quiet, isolated Village mews off Sixth Avenue and West 11th Street. Number 1 Patchin Place had its drawbacks — it was heated by a potbellied stove and had an outhouse but no bathtub, and it was really too small — but the location was charming and convenient, and the rent, at $20 a month, was low. They took out a long lease, and the apartment would remain Louise's for many years, the closest thing she had to a permanent home. Friends visiting would find the large-boned Jack reclining on the sofa bed, typing, with Louise at his side, and wonder how he got anything done. He didn't, and eventually rented a room over Polly Holladay's restaurant in Sheridan Square as a workplace, swearing Louise to secrecy so there would be no distractions from well-meaning friends.

Almost immediately they ran into a series of troubles. On September 13, Jack gave a speech at Hunt's Point in the Bronx denouncing the landing of Allied troops in Russia, a move he believed, with single-minded devotion to the radical cause, was motivated only by the wish of the forces of capitalism to destroy the Bolsheviks, whatever the official Allied justification. (Their stated aim was to keep munitions shipments out of German hands.) Jack was arrested the next morning, charged with using "disloyal, scurrilous and abusive language about the Military and Naval Forces of the United States," and released on $5000 bail.

The first trial of *The Masses* editors — the one Jack had wanted to get home from Russia for but had missed — had resulted in a hung jury. The second opened at the end of September, with the business manager, Merrill Rogers, Max Eastman, Floyd Dell, and the cartoonist Art Young standing trial with Jack, whose offense was writing the following headline over an article on mental illness among the troops, reprinted from the *Tribune:* "Knit a Strait-Jacket for Your Soldier Boy." The whole trial seemed a farce; so trumped-up were the charges that Jack said to Art Young in mock earnestness as they entered the courtroom, "Well, Art, got your grip packed for prison?" But as the proceedings went on it became clear that if the defendants said anything against the war they might go to jail. Louise herself was questioned briefly on October 3, asked to identify what parts of her and Jack's jointly written *Masses* story on France she had composed. The high point of the trial came when Jack, having embarked on an oratorical flight, spoke about a young friend in France: "Somewhere he lies dead, and he died for you and he died for me. He died for Max Eastman, he died for John Reed, for Floyd Dell, for Merrill Rogers." At that point, Art Young, who had been dozing at the defense table, lifted his head, and said, "Didn't he die for me too?" and the courtroom erupted in laughter. Again the jury was hung, and on October 5 the defendants went free.

The trial set in motion a strange course of events, one that sounds apocryphal but that different sources bear out. At the trial, with other cheerleading bohemians, was the beautiful and talented young Edna St. Vincent Millay. Seven years younger than Louise, Millay was a formidable rival in Village circles. A celebrated poet and playwright (she was a member of the Provincetown Players), she had an intoxicating effect on others, according to Edmund Wilson, who would later model the heroine of his novel *I Thought of Daisy* on her. At the time of the *Masses* trial she was breaking the heart of the defendant Floyd Dell. Delighted by her presence, Dell introduced the red-haired, green-eyed beauty to Jack.

A few weeks later, late in October, Jack was with Dell and Millay when rumor of an armistice surfaced. They decided to celebrate by taking a late-night ride on the Staten Island ferry. As the ship passed through the foggy harbor, Jack regaled Millay with the story of his life — revolutionary version. As Dell later wrote, Jack "was telling her his most thrilling adventures as a war correspondent and Communist conspirator, and she said, like Desdemona, 'I love you for the dangers you have passed.'"

Dell believed this was not an isolated episode, and that Millay was for a time quite in love with Jack. His story becomes more speculative at this point, however, and is based on other people's reports. But it does seem likely that the romantic Millay was seriously attracted to Jack, and that he might well have reciprocated her feelings.

And in any case, Dell's story is very colorful, not one that might easily have been fabricated. Once when Louise was off on a speaking engagement, Jack entertained Millay at the Croton house. He was gathering wood in the basement, into which the back door of the hillside house opened. He looked up and saw Millay — or Vincent, as Dell and others called her — descending the stairs, holding a lighted candle, entirely naked. At that moment Louise came in through the back door, according to Dell. She then went shrieking off, running into the kitchen of her neighbor Sally Robinson, crying and swearing Sally to secrecy.

There is no other record of Louise's response to this incident, which could well support the argument that it is apocryphal. But accepting her husband's brief infatuation with the poet would be consistent with Louise's new maturity on the subject of free love. If she wished, she could believe the affair was never consummated — there is no hard evidence that it was — or that it was fairly one-sided, that Jack was not the pursuer but the pursued. Secure in her secret love for Andrew Dasburg, well used to Jack's charms and the effect they had on women, she may have gamely decided to dismiss it.

On the other hand, the poet would have appeared a considerable opponent, rivaling Louise in beauty, brains, and dramatic intensity.

The incident — or unfounded rumors of such incidents — might have eroded the firm ground Louise had only recently begun to feel under her feet.

Professionally, Louise was flourishing. *Six Red Months in Russia* was published by George H. Doran on October 19 in a lavishly illustrated edition, with endpapers reproducing some of the official and unofficial Russian documents, passes, and other memorabilia she had brought back.

The book met with mostly favorable reviews, but some were, to Louise and Jack, annoyingly predictable. At least three reviews called the book hasty — which was indeed true. *The Dial* made much of the fact that she was pro-Bolshevik, but went on to say that her bias "fortunately, does not mitigate her reporter's gift for accurate observation" and called the book "exceedingly valuable. . . . She lived through the weeks before, during, and after the Kerensky regime — lived through, that is, literally, and not by clinging to the American Red Cross and Embassy. She risked her life; she interviewed the organizers and leaders personally; she was on the 'inside' of every movement; she saw from the eyes of the people themselves. Here her original romantic sympathy enabled her to see the facts as a cold-blooded observer could never have succeeded in doing."

Another review, again favorable, thought the book's strength was that Louise was *not* partisan, praising her for presenting the revolution "fearlessly, without prejudice and without any preconceived theory. Indeed, she has no theories and because of that the impact of her sincerity is overpowering and her reading of events singularly convincing." The Socialist *New York Call* loved it. *The Nation* found many errors in it, some in the Russian language, but felt it contained a "wealth of information."

Floyd Dell, whose connection to any involvement between Jack and Millay was no doubt unknown to Louise, wrote his review in *The Liberator* in the form of a letter: "Fortunate you," he began, "you were there and made us see it with your eyes . . . the panorama of those six tremendous months passes like living reality before us."

Responses from friends like Dell were especially gratifying, for Louise could feel she was at last being taken seriously in her own right, not just as Jack's wife. Upton Sinclair, the muckraking novelist and Socialist who had achieved international fame with his 1906 exposé of

Louise, circa 1887, at about
age two

Louise in the 1908 Nevada
State University *Artemesia*

The young John Reed, circa 1913, shortly before he met Louise

Left: Louise, newly arrived in Greenwich Village to join Jack, circa 1916

Below: Mabel Dodge, the hostess of a celebrated Greenwich Village salon and Jack's great love before Louise

Right: Eugene O'Neill, the young playwright, with whom Louise began an affair in 1916

Below: Louise on the dunes in Provincetown, summer 1916

Above: The Provincetown Players' 1916 production of O'Neill's *Thirst*. From left to right, Louise, "Jig" Cook, and O'Neill. Louise's affair with Gene was at its height.
Below: The Wharf Theatre, home of the Provincetown Players

Jack in his Greenwich
Village study, circa 1917

Louise and Jack at their
country retreat in Croton-
on-Hudson, circa 1917

Louise, in her "George Sand haircut," in 1919, during a nationwide lecture tour

The artist Andrew Dasburg, with whom Louise trysted in Woodstock, New York, from 1918 to 1920

The anarchist Emma Goldman, who was a close associate of Louise's, though she wasn't always sympathetic to her

Max Eastman, the *Masses* editor, and neighbor and friend to Jack and Louise

Patchin Place, Greenwich Village. Louise and Jack lived at Number One, the first door on the left.

the meatpacking industry, *The Jungle,* had been a longtime acquaintance of Jack's. But when *Six Red Months in Russia* appeared, he wrote Louise offering to review the book in his new periodical, *Upton Sinclair's.* A long correspondence ensued, with Louise writing in deadly earnest over many scrawled pages about political matters — for instance, the suffering of American soldiers in boxcars under a Japanese command — and relaying almost nothing of a personal nature.

She and Jack were more in demand than ever at Village parties, and Louise won scores of new admirers. She was beautiful, passionate, warm, and witty; now she had shown her mettle by living through the Russian Revolution and writing a book about it that was the talk of the moment. Art Young called her "a picture of flaming youth" and remembered her "joyous laughter at official stupidity." Describing a party at which Jack and Louise were present, William Carlos Williams conveyed a vivid sense of the couple's style:

> [Jack Reed, a] plump, good-natured guy who had taken the bit in his teeth and was getting out. . . . The story went around that he was a sick man, had already had one kidney resected, but it didn't seem to put much of a crimp in his style. He looked at us as if he couldn't quite make out what we were up to, half-amused, half-puzzled. Louise Bryant, his wife, who was with him that night, had on a heavy, very heavy white silk skirt so woven that it hung over the curve of her buttocks like the strands of a glistening waterfall. There could have been nothing under it, for it followed the very crease in her buttocks in its fall. No fault there. She too looked to be outward bound.

Louise in 1918 made an indelible impression on others, more even than she had in her twenties. On her return from Russia she had her hair bobbed in what one newspaper called "a George Sand haircut." It was straight, glossy, and hung in bangs over her forehead, giving her a youthful, gamine-like appearance. Like many of the American contingent in Russia, she had bought all kinds of Russian treasures for next to nothing. She specialized in clothes and accessories, including a pair of knee-high embroidered boots, silver belts, bracelets, sable coats, and seal hats. She cut a striking figure in her exotic, almost outlandish Russian costume.

This new visibility and attractiveness cut both ways, however. There were those in the *Masses* crowd — mostly women — who viewed her with suspicion and even scorn. To Isobel Soule, an idealistic Barnard College graduate, Louise was "frivolous." And Mary Heaton Vorse said, "Exactly. Louise is fighting for the revolution. That's what it's for — so everyone can have a fur coat." Susan Jenkins Brown ran into Louise in "Cossack garb" on Charles Street one afternoon and noted disdainfully how Louise showed off her outfit "as if she were a model" and bragged about how the Bolshevik men took to her. "What a pain in the neck she was," Brown said years later.

The tone of comments like these could be attributed in part to envy. Louise was beautiful, talented, accomplished, stylishly dressed, had more than her share of male admirers, and she was married to the man of the hour in the circles in which they traveled. The success of her book and newspaper articles had launched her into the national spotlight, out of the narrow Village sphere to which many had expected her to confine herself.

But something else seems to have been at work here: envy is not enough to account for the persistent nastiness of Louise's detractors. The politics of the left also came into play. To care about your surroundings or your clothes was considered highly bourgeois. Emma Goldman, who otherwise liked Louise, explained why she couldn't "take her seriously": "she powdered her nose and rouged her lips and she was careful of her figure." To these people, Louise's attention to her appearance rendered her suspect, suggesting that her revolutionary politics were a sham.

Several paradoxes are operating in this kind of situation. What harm did it really do the cause when a woman wished to dress well? Did it help the cause to wear sackcloth and ashes, or the modern equivalent, every day? Other radical Village women wore more conventional downtown garb, dreary and usually black. Protest and clothing were inextricably bound up: you were what you wore.

Another paradox was even more obvious. Louise had won the approval and friendship of no less than Lenin — the sun-god of the radical left — and yet these people talked about her clothes. Their attitude certainly was as bourgeois and frivolous as the values they faulted in Louise. These radicals were supposed to be comrades, after all, and their nastiness was not only uncomradely but counterproductive. This sort of thing, some might say, will always remain a problem in radical circles, when activists who are not themselves working-class choose to fight the battles of the working class. Ultimately, Louise had to conclude that it didn't matter. She could do more for the cause — meeting with newspaper editors to get stories, for instance — if she presented herself attractively.

Her marital status lingered in the background as another point of debate. On the one hand even a friend like Emma Goldman could say, "Louise was never a communist, she only slept with a communist." If she was only sleeping with members of the dominant group, like O'Neill or Reed, she was reduced to the status of "girlfriend." Yet marriage was a deeply suspect institution in radical circles in the teens and early twenties. It bespoke outmoded Victorianism, a rejection of personal liberty (and, as such, in popular Freudian thought, neurosis), and acceptance of traditional sex roles. It was, in short, bourgeois. Louise and Jack were aware of this view: both were studiously nonchalant, and at other times frankly apologetic, about their marriage. Jack told his friends he needed to marry Louise on the eve of his kidney operation so that she would be his legal heir; Louise said she was marrying Jack to make traveling easier. They kept their marriage secret for as long as they could, about six months, and as late as the year they returned from Russia Louise was writing to Upton Sinclair, "Yes, I'm really *Mrs.* Reed. One has to do that, you know, in order to get passports and be comfortable. Besides a marriage certificate never seemed of sufficient importance to us to make a fuss about — one way or another." It is, of course, difficult to distinguish such explanations from rationalizations. Louise and Jack, deeply in love, and with their mutual ambivalence about nonmonogamous relationships, may well have wanted very much to be married, but still they felt the need to apologize for it.

On the other hand, it had to have been common knowledge that both Louise and Jack slept with other people. The O'Neill affair was well known, of course, and Jack's womanizing was notorious. By the logic of the day, this should have been generally accepted behavior, and most likely it was. But the double standard, as time has shown, is extraordinarily difficult to eradicate, and a woman's extramarital activity was only grudgingly tolerated. Jack's sexual exploits, as a well-liked, handsome, charismatic man and a virtual hero among radicals of the day, were not only expected and accepted but something to be proud of, part of the legend. For Louise, it would have been another story entirely. Married to such a man, the talk must have had it, what need had she to turn to others? Among those women who either treated her with suspicion or barely tolerated her, there must have been considerable resentment over her freedom, her ability to remain in a marriage with a man of Jack's stature and at the same time to take lovers who were equally, though very differently, attractive. Again, jealousy would have entered into the equation, but so too did the strange need to find fault with such a woman, a woman who seemed to threaten the status quo of the bohemians, a group who were by definition not supposed to have a status quo to begin with. In matters of style, professional achievement, appearance, and sexual comportment, Louise was damned if she did and damned if she didn't. It had never been easy for her to persevere in living her life in the way she wanted, and her newfound success and fame had not made it any more so.

9

A Defiant Witness Speaks

T he year 1919 found Reed still holed up finishing *Ten Days That Shook the World* while Louise, very much in the limelight following the publication of her book, was entering into the most intense, committed, and sustained period of activism in her life. Royalties, as well as the modest $25 and $30 sums she and Jack commanded for addressing mostly partisan groups, sustained the household in minimally comfortable fashion. But Louise sought a wider stage, a move that took considerable courage in the climate of the coming Red Scare, when deportation of radicals was reported almost daily in the pages of the national press and in Washington.

Louise committed herself naturally to adversarial politics. As a college student, when she was asked to watch her behavior in light of the recent controversy surrounding the college's association with controversial Darwinist thought, Louise took the suggestion as an assault on her civil liberties and deliberately flaunted her unconventional habits, bringing down the wrath of the college authorities. A passionate defender of individual rights and the cause of the oppressed, she was inflamed by hypocritical or repressive responses to expressions of her beliefs. Louise's passionate approach to politics — it could even be called romantic, though the term belies the high seriousness Louise brought to the arena — would from time to time, arouse intense opposition against her and her causes.

Louise leaped into the debate over how the West should deal with revolutionary Russia with a speaking tour of the Middle Atlantic states in January and February 1919. On February 2, she commanded her biggest audience yet. Sharing the stage with her old compatriot from Petrograd, Albert Rhys Williams, she addressed a crowd of thousands at the Poli Theatre in Washington, D.C., speaking on "The Truth about Russia." Her mission was simple: she wanted to correct the rampant untruths about the new Russia circulating among critics in the U.S. The Bolsheviks were not in collusion with the Germans; there had not been widespread slaughter during the revolution; the majority of the Russian people — the peasants — considered themselves Bolsheviks; there was no widespread "nationalization" of women. She spoke passionately, and with wit. Answering the charge that Trotsky's daughter had taken large sums of money out of the country, she pointed out that the girl was only six years old, "and she is a very precocious child, but, I am sure, she is not able to do that."

Even the most hostile accounts indicated her effectiveness as a speaker and her general charm. The *New York Times,* in a belligerent piece, admitted her charisma grudgingly: "Miss Bryant appears a demure and pretty girl, with a large hat, a stylish suit, and gray stockings. Her voice is high, and it has a plaintive note to it. She amuses the crowd because, with the air of an ingenue, she hurls darts at Government departments, holds people up to ridicule, and with a fearful voice appeals to American fair play to be just to a beneficent Bolshevist Government and give it a chance."

Yet the climate of Washington in early 1919 was far from sympathetic, and accounts of her appearance were drenched in withering sarcasm. The gist of the *New York Times* coverage was that the speakers had reported not the truth, but gross distortions, about Russia. The editorial continued by pointing out that "Miss Bryant" was in fact "Mrs. John Reed . . . an extreme radical, whose speaking and writing in America were considered several times to be so dangerous to the winning of the war that he was arrested and forbidden to keep on — that she shares and has shared his views, and that during her six months in Russia she was in no wise a disinterested, objective observer, but a partisan of the fiercest sort."

Moreover, at least some members of her audience were decidedly not partisan. The *Times* account noted that the first rows of the theater were set aside for congressmen and darkly implied that they were present out of sympathy for the Bolshevik cause. Such was not the case at all. Legislators in Washington were thrown into increasing hysteria over the "Bolshevik threat," as events around the world seemed to suggest world revolution was imminent. Russia was not the only country experiencing turmoil in the aftermath of a massively dislocating war. Italy, Austria, Hungary, and Bavaria were all exploring the possibility of government by soviets, and some would actually adopt such a government in the months to come. Other parts of Europe were racked by strikes and uprisings. The French navy mutinied in the Black Sea rather than fight to suppress the Bolsheviks. Closer to home, strikes occurred across the country: the first general strike ever in the U.S. developed out of a Seattle shipyard walkout, and in Portland, Oregon, unions formed a soviet. In all, thirty-six hundred strikes occurred in the U.S. in 1919. Capitalist interests joined forces in Washington to defeat the closed shop, masking their efforts as patriotic measures to stamp out Bolshevism.

Congress rose to the challenge with relish. The Judiciary Committee of the Senate, which had, under the guidance of Senator Lee S. Overman of North Carolina, been investigating liquor-brewing interests and German propaganda in wartime America, was directed "to begin an investigation of Bolshevism and all other forms of anti-American radicalism in the United States." The resolution was passed unanimously the day it was introduced, February 5.

Thus began the grand and ignoble tradition of witch-hunting in the U.S. Congress, a tradition that would culminate in the 1950s with the House Un-American Activities Committee and Wisconsin Senator Joe McCarthy's hearings before the Armed Services Committee. Louise, Jack, and other radicals watched in disgust as a parade of superpatriots, including David Harris, U.S. ambassador to Russia, whom Jack and Louise intensely disliked, testified. First they asserted a connection between pro-German and Bolshevik activity. Later they more frankly asserted that the Bolsheviks were ruining Russia, in particular its women, who were supposedly forced to participate in free love or otherwise be raped and ravished. Furthermore, on American soil, "several avowed agents of the Bolsheviki [are] here — avowed propagandists" — among them John Reed.

Jack, Louise, Rhys Williams, and their friends were dismayed by the

misinformation daily brought before the Congress and concluded that
the committee was not interested in hearing any witness sympathetic to
the Bolsheviks or, perhaps more importantly, even remotely informed as
to events in Russia. They began to inundate Senator Overman with
telegrams demanding to be called before the committee. Each was
insistent on his or her right to be heard, despite the dangers of identify-
ing themselves with the Bolshevik cause before a thoroughly unsympathetic governmental body in full public view. Louise Bryant's testimony
was to be one of her finest hours.

In Washington for her brief speaking tour in the area, Louise had new
reason to linger there, waiting to be called to give testimony. In the
meantime, with Anna Louise Strong, a Socialist then active in organizing Seattle's general strike, she projected plans for a nationwide lecture
circuit. She was in Baltimore, again speaking on "The Truth about
Russia," when she was called to defend a different cause, but one that
aroused her passion just as surely. Clara Wold, her old feminist friend
from Portland and a Patchin Place neighbor, telegraphed to Louise from
Washington that her presence was needed there in the cause of woman
suffrage. The National Woman's party would pay her way. Louise was
off on the next train.

The battle for suffrage, which Louise had followed avidly since her
direct involvement in Portland in 1914 and 1915, had reached a critical
juncture. A national woman's suffrage amendment had been continu-
ously brought to the floor of Congress since 1914 but was blocked there
procedurally for years. During the 65th Congress in December 1917,
President Wilson had declared his support for the amendment, and it
was passed in the House in January 1918 by a vote of 274 to 136. But
efforts to get it passed in the Senate were unavailing (it would take all of
1918 and half of 1919 to achieve passage, and ratification would not
follow for another fourteen months). When Louise was in Washington
in February 1919, suffragists' hopes were pinned to the lame duck session
of the 65th Congress. It was to this battle that Clara Wold called
her friend.

The National Woman's party, which housed and funded Louise during at least part of her stay in Washington, had long before become frustrated with the relatively conventional tactics of the more mainstream
National Woman's Suffrage Association, led by Alice Paul. Founded in

1916 by the prosuffrage Congressional Union in the twelve states where women had the vote, the NWP was fundamentally a more radical group: because a large proportion of its membership were Quakers, the party did not support the war effort; because women were given the vote in Russia after the revolution, they supported the Bolsheviks. Moreover, they had borrowed the example of the British and had adopted increasingly militant tactics, picketing before the White House and on Capitol Hill. In response, they were persecuted regularly by the police and thrown into jail, with the result that a secondary cause became the civil liberties increasingly denied them.

In its militancy — it was called by the mainstream press "the I.W.W. of the suffrage movement" — the National Woman's party was an organization toward which Louise instinctively gravitated. Moreover, the aims of mainstream feminism aroused her natural suspicions as an "equality feminist" — a feminist who believed that the principle of equality overrode any other consideration in furthering women's rights. So, for instance, while many feminist and other labor leaders were lobbying for protective legislation that emphasized women's distinctness from men, she saw that such legislation undercut the principle of equality — paving the way, perhaps, for discrimination against women. As one feminist historian explains, "At a time when most feminists believed in women's superior ethical insight and nurturant qualities, the NWP derided any reference to feminine distinctiveness, and in fact worried that such ideas would prohibit women's political advancement."

As the Senate vote on suffrage approached, Louise and the NWP became increasingly frustrated by what they saw as Woodrow Wilson's tepid support for the amendment. The statements he made on woman's suffrage didn't go far enough, they felt, and he was not bringing enough influence to bear on individual senators to get the bill passed. It was a question of "doing too little too late," they felt. They decided on serious action.

On the eve of the Senate vote, about seventy-five women assembled outside NWP headquarters on Jackson Place and marched to the White House. Carrying the party's gold, purple, and white banners as well as the American flag, following a young woman who carried an urn of fire, the members brandished signs reading, "The president is responsible for the betrayal of American women" and "He preaches democracy abroad and thwarts democracy here." After the requisite galvanizing speeches

on the White House lawn, they flung a two-foot effigy of President
Wilson into the flames. Immediately the police descended, and at least
forty women were rounded up and brought to the house of detention.
The NWP released a report describing the scene: "Through the smoke
of the flames, from the stone rail of the White House fence and from
the steps of the patrols in which they were carried off, the women
denounced the President, declaring him to blame for the threatened
defeat of the suffrage amendment." The statement went on, "We burn
not the effigy of a president of a free people, but the leader of an
autocratic party organization whose tyrannical power holds millions of
women in political slavery."

Among the forty or so arrested was "Miss Louise Bryant"; she was
also one of "seven New York women" who refused bail; the women were
arraigned the next day in the district police court and sentenced to five
days in jail.

The arrested women promptly went on a hunger strike. By then, this
was a common suffragist tactic and won the women popular sympathy
(as well as, usually, an early release), but it was undertaken with the most
serious of purposes. Because civil liberties were routinely denied arrested
suffragists, they refused food in order to have themselves declared political prisoners. Enough of them — including Louise — were aware that
political prisoners were treated differently in countries where the phe-
nomenon was common, such as prerevolutionary Russia. Political prisoners were allowed to receive mail, books, and visitors, to wear their own
clothes, purchase their own food, and see their own lawyers.

Over the protests of Jack, who wrote her from Croton immediately
after the arrest, worrying about her health, Louise joined the hunger
strike. It was, of course, a matter of principle; moreover, as a celebrity-
of-the-moment, she was well aware of the publicity value her involvement in the strike — and the women's movement in general — would
have for suffrage.

It cannot have been a pleasant time, despite the camaraderie of the
other suffragists. Dorothy Day described her hunger strike for the cause
in the same Washington jail:

> There were no meals to break the monotony, and if the women tried to
> call to one another, there were always guards on hand to silence them
> harshly. In the morning we were taken one by one to a washroom at the

end of the hall. There was a toilet in each cell, open, and paper and flushing were supplied by the guard. It was as though one were in a zoo with open bars leading into the corridor. There were only narrow ventilators at the top of the rear wall of the cell, which was a square stone room. The sun shone dimly through these slits for a time and then disappeared for the rest of the day. There was no way to tell what time it was. . . . The place was inadequately heated by one pipe which ran along a wall. Suspense and fear kept one cold.

After a few miserable days — at least three — Louise was released. Though she later wrote of "the horrors of prison," she cheerfully (or defiantly, because Jack had been adamant that she not hunger-strike) told Jack that she actually thought going without food had helped her recover from a lingering cold, and that the only aftereffect was that she was a little shaky on her feet.

Word had reached Louise in jail that the vote on suffrage had not passed in the Senate, as feminists had expected. Not much could be done until the next session of Congress. The most pressing matter, therefore, was testifying before the Overman Committee. Louise wrote to Jack of the importance of correcting errors in the testimony already given and urged him to collect as many newspapers and magazine accounts as possible giving the real story about events in Russia. She pored over her own materials, piling up documents she hoped to show to the senators: copies of *Die Fackel,* for example, the German propaganda newspaper Jack had worked on in Moscow. She eagerly awaited her day in court, which she came to think of as the cause's day in court, and with what seems in retrospect a touch of naiveté, she believed she would have it.

Eventually — and only after bursting into the hearings and demanding that her testimony be scheduled — she was called before the committee. On February 20 the gallery was packed with an audience of mixed sympathies, the radical observers mostly women, presumably Louise's suffragist friends. The tone was set from the moment her testimony began, when the senators questioned her at length about her belief in God. Though she said at the outset that she believed in the sanctity of an oath, Senator William H. King of Utah pushed on, stating that "a person who has no conception of God does not have any idea of the sanctity of an oath, and an oath would be meaningless." Not satisfied with her concession that she believed there was a God, she was asked if she believed "in a punishment hereafter and a reward for duty." Exasperated, she responded, "It seems to me as if I were being tried for witchcraft. . . . Very well; I will concede — I concede there is a hell."

When asked about her NWP affiliation and her involvement in the effigy-burning demonstration, she replied straightforwardly, adding, "I do not know what that has to do with the truth about Russia. . . . I believe in equality." When the senators delved into her past, including her marriage to Trullinger, she protested that she believed she was there to tell the truth about Russia. "We want to know something about the character of the person who testifies," said Senator King, "so that we can determine what credit to give to the testimony."

Observers noted that her cheeks reddened with the first exchange about her religious beliefs, and her color remained heightened throughout the long day. When she attempted to elaborate beyond the usual yes or no in her answers, she was ordered, "Don't be so impertinent." Hisses from the gallery led Senator Overman to clear the room temporarily. Where anti-Bolshevik witnesses who had come before the committee earlier had been allowed to testify freely, she was continually admonished to "never mind that" and "answer yes or no to the question."

For the most part, she more than held her own. Asked to explain under what circumstances she went to Russia, she told them of her financial arrangements, adding, "I did not go to Russia for money. I went because I am a reporter, and because I wanted to see the revolution." The committee responded with "You didn't go for money, you went for love, hey?" When asked about her speech at the Poli Theatre, she answered, "The purpose was to protest against intervention in Russia. I, as an American, believing in self-determination, cannot believe in intervention. I do not see how we can fight for democracy in France and be against it in Siberia."

Relieved that she was at last being allowed to make a statement of any length, she fielded a question about whether she was "anxious" for the Bolsheviks to remain in power. "I am anxious," she began. "Answer my question," Senator Knute Nelson interrupted, "Are you anxious to have the Bolshevik government there as a personal thing?" She replied that she believed the Russians should settle that. Questioned again, she reiterated that she believed in self-determination. "Self-determination at the point of a gun?" she was asked. Yes, she answered. "All governments have had to be self-determined at the point of a gun. There has never been a government established except after a war." (True or not, this last was a firmly held and oft uttered belief of both Louise and Jack, who would say the same thing in his testimony before the committee the next day.)

Questioning continued along these lines, and it became abundantly clear that the committee wanted to hear only incriminating facts about Louise, Jack, Rhys Williams, Raymond Robins, or any other radical sympathizer. At the end of the day, Louise was allowed to make some general observations about conditions in Russia, but again the committee seemed less eager to hear them than to see how far she would go in incriminating herself. She handled them adroitly, insisting that she did not advocate a Soviet-style government for the United States. Nevertheless, it was an exhausting and humiliating experience, and she was dejected at the end of the day. More than that, she was angry.

The next morning, when proceedings again convened, she told them so. She had been treated "like a traitor," she said, pointing out that all previous witnesses — those who did not support the revolution — had been allowed to talk at length while she had barely been allowed to answer questions fully. Senator Overman chastised her: "You seem to want to make a martyr of yourself, when you have not been treated unfairly as far as I can see. You are a woman and do not know anything about the conduct of an examination such as we have in hand here. We are going to treat you fairly and treat you as a lady." These were fighting words, and Louise shot back, "I do not want to be treated like a lady, but I want to be treated as a human being."

She wanted it in the record that she believed she had been "lectured at" ("You were not given lectures. You were cross-examined") and subjected to "a sort of third degree." She complained that she was patronized for her commitment to her principles: "Even my morals have been suggested [sic] by Senator Nelson. He has given me regular lectures as to what I ought to think, and how I might, somehow, come out of this terrible slump I have gotten into." Indeed, at the end of the previous day, she had been told she was "deluded," the senator adding, "You are young, too, and I feel sorry for you."

Pressing her advantage, she protested that the committee had not called many who had come forward to testify before them, most notably her husband. When Major E. Lowry Humes, who was participating in the investigation on the part of the War Department, denied that Jack had ever applied to testify, Jack spoke up from the audience, and Overman conceded that perhaps his telegrams had been overlooked. Louise carried the day, and when Jack succeeded her on the stand, he was treated respectfully if not gingerly — and dismissed as soon as decorum would allow.

Louise felt no sense of personal triumph after her testimony. It was a frustrating exercise, and she believed, rightly, that she had made few inroads in convincing the committee to explore the issue without prejudice. In an interview a few weeks later, she said, "When I . . . realized how old and stupid [the senators] were in their blindness, and yet how full of bitterness and rancor, then I began for the first time to fear for my country. I have always said, 'In America we shall manage our changes without violence. We have political methods. We can get together and discuss.' But when I saw that senate committee I lost hope. There will be violence in America, but it will not be from the workers; it will be from the ignorant reactionaries."

On the other hand, Louise's purposefulness and determination were admirable and won the respect of fellow radicals. The image of the browbeaten young woman who refused to be cowed by the overbearing senators caught the imagination of such observers as Boardman Robinson, who produced a delightful cartoon of a brave but small Louise surrounding by looming, finger-pointing elder statesmen, peppering her with questions like "Do you believe in infant damnation?"

But Louise knew that hers was a hollow victory, and she turned her attention to her speaking tour. Having tried her hand at correcting the misperceptions of those in power, she looked forward to preaching, if not to the converted, at least to the educable: the workers who were agitating for improved labor conditions, left-leaning individuals interested in social change, and the many who were simply eager to hear about Russia and its great experiment. Anna Louise Strong, finding that Louise was in demand as a speaker across the country, was putting together a grueling tour under the auspices of the Central Labor Council and their Russian information bureau. A woman of considerable energy herself, she expected a lot from Louise. Inevitably, the two would clash, but Louise shared Strong's pragmatic determination to strike while the iron was hot and generally tried to comply with the Seattle organizer's wishes. She asked only that Strong space out her early engagements, taking into account her fatigue after the busy month of February, and to schedule some meetings in California so that she could see her mother.

As preparations were being made, Louise and Jack took the train to Philadelphia for Jack's trial on the "inciting to riot" charge. Both were deeply pessimistic about the outcome, and Louise was almost frantic with worry, fearing Jack would get the maximum penalty, a five-year jail sentence. But they found David Wallerstein, a competent lawyer willing to defend Jack without charge, and who was determined to plead the case solely on the basis of free speech. On September 24, he put Jack on the stand in his own defense, and to everyone's great relief the jury voted for acquittal. Several weeks later charges were dropped in the Hunt's Point case. But Louise, always fearful that Jack would get into serious trouble, was still uneasy. She found herself half agreeing with Jack's mother, who was bombarding him with cautionary letters, one warning him to stay away from Portland because "they are arresting Bolsheviks out here."

Mrs. Reed was quite right. Bolsheviks were being arrested in Portland in 1919 — as well as in scores of cities and towns across the country. The large and bloody flowering of the Red Scare was beginning. In the wake of the Russian Revolution and of the revolutionary experiments in Europe, patriots viewed American radicalism with what eventually amounted to paranoia. Events that Louise and Jack had so cheered, like the Seattle general strike early that year, had put the government and law enforcement on the offensive. Attoney General A. Mitchell Palmer, running for president on a red-baiting platform, had joined league with the young J. Edgar Hoover, then head of the Bureau of Investigation's newly formed Radical Division at the Justice Department, and was busy convincing Congress — to the tune of a $2.6-million appropriation for his people's activities — that revolution in the U.S. was imminent. (In fact, with the fervor of a millenarian, he predicted the date on which it would begin — July 4, 1919; when that date passed he named the day May 1, 1920.)

When the scare was well under way, a piece by Palmer in the popular magazine *Forum* explained how he saw the events of early 1919: "Like a prairie-fire, the blaze of revolution was sweeping over every institution of law and order. . . . It was eating its way into the homes of the American workman, its sharp tongues of revolutionary heat were licking the altars of the churches, leaping into the belfry of the school bell, crawling into the sacred corners of American homes, seeking to replace marriage vows with libertine laws, burning up the foundations of society." Later in the year, Palmer and the man known as "Palmer's assistant," Hoover, proved their seriousness with the mass arrest of IWW workers and the deportation of the foreign-born, establishing 1919 as one of the bloodiest and most barbaric years the U.S. had seen. For Louise to lecture in such a climate required consummate courage. Though she was technically lecturing independently, the fact that her expenses were paid by a radical group did not escape the federal authorities, who monitored her movements rigorously.

On the other hand, the very radicalization the authorities so feared was galvanizing to Louise and Jack. However repressive, 1919 was a time of great energy and promise as well. Later in the year the Boston police strike, the coal strike, and the steel strike seemed proof that the workers of the U.S. were ripe for revolution. A lecture tour that reached the people and that provided a source of information alternative to the press excited Louise and Jack equally. For a time they hoped they might speak together. Jack was as much in demand as Louise, in spite of the fact that his Russia book had not yet appeared. Anna Louise Strong arranged successive engagements for the two of them. But during a short visit to Croton at the end of the month, it became clear that Jack was needed by the Socialist party. The recently organized left wing was looking to him as a leader, and he made it a priority to see that the radical left organize a pro-Bolshevik united front in the interests of supporting Russia and world revolution. Failing that, he hoped at least to organize a party that would be recognized by the Soviet government, the Communist International (the Comintern).

Louise left very reluctantly in early March, making Jack promise not to do all the spring gardening work without her. In a letter a few days later, she also urged him not to go off on political business on her return: "I *do so want to visit you!* And it would be wonderful to work together, *even a week,* in the garden." The new tenderness that had sprung up between them after his return from Russia translated into real misery at being apart. Louise wrote to Jack almost daily, addressing him as "dearest Big." He reciprocated, inventing a new nickname for her — "dearest Small."

Louise's tour was a resounding success. At her first stop, in Detroit, she wrote Jack, "They gave me a grand reception. . . . The papers carried *big* stories." She outlined her schedule: Chicago, Minneapolis, Yakima, Seattle, Tacoma, Portland, and San Francisco. (Many cities were added later.) Anna Louise Strong had sometimes scheduled two meetings a day and yet could guarantee her only $50 a week over expenses. Meanwhile, most of the cities she spoke in on her way west had booked her for engagements on the way back. Even this early in the trip, she worried about her fortitude, and resolved to "have it out" with Anna when she got to Seattle. She closed the letter to Jack with, "Old Darl, how I'd love to be there in the country. I don't want to *think* at all."

But her successes buoyed her up. The welcome she received at each stop was so warm that she was overwhelmed. In Chicago she met Jane Addams at Hull House, the settlement home she had founded in the midst of Chicago's slums. When Addams saw how tired Louise was, she offered her the use of her own room. Sinclair Lewis turned up for her talk in Minneapolis, bringing with him "a flock of newspapermen and the Socialist bunch." He introduced himself after the meeting and took her home with him to meet his wife. The crowds everywhere were huge: in Minneapolis, many had to be turned away, and the next day, in St. Paul, "people sat in the aisles and on the stage and I had room only to speak and not to promenade." Her book, boxes of which she had brought with her, was selling out fast. Most gratifying was the warm reception she got, at nearly every stop, from Russian refugees.

As she headed west, she grew uneasy, thinking of revisiting Portland and other scenes of her youth. She was also sick, writing Jack from the train: "Everyone is sneezing, and I am among the sneezers, my beauty being somewhat enhanced by a large coldsore on the right side of my face. If I go on this way I will appear sinister." The cold grew worse and she developed a throat infection, which later spread to one of her lungs. From the Davenport Hotel in Spokane she wired her Patchin Place neighbor that she might need to be hospitalized, asking him to relay to Jack the message "not to worry excellent care just lonesome." On the heels of the infection she came down with influenza, which in 1919 was raging, as it had on a larger scale the year before, in epidemic — and killer — proportions. It set her back a week, and when she reached Seattle — a key stop because of its recent general strike — Anna Louise Strong suggested she take off a couple of days. But she was so much in demand at informal gatherings that it was difficult to get any real rest. "Anna Louise is belligerently entertaining me. Parties, house parties, god knows what. Was dragged here to a country place across the Sound last night. Uncomfortable, but what a crowd. Everybody sits right by my elbow so they won't miss anything *interesting!* I'm afraid lionizing is too nauseating for me to bear."

But the audiences in the West were the most enthusiastic yet. One of her five speeches in Seattle was given in the Longshoremen's Hall near the docks. The audience was "the roughest, finest, most wonderful!" she wrote Jack. The hall was a big old barn and she had to struggle to make herself heard, but the crowd loved her. She stopped speaking at ten-thirty but didn't manage to leave until midnight. It filled her with emotion, she said, "the same kind of emotion I feel when I look suddenly at the purple blueness of these great mountains of the West."

In Seattle she came into direct conflict with the managers who worked for Anna Louise Strong. They had scheduled some dates in several cities in western Canada, to which Louise had agreed. But as the dates approached she learned that she had to declare her intentions when crossing the border. The managers told her to say she was visiting friends, but she flatly refused to lie, she told Jack. "I was going there to speak on Russia and *against intervention!* What a mess I'd get into by trying to evade the facts."

And she was dreading Portland, where, as it turned out, she was booked into the Multnomah Hotel, where Jack's mother was boarding. "Isn't it funny?" she wrote Jack. "I'll do the best I can with your mother but it gives me cold shivers to think of even *being* in Portland." For all she knew, Paul Trullinger might show up. And Mrs. Reed was a formidable prospect: Louise wasn't sure whether Jack's mother approved of her, and she knew she didn't approve of Bolshevism. Moreover, the Portland City Council wanted a copy of her speech in advance, which she had resolved to provide to them rather than risking being barred from appearing — "because *no radical* has been able to open his mouth in any big hall there."

But her visit in Portland was one of the high points of her trip. Reporters with photographers met her in the hotel and wrote up favorable profiles. "So much for the return of the prodigal daughter," she wrote Jack. In fact, *The Oregonian* treated her very much like one, writing that she "has changed little . . . since she left Portland several years ago. . . . she is very much the same little radical and vigorous reformer." The talk itself was a great success. People began showing up at five o'clock, and by seven, when the talk was scheduled to begin, there wasn't even standing room.

Moreover, her visit with Mrs. Reed went off well, which "*much* relieved" her. Mrs. Reed had become a thorn in her son's side, fretting about his activities and complaining of abject poverty. Louise reassured Jack that his mother's financial situation wasn't as dire as Mrs. Reed had described it, that in fact she lived quite well. She told him she had met his brother Harry and his wife, Polly (the former she liked, the latter she didn't). "I seem to stand high with the family," she wrote Jack, later inserting the words "at the present moment," as if in afterthought. She also reported that their mutual Portland friends, the artists Carl and Helen Waters, hoped to join them that summer in Truro and spend the entire time lying in the sun and painting. She hoped it would happen.

Her next stop was the San Francisco area. She lunched with the *San Francisco Call*'s crusading editor Fremont Older, who wanted firsthand news of the revolution. He in turn told her about his long battle to clear the name of the anarchist Tom Mooney, wrongly imprisoned for bombing a Preparedness Day parade in 1916. It was a cause familiar to her, but Older's spirited belief in Mooney's innocence inflamed her anew, and she was pleased when Older told her he would escort Mooney's wife to hear her speak.

By now her tour had picked up plenty of momentum and the attendant publicity. The mayor of Berkeley, on the other side of San Francisco Bay, said he would not allow her to speak there because any Bolshevik sympathizer, as he saw it, was "an emissary of the Germans." Increasingly wise to the ways of the press, Louise immediately called a press conference, with the result that "every paper carries a big story." A friend in the Department of Justice let her know that she was probably being set up to break a city ordinance (Jack had been subject to the same ruse in Philadelphia), so she canceled her Berkeley appearance. She was getting used to rooms full of photographers, smoke, reporters, and people who wanted her autograph — but, she wrote Jack, she just missed him.

Her appearance in San Francisco involved two major reunions — the first with her family and the second with her Portland friends C. E. S. Wood and Sara Bard Field. Her mother made the long trip from her new home in Roseville, near Sacramento, to see Louise at the St. Francis Hotel; her sister might have come as well. (Her brother and half brothers were overseas in the army.) Her mother loved hearing her speak, Louise wrote proudly to Jack: "My mother is absolutely *bewildered*. She isn't sure if I'm a Bolshevik or a patriot or what it is all about. But she likes to have me get an ovation anyway." Still, in another letter the same day, she complained of having "not even a minute to myself — and *relatives* — God — they are all alike — I only want my honey for a family — and his dog and our cat." No doubt she had in part adopted Jack's attitude toward relatives (his mother was a constant bother), but she had also simply grown away from the mother and siblings she had not been especially close to in the first place.

C. E. S. Wood had finally left his wife to join Sara in California. Sara had recently suffered a major tragedy, a car accident in which her son was killed and her leg nearly severed, and her first foray out of the house was to see Louise speak. Wood had tried to give Louise a royal welcome, inviting her to dinner with the French consul, but she had declined, pleading exhaustion (though she wrote to Jack that she was "quite immune" to such requests, "this trip being devoted *entirely to the proletariat*"). But she was deeply moved to see Sara hobble down the aisle on Wood's arm, taking her seat between Wood and the wife of Tom Mooney. Wood was so carried away by Louise's speech that he wept openly. The Mooneys and the Woods arranged to have masses of flowers presented to her on the platform, and she too was moved almost to tears. Their generosity, her knowledge of Sara's tragedy, Mrs. Mooney's presence, and, perhaps most of all, the momentousness of her success before the two early idealistic influences of her life, raised her to a pitch of emotion.

Somewhere along the line, however, she laid down the law with Anna Louise Strong. She canceled most of the dates scheduled on her return trip home and wrote Jack from San Francisco, where she stayed the first week in April, that she hoped to be home in ten days. But certain dates could not be canceled. She spoke twice in Los Angeles, where she finally met her correspondent Upton Sinclair, who came to visit her with his wife at the Hotel Rosslyn. Her two remaining appearances were in Salt Lake City and Detroit, both of which she described at length in a letter to Sinclair after she returned home.

In Salt Lake, she met her old nemesis, Senator King from the Overman Committee, who, she reported, tried to have her arrested on her arrival. It didn't work: "The Mayor and the Chief of Police came to the train, looked me over, smiled sheepishly and for some unknown reason, did nothing at all." Her victory over the senator was sweet, and she indulged in some very understandable gloating: "We routed King. It was easy and I deserve no credit because organized labor absolutely backed me up. It was the first meeting held in Salt Lake in God knows how many years. All speakers avoid it and the people there are as thirsty as a desert. I'm going to direct everyone that way from now on. A little truth in that arid spot will do a lot of good."

In the same letter she described another satisfactory rout in Detroit. AFL president Samuel Gompers, long an enemy of Bolshevism, sent Peter Collins, "his old standby, to counteract the effect" of her appearance, scheduling him to speak after Bryant under the auspices of the patriotic Security League. They spoke on Easter Sunday, and Louise found the crowd "wonderful." But after Collins denounced Karl Marx and the red threat in general, "the audience lost patience and showed its teeth." Booing the speaker off the stage, "the audience gave three cheers for the Soviets and called it a day."

Though she would make a short stop in Chicago — where she met Carl Sandburg, who had also been in Russia for the revolution — Louise's trip was effectively over, and she was eager to get back to Croton and spend some time with Jack. The letters had flown between them — always tender, sometimes passionate. They lingered over domestic details: Jack had decided to buy a dog, much to Louise's delight, and while in Portland she had looked into getting the pick of a Persian cat litter. There was discussion in almost every letter about the garden: Louise was frustrated because all the seed catalogs she came across on her trip offered only western varieties, but from San Francisco she sent some hollyhock and delphinium seeds, hoping it wasn't too late to plant them.

Throughout, each was supportive of the other's career. He asked how her book sales were going, and whether local bookstores had copies in stock. He happily reported that a Village bookstore had sold more than three hundred copies and had orders coming in all the time. When *his* book appeared, in late March, she wrote, "I'm so glad yours is out. I'll see to it that it is mentioned *at every single meeting!*" Jack wrote her that he found her letters "full of enthusiasm and emotion over the meetings . . . simply wonderful."

With the reception each was receiving, Louise and Jack felt more optimistic than ever that the essential message of the revolution — that experiment could lead to a better society — was reaching the American people and making a difference. They themselves felt like more than just a couple in love: they were *working* for something together, and the thrill of this collaboration comes through in their letters. Their physical passion remained strong: "How hard it is to be away from you in the Spring! Last Spring you were in Norway and the year before the wine of the first warm breezes carried my honey away and wounded us both deeply. I refer to this, dear, not as a warning but to tell you that it [is] as difficult for me as it is for you. . . . I toss about restlessly all night and fall asleep only to wake from troubled little dreams of desire. Oh, my dear honey — try to wait for me! I am a prisoner bound. Without you I have no outlet."

Louise returned home strengthened in her convictions. Yet her experience of these dramatic days of 1919 was sharply different from Jack's. While he was becoming more and more closely drawn into the internecine politics of the Socialist party and its pro-Bolshevik and anti-Bolshevik offshoots, she was getting a broader sense of the country, of what the Russian experiment meant to various people. So while they were working for the same cause, she was forming some quite distinct views of her own. She had spent much time with radicals sympathetic to the Bolshevik cause who were not wracked by infighting as the New York radicals were beginning to be. More gratifyingly, she was heartened by the solidarity she had seen, and the overwhelming support she had found for radical views across a broad spectrum of people: laborers, Russian refugees, left-leaning reformers, and even middle-class, seemingly indiscriminate lecture-goers. At many meetings, hats were passed for Russian relief funds, and more than once resolutions were passed unanimously demanding the withdrawal of American troops from Russia. Set against the ugly, red-baiting mood that prevailed in the courts and in Washington, her enthusiastic reception was at once a relief — especially after her showdown with the Overman Committee — and a confirmation of revolutionary theory.

Her constant theme, with variations, was stopping Allied intervention: "There was no military reason for the invasion of Siberia. The general staff of the United States Army advised against it. It's a national disgrace, a national scandal." She announced that the politicians had betrayed American soldiers who had — here she often cited her brothers — "enlisted to fight Germany, not Russia." And over and over again she tried to counter the lies about Russia circulated by politicians and, all too often, believed by the press. In the West, she appealed to supporters of Seattle's general strike, which had been reported as a Bolshevik movement. "The reason [the newspapers] lie about it," she said, "is that Soviet Russia is one great general strike against all the governments of the whole world" — which was, in fact, a fairly insightful analysis of the situation. And she provided the truth about Russia: information about maternity leaves guaranteed by the Soviets, for instance, or Lenin's plans for trade. She modified her speech at each stop according to the makeup of her audience, local concerns, and recent victories — and defeats — on the radical front. After the Supreme Court confirmed the conviction of Socialist party leader Eugene Debs on charges of espionage, she began two speeches in Los Angeles, saying, "Today Eugene Debs is on his way to prison" — which, she said, made many listeners weep. Always she was partisan, but, as she said in closing in one speech, "After what I've seen, I wouldn't have a drop of red blood in my heart if I was not touched by the greatest thing in the world — the Russian Revolution."

One feature of her appearances was almost always remarked upon by the press: she wore a long black cloak, lined in red. It was not permitted to fly a red flag — and in fact she commonly spoke in halls decorated with American flags — but Louise used the cloak's lining to great effect. At the end of a speech, when the applause began, she threw back the cloak to flourish its red lining, giving a dramatic twirl as she left the platform. It was as if she had wrapped herself in the red flag of red Russia, and it was an image that few forgot.

10

Working for a New World

"Separations," Jack said, "are the cruelest things in the world."
After Louise returned from her lecture tour in May, elated but
exhausted, she and Jack retired to Croton to regroup. Louise
simply collapsed, later writing to Upton Sinclair, "I had a sort of physical and spiritual breakdown after I came home — just tired I guess."
For a few days they relaxed, sitting in the garden and playing with
the new German shepherd, conditionally named Puppy. They ordered
plants and laid a flagstone terrace. At their happiest, as Louise had
written earlier to Sara Bard Field, they felt "like children who will never
grow up."

Croton provided a refuge, but it was also a congenial community
made up of likeminded souls seeking quiet in the country. As one
observer wrote, "There is a sort of Colony at Croton, and every other
house is inhabited by someone one knows, or who knows the other. All
work-worn journalists, artists and Bohemians generally, who come there
with their children for a rest." Describing one idyllic summer afternoon
at Boardman and Sally Robinson's cottage, she continued: "It was as
though Greenwich Village in summer array had been dumped down
with deliberate pageantry upon the grass. There were men in open-
necked shirts, and there was one in a green sweater, another in a butcher
blouse shirt and corduray [sic] trousers like a French *ouvrier*. Women in

yellow, and orange, children in royal blue, or bare-armed and bare-legged in bathing suits; lovely splotches of color among the tree stems."

Besides the Robinsons, Jack and Louise's neighbors on hilly Mt. Airy Road included Floyd Dell and his wife, B. Marie; Max Eastman and, in another house, his feminist sister, Crystal; the radical lawyer Dudley Field Malone; and the radical political cartoonist Robert Minor. The street came to be known as Red Hill, and Jack was said to have strolled down Mt. Airy Road to greet a visitor, exclaiming, "Welcome to the Mt. Airy Soviet!"

At no time were Jack and Louise more at ease than when they were at Croton, playing house. Both were intensely domestic. In sharp contrast to their working lives, when they functioned in the starkest material conditions, at home each greatly enjoyed their modest creature comforts. Perhaps influenced by the relatively untroubled lives of their neighbors, who were less actively involved in politics and generally led more settled family lives, at such times they thought of having a child. Louise had spoken of this as early as the summer of 1916 to Sara Bard Field: "I want sometime — so much — to have at least one child."

In early 1918, when the Storrses wrote of the birth of their first child, Louise responded with effusive congratulations. She truly envied Marguerite, she said, and she realized it was time for her to think seriously about having a family. She said she wanted just one more trip abroad and then hoped to go to the country and stay "until I have *one* baby anyway." For the moment, however, she and Jack were too active in their careers. They could not comfortably have afforded a nanny, and even radicals in those days did not think of men sharing child care responsibilities. But the major obstacle to their sincere desire to have "just one" baby was the uncertainty of their lives and the dangers associated with their work — not only the dangers involved in covering stories in countries wracked by turmoil, but the dangers of being radicals in the U.S. while the Red Scare was heating up.

Their domestic interlude was interrupted when Jack fell perilously ill with influenza. An epidemic was under way, and no doctor or nurse could be found to care for him, so Louise devoted herself to nursing Jack full-time. She relied on telephoned instructions from a New York doctor, who directed her to give him aspirin, eggnog, and plenty of brandy. She propped her patient in front of the fireplace and tried mightily to keep the small house warm, chopping wood to keep the fire going day and night. In spite of her ministrations, which included a daily alcohol rub, Jack did not improve, falling into delirium, and Louise felt alone and frightened as she struggled to turn him repeatedly, slipping out only when he was unconscious to get supplies from the village, half a mile away.

As the snow melted and unmistakable signs of spring began to appear, Jack seemed a little stronger and she moved him to a bed by the window. The trees they had ordered arrived, and Jack was able to supervise their planting from his open window. Boardman Robinson came by and helped her plant a small red hawthorn, as Jack pointed out a spot for it. Later, perhaps still influenced by her tender and maternal mood in these days, she wrote a poem called "Spring in Croton," which appeared in *The Liberator:*

All the fruit-trees were in bloom
They were little girls
Going to communion
But the hawthorn broke my heart
It was the little son
I dreamed about and never had.

Though she urged Jack to take things slowly after his illness, both were turning again to writing: Jack covered the AF of L convention in Atlantic City in early June for *The Liberator,* and Louise wrote editorials, mostly about intervention, for the American Soviet organ the *New York Communist,* of which Jack was editor. Conditions in Russia horrified her. Reports of suffering in Siberia made her so ill, she wrote Upton Sinclair, that she "stayed awake night after night and woke up out of crazy nightmares when [she] did go to sleep." She continued, "If I hadn't *been* there, I wouldn't be able to visualize it so well. I think the most difficult thing to hear is the fact that I am here *secure* — in bitter safety — and those wonderful people are dying this way."

It is impossible to understate the effects of world events on Louise in 1919. Having seen the revolution, written about it, and testified about it before a hostile Senate committee and to enthusiastic audiences across the country, she felt caught up in the great current of events. When news that a revolution in Hungary had installed a Communist government — the short-lived regime of Béla Kun — reached her on her speaking tour, she wrote Jack a letter in which her desire for him mingled with her passion for world change: "Dearest lover . . . White stars hang from a cold sky. I have read the news about Hungary — the *Great News!* I look out of my windows at the stars and the winds of spring fan my hot face. It is wonderful — all this my lover, all this new awakening — all *over the earth*; and this *other awakening*. I can hear the feet of that great army across the world."

Though Jack, of course, shared her passion, he was caught up in left-wing politics at home. In the wake of the March publication of *Ten Days That Shook the World*, he was regarded in many circles as the single most important expert on the revolution. Reviews had been uniformly positive, even in conservative strongholds (though the *New York Times* commented that "It cannot be said that he adds anything to the essentials of the narrative already told by his talented wife"), and five thousand copies sold in the first five months.

Jack was clearly in demand: the Bolsheviks saw the need for international support and looked to the American left expectantly. But the Socialist party, which he had joined on his return from Russia, was torn apart over how to pursue the opportunities presented by a domestic postwar economic downturn, labor unrest, and seemingly historic shifts in eastern Europe. In February, Jack had been elected by the party to its fifteen-person City Committee and accepted a nomination as international delegate — though exactly whom he would represent was becoming increasingly less clear. He had never liked party politics. The political organization that had always most closely held his imagination was a grass roots labor union, the IWW, but the Bolsheviks' success convinced him that the time had come to commit himself.

Pressures within the political ranks were escalating in the spring of 1919, as a left wing within the Socialist party swept its elections, with the result that it tried to purge itself of left locals. When the left wing held its own convention in New York City in June, factionalism again reared its head. A split in the left began to emerge. The foreign-language, largely immigrant federations, led by the twenty-seven-year-old Louis Fraina, called for immediate adoption of Communism; while another group, led by the twenty-nine-year-old Benjamin Gitlow, determined to win back the Socialist party for the cause of revolutionary Socialism.

The first group would call itself the Communist party, while the Gitlow-led group, which included Jack, would become the Communist Labor party. Both groups realized the Third Socialist International, or the Comintern — the international association of Communist parties now being formed in Moscow — would most likely recognize only one party, so the stakes were high.

Jack had become increasingly preoccupied with such matters, and while Louise understood, she was sometimes impatient. Subtle differences in their political commitment had begun to arise during this year, and they would become more pronounced in the months ahead. Basically, Jack chose as his course making an outright commitment to an organized political party, and Louise as hers remaining outside party politics and focusing on the specific causes she cared about — intervention, feminism, famine conditions in Russia. She never forgot why the Bolsheviks had so thrilled her — their support for women's rights, the possibilities they laid open for a new society — and she supported fiercely their right to pursue their path against Western efforts to swing the balance toward the reactionaries. If little conflict developed between Louise and Jack over dedication to a specific party, it was because divisions on the left had not yet become rigid, and both knew that the important thing was to forestall Allied intervention. Otherwise, who would ever know what might come of the exciting events Lenin had set in motion? Also, they both saw the vital link between the Bolshevik Revolution and chances for revolutionary change in America, and insofar as Jack worked to maintain that essential connection, Louise could support him.

Still, she seems to have hung back a little in these months, her presence somewhat shadowed by Jack's frenetic mood. Benjamin Gitlow later wrote a description of a visit to the Patchin Place apartment, one worth quoting at length for the atmosphere of intense activity it conveys:

> Strewn all over [the] living room were newspapers, pamphlets, letters, torn envelopes, manuscripts, and books. Ashes obscured the base of the little wood-burning fireplace. Heaps of dust covered newspapers, and printed matter lay piled high in utter confusion on the large flattop desk. On a little table stood a dirty, smudged enameled coffee pot, an ashtray full of cigarette butts and a couple of unwashed plates and saucers. The

cot against the wall of the small room directly across from the fireplace was always mussed, with a few pillows scattered on its untidy surface.

On this visit, Louise, "perched upon the couch . . . a miniature of well-shaped daintiness and charm, with large dreamy eyes that looked straight at you," confided in Gitlow while Jack turned his attention to some papers. She was concerned that Jack had put aside his writing — "what he can do best" — for party politics. She trusted his instincts, she said, but worried about the consequences.

With Jack preoccupied with party politics that would be very difficult for her, as a woman, to enter into and that did not particularly interest her (in part, perhaps, *because* they excluded her), Louise turned her attention to practical matters — namely, earning money. The couple's bank accounts were routinely overdrawn, and Jack was suspended from the Harvard Club for a $34 debt. Except for small sums for lecturing, his income consisted mostly of token payments received from *The Liberator*. More mainstream outlets would not touch his work any longer. Louise also contributed to *The Liberator*, but at the same time she was trying to branch out into the more lucrative fiction market. She had tried for years to break into the pages of the *Metropolitan*, run by her friend Sonya Levien, and *McCall's*, where Bessie Beatty was now an editor. Despite her connections and persistence, she never succeeded. She looked elsewhere, traveling briefly in July to Washington, where, as she wrote Jack, she had "about 15 jobs on the string." She would have taken a job in the suffrage movement if funds could be found to pay her, but evidently they could not. She also consulted her quasi-literary agent, a woman named Millie Morris whom she had met in Washington, to see if she was making any progress selling her plays — particularly her Provincetown Players' hit, *The Game* — to Hollywood. The movies evidently drew her, for back in Croton she wrote Upton Sinclair that she had — inexplicably — two offers to "ride horseback" in films. ("It's the one thing I *do* know how to do," she wrote, remembering her girlhood on Grandfather Say's ranch.) She had heard that Sinclair was starting a movie company — would he consider her for roles or scripts?

In this context, it is difficult to understand a curiously high-handed letter she sent to the editor of *Soviet Russia*, returning a $15 payment for an article she had contributed: "I have never taken a cent for any work I have done to help Soviet Russia and to prevent my country from continuing in its criminal efforts to destroy the Russian revolution. I have a feeling that if I ever did take money it would seem too much like a job." Noble sentiments, perhaps. But Louise's statement that she had never taken any money for her efforts to support the cause was blatantly untrue. The only significant sums of money Louise had made in her life had come from her book and syndicated columns on Russia and her speaking tour — and, since all these ventures did in fact further the cause, this was nothing to be ashamed of. But perhaps the real motive behind her lofty claim of disinterest in money is revealed in the statement that followed. She had never kept herself "within the limits of any organization — not even the Socialist Party," she wrote, in order "to be honest with my own conscience." This sentiment, of course, was consistent with Louise's journalistic ethos: although fiercely partisan in spirit, she always insisted on her reportorial objectivity, and this seemingly paradoxical position had driven the success of her writings about Russia.

In this, however, she may also have been conducting an internal argument with Jack. He, of course, was deeply involved with an "organization" — the Socialist party, in fact. And he had virtually put aside journalism; any writing that he did in these months was more in the nature of commentary or even propaganda. She might have been questioning whether *he* was being honest with his own conscience — or, more to the point, his own talent. Louise was trying, not very successfully, to make a distinction between what she did for the cause and her *real*, reportorial writing — of which she was doing little — but her foremost concern may have been that Jack was hiding his light under a bushel.

And larger battles loomed. The Socialist party's left wing had scheduled a convention in Chicago for September, and Jack was anxious that his faction should prevail there. He and Gitlow had been plotting with Jim Larkin and Eadmon MacAlpine, even though they knew that their group was no longer a majority in the left wing. Louise took a longer view. Jack had become, with *Ten Days*, the one American radical with mainstream recognition as an authority on Russia. The Russians themselves respected and admired him, and Lenin considered him a personal friend. Aware of Russia's need for international support, Louise knew it was inevitable that a delegate would be sent to the Comintern, and that the delegate would most likely be Jack. Given the increased overt hostility to radicals over the past two years, she doubted that U.S. officials would look the other way were Jack to make such a trip. If he were to go to Russia, quite simply, there was a real possibility that he might never come back.

She knew from experience that she could not sway him once his mind was made up. So she sought a respite — a couple of weeks at the little cottage in Truro on Cape Cod. Their Portland friends, the artists Carl and Helen Waters, sent word that they could join them there. Jack pleaded poverty, but Louise wouldn't hear of it: she marched off to pawn his prized possession, his great-uncle's gold watch, telling him that a pretty woman could strike a better bargain. She was convinced that this respite was essential to his health, confiding to the editor of *Soviet Russia,* "He is not well and has no idea how to take a vacation near New York. Here he cannot even hear the rumblings of battle."

Yet the trip was also essential to her own well-being, for she needed time with Jack to dispel her fears of yet another desertion. They enjoyed nude sunbathing on the dunes, long ocean swims, and picnic dinners on the beach with the Waterses. The Portland couple, though sympathetic, had no inkling of the technicalities of left-wing support for Russia, and when politics came up at all in conversation, it was of the most idealistic sort. There was no telephone at the cottage, and, because of the shortness of their stay, no mail; the papers that reached them carried yesterday's news.

One warm night their old friends Jig Cook and Susan Glaspell walked over from their house in Provincetown. Sprawled out under the big tree in the back yard, Jack confided that he wished he didn't have to leave. "It may surprise you," he said, "but what I really want to do is write poetry." They weren't surprised, said the Cooks — why didn't he? "I can't," said Jack, shaking his head, "I've promised too many people."

Indeed, it was politics that called him away and brought their brief holiday to a close. Louise and Jack had expected to stay until just before the Chicago convention, but news of a fresh split in the left wing reached Jack at the end of July, and they packed their bags after just two weeks.

The new split meant more frequent and fevered meetings for Jack, long nights in the Patchin Place apartment strategizing with Gitlow, MacAlpine, Larkin, and Ben LeGere. If factionalism was the pressing concern, the mood was nonetheless spirited: the formation of the Comintern had signaled that a program for world revolution was in the making. This, together with the Socialist party's overall shift leftward and the thousands of worker strikes all over America in 1919, heartened Bolshevik sympathizers regardless of where they stood on the party political spectrum. In this general optimism, Louise could find common ground with Jack, and she sat in tolerantly at numerous informal strategy sessions. She had a particular fondness for Jim Larkin, who often grew impatient when discussion took an abstract intellectual turn. He was a simple man, very effective with the workers, and for this gentleness and his Irishness Louise often sought him out in his apartment just around the corner in Milligan Place.

Often, when she got fed up, Louise went out to Croton. There was much lugging of typewriters back and forth. Other occasions might find her in Patchin Place, trying to finish a short story, and Jack in Croton. During one such interlude she wrote Jack that she hoped he'd found the house tidy and that he'd liked the flowers she'd picked: "I wanted everything to be that way when you arrived." She hoped he was resting, she wrote, but if he wasn't, could he give the German shepherd a bath? She promised to send Caroline up to do some real cleaning before long. In the meantime, she vowed, she wasn't leaving the apartment before her story was finished. Jack was similarly solicitous, writing her of the puppy's antics and urging her to get her work done.

At the Chicago convention at the end of August, the optimism of the previous weeks was dashed. Jack would go to Russia as Louise had suspected, but under the worst circumstances politically — as the representative of a faction, not a united American Communist party. The left wing had indeed officially split. As delegate for the Communist Labor party, Jack asked his cohorts to arrange for his departure as soon as possible. There was a chance that the delegate who reached Moscow first would win the Comintern's recognition, and rumors floated that the Communist party leader Louis Fraina was on his way. It was imperative that Jack set out.

But as Louise had again foreseen, it was not that simple. Disturbed by the emergence of two Communist parties seemingly overnight, the U.S. government quickly outlawed them, arresting scores of Communists and those they believed to be Communists. Jack was under surveillance almost constantly. He holed up in a loft occupied by the anarchist

Carlo Tresca on 12th Street, where he edited the newly formed *Voice of Labor* and waited for word that arrangements for his departure had been made. He lived virtually underground: the columnist and humorist Don Marquis, sighting Jack from a Fifth Avenue bus, climbed down and asked where he'd been. Jack replied that he was in hiding, to which Marquis commented that he'd picked a hell of a place to hide. "None better," said Jack, "and besides, the red-hunters never catch anybody."

With Russia blockaded, Jack couldn't just sail aboard a passenger liner, of course; moreover, he would be arrested if he traveled under his own name. Finally, the Communist Labor party worked out a plan: he would travel as a coal stoker on a Scandinavian ship, bearing the papers of Jim Gormley, a seaman who had jumped ship. The journey would not be easy, and not only because Reed was a marked man: overworked constantly, he had never really been well since he had lost his kidney, and shoveling coal convincingly for almost two weeks would test his endurance. Getting into Russia after he landed in Christiania would be, for all Louise knew, nearly impossible.

Nevertheless, Jack was his usual sunny self at the end of September, when he invited friends to see him off at the dock. Dressed in seaman's garb, with a dark knit cap and a backpack, he was a hearty host, exchanging jokes with the men and smiling at Louise, who stood a little apart. After a quick kiss, he sailed out of her life.

Jack had told Louise that he would be back in just three months, by Christmas. Yet she knew he would not likely return as early as that. Indeed, with the red-baiting climate at home heating up, it would be extremely dangerous for him to do so.

On November 7 — the second anniversary of the Russian Revolution — Attorney General Palmer, with Hoover's help, sent federal agents to infiltrate such radical groups as the Communist and Communist Labor parties, the Socialist party, and the Union of Russian Workers. The raids struck in more than ten cities across the country and resulted in the mass arrests of hundreds of radical sympathizers, most of them foreign-born. After being detained under oppressive conditions for almost two months — and, under the 1918 Alien Act, denied a trial — 249 of the foreign-born radicals were deported on the SS *Buford* to Finland — among them Emma Goldman and her onetime lover Alexander Berkman.

Another raid the next day, conducted by Clayton R. Lusk and his New York State Committee for Investigating Bolshevism, struck very close to home: thirty-five members of the Communist and Communist Labor parties were arrested for questioning. The three eventually held — Jim Larkin, Benjamin Gitlow, and Harry Winitsky — were charged with and then indicted for criminal anarchy. Louise threw herself into working for the defense of Larkin. Various groups pitched in, among them Elizabeth Gurley Flynn's Workers' Defense Union. Months later Louise would cover Larkin's trial.

In the absence of Jack and the jailed Gitlow, Louise kept *Voice of Labor* running almost single-handedly, performing all editorial and managerial tasks. Her first contribution appeared in the November 1 issue, a poem called "Out of the Sunset (Dedicated to British Diplomacy)." The poem's "speakers" are the children of Russia, and the refrain, "We are the Russian children / Murdered by British guns." Mediocre in its execution, the poem is remarkable for its overt militancy. The children vow they will exact revenge for British aggression in Russia. One verse reads:

> We shall raise a phantom army,
> We shall march on silent feet
> Into every British household,
> Into every British street.

Another, even more ominous, verse reads:

> Into every sun-filled morning,
> Into every star-filled night,
> Till the blossoms wither blackly
> And your blood is cold with fright.

The lines represent Louise's anger rather than a belief in a militaristic solution; more than that, they suggest that she had gradually come to accommodate herself to and accept the value of propaganda. Not since the days of the Provincetown Players had she drawn so clear a connection between art and revolution.

She also twice contributed the lead editorial to *Voice of Labor*. Always sympathetic, as was Jack, to the Wobblies, she was appalled to see advocates of the open shop — most prominent among them the National Association for Manufacturers — using Red Scare tactics against workers. Speaking of the hundreds of jailed IWW members across the country, particularly in the West, she wrote in a lead editorial on November 15: "The jails are filling up. JAILS FULL OF POLITICAL PRISONERS ARE THE MOST FAITHFUL INDICATORS OF HOW NEAR A COUNTRY IS TO REVOLUTION." Another lead editorial declared that the forces of intervention, lynching, and red-baiting were giving birth to the revolution of tomorrow — and by violence.

Yet Louise continued to believe that she could best maintain her journalistic integrity by remaining, on the face of it, nonpartisan. The subject she most commonly lectured about in 1919 and early 1920 was the food blockade against Russia. Wracked by famine and disease and weakened by civil war, Russians were suffering under conditions even worse than those that had preceded the revolution. Deaths from these causes were estimated at four million in 1919 and five million in 1920. Aside from her anger that the Western powers, including the U.S., would try to squelch the experiment in social change that had so inspired her, this was a humanitarian cause about which something could be done — a cause that even the most hardened anti-Bolshevik could ignore only with difficulty. In an interview with the Socialist *New York Call*, Louise referred proudly to the year and a half she had spent agitating against the food blockade. In the same article (accompanied by a photograph of Louise in her Russian garb), she emphasized that she never took sides; that's why, she said, she was a good reporter. Asked pointedly about her political affiliations, she said she considered herself a Socialist, but did not like organizations in general — an observation perhaps rooted in the months when she saw Jack almost swallowed up by them. The article, in fact, was titled, "Louise Bryant Prefers Reporting to Propaganda."

But at the same time, she was producing far more propaganda than reportage, and the chief outlet for her writing was a party newspaper. It seems clear that Louise spent the early months of Jack's absence very much as he had spent the months before — intellectually working through her political views as well as her career, balancing her desire to write and her desire to effect change. She and Jack had been happy together in the days before his departure, but she had seen the toll his divided instincts had taken. She had disapproved of the internecine party politics he had perforce taken up, and yet she, like her husband, was desperately aware of the immediacy both of revolutionary action and of governmental persecution. Her friends were being arrested and deported with alarming frequency; she could hardly stand by. And, of course, there was the strain of Jack's absence: she not only missed him terribly and must have felt abandoned once again, but she also feared for his well-being. In the grim winter of 1919 to 1920, in the face of these troubles, she threw herself into her work.

In a coded message to her friends John and Marguerite Storrs in Paris, Louise wrote guardedly that they could guess where Jack was now: "the place where we would all like to go — where there is new life and real freedom." Shortly after his departure, she set in motion plans to join him in that place, to share the "real freedom" of the Bolshevik adventure. Perhaps she hoped for more journalistic coups as well. But as letters from Jack arrived more erratically and became more confusing — to the point where he warned her repeatedly *not* to come — she also wanted to watch over him, to see that his health was good, and to keep him from making any hasty moves.

His first letter, written in Christiania after he had jumped ship at Bergen in northern Norway, indicated some uneasiness about what he might find in Russia. Swedish sympathizers had warned him that the political situation in Russia was "frightfully mixed up," news he found "heartrending." The White Army, its supplies and arms furnished by the Allies, was nearing Petrograd — an advance Jack called "a last desperate effort to crush Russia" that "may succeed. Something appears to be wrong internally." He hoped, he said, to start for Stockholm that night, and from there to pass through Finland and then to Russia.

The letter was full of praise and reassurance, for Jack was by this time well attuned to Louise's fears of abandonment or effacement in his shadow. He wrote that he had met two Swedish intellectuals who had been very interested in his wife's work; he had given them a photo of Louise that would be printed in a popular Swedish magazine "which has a large influence," together with excerpts from *Six Red Months*. "I have also told everybody about how my honey broke the Overman blockade, and shall tell at headquarters [the Kremlin]." (He added that he, as the editor of the *Voice of Labor*, which was greatly admired in Sweden, was "the big cheese in these parts.")

Jack wrote next from Finland, where he had encountered some trouble. He had been smuggled into the country aboard a ship crossing the Baltic, but had difficulty locating his contacts in the port of Åbo. He finally ended up, half frozen, in a safe house near Helsinki — stranded, as the Finns had stepped up persecution of local Bolsheviks. "I fret and fume at my delay," he wrote to Louise, "and spend the time thinking about my honey and wanting her. It is awful. I can neither go forward or go back. . . . If this hadn't happened I should now be in headquarters, and almost ready to start back. . . . I do nothing but long for my honey. Other people don't matter at all." He advised her to approach the Communist Labor party if she needed money, reasoning that he was working for them "on urgent business" and that they had an obligation to watch out for her. He would love to see her, he wrote, but "it would be ghastly for you here now."

In December, Jack was finally able to leave Finland, and made his way by sleigh and even on foot across miles and miles of frozen wilderness to the Russian border, where he was greeted warmly by Soviet soldiers with red stars sewn onto their uniforms. Slowly, he made his way to Petrograd, where he enjoyed several nostalgic days before moving on to Moscow, which, because of its relative distance from the major outbreaks of civil war, had just been designated the new capital. He gained an audience immediately with the Executive Committee of the Comintern, reporting on conditions at home and — his real mission — seeking recognition of the Communist Labor party. The committee promised to review his request, but Jack sensed that a decision would be a long time in coming and embarked on a protracted tour of the country, fascinated by the changes wrought by the revolution and at the same time horrified by the famine and suffering in what was perhaps Russia's cruelest winter.

Louise did not receive word from Jack after those early letters from Sweden and Finland, but he was very much in the news. The first "real" Palmer raid, conducted on January 2, rounded up more than ten thousand suspects. Included in the four thousand who were held in custody were Jack's friends in the Socialist party left wing. Three weeks later, on January 21, he and thirty-seven other members of the Communist Labor party and eighty-nine members of the Communist party were indicted in Chicago on charges of criminal anarchy, which was punishable by up to five years in jail. The next day the *New York Times* reported that Jack had illegally left the country some time before, disguised as a coal stoker and headed for Denmark and then Russia.

Louise took in the news with dread. Of course, it was far preferable that Jack be in Russia than in Finland, where the White Army was known to be brutal to captured Bolsheviks. But the news of his indictment troubled her even more. If he returned, he would almost surely go to jail. She remembered Jack's insistence that he return from Russia in 1918 to face charges against him in the *Masses* trial, and she feared his righteous and self-destructive instincts would lead him to respond in the same way now. The alternative was that he stay in Russia for a very long time, perhaps forever. If that were to be the case, she wanted to join him there. At the very least, she wanted to go to him to keep him from making any impulsive moves. Faced with an array of imperfect options, she tried to busy herself with work, while uppermost in her mind was her desire for word from Jack himself.

Instead, she received, again through the press, absolutely terrifying news. On March 17, she read that Jack had been arrested in Åbo in Finland for smuggling, carrying Bolshevik propaganda and letters from those who had been deported on the *Buford.* Louise was filled with indignation. Jack seemed to have become a mysterious bargaining chip in a very dangerous situation in international politics. She feared as well the treatment he might receive at the hands of the Finns.

On April 9 the worst news of all reached her: John Reed, the newspapers reported, had been executed in Finland. Though Louise was well acquainted with the ways news could be distorted for propaganda purposes and had an instinctual distrust of reports in mainstream papers, how she felt at this news is almost impossible to imagine. It brought together all her old fears — of abandonment, of being left alone without an ally. She simply froze in horror.

Her anguish was mercifully short-lived, giving way to exultation when she read the next day that the news of Jack's execution was false. And on April 16 Secretary of State Bainbridge Colby cabled her that Jack was indeed well, though confined to a Finnish jail. It had been a freakish couple of days, an experience cruel beyond measure.

What had actually happened was this: as Jack had prepared to leave Russia in early February, the Comintern had made a decision. The two American Communist parties should be merged. Naturally, Jack thought he could best accomplish this by returning home — characteristically, without concern for his indictment. In fact, as Louise had suspected, his first reaction to his indictment was to return to face the charges. And he very likely feared that Louise would be wracked with worry. To further the American Communist cause, he took what the Comintern leaders could provide: 102 diamonds worth more than $14,000, and $1500 in various currencies.

Setting out, he stopped first in Petrograd, where he had a reunion with Emma Goldman in the Astoria Hotel. They brought each other up to date on events in Russia and government persecution in the United States. They quarreled a bit: Emma, as an anarchist, feared growing statism in Russia, particularly as manifested in the organization of the Cheka, a secret police force known for its brutal tactics. Exasperated, Jack burst forth: "You are a little confused by the Revolution in action because you have dealt with it only in theory."

Carrying the diamonds, money, and assorted documents, including an introduction Lenin had written for a new edition of *Ten Days That Shook the World*, as well as the seaman Jim Gormley's forged papers and a passport in the name of Samuel Arnold, Jack tried valiantly to get out of the country. A route through Latvia had to be abandoned because civil clashes prevented him from reaching the coast. Returning to Petrograd, Jack then made his way into Finland in a blizzard, returning to the same safe house where he had stayed on his way over. In Åbo, in mid-March, he stowed away in the engine room of a freighter, only to be routed out by two customs officers just before the ship sailed.

Jack was accused not only of smuggling: reports that he would be charged with treason surfaced alarmingly during his day in court. The absence of letters from Louise confirmed his belief that the State Department was concealing his whereabouts. With foresight, he decided he had to make his plight public — especially to American officials who might intervene. It was Jack himself who leaked the story of his own execution, though it remains a mystery how he did so.

The strategy backfired. He was found guilty on April 26 and fined $350; the smuggled goods were confiscated. Though letters from Louise did begin trickling in, he found himself languishing in a Finnish prison: it seemed his country had abandoned him, or, worse yet, that U.S. authorities were asking the Finns to continue to hold him.

He spent three miserable months in solitary confinement in jail, deteriorating physically and, under the continued deprivation, mentally. His meals consisted of bread and salted fish, a dangerous diet for a man with one kidney who needed to avoid salt altogether. He could sleep only five hours a night, he wrote Louise, "and so am awake, penned in a little cage, for nineteen hours a day." He worried about his emotional state: "The thought of you drags at me sometimes and my imagination plays tricks, and I almost grow crazy." He returned almost obsessively to the subject of his gold watch — the watch he had pawned the summer before to send them to Truro. First he asked that she try to save it at all costs, and then he told her to pawn it again to make the payments on the Croton and Truro houses; later he would ask her repeatedly where it was.

Newly independent Finland, under a conservative government, considered the Bolsheviks its most deadly enemies, and it made no difference that the prisoner John Reed was an American. His release was delayed many times. In early May he threatened a hunger strike, and the tactic worked: the date for his release was scheduled. Inexplicably, however, the day receded. It was not until June 2 that he cabled Louise, in great excitement, that he would be released and put on the next boat for Revel. Returning home was impossible; his request for a passport was denied. On June 7, from Revel, he wrote Louise that he was "temporarily returning headquarters." Any misgivings Louise may have had about the news evaporated as soon as she read the next line: "Come if possible."

11

A Last Separation

*I*n the spring of 1920, Louise and Jack wrote as if under a cloud, talking of death, speaking of reunions as final ones. Jack composed a poem in his cell in Finland, which he wrote out compulsively, over and over, and later repeated for Louise:

> Thinking and dreaming
> Day and night and day
> Yet cannot think one bitter thought away —
> That we have lost each other
> You and I. . . .

For her part, Louise wrote a poem echoing a similar note, which was accepted by the prestigious *Dial*. Its last stanzas read, ominously,

> Three ikons
> And your photograph
> Hang on the wall.
>
> You've been there so long, dear,
> With the same expression
> On your face
> That you've become an ikon
> With the rest.

Ikon, ikon,
I can think of only one prayer.
One more time before I die
I want to see you.

Of course, Louise had endured the false report of Jack's death, and there
was no question that his situation was dire. A newspaper editor tried to
cheer her up by saying that he was glad to hear news from Jack — as
long as he was alive, the editor said (perhaps meaning that now the U.S.
knew of his imprisonment), at least the Finns would not shoot him.
Louise can hardly have been heartened by this reasoning.

For Jack's part, he knew how seriously his health had been weakened
by his ordeal, and how difficult it would be to get to a safe place. He
wrote Louise on June 7 telling her to join him in Russia, but he changed
his instructions several times after that, mysteriously urging her to wait
for a particular message from him or news from unnamed persons
before she undertook the journey.

Despite this uncertainty, or because of it, Louise was making concerted efforts to plan her trip to Russia. Though her days were given
over to covering Jim Larkin's trial for *The Liberator,* as early as April she
had made an application for a passport. This was almost a preposterous
request at the height of the Red Scare — and yet she persevered. The
State Department proved obdurate. On April 10, the office of the undersecretary issued a memorandum citing the reasons why the request of
"Louise Bryant, Anne Mahon [sic], or Louise Bryant Reed" should
be denied. As the "wife of John Reed, the notorious Bolshevik sympathizer, propagandist and lecturer," she was guilty first by association. The
memo did go on to cite her appearance before the Overman Committee, but then returned to Jack's "crimes," most notably his indictment in
Chicago.

What would become a persistent charge surfaced in this memo: that
Louise and Jack had obtained passports in 1917 — after having them
withheld at the last minute — by swearing not to become involved in
"political agitation of any kind." The Reeds had abused the privilege of a
passport by breaking their promise, the State Department haughtily
implied, and therefore a passport should not be issued to either one of
them again. A remark at the end of the memo noted that the Justice

Department had "informally requested" holding up issuance of a passport to Louise. No doubt this request came from J. Edgar Hoover himself, in his capacity as Palmer's assistant.

An April 16 memorandum from the State Department's Division of Foreign Intelligence elaborated on Louise's "abuse" of her 1917 passport, noting that she had admitted before the Overman Committee that she had acted as a courier for the Bolsheviks when leaving Russia in 1918. Like the first, this memo noted that Jack had been appointed "Consul-General" for the Bolsheviks, with no mention of the highly ridiculous nature of the post or the fact that it was withdrawn immediately. The memo stated that there was a "probability" that Louise, if allowed to leave the country, "would immediately reengage in Bolshevik propaganda aimed directly or indirectly against the United States. . . . To issue this passport might set a precedent for the issuance of passports to others equally radical whose activities might prove embarrassing to this Government."

A supporting document was churned out, a "supplemental memorandum re Louise Bryant (Mrs. John Reed)," on April 22. It cited her 1919 lecture tour, calling it "in the interest of the Communist Labor Party," though the party did not exist at the time she made the cross-country trip. It stated, rightly, that she had spoken in support of the Soviet system and against U.S. intervention in Russia, and reiterated the general view that she was, though not a member, sympathetic to the goals of the Communist Labor party, "one of which is the advocacy of the overthrow of organized governments by force."

If her two-page appeal written in April to the secretary of state himself is any indication, Louise seriously underestimated the force of the State Department juggernaut. On the other hand, she and Bainbridge Colby were such old foes that they were almost old friends: it had been Colby who sorted out the confusion surrounding Jack's imprisonment and the accounts of his death. In appealing to him, she was remarkably candid about her position, but she either disingenuously or naively tried to convince Colby of the innocence of her actions. The letter began with a word of explanation for an embarrassing feature of *Six Red Months in Russia,* a copy of which she sent him along with the letter. The documents reproduced on the book's endpapers identified her repeatedly as "*tovarisch* Bryant," or comrade. The Russian guards who inspected documents at checkpoints, she said, were "very serious," dividing people into two classes: comrades and czarists — "very much like it was during the French Revolution when there were only 'citizens' and 'royalists.'" So Colby should not assume, just because of the term "comrade," that Louise was herself a Communist.

It was her livelihood that called her back to Russia, she argued. The International News Service was willing to send her "immediately upon your consent." Louise hoped Colby would not deny her request because he was busy with "a million more important matters. It means to me," she wrote, "my whole future and my whole chance of expression."

Before turning to a defense of Jack, she told a curious and probably untrue story, but one calculated to disarm with its honesty. Just yesterday, she said, she had resigned from the American Women's Emergency Committee ("the only organization I am connected with," she added, with her usual pride in her independent position), which was working for the lifting of the blockade against Russia so that medicine and supplies could get through to the "women and children" there. This "honest and energetic organization," she wrote, would in the near future have to speak out against Colby and the State Department for withholding papers for relief ships, "and I cannot take part in such a campaign and at the same time ask consideration of you."

Louise took an interesting tack when she turned to Jack's case. After addressing such issues as his supposed smuggling (she maintained that journalists needed to carry many documents, including propaganda, around with them to write their stories), and arguing that he always tried to get home to defend himself when he heard of indictments against him (which was true), she pleaded his general impracticality, claiming that there were poets and there were revolutionaries, and Jack was the former: "Jack is a poet. Poets, as you may know, are beautiful and also difficult. He is a dreamer and has been too shattered by frightful war experience to believe in any of the violence Mr. Palmer's exotic imagination gives him credit for. Reed has high ideas of honor and somewhat impractical ones." She compared Jack to Carl Sandburg, who was caught returning from Scandinavia with film reels and $10,000 from the Bolshevik government. When Sandburg was questioned by military intelligence, he said only, "I am the son of a peasant." This was a story she relished telling, and for Colby's benefit she added, "If he had said, 'I am a poet,' he would have given the proper reply. Only a poet would have been impractical enough to let himself be so misunderstood."

It was an ingenious letter, but it did not sway Colby. By the time Reed wrote her in June telling her to come at once, she had decided the wiser course was not to draw the authorities' attention to herself any longer. Like Jack, she would have to leave the country illegally, without a passport. As conflicting messages from Jack continued to arrive, she spent the month of July trying to arrange secret passage to Russia. Friends finally arranged for her to travel on a Swedish steamer, traveling as the wife of a Swedish businessman.

She spent a last, bittersweet weekend with Andrew Dasburg in Woodstock. To Dasburg she seemed driven, determined to reach Jack and convince him not to return to America and face the certainty of a long jail term. Jack's health worried her too, but the urgency she felt seemed fueled by a greater sense of purpose: it was as if the entire course of revolutionary progress worldwide depended on Jack's welfare. Andrew drove her down to the pier and left her with her friend Esther Andrews; his presence might have given away her camouflage. The boat's departure was delayed for five hours, however, and Esther had to leave her to wait alone. It was a confusing, hectic departure, and Louise regretted that she had not had time to say a proper goodbye to Andrew.

She wrote him on her fifth day at sea trying to explain some of her feelings. The journey had been rocky at first, but after days of lying on the upper deck "where the officers go to smoke and the passengers never come," feeling the sun and gazing at the smooth sea, she was more at peace. "Everything was so difficult at the end," she wrote. "I felt very cruel leaving you — and that made me incoherent and edgy. Now I am still worried. Will I really get through? At night I dream that everyone is clawing at me and shouting: 'Who are you?'" She explained again why she had to join Jack and keep him from coming home, this time couching it in terms of what it would mean for her and Andrew's future as well. "If J. comes back he will only go to prison and that will be horrible. Always to know he is there — more dependent than ever — it would destroy us. You can see that. It would destroy all three."

She enjoyed the company of the Swedes on board. She read and darned stockings while they danced and played cards, which caused one elderly lady to comment, she noted with amusement, that she was "of good conduct." She was surprised to find herself admiring "the sweetness of their family life, which does not seem to stifle them." But she knew difficult times lay ahead.

Indeed, when she arrived in Gothenburg on August 11 she learned from underground friends that it would be wisest to change her plans. She should avoid Finland entirely, they said, and enter Russia by sea, from the north. She left that evening for Stockholm. Writing on the train to Stockholm, she described her plans to Dasburg: "I will go all the way to Murmansk — across Norway first and then up and around the coast by devious routes. I feel as if I shall eventually arrive at the moon instead of Moscow." She had been giving some thought to inventing a cover story for friends to tell the authorities in the U.S. when they discovered her departure: "When the Woodstock and Washington Square sleuths find that I am gone — it is best to say I went *without* a p+port and say I worked my way over. They will try to prove some other *act* against me and I see no reason for that. Say I went as a boy if you wish. It will at least throw them off the track." The image of her disguised as a boy working her way over as a seaman was a romantic one, and it was persistently repeated in histories of the period and biographies of Jack — and by Louise herself. The reality — that she posed as the bourgeois wife of a Swedish businessman — was far too mundane for her purposes.

She was bound for the port of Narvik in Norway, the farthest north she could get by rail. From there she wrote Andrew a postcard: "I am north of the Arctic Circle and it is hard to think that it is still summer in New York — here all is white again." From there she made her way to Vardö, near the Russian border, by boat, skirting the rocky northern shore. She would take a different boat to Murmansk, a port just over the Russian border. From Vardö, Louise wrote Andrew, "It is the most dangerous part of the trip — entirely an underground one." She had to remain in hiding in Vardö, waiting for a storm to blow over, in a room without a bed with three men who did not speak English. The weather was clearing as she wrote, and she said that they would be leaving that night at midnight "in a small boat on the open sea." Still, the most perilous part of her journey lay ahead, for Murmansk was in Allied hands.

Jack received word that Louise was on her way in the middle of August; he cabled her to remain outside Russia, though he was well aware the message probably would not reach her. The news threw him in a quandary as he was once again forced to contemplate going home "without giving the impression that he was escaping defeats, and without losing his effective voice in the Comintern."

For Jack was now deeply embroiled in upper-echelon party politics. Since June, he had been involved in planning the Second Congress of the Communist International, known as the Third International, to be held in mid-July. He took a room in a small hotel set aside for delegates to the congress, the Dielovoy Dvor in Petrograd. He was elated to be among revolutionaries from all over the world, of every stripe. Though they did not all espouse Leninism, they were all dedicated to the ideals of the revolution. The first session of the congress was held in Petrograd for symbolic reasons, but then moved to the new capital, Moscow.

Jack was disappointed to find the mood of the congress not as broadly ecumenical as the range of delegates seemed to suggest. Instead, it was dominated by the Bolsheviks, and he, like many other knowledgeable radicals from outside Russia, had difficulty being heard. Lenin had recently produced a pamphlet called "Left Wing Communism: An Infantile Disorder," which spelled out the policy behind this new mood. As the promising European revolutionary movements of the late teens were failing or being suppressed, Lenin found it expedient to play down the idea of an imminent world revolution, instead concentrating on establishing the power of the Bolshevik party — the executive committee at the congress — over all foreign revolutionary parties. Since other left-Socialist groups could not achieve the same success as the Bolsheviks, they would have to submit to a more disciplined approach, set by Moscow.

Jack had no quarrel with the policy in and of itself, but in practice he found it extremely frustrating. When he proposed English as one of the official languages of the congress — a reasonable request, given the numbers of English-speaking delegates — the proposal was defeated, thus cementing the impression that the Russian leadership was bent on controlling the congress. But trade unionism was the issue on which he clashed directly with new Soviet leaders like Grigory Zinoviev. In brief, the Bolsheviks believed it was vital to infiltrate and capture the trade unions, especially the AF of L, for Communism, while Jack thought such groups were far too conservative for the plan to work and proposed instead that the party replace trade unions with revolutionary unions like the IWW. It was a bitter fight, and Jack lost.

But Jack was still willing to work with the Bolsheviks even after the somewhat dispiriting congress, which after all had succeeded in bringing many delegates into the party and establishing a centralized body of revolutionists that workers of the world could look to for guidance. Jack was named the American representative on the ECCI, or Executive Committee of the Communist International, where he continued to fight the trade union battle. Though he found the new Soviet leaders somewhat intractable — he especially disliked Zinoviev — he finally decided, after submitting a resignation that was not accepted, that he could work with them.

The high-handedness of these new bureaucrats made itself felt in a more personal way, however, when he learned that Louise had, miraculously, passed safely through Murmansk and was in Petrograd. He wrote her from Moscow on August 26, saying, "I had made all arrangements to go to Petrograd, and if possible farther on the road north, in order to come back here with you." But the day before he had been told that he must join the ECCI for a conference of the Peoples of the East at Baku in the Caucasus, and he was leaving that night: "To this I thought my honey would love to go. I asked for permission to stay and come later with you. But they refused. Then I asked that you be sent after me. That also cannot be done, because there is civil war going on down South, and we are going in an armored train, which is the only one to go." He added that he worried about one thing: "I must soon go home, and it is difficult to get out of here, especially for a woman. That is why I tried to get word to you to wait for me outside [Russia]. But as soon as I found out you were coming, I was so glad that I was to see my honey sooner."

He recommended that she go on to Moscow, unless she would be more comfortable waiting for him in Petrograd, and he made out a list of people she could see in the capital, including Aleksandra Kollontay and Angelica Balabanov. He closed the letter, "I love my honey with all my heart and am happy to be able to see her again," and signed it, "Your Big."

Presumably — though she left no record of it — Louise followed his instructions and made herself busy in Moscow seeing the people he had mentioned, while he made the long train journey to Baku. The conference there was historic, the first step in Soviet Communism's long quest to woo developing countries, building on Lenin's the-sis that revolutionary movements in the capitalist West could link up with nationalist movements in the undeveloped world to achieve world revolution. Most immediately, however, the Bolsheviks wanted to capi-talize on the growth of nationalist movements among the Eastern, mostly Muslim peoples of the former Russian empire by giving their separate struggles a unity and a goal. Zinoviev, accompanied by Karl Radek and the Hungarian leader Béla Kun, attempted to rally the gath-ered Turks, Persians, Arabs, and Armenians around the cause of anti-imperialism, urging an all-out "holy war." Cynically, they were mani-pulating the Muslims who had just thrown off the czarist yoke into a holy frenzy, hoping to harness that unleashed energy to the Bolshevik cause.

The conference lasted ten long days, and left Jack again frustrated by the tactics of Zinoviev and his colleagues — tactics that had been unde-niably effective, as the assembled peoples had responded with fervor, holding aloft swords and rifles at every speech. As the Bolsheviks cele-brated the conference's success on the way back to Moscow, the train was attacked by bandits on horseback, who were fought off by a Red Army squad. When they attacked again, Jack, characteristically, leaped off the train and into the fray.

On the morning of September 15, Jack ran shouting into Louise's hotel room. As she later wrote simply, "We were terribly happy to find each other." They had much to tell each other, but for the first few days they passed their time making renewed pledges of love. They vowed there would be no more separations. In the evenings they walked in a nearby park under birch trees, and, wrote Louise, "Death and separation seemed very far away." Jack repeated for her the scrap of rather desperate poetry he had written out obsessively in the Finnish jail, the one about the "bitter thought" that would not go away, the thought that they were lost to each other. But he also showed her another, happier poem he had written in the same bleak period, called "Letter to Louise." The second stanza began:

> White and slim my lover
> Birch tree in the shade
> Mountain pools her fearless eyes
> Innocent, all-answering

Were I blinded to the Spring
Happy thrill would in me rise
Smiling, half-afraid
At the nearness of her.

. . . .

Let my longing lightly rest
On her flower-petaled breast
Till the red dawn set me free
To be with my sweet
Ever and forever . . .

Louise fought the urge to question Jack about his experiences; he was obviously much the worse for them. She found him "older and sadder and grown strangely gentle." He was terribly thin, and his clothes were ragged. It was clear that he was still malnourished from his imprisonment, and had not had the chance to rest and gather new strength. "He was so impressed with the suffering around him," Louise wrote, "that he would take nothing for himself. I felt shocked . . . unable to reach the pinnacle of fervor he had attained." He seemed to inhabit another realm. But Louise hoped that her presence and her attentions would restore him.

Jack did forget his troubles for a time. He recovered his usual ebullience, taking her around Moscow, to the opera and the ballet. He had meetings of the ECCI to attend, but he found time to take Louise to see Lenin and Trotsky, and introduced her to Béla Kun and the Turkish adventurer Enver Pasha. The mood of the Soviet leaders, in the wake of the Third International and the Baku conference, was confident, and Louise and Jack felt that despite the cynicism of some of the Bolsheviks, they may have been coming close to putting together an unprecedented revolutionary alliance. The "red dawn" that Jack had written of in "Letter to Louise" seemed, they thought, to have come, and they would be together "ever and forever."

Their time together was short. Just a week after their reunion, Jack fell sick, complaining of dizziness and headaches. A doctor diagnosed influenza, which greatly relieved Louise, who had nursed him through that illness in Croton the year before. Nevertheless, she made him promise to rest and recuperate fully before going home, where he would surely go to prison. Jack knew that she was really asking him not to return to the U.S., and said, "My dear little Honey, I would do anything I could for you, but don't ask me to be a coward."

But Jack's condition worsened, and his fever raged. Louise called in more doctors, who diagnosed typhus, which was then epidemic in southern Russia, and admitted him to the Marinsky Hospital. Louise fought to be allowed to stay with him — she later said she kissed him on the mouth in front of the doctors, so they could not plead the dangers of contagion — and did not leave his side thenceforth.

In a letter to Max Eastman, Louise wrote, "He would have died days before but for the fight he made. The old peasant nurses used to slip out to the Chapel and pray for him and burn a candle for his life. . . . Spotted typhus is beyond description. The patient wastes to nothing under your eyes." Still, she continued, "He was never delirious in the hideous way most typhus patients are. He always knew me and his mind was full of poems and stories and beautiful thoughts. He would say, 'You know how it is when you go to Venice. You ask people — Is this Venice? — just for the pleasure of hearing the reply.' He would tell me that the water he drank was full of little songs. And he related, like a child, wonderful experiences we had together in which we were very brave."

But after two weeks, during which, as Louise wrote in a letter to Jack's mother, "he fought so hard for his life . . . trying and trying to smile and breathe," he had a stroke, and his right side was paralyzed. He could not speak, Louise said, "but he held me tightly by the hand through the hardest hours." Louise still prayed he might live.

On October 17, at two in the morning, Jack died. Louise would not leave his body for an hour, until it was cold. Even then she had to be carried from him.

12

Toward Another Life

John Reed's death and burial became the stuff of legend. The Bolsheviks put on a magnificent show, in keeping with their abiding respect for the man who had brought the story of their revolution to the world. His body lay in state in the Labor Temple, or Trade Union Hall, from October 20 — two days before what would have been his thirty-third birthday — until the day of his funeral, Sunday, October 24. The hall was draped in revolutionary banners in brilliant colors, and the coffin was raised on a dais. It was guarded by fourteen soldiers, Louise wrote Max Eastman, "standing stiffly, their bayonets gleaming under the lights and the red star of Communism on their military caps. Jack lay in a long silver coffin banked with flowers and streaming banners. Once the soldiers uncovered it for me so that I might touch the high white forehead with my lips for the last time." Another observer noticed that interspersed among the fresh flowers were others made of tin and gaily painted, clearly doing double duty for many a revolutionary burial.

The day of the funeral dawned cold and dark. A great crowd gathered in the Labor Temple, and from there made a procession to Red Square, while a military band played Russian funeral marches. It began to snow on the way. Louise had made some halfhearted attempts to get Russian officials to return Jack's body to the States — or so she told his mother

— but had been refused, because of the blockade and the chance of contagion. He was, instead, to be honored by burial under the walls of the Kremlin, next to other revolutionary heroes. Behind his gravesite hung a large red banner, its gold letters reading, THE LEADERS DIE, BUT THE CAUSE LIVES ON.

The service was stately indeed, with speeches read in English, French, German, and Russian; among the speakers were Nikolai Bukharin and Aleksandra Kollontay. The snow began to change to rain, and Louise grew faint, eventually leaning back, white-faced, against the supporting arm of a Russian official. Louise's account suggests an anguished ordeal:

> On [the funeral] day I felt very proud and even strong. I wished to walk according to the Russian custom, quite by myself after the hearse. And in the Red Square I tried to stand facing the speakers with a brave face. But I was not brave at all and fell on the ground and could not speak or cry.
>
> I do not remember the speeches. I remember more the broken notes of the speakers' voices. I was aware that after a long time they ceased and the banners began to dip back and forth in salute. I heard the first shovel of earth go rolling down and then something snapped in my brain. After an eternity I woke up in my own bed. Emma Goldman was standing there, and two doctors and a tall young officer from the Red Army. They were whispering and so I went to sleep again.

Louise later characterized what happened to her as a heart attack ("my heart went back on me"); the doctors told her that the strain of the last months, her arduous trip through Finland, and the shock of Jack's death made it imperative that she rest completely if she wanted to recover her health.

"Jack's illness and his death brought me closer to him than all our life together did," Louise wrote Andrew Dasburg some time later. "I found myself all alone in a strange world and everything smashed to hell." She had lost all direction, but stayed on, numbly. Years later she told the lawyer Clarence Darrow a fantastic story about visiting Jack in the typhus ward wearing a Russian dagger at her belt. She told Jack she would use it to kill herself after his death, she said. But Jack told her gently no, that they all must live out their lives: "That's why I'm still here." To Mrs. Reed she wrote, "[F]or myself — my life is nothing now. Do not think I shall go out seeking new life." She had turned gray overnight, she said, and added somewhat ruefully, perhaps remembering the old controversies raised in her college days about her high coloring, "I have no silly red cheeks now."

Yet she was fiercely proud of her husband and of the regard borne him by the Russians, who, as she wrote Mrs. Reed, "loved Jack greatly and . . . give him every honor in their power." She ended her account to Max Eastman of Jack's funeral in Red Square on a note of pride:

> But I have been in the Red Square since then — since that day all those people came to bury in all honor our dear Jack Reed. I have been there in the busy afternoon when all Russia hurries by, horses and sleighs and bells and peasants carrying bundles, soldiers singing on the way to the front. Once some of the soldiers came over to the grave. They took off their hats and spoke very reverently. "What a good fellow he was!" said one. "He came all the way across the world for us." "He was one of ours —" In another moment they shouldered their guns and went on again.

But she closed her account with a sharp cry of despair: "I have been there under the stars with a great longing to lie down beside the frozen flowers and the metallic wreaths and not wake up. How easy it would be!"

As with so many legends, the story of John Reed's death and burial is shrouded in uncertainty. One of the more enduring aspects is that he is the only American to be buried in the Kremlin. Not so — Big Bill Haywood, present at Jack's funeral, would be buried there as well in 1928. Other facts are equally confused. Did Louise fall into the arms of a Russian foreign minister, as the British observer Clare Sheridan reported, or to the ground itself, as Louise said? Louise claimed Jack had been alert and aware during the last days of his life; Emma Goldman said Louise had told her that he was not aware of her presence. In one account, Louise said Lenin had intervened and saw that Jack got competent medical care; in another she said that Lenin did not know of Jack's illness until it was over. Then there is the story of Louise shipping out to join Jack dressed as a sailor, a story she encouraged and, according to Emma Goldman, told herself.

These minor issues threaten to obscure — and perhaps arose because of — the larger controversy surrounding Jack's death. Almost immediately afterward the question of his continued loyalty to the Communist party, of what many called his "disillusionment," became a burning issue among his friends and foes. It was, according to Theodore Draper, perhaps the best authority on the subject, something that "everyone has written of . . . differently in his or her own image." Simply put, many rushed to conjecture what Jack's last thoughts were, and their conjectures served their own ends. Emma Goldman, who had become critical of the Bolsheviks at the first sign of authoritarian tendencies, told several versions of a story about hearing with amazement that among Jack's last words were "Caught in a trap, caught in a trap" — words that she often used to articulate her experience in the Soviet Union. It was a story she claimed to have heard from Louise.

Later, Benjamin Gitlow, who would become a virulent anti-Communist, literally invented a story that he said Louise related to him when she visited him in Sing Sing in 1921. Explaining, thirty years later, "I will give the story of his last days in her own words as they were imprinted on my memory," he proceeded to devote three pages of his book to "Louise's Story," written in the first person. And a vivid story it was, complete with a report of Jack's puritanical revulsion at the prostitutes and vodka on the train back from Baku.

Max Eastman entered into the fray long after Jack's death, using as his authority Louise's testimony — though he too told the story differently every time; eventually, in his last book, he admitted, seemingly undone by his own confusion, "There are so many of these versions, and they differ so widely, that it is impossible to decide what happened."

What happened was rather obvious: no one could have known what Jack was thinking in his last days. No one, that is, but his widow, who had been at his side. Other friends and colleagues, in turn, heard what they wanted to hear — or, in some cases, fabricated it seemingly out of whole cloth. In some cases such behavior was not entirely their fault. Louise did indeed repeat various versions of what Jack's last observations were — although nowhere did she say outright that he had broken with the Communists. There was no doubt he had been frustrated by

Zinoviev and the ECCI, but his belief in Bolshevism grew so naturally out of his own experiences and convictions that it was unlikely that impatience with the methods of the new leaders would have shaken his course.

Moreover, given the likelihood that Jack's dissatisfaction amounted to little more than complaints about bureaucratic annoyances, Louise may not have known of Jack's general feelings about the great Soviet experiment. If anything, she would have been inclined to assume that his general commitment to the ideals of the Bolshevik revolution had not wavered, as hers had not. Questions about Jack's loyalty or disillusionment would simply have confused her, and in her grief she was in no shape to comprehend that a battle was being fought over Jack's political soul.

In short, the responsibilities of being Jack Reed's widow arose almost immediately after his death, and Louise was ill equipped to rise to the challenge. She was extremely vulnerable to the claims of revisionist historians who wished to make Jack over in their own image. Naively, she believed that Jack's friends shared his beliefs and would continue to do so. Her fullest account of Jack's last days and his death she recounted for Max Eastman, who would later provide the most egregious revisionism. It took the form of a long letter that he would soon after publish in *The Masses.*

Moreover, valued though she was as an eyewitness to Jack's last days, her stock in radical circles plummeted after his death. Little of this reached her in Russia, but she was fast losing credibility among those who had always been ready to denounce her as a superficial hanger-on dependent on Jack's reputation. The old nastiness that had clung to many observers' views of her began to surface. Dorothy Day, the same woman who perceptively noted that the *Masses* folks never liked Louise because she "had no right" to have such beauty *and* brains, reported a telling instance of this kind of bad blood. She was in *The Liberator* offices with Floyd Dell and Max Eastman when news reached them of Jack's death. Max, on whom Louise was relying in her darkest hours, "said with a slight sneer in his voice, 'And I suppose Louise got hysterical and threw herself over his coffin.'"

Eastman knew his target: Louise was indeed emotional and given to drama, and she did collapse at Jack's funeral. But Eastman's cynical response to the widow's plight suggests that a script was developing: a script in which Louise was minimized and even dismissed, written out of history as a hysterical woman. She never really fit others' idea of a proper professional widow, though she would do her best to honor Jack's memory by serving the truth. She was, for the moment, undone by his loss, but she kept on muddling through.

Physically recovering from shock, with the aid of an American doctor brought to her bedside by Emma Goldman, Louise moved into the so-called Sugar Palace, a small hotel maintained by the Soviets for visiting foreign diplomats. From there she wrote Andrew Dasburg a mournful, elegiac letter that spoke of how close she and Jack had been at the end. She could not resist testing the waters, however, closing the letter by asking "What shall you do, Andrew?" She would be back in the early spring, she said, and perhaps he would tell her then.

A note of determination crept into the letter, however, as she talked about her own future. She was to go to the Crimea and then to Persia as soon as her health allowed, she said. Though she did mean to come back to America at some point, she wrote, "I make Moscow my permanent address."

Another, more ominous note also appeared, one that would characterize her personal communications in the weeks to come. Speaking of conditions in Russia, she wrote to Mrs. Reed, "The only way to endure it is to become utterly reckless and live each day as if no dawn would come." She wrote in the same vein about Jack's death, stressing both her determination to carry on and her utter indifference concerning the future: "I shall work very, very hard and hope Fate will be kind to me and not make my life long."

A poem for Jack, called "Aftermath," which would appear in *The Liberator* in 1921, sounded the same desperation in its central stanza:

> Faster and faster I whirl
> Toward the end of my days.
> Dear, I am drunken with sadness
> And lost down strange ways.

Drunken with sadness, lost down strange ways, she would become entirely reckless, hoping only that fate would be kind to her and the dance of life would soon finish. It was an attitude that, to varying degrees, would color her life to the last of her days.

Yet she set out, grimly but with great energy, to work. As soon as she was on her feet, she began filing cables with the INS, the International News Service, from the Sugar Palace. For eight months, and periodically thereafter, her stories appeared without a byline; she told Andrew Dasburg that any story he saw in the papers datelined Moscow had been written by her. While this cannot have been true — several capable American reporters still covered Russia — the record indicates that she may indeed have been the foremost American correspondent there. Most of her cables were written in shorthand that to the uninitiated sounds distinctly Orwellian: "12020 exlouise bryant moscow january first litwinoffs [sic] appointment representative estoniaward indicates important reorganization russias diplomatic service stop reval remains principal russian door europeward importantest political financial matters handled reval by representatives exevery country stop."

Louise filed nearly every day, keeping up a grueling schedule. The entire process was somewhat confused and confusing, as frustrated cables from Frank Mason, her INS editor, reveal that much of the time hers did not get through. Many were routed through Berlin. Perhaps because they were written in shorthand, Mason often misunderstood her and she had to correct him forcefully.

But the fault may have lain with her bosses as well. The INS, as one cynical newspaperman commented, was "a ramshackle affair" whose unofficial motto was "Get it now, correct it later." He nicknamed it the Unintentional News Service, so disorganized were its methods and dispatching of reporters.

Other factors made reporting difficult, but these had more to do with the people she was covering and the conditions under which she had to work. As Louise wrote in a byline article the following summer, the commissar for foreign affairs, Georgi Chicherin, worked during the night rather than the day and in fact would not allow stories to be submitted until after midnight. He read every single wire, and sometimes he would not get to a reporter's story until five in the morning. "The plain truth is that correspondents are far from welcome [in Russia]," she wrote.

But the cables between Louise and her news service also indicate just how indispensable she was to American reporting on Russia. When rumors of Lenin's death began to circulate in America, Mason sent a series of urgent cables to her. Because of Louise's unparalleled access to inside sources — including Lenin himself — she was able to clarify the state of his health. (He had never fully recovered from being wounded in an assassination attempt in 1918, but he was nowhere near death.) Moreover, her reporting was detailed and often technical, indicating her close familiarity with internal and foreign policy issues in Russia. Often her acerbic sense of humor revealed itself. She covered the Kronshtadt rebellion in March in detail; she reported on rumors of counterrevolution ("only fighting ive seen done by mischievous schoolboys snowballing each other stop seriously speaking ive not heard single shot stop"); she wrote long cables giving convincing proof that war between Russia and Romania — though expected by the West — was not imminent.

Her specialty was the East. As the Baku conference had shown, the Soviets were eager to reestablish close ties with the Central Asian, Muslim, and Turkic-speaking Central Asian territories of the former Russian empire, now in the throes of organizing themselves into independent republics, especially in light of the British presence in the nearby Middle East and India. Aware that any activity in those regions would be breaking news, Louise went to the Foreign Office for permission to travel there about a month after Jack's death. Her request was flatly refused. Typically, she went directly to the top — to Lenin. As she later related, he looked up from his work and smiled. "I am glad there is someone in Russia with enough energy to go exploring," he said. "You might get killed down there, but you will have the most remarkable experience of your life; it is worth taking chances for."

On January 11 Louise set out, carrying with her a pass, or *probsk,* enabling her to ride on all trains and to stay at government hotels, along with a personal letter from Lenin. For the first leg of her journey, to Bukhara, the Russians provided her with an escort of two soldiers. It was indeed a perilous journey, as she wrote in another byline story that appeared in the summer of 1921. "The trains running out of Riga and Reval to Petrograd and Moscow are quite clean and one runs small risk traveling, but to go to the Caucasus or Turkestan means to take a tremendous chance of contracting typhus. It is impossible to escape the vermin, especially in the fourth-class carriages," a real concern, given the precarious state of Louise's health. She also ran the risk of encountering bandits such as those who had attacked Reed's train on the way back from Baku.

Often mistaken for a Russian because of her costume — an old fur hat and *shuba,* a shabby dress, and Tatar-embroidered boots — Louise made her way through all the Near Eastern parts of the former czarist empire, "clear down to the very edge of India," she wrote. She described it as "a hard but intensely interesting journey over the Kirghiz Steppes, the Desert of Kizil Kum, through Turkestan, Bokhara, and to the edge of Persia and Afghanistan." Her mission was to see the effect of the treaties the Soviets had made with the Eastern nations. At the time of the revolution, the Bolsheviks had declared that the religion and cultural practices of all Muslim peoples would be respected, and she was able to report that the strategy had, by and large, been effective: "The present fine crop of treaties is the legitimate outcome of that early planting." But the reality of Russia's treatment of the Muslims was more complicated; while they had generally respected the integrity of Muslim countries, there were exceptions.

Louise claimed to have been the only Western reporter in the area in six years, and that may not have been an exaggeration. There is no doubt that she returned to Moscow after her two-month trip a seasoned expert on Eastern affairs. She had also developed an intense interest and respect for Middle Eastern peoples and the region in general. For several months her reporting focused almost exclusively on the East; when the Soviets spent weeks negotiating a very difficult treaty with Persia, Louise covered every complicated step.

Her involvement with the Muslim world took personal shape in her relationship with Enver Pasha, the Turkish leader who could perhaps best be described as a political soldier of fortune. An organizer of the Young Turk revolution of 1908 and a leader in the Ottoman government from 1913 to 1918, Enver had been active in the cause of Turkish nationalism and then came over to the Bolshevik side, convinced that Leninism and some form of third world nationalism were not incompatible. The Russians were naturally suspicious of him, but they understood he might have considerable influence with the Turkic-speaking Central Asian republics of the old czarist empire, which they were eager to cultivate.

In short, Enver Pasha was a remarkable man — the first leader who would attempt to use Marxism-Leninism as the theoretical route to a new kind of third world nationalism, and in this sense a precursor of Ho Chi Minh, Mao Zedong, Kwame Nkrumah, and other postcolonial nationalist leaders. It is an indication of Louise's political astuteness that she saw Enver's potential and was drawn to him. She first met him at the Sugar Palace, where he too had been given rooms. They became friends — in spite of, or perhaps because of, Enver's volatile personality. For six months, whenever Louise was in Moscow, they ate at the same table and often went together to the theater and the Turkish embassy. Their friendship was cemented when Louise actually saved his life, coming upon a man with a pistol outside Enver's door and calling out loudly and forcefully enough that the always armed Enver was able to emerge from his room and disarm the man.

Louise wrote a byline article about the Turkish leader that she later included in her 1923 book, *Mirrors of Moscow*. It was a vivid portrait that revealed both her fondness for and her distrust of the man. It began:

> No man I ever met lives so completely in the moment as Enver Pasha; the past he puts behind him, the future he leaves to Allah. His only hero is Napoleon. In Moscow he was the *avant coureur* of the new under-standing between Russia and the Mohammedan world. . . . Any man who has brains and gives all his being to the task in hand is bound to possess personality and power and, very likely, charm. Enver Pasha cer-tainly has charm, in spite of his obvious opportunism, and the cruelty and lack of conscience which a fatalistic belief inspires.

She went on to describe his position as the "social lion" of postwar Moscow, of such magnetism that when he attended the theater the Russian actresses played to him across the footlights. Louise's friendship with him was enhanced by her brutal frankness, which she said he liked; he praised her "arrogance" when she roundly criticized a pencil sketch he made of her.

The inevitable question is whether their relationship progressed be-yond friendship. Enver was a full-fledged ladies' man; married to an Ottoman princess, he was said to have other wives as well — all safely stowed away in Turkey. Louise, never long without a man's company, wrote of him in fascinated tones that seem to express at the very least a romantic infatuation. Certainly he was her type: he was another larger-than-life, robust figure. Louise frequently asserted in later years that she had had many proposals of marriage after Jack's death — "and not all with Americans." Some years later Louise would tell her daughter that Enver died with her photograph next to his heart, and she carried with her to her own death an envelope marked "secret password" containing an inscription from Enver in Arabic.

The romance of her acquaintance with the dashing Turk no doubt lifted Louise's spirits in the bleak days after Jack's death, and her constant, almost frenetic reporting duties certainly kept her mind occupied, if not her heart. She remained bereft. That she could not quickly forget him is indicated by a sonnet she wrote that Max Eastman included in a February 1921 issue of *The Masses* dedicated to Jack, which read, in part:

> Jack, you are quiet now among the dead.
>
> . . . .
>
> They say you died for Communism — they
> Who to some absent god must always give
> The choicest even of the fruits of youth.
> Your god was life. Because you chose to live,
> Death found you in the torrent of the fray,
> Exulting in the future and the truth.

For Louise, herself caught up in "the torrent of the fray" of life, the future was no cause for exultation, but the truth — what she saw and reported so diligently to the American public — served her as reason, in these dark days, to continue.

Louise had told Andrew Dasburg that her permanent address was Moscow and had emphasized to Jack's mother that she would never again live in the United States ("I could never bear to be far away" from his grave, she wrote "darling Muz"), but she was driven by a strong sense of duty toward Jack's memory. However unsuccessful she would turn out to be as a professional widow, she would devote several months of 1921 and early 1922 to seeing that Jack's life was properly recorded and all respects duly paid. She admonished Mrs. Reed to "be brave," adding "Jack was a beautiful and wonderful person and his memory demands that at least of us." For her part, she wrote, "I just want to do one thing — and that is to come home and get his papers in order. Most everything he wrote here was lost. He sent twelve articles (a whole book) home — but not one reached America — and there are only loose notes here. In his studio at Croton his manuscripts are quite in order and I do not want anything he has written to be lost. . . . The only plan I have in the world now is to do as well as I can this last service for Jack."

By April 1921 she was ready to return to America, though she planned to stop in Berlin for a month, see some good doctors, and recuperate from her collapse and "heart attack" after Reed's death. But, as always when she tried to leave or reenter her country, she encountered significant obstruction from the State Department and, indirectly, J. Edgar Hoover. On April 30, a U.S. official named Gray wrote to the secretary of state saying Louise had arrived in the Latvian capital of Riga with the intention of returning to America via Berlin and asking whether he was authorized to issue her an emergency passport. There was no response, and Louise evidently asked her U.S. lawyer, Arthur Garfield Hays, to intervene, for he wrote to the secretary saying if the delay was due to any question of her citizenship, he could vouch for her.

At this point U.S. officials decided to raise the issue of why Louise had no passport in the first place — that is, how she had managed to leave the country in 1920, when she traveled to Reed's side posing as the wife of a Swedish businessman. Accordingly, the State Department sent a telegram on May 25 authorizing issuance of an emergency passport, but stipulating that she must provide "full affidavit showing document she used in leaving United States." The passport was issued, but officials would not deliver it until Louise produced such an affidavit.

Naturally, she drew the line at this. Hurley, an official with the consul at Riga, cabled the State Department, explaining Louise's claim that "she left United States 'for certain papers' but objects to execution of any affidavit and to investigation of matter here, contending that she is an American citizen and, as such, entitled to admission to United States."

A flurry of internal memos at State ensued, indicating that they were having second thoughts about the advisability of blocking Louise's return. "I think that the Secretary should be informed of this situation," one official wrote. "A refusal at this time would raise a hornet's nest. P.S.," he added, "It will undoubtedly be alleged that we are persecuting a widow on account of her husband's opinions. It would be wise to go slow in this matter I believe."

Confusion ensued between Riga and Washington as to whether she would be issued a passport without the affidavit, issued an emergency passport, or told she did not need a passport. Louise evidently won this battle, for on July 13 Consul Gray informed Secretary of State Charles Evans Hughes: "Louise Bryant Reed sailed direct to United States Steamship LATVIA from Libau July 11th. Having declined to execute required affidavit she sailed without passport." In spite of their deep distrust of her, the State Department appears to have backed down. But, over at the Justice Department, J. Edgar Hoover still had his eye on Louise Bryant. Another official, on receiving the news that she had sailed from Riga, wrote "Informed Mr. Hoover 7-20-21. He said he would let me know if anything was done in the matter."

Louise would be in America for almost a year, but little is known of her movements during this time. She wrote few letters, appeared in public seldom, and does not seem to have taken up an active social life. Certainly her return was quiet; she slipped in with no one to meet her at the dock. The apartment at Patchin Place was vacant, and she moved in to work. The thought of Croton was too painful. The subtenant there, a man Frank Walsh had found named Diamond, had left, breaking his yearlong lease, and the cottage stood empty. Clare Sheridan described a visit to Mount Airy Hill in the month Louise returned. The entire area was charming, but run-down, she noted: "The houses have no gardens, the grass grows long and the rose bushes are weed tangled. Now and then a bunch of peonies survives. . . . Towards the hill summit I noticed a wooden veranda'ed cottage. Looking rather neglected and lonely, the ground sloped down to a stream where some yellow and purple iris bloomed amid the waste. On the post box at the gate were inscribed the two names: Reed, Bryant, and sure enough it was the summer cottage of Jack Reed and his wife." Louise visited the cottage only to gather what papers she needed, and cast barely a glance at the grounds she and Jack had so lovingly tended.

She had her work; indeed, she had her work cut out for her. William Randolph Hearst planned to run in his newspapers a series of byline articles based on her reportage from Russia. She had filed some full-length stories while she was there, but she had to reconstruct others from her records of cables and the stories that had been fashioned from them by INS editors. The first story in her sixteen-part series appeared on August 16 in the *New York American* and on the next day in the *San Francisco Examiner*. She explained, in that piece, her somewhat mechanical view of what was required of a reporter: "to be a sort of phonograph, with a motion picture attachment." She added, "It is not necessary to exaggerate about Russia to be interesting. The days are too swift and the life too stark and terrible to be dull. Personally, I feel as if I have lived ten years in one."

Louise's series covered a broad range of topics, from the New Economic Plan, which Lenin had introduced in March, and which she correctly described as a modified form of capitalism, to an interview with Trotsky in which she lavishly praised his organizational skills. The one exception to the otherwise unstinting objectivity of her work was a story about Emma Goldman in which Louise mourned the anarchist firebrand's denunciation of Bolshevism. Louise wrote scathingly that Goldman's attacks on the Bolsheviks "were more virulent and hysterical than those of the extreme reactionaries" and "charged with virulent hatred." Whatever misgivings she herself may have had by this time, Louise still felt it vital to defend the survival of the new revolutionary society in Russia — especially in the face of the threat of military force by Western capitalist powers.

Otherwise Louise was far more sober about conditions in Russia, and her observations had more weight than Goldman's in that they were backed up by interviews with Soviet officials themselves. Her old hero Aleksandra Kollontay, for instance, told her, "Remember that these are the gray days of the revolution. Everything has settled down into the momentous, undramatic task of reconstruction. If you look for that elation you saw here in 1917 you will be disappointed."

The series brought Louise's name into the public eye again, and certainly gained her great credit in newspaper circles, as subsequent events were to bear out. It must also, of course, have given her great personal and political satisfaction once again to get out "the truth" about Russia. But she seems to have retreated into her professional role: there were no more quasi editorials for marginal magazines like *Soviet Russia* or *The Liberator*, no talks late into the night with radical sympathizers. The left had dispersed, turning inward or, increasingly, becoming expatriates; it had reached the point that, as Max Eastman later wrote about the early 1920s, "Few now can imagine what an insular, irrelevant, hole-in-the-corner thing socialism was in the America of those days." It seems that Louise did not seek out Jack's radical friends and in turn was not sought out by them. Her relationship with Andrew Dasburg reached a denouement as she learned that he and his son had moved to Santa Fe to live with Ida Rauh and her son by Max Eastman.

There is one prominent exception to Louise's low profile in what radical circles remained: her appearance (duly noted in FBI confidential reports) at a John Reed memorial meeting on October 17, 1921. Held in the Central Opera House in New York, the gathering drew some two thousand people, who rose to their feet to sing the "Internationale" and the Russian funeral song written for the martyrs of the 1905 revolution. As the *New York Call* reported the following day, Louise gave a stirring speech: "The splendid stand of Russia caught the imagination and great heart of John Reed and sent him to Russia to fulfill the mission of the most humane government the world has ever seen. For a year he worked and starved and suffered in Moscow; now for twelve months he has been lying in a grave in the Red Square." Then, moving on to a larger plea for Russia, she concluded by saying: "Today Russia is being crucified for its ideals. Only one country kept before it the ideal of brotherly love and righteousness and that was Russia. Now we must work for Russia. Russia has no time for propaganda in this country while 25,000,000 starve within her own borders."

But Reed more than Russia, for the time being, was foremost in her mind, and she turned her attention to gathering his papers with a view to collecting and publishing them, and perhaps one day writing his biography. First she applied to the American legation in Helsinki seeking personal papers she believed had been taken from Jack during his jail term, but to no avail. She appealed to Jack's old friend Lincoln Steffens for guidance. He suggested that she try Fred Bursch, a small publisher in Greenwich, Connecticut, who had been a Harvard classmate of Jack's and who might be willing to issue the unpublished material she had.

But Louise had already applied to Bursch, who had in 1917 published a collection of Jack's early poems, *Tamurlaine*. Nothing more would come of it, though a back-and-forth of letters between Greenwich and Patchin Place ensued. Louise gave up when she got a passionate letter from Bursch's wife, Anne, in May 1922, stating that she had known of many dead people who spoke from beyond the grave and that she absolutely knew, without reservation, that Jack was alive.

There were other, fresh hurts. Boni and Liveright wanted to reprint *Ten Days That Shook the World* — welcome news indeed. Louise had been busy with *Ten Days*, trying to get some movie producers interested in it, and agitating for just such a reissue. The publishers wanted to use a blurb from Louise on the back. Would she mind, they asked, if they put after her name, in parentheses, "Mrs. John Reed"? Louise's response is not recorded.

With this string of disappointments, she put aside, temporarily, her mission to gather and publish Jack's papers. By the spring of 1922 she wanted only to go back to Russia; America held nothing for her. "It has been terrible to come back," she confided to Bursch, "more terrible than I ever dreamed. I mean to finish all these things I have to do so I can go away and not come back."

To her personal disappointments and grief was added the distinct sense that there was no place for her in the United States. It was a conviction shared by scores of other young radicals and intellectuals in the early years of the 1920s. The writer Harold Stearns had ushered in the new era with a 1920 article in *The Freeman* called "What Can a Young Man Do?" His forthright answer was "Get out!" America offered nothing to "imaginative and adventurous and artistically creative young men" — or women. With the election of the Harding-Coolidge ticket in 1920, a new conservatism had taken hold in the country. The Red Scare was in full flower, the days of the Palmer Raids seemed like a picnic, and Wilsonian internationalism a distant memory. The country was preoccupied with the evangelism of Billy Sunday and Aimee Semple McPherson, with mindless fads like goldfish swallowing and flagpole sitting, with Prohibition, bathtub gin, and speakeasies. Babbittry — derived from Sinclair Lewis's 1922 instant classic — ruled the land. "A strange, brittle, cerebral aristocratism has succeeded the robust democratism of the last age," complained the critic Van Wyck Brooks in 1923, attributing it to the dehumanization of the Great War. The energy of the intellectual and radical left had dissipated, with most radicals turning inward, or, with a huge wave of artists and writers, going abroad. Malcolm Cowley, writing from the perspective of the younger, less political bohemians who would forsake the Village for Europe, wrote that there "was one idea that was held in common" by the older and younger groups — "the idea of salvation by exile. 'They do things better in Europe: let's go there.'"

Louise, of course, with the experience of her sedate married days in Portland, Oregon, was no stranger to this kind of bourgeois complacency, and she would have none of it. It pained her that the Village, where she had experienced such joy, activity, and freedom in her years with Jack, had now degenerated into a commerical tourist trap. The world she had inhabited no longer existed, and it must have been, as she had said, terrible to come back and find that it had vanished.

Going abroad seemed her only hope. She was friendless, disconsolate — and she was broke. "Of course when Jack died I not only had nothing left," she wrote a friend, "no will to be and no enthusiasm. I just had bad health and a lot of debts." Mercifully, because of her good standing in newspaper circles, she was again offered the chance to return to Russia — this time for King Features, another Hearst agency. Her standing as a professional woman was all that she had left, and it was with great effort — and a belief that there might still be a world elsewhere — that she gathered the energy to take up her career again in earnest.

Much to Louise's disgust, U.S. officials again threw roadblocks in the way of her plans. When they denied a routine passport application, she went personally to Washington to fight her case. Writing from there to Anne Bursch in Connecticut, she declared, "Am down here in D.C. now because I have a chance to go abroad. But they regard me as dangerous. What stupidity! There was a time when I had enough fire and spirit to care about justice and liberty and all the words men die for, but I really don't care any more."

The State Department, even more conservative in Harding's shadow, took care that they not be put into the same tight situation they had found themselves in when John Reed's widow sought to return from Russia. First, they could delay her recommendation, as Undersecretary of State Hurley wrote in a May 22 memo, noting that "surely there are other applications filed previously to this which should receive precedence." In the meantime, Hurley was making a thorough investigation of King Features, presumably to determine whether it was some kind of Communist front. But, first and foremost, he wanted the affidavit Louise had refused to provide when she had sought a passport in Latvia, especially given that she had, he said, played "fast and loose" with State in the past: "Having persistently refused to give a satisfactory explanation to the Department . . . as to the methods employed in leaving this country and also reasons for same, I think it about time she should be made to do so and, failing this, her application should receive consideration with this condition in mind."

While Louise had understandably resisted filing such an affidavit when she simply wanted, as an American citizen, to return to her own country, she at this point felt no compunction about issuing whatever statements authorities demanded in order to leave. In fact, she made two affidavits, one on May 23 and the second the following day. The first was forthright and quite mild, stating "Miss Bryant has followed the vocation of journalism for the last five years and this is her only means of making a livlihood [sic], and should she be denied a passport at this time, great hardship would be worked upon her." It concluded, "Miss Bryant is not a member of any political party or organization and is not interested in politics except as an observer."

The next day she wrote another, stronger affidavit that addressed more directly the concerns of the State Department. In it she admitted that she had been abroad in 1920 and 1921, though she deliberately did not say whether she had traveled without a passport. She stated "that the reason for her last visit to Europe was for the purpose of seeing her husband who was critically ill." She also swore that she was "not opposed to organized government, nor . . . a member of any radical organization or society." Evidently this show of compliance satisfied the authorities, who seem to have been motivated at least in part by irritation at her insubordination. A passport was issued.

It was a compromise of sorts, but consistent with Louise's decision, in 1921 and 1922, to put her work above all else. In no way was it a renunciation of her principles. Unlike Reed, she had never officially attached herself to any organized political party. By now it should have been clear from her public statements that her support for the Soviet Union was based on the fact that it was a great experiment in the creation of an alternative to capitalist society, an experiment that should not be snuffed out, and that some of its best elements were actually manifestations, to her, of her most deeply held beliefs — equality for women and a better life for workers, for example.

In any event, her decision to concentrate on her journalistic career was finally pragmatic: the arrangements were conducive to unparalleled journalistic freedom. Her agreement with King Features seems to have been somewhat different from that with the INS, perhaps because of the prestige she had gained from her sixteen-story byline series. There would be no cabled wire stories; instead she would draw on previous material and new interviews to create several portraits of the Russian leaders and people. Louise may have had plans for a future book, and, in fact, these portraits would be published in 1923 as *Mirrors of Moscow.* King Features supplied the title of the embryonic book, running four stories about Lenin and the men around him under the same title and designating Louise as the "Famous American Newspaper Correspondent — Author of 'Six Red Months in Russia.'" The first of the articles ran on June 4, 1922.

By that time Louise was most likely on her way to Russia, for her next piece of correspondence on record is a cable from Moscow to New York on June 22. That an article on Lenin should appear while she was still en route to Russia was typical of the irregularities of the publication of her stories. They appeared at odd intervals. Much material came from her previous visit to Russia and often discussed news events that had occurred long before. Were her "Mirrors" pieces reportage, or impressions previously collected and fleshed out for the series? The answer is compounded by the difficulties of tracing her movements in 1922. The published book *Mirrors of Moscow,* for instance, contains a long story about Enver Pasha, who was not in Russia during Louise's stay there in 1922. She had met him the year before.

It is possible, however, to piece together from the book some of her activities in Russia in the summer of 1922, in part because they do contain significant reportage about specific current events. The New Economic Plan was one. With the economy crippled by the long civil war and still cut off from trade with the West, Lenin was attempting a radical jump-start of sorts, introducing in measured fashion some forms of free enterprise. Of course, the attempt was met with great resistance by Bolsheviks and Communist sympathizers, but it was also becoming clear that it was accompanied by a loosening of restraints on free speech and artistic expression that were already igniting the great Russian cultural renaissance of the 1920s, encouraging many to believe again that the Bolsheviks really could create a vibrant new society. For Louise, the NEP certainly seemed a bit of a retreat, but she sensed its potential reverberations, experiencing a new admiration for Lenin's astute leadership.

Louise also interviewed Feliks Dzerzhinsky and Jacob Peters, the head and the de facto head, respectively, of the Cheka, Russia's increasingly notorious secret police. She questioned them closely, and wrote with great care about the issue of the recent executions that had so horrified many Russians and the rest of the world. She tried to be fair-minded about the perceived necessity for the Cheka, but, as she concluded dryly, "There is always something appalling when one comes face to face with such a display of law and order."

Mirrors of Moscow also indicates that Louise traveled to the provinces to meet the peasant Mikhail Ivanovich Kalinin, who had been appointed the second president of the Russian Socialist Federated Soviet Republic. She particularly admired Kalinin's wife, a peasant who managed her tiny farm and had at the same time been elected president of the local soviet: "Madame Kalinin is an individualist; a modern feminist of the type of professional woman who, in America, insists on keeping her name and continuing her work after marriage."

That feminist causes preoccupied Louise during her 1922 trip to Russia is borne out by her long piece in *Mirrors of Moscow* about Aleksandra Kollontay, once a member of the cabinet but now in official disgrace after the arrest of her husband, a leader of the Kronstadt rebellion. Louise interviewed her in her tiny room in a Moscow hotel, where they discussed Kollontay's new work in educating women to take an active part in politics. However far Kollontay had fallen, Louise realized that at least Communism was giving her the chance to make a difference that capitalism would never have allowed in the conservative 1920s, and she found Kollontay an inspiring example of exactly the sort of new Socialist the revolution accommodated. "As champion of her sex," Louise wrote, "she cries to the women of Russia: 'Cast off your chains! Do not be slaves to religion, to marriage, to children. Break these old ties, the state is your home, the world is your country!'"

Mirrors of Moscow has a far more sober, unemotional tone than *Six Red Months in Russia*. The NEP was a factor, as well as Louise's understanding that Lenin would have to settle for socialism in one country rather than the world revolution American leftists (and Trotsky) had hoped for. Her concern was to sort out what *mattered*, what was good and progressive about Communism, from everything else. She had interviewed Lenin and Trotsky at length and assessed them as though their important work was over — which, in a very real sense, it was.

It is a mature, responsible piece of reportage. All of Louise's portraits of Russian men and women are informed by a fair yet passionate, thoughtful, and original mind, indicating that Louise had grown professionally since Jack's death. Devastated though she may have been, and cut off from her American friends by her own doing, she persevered alone.

Or perhaps not quite alone. Another, scanty record, reveals a little more about Louise's activities in the summer and fall of 1922. A series of cables and letters between Louise and Frank Walsh suggests a close friendship and a probable romantic involvement, though one in which she may not have fully reciprocated.

Frank Walsh was a full-blown radical hero — though of the most highly respectable sort. A labor lawyer, Walsh had approached Woodrow Wilson immediately after his presidential nomination in 1912, convinced of Wilson's sympathy for improvement of social and industrial conditions. Under Wilson, as chairman of the U.S. Commission on Industrial Relations, Walsh went after such leading figures as John D. Rockefeller, J. P. Morgan, and Andrew Carnegie. Later, he served as a joint chairman of the National War Labor Board, which fought for the rights of workers to organize, equal pay for women, an eight-hour workday, and the rights of all working men and women to a living wage.

Louise saved Frank's letters, and on them she noted proudly, "Head Labor War Board." But it was in his capacity as a fierce advocate of radical causes that he would have caught her sympathies most. He had been active in defending radicals persecuted in the Palmer Raids, most notably William Z. Foster, who had been brought up on charges of criminal syndicalism. Perhaps even more important to Louise was his defense of the anarchist Tom Mooney, whom she had befriended in San Francisco on her speaking tour, which was taken by Walsh at his own expense and carried out over a period of twenty years. (Mooney would write, at Walsh's death in 1939, "In his passing . . . the common people have lost one of their great friends and champions.") But what may have really won Louise was his avid support for Irish independence, signaled by his (vain) attempt to gain an independent Ireland recognition at the Treaty of Versailles. Louise had always been drawn to the Irish cause; now, as Ireland emerged as the one place in Europe where actual revolution was happening, she was determined to get there.

Louise's path would have naturally crossed Walsh's in her Greenwich Village years. In 1921, adrift, alone, and looking for advice, she may well have sought him out. By coincidence, Walsh was traveling to Russia at the same time as Louise, acting for three organizations, the American Committee for Relief of Russian Children, the Amalgamated Clothing Workers of Europe, and the American Committee for Russian Famine Relief. Louise's immediate political concern was the suffering of Russians under the blockade, so it was natural that they should join forces.

On the other hand, it was hardly a likely match. Walsh was fifty-eight — to Louise's thirty-six, or, in her version, thirty — and married. *Very* married, with a wife of thirty years and eight children. He was heavyset and not particularly handsome. Their involvement may have been an indulgence on his part, the attraction of a confirmed family man to a fascinating, charismatic, and independent woman. A paternal impulse seems to have been at work as well, as Louise, capable as she was, may have appeared to a man of another generation as a widow in need, or, even more attractively, as a damsel in distress.

If Louise was an unlikely damsel, Frank became, for the summer of 1922, her unlikely knight. On June 20, Louise cabled Frank in Berlin — the de facto headquarters of American news organizations in Europe, and by the early 1920s a common stopping-off place for Americans on the way to Russia — "When are you coming." Subsequent cables back and forth indicate that Walsh arrived in Moscow on July 14.

Louise and Frank were together in Russia for a little over a month. There is no record of what passed between them, or what their movements were, but during this time Louise continued to gather material for her Russian portraits, while Frank wrote four articles for the New York papers. Very likely she worked closely with him during his investigation of famine conditions. Much of this worked its way into her writing, as, for instance, when she investigated the newly formed women's congresses, which were focused less on politics than on famine-related issues like hygiene education and child care.

But the most concrete evidence of the relationship between Louise and Frank dates from after their time in Russia together. On August 26 Louise traveled to Riga and from there went immediately to Berlin; Frank left for the U.S. on September 7. Throughout September they were in almost daily contact by mail and cable. Louise had set in motion her plans to go to Ireland to cover the Irish civil war and the efforts of the Irish Republican Army to install an independent provisional government, and Frank Walsh, an active, well-connected supporter of the Irish cause, was an excellent source for contacts. Louise cabled him from

London asking for credentials to be presented to Irish leaders; Frank responded with letters to some ten leaders, including William Cosgrave, the recently named chairman of the provisional government after the deaths of Michael Collins and Arthur Griffith.

Plans for the Irish trip seemed to be on hold, however, despite Walsh's efforts. Louise had begun instead to move in seemingly aimless fashion from one European capital to another. On September 11 she wrote to the Storrses in Paris saying she hoped to visit them there briefly on her way to Rome. She made a quick trip to Paris, in fact, but then returned to London. In the meantime Frank Walsh was taking care of all domestic details for her, dealing with the subtenants in Croton and Patchin Place and making all necessary rent and mortgage payments.

But by the end of the month Frank evidently grew impatient with his role of facilitator and caretaker and wrote Louise a long passionate letter, addressed to her in care of the INS in London. It is a curious document, at once intimate and awestruck, a kind of paternalistic mash note. First, he apologized for sending an unnamed but clearly compromising gift to her in Paris: "I hope you had a few days in Paris and liked the little offering — Somewhat 'personal' but I was far away which emboldened me." The theme of the letter was not Frank's feelings for her but the feelings of other men. In over ten pages he catalogued the men who, he said, were in love with her. Of one admirer, he wrote, "When he gets on the subject of you, there's no stopping him — he says you're the finest girl in the world." A certain Bradford Merrill — a Hearst editor — felt the same way, he said — "he says you radiate honesty." There were those who admired her beauty and her bravery, he wrote. He was sorry there were so many "snapping at your heels."

She should remember, however, that his was the truest love: "[S]ometime, maybe, you will know that I am the *most* dependable, as well as the one who appreciates and loves you most of all." Addressing her as "you independent little soldier!" he wrote that he wished she would ask him to do more for her — though he knew she wouldn't. He assured her that things had not changed since their interlude: "Do know that away over here in the old New York ways I still think you are the lovliest [sic] and have the same feeling of affection, only more so."

The letter reveals Frank Walsh as thoroughly smitten (if a bit reserved — it has the tone of a married man writing to his adored young mistress), but Louise's feelings are less clear. Frank certainly knew what she liked to hear. She thrived on hearing that other men admired her. Despite her success, she was alone and shouldered considerable responsibilities for a single person — a full-time reportorial career, a house, an apartment, and the legacy of an increasingly mythical husband. She was lonely and needy, and, to be sure, she greatly appreciated Frank Walsh's help with Irish contacts and her domestic situation. But she liked to think of herself as independent, and Walsh's perception of her as someone who would not accept favors would have pleased her. The unbridled frankness of the letter must have also pointed out how faintly ridiculous the whole involvement was. Walsh was an older man with no intention of leaving his wife; whatever his politics, he was very much part of the establishment, and Louise had no truck with those in authority except when she needed something from them. Finally, Louise's life was decidedly peripatetic, driven by her career and her longing for adventure; to settle down in Patchin Place as a kept woman was most definitely not her style.

Louise last wrote to Frank in late October. She was in Rome, and she needed him to get the keys to the Village apartment from her tenant, Rebecca Hourwich. The tone of their letters became businesslike in the extreme; any spark between them, it seems, had been extinguished. But Louise found herself in Rome with a new man at her side — a man fully as robust, captivating, and dynamic as Jack Reed. His name was William Bullitt, and Louise's life was about to undergo a sea change.

PART III

Among the Rich

13

Enter Bullitt

I'm going to be a lawyer and Governor and Secretary of State and President," said Bill Bullitt when he was a very young boy. For the man who would become Louise's third husband, certainly all these things seemed possible. He had been born in the lap of luxury and lacked for nothing material, he had enormous intellect and talent, he loved power and wore it well. And, as his precocious remark well illustrates, he did not lack self-confidence. In fact, his utter self-assurance, just shy of arrogance, was, in his youth, his most distinguishing characteristic.

William Christian Bullitt, Jr., was taught at an early age that his ancestry was one to be proud of — indeed, one that marked him out for greatness. His distinguished forebears included Pocahontas; Annie Henry, the wife of Patrick; Augustine Washington, the father of the first president; Thomas Walker, a close friend and neighbor of Thomas Jefferson; and Thomas Bullitt, the founder of Louisville, Kentucky.

On his father's side, he was directly descended from Joseph Boulet, a French Huguenot who settled in the Potomac Valley in Maryland in 1635. On his mother's side he was descended from a Hebrew scholar turned doctor, Jonathan Horwitz of Berlin, and the eminent surgeon Samuel Gross, the subject of *The Gross Clinic,* Thomas Eakins's best-known painting. His mother's family were devout Episcopalians, though evidence suggests that they were originally Jewish. The Bullitts always denied this vehemently, but the possibility of Jewish ancestry would be seized on by detractors like Ernest Hemingway for the rest of Bill Bullitt's life.

The sharpest memory Bill was to have of his father was a story he heard at his knee, about a Spartan boy who had his insides ripped out by foxes while he stoically stood at attention. The senior William Bullitt was an efficient, distant man, and for most of his life a solidly respectable citizen. A lawyer, he became an executive with the profitable Norfolk and Western Railroad and an investor in coal mines in Virginia and West Virginia, including, appropriately, the Pocahontas Coal Company. In 1889, after a first marriage that produced a son, John, William Senior married Louisa Gross Horwitz, and on January 25, 1891, William Christian Bullitt, Jr., was born.

The Bullitts were old Philadelphia incarnate, making their home at 222 Rittenhouse Square, the preeminent center of Philadelphia society. Young Bill and, three years later, his brother, Orville, were raised to speak French at the table, say their prayers in their mother's room every morning, and attend church each Sunday at the Holy Trinity Episcopal Church not far from the square. Each summer Louisa Bullitt took Bill — usually not Orville, who was sickly, or their half brother, John, whom Louisa did not favor — to visit her mother in Paris, and the result was, at a very early age, a very worldly young fellow.

Bill had an independent, even rebellious streak, as evidenced by his refusal, on the eve of his departure, to go off to the elite boarding school Groton: "Every Groton fellow I know is a snob," he growled. Instead he stayed at home and attended Delancey School, and, as he moved into his teens, spent his summers being toughened up at a New Hampshire camp. He later credited Camp Pasquaney as the institution with the greatest influence on his life.

When he entered Yale in 1908, Bill Bullitt shone. His accomplishments were striking, indeed, almost overwhelming: he was the head of the Debating Club; an editor of the *Yale Daily News;* and director, with his friend Cole Porter, of the Dramatic Association. The Dramat, as it was called, was his first love: he took several leading roles, often women's parts, the most notable perhaps being that of Katherine in *The Taming of the Shrew.* His classwork did not suffer; he made Phi Beta Kappa and impressed his classmates with the formidable intellect and the boundless energy he brought to almost every activity he took up. They voted him the most brilliant member of the class of 1912. The world seemed to lie at his feet.

He stumbled slightly with his next step. In accordance with his father's wishes, he enrolled in Harvard Law School in the fall of 1913. Despite his childhood bragging, and the suitability of a Harvard law degree for the kind of career that seemed ahead of him, Bill found quickly that he had almost no affinity and very little liking for the law. When his father died in the spring of 1914, any sense of obligation about continuing his studies vanished. The story goes that Bill's law school career climaxed during a long classroom exchange with the eminent Professor Joseph Beale. After long, hairsplitting questions about the legal culpability of a woman unknowingly carrying an unregistered gun in her purse, Beale finally backed Bill into a logical corner and asked him point-blank if the hypothetical woman wasn't committing a criminal act. "No!" resounded Bill. "It isn't just!" To the great hilarity of the class, the professor smiled and told Bill that he could find the divinity school three doors down the street. Bill didn't laugh. He flounced out of the classroom and caught the next train to Philadelphia, arriving in time for dinner at Rittenhouse Square.

In 1914 Bullitt joined his mother for a tour of Russia and stopped on the way in central Europe, where he made the acquaintance of many officials who were longtime friends of the Bullitt family, including the ambassador to Germany, James W. Gerard. The trip to Russia was cut short by the outbreak of war, but Bullitt delayed his return to the States, stopping first in France. There he dramatically recovered family jewelry from his deceased grandmother's Paris apartment at a time when German occupation of the city seemed imminent.

On his return Bill made what at first seems a somewhat puzzling career move for someone so well placed and full of promise: he took a job as a ten-dollar-a-week reporter for the conservative *Philadelphia Public Ledger* (the city's largest paper, it later merged with the *Inquirer*), covering the police beat in South Philadelphia. Yet the move was motivated by Bullitt's special blend of idealism and ambition. The muckraking journalists of the first decade of the century, men like Upton Sinclair and Lincoln Steffens, had prepared the way for a new breed of socially engaged reporters, men and women who could make a difference in their coverage and analysis of the news. As would become even more clear in subsequent years, Bullitt deeply identified with men like John

Reed; in fact, in 1914 he would have been reading Jack's groundbreaking series in the *Metropolitan* about traveling with Pancho Villa, as well as his early reports from central Europe. And Bullitt saw journalism as having a special impact on foreign affairs, for in these years, before the U.S. had developed a fully formed espionage division, reports from foreign countries carried the full weight of "intelligence." He quickly grew bored with the narrow reach of the police beat; soon, in fact, he was publishing analyses of the war on the *Ledger*'s editorial pages.

Journalism came easily to him, and his considerable talent showed itself early. In 1915 he was assigned to cover the journey of Henry Ford's ill-fated Peace Ship to Europe, which had as its goal a vaguely planned peace conference in Norway. (He may have first met Jack, in fact, during the planning stages of the Peace Ship, as Jack was working with Ford on a never-realized plan to start a "peace newspaper.") His pragmatism quickly won out over any idealistic admiration that Ford's project may once have held for him, and the reports he filed for the *Ledger* were biting and sardonic — and always witty. The *Ledger* promoted a subsequent series by Bullitt with a photograph and a caption that emphasized not so much the thoroughness of his reporting but the force of his personality: "a descriptive writer whose racy and distinctly humorous articles have . . . given a hearty laugh to all Pennsylvania."

On the heels of these modest — for a man like Bullitt — successes, he married, in March 1916, the renowned beauty Ernesta Drinker. Her lineage was, if possible, even more distinguished than her husband's. A Drinker was said to have been the first child of European descent born in William Penn's Quaker colony, and the family — her father was president of Lehigh University — were, like the Bullitts, among the mainstays of old Philadelphia society. But it was Ernesta's great beauty that held her apart. "I have seen men catch their breath, looking at Ernesta," her sister, who would become the eminent biographer Catherine Drinker Bowen, later wrote. By the age of twenty-two Ernesta had had so many marriage proposals, she told her mother, that she had stopped counting when the number reached fifty.

Bill Bullitt and his young wife were a striking and compelling presence. As if on cue, with his marriage his career began to take off — and Ernesta held her own as well. They combined their honeymoon with Bill's new assignment to cover the war in Europe from the point of view of the central European powers. It was a felicitous move, drawing on Bill's excellent contacts in Germany and Austria-Hungary, his fluency in German, and his deep interest in the area — for central Europe was at center stage right now. For her part, Ernesta produced a lively and incisive book of observations, *An Uncensored Diary from the Central Empires.* Already Bill was exploring the relation of journalism to diplomacy, sending home dispatches concerning the likelihood — or not — of German peace proposals.

His reporting earned him, on his return in the fall of 1916, eminence as one of the single most knowledgeable authorities on Germany and Austria-Hungary. Walter Lippmann called him "the sharpest of the American correspondents," adding, "His intuitions as to coming events," evidently meaning, particularly, U.S. entry in the war, "prove to be extraordinarily accurate." In November 1916 Bullitt was picked to head the Washington bureau of the *Public Ledger,* an important job, with the country on the brink of entering World War I.

The power of this position — or perhaps its proximity to real power — acted on Bill almost as an intoxicant. Journalism was not a large enough sphere for him; he became impatient with writing "editorials no one ever read." Ironically, his reporting was more successful than ever — to the extent that rival papers hired a personal detective to follow him to see where he got his information. Indeed, Bill had a pipeline to the path of power, having won the admiration and respect of Edward M. House — known always as "Colonel House" — the intimate adviser to President Wilson. Before long he was sending lengthy memos to House, many of which made their way to the president, analyzing the European situation and speculating on future events.

Bullitt was tired of journalism now and ready to play a role in the making of a new world order — which Wilson and House certainly believed would be the ultimate justification for U.S. entry into the war. The *Public Ledger* had been his ticket into the circles that were already making plans for the postwar world. Now that he had found his way in, and gained access to powerful men, he first tried in vain to get a position as a secretary to Wilson, whom he greatly admired. But in late 1917 House engineered for him instead a position as assistant secretary of state, reporting to Joseph C. Grew, chief of the Division of Western European Affairs. Bullitt took full advantage of his new position, keeping up a steady stream of memoranda to House on subjects ranging from the Bolshevik Revolution to points he thought Wilson should make in his next speech to Congress.

His persistence — and his talented appraisals of the global picture — paid off in 1918, when he was ordered to Paris with the American Commission to Negotiate Peace, a group of scholars and specialists informally known as the Inquiry. He sailed for Paris on December 4 on the *George Washington,* with President Wilson himself on board.

In Paris, Bullitt became secretary to Colonel House as well as chief of the Current Intelligence Section of the mission, briefing the peace commissioners on each day's news. It was an extraordinary time and place for a talented and ambitious man of just twenty-seven. The future itself was being forged in Paris. The old world order was finished, the empires of Germany, Russia, Turkey, and Austria-Hungary in ruins. New nations were scrambling to be born. Wilson's immediate agenda was to draw up a proposal for Europe's future that could be presented to a group of delegates representing the new German government; his larger agenda, embodied in the League of Nations, was nothing short of a new world order.

There were two pieces in this extraordinarily complex diplomatic situation that would have considerable impact on Bill Bullitt's future. The first was the domestic unpopularity of the League of Nations, which led Wilson to return to Washington for a month at a critical stage in the peace negotiations, leaving Colonel House as his representative at the Versailles conference in early 1919.

The other critical factor was the question mark that was Bolshevik Russia, which had withdrawn from the war against the Central Powers after the 1917 revolution. In response to widespread fears in Europe as well as the U.S. about the spread of Bolshevism, the U.S. had recently sent Allied troops into Russia to intervene in the ensuing civil war on the side of the White Army against the Bolsheviks. But the end of the war had rendered this intervention questionable, and continued war in Russia loomed as a major obstacle in the process of making peace in Europe.

Bullitt had early on foreseen the complexities of the Russian situation, and he was gratified to see the peace conference turn its attention to the topic. He had avidly watched the revolution unfold in Russia, first with wariness and later with unmitigated enthusiasm. In May 1918 he had written to House that he wished he could see Russia "with as single an eye" as Jack Reed, but that he had not yet formed solid convictions about it. Yet at the same time he was firmly opposed to intervention in Russia, influenced at least in part by a memo from Jack in his capacity as director of Revolutionary Propaganda for the Bolsheviks, which Bullitt forwarded to Colonel House. The prospect of intervention made him, as he wrote to House, "sick at heart because I feel that we are about to make one of the most tragic blunders in the history of mankind." Like Jack Reed, Louise Bryant, and other radical sympathizers of the Russian situation, he deeply mistrusted Ambassador David R. Francis. The insanity of sending troops into Russia when European peace looked imminent horrified him. In the last months of the war Bullitt wrote, in an unpublished piece of fiction, about his hopes for seeing peace come about:

> No machinery for peace on earth can bring good will to men unless the hearts of the people of the world are changed. . . . There has got to be a spirit and conversion. . . . I know a lot of men who have been to Russia since the Revolution began, and they have all suffered conversion. They are done with Emperors — political emperors, financial emperors and moral emperors. They have exiled the Czar. Taken over the banks and buried Mrs. Grundy. As a nation they have become brotherly, open-hearted, free from convention and unafraid of life. Is it possible that war may end in a similar state of grace in the rest of Europe and America?

In the early months of 1919 plans began to surface in Paris and London for a commission to be sent to Russia, as officials realized they simply did not have enough information to deal with the Russian question in their peace plan. The journalist Lincoln Steffens later said he initiated the plan, but House was so enthusiastic early on that it is difficult to sort out its origins. At every stage Bullitt was to be included in any group that went. With his usual prescience, he had made Russia his field of expertise. He was appalled that the conference had no Russian policy. Also, again perhaps influenced by John Reed, he was passionate about going. He seemed an ideal candidate — not only for his knowledge, but also because his youth and relative obscurity made him less likely to attract notice.

The mission shortly became Bullitt's mission. He chose the colleagues who would accompany him: Steffens, whom the Soviets trusted as a left-leaning observer; Captain W. W. Pettit, a military intelligence officer specializing in Russia, and R. E. Lynch, a naval secretary. He also seems to have formulated the group's purpose. This is a matter of some controversy, as Bullitt certainly did get a lot of mixed messages about what he was being asked to achieve. He would later claim that the U.S. and British governments sent him expressly to negotiate terms on which the Bolsheviks would stop fighting and begin talks with the Allies. The official line was that he was going to gather information — but the list of questions he was given to ask constituted a virtual proposal for peace. This misunderstanding was to prove a decisive factor in Bullitt's future.

For he went to Russia and succeeded brilliantly, accomplishing something that startled the Western leaders who had — directly or indirectly — sent him. Meeting almost daily with Lenin, Litvinov, and Chicherin, he helped hammer out a plan to which the Russians could agree. He later remarked that once he sat down with Lenin on March 14, of the eight terms outlined for him by David Lloyd George's secretary, not one clashed with the conditions set forth by the Bolshevik leader. Basically, Lenin offered to give up, at least for the time being, all of Siberia, the Urals, the Caucasus, the Archangel and Murmansk regions, Finland, the Baltic states, and most of the Ukraine, agreeing as well to repay the financial obligations of the former empire. Bullitt had to turn down only one request — that France would live up to the conditions of the armistice — getting the Bolsheviks to concede the point by arguing that France would reject the treaty otherwise. The only Russian condition was that the Allies formalize this proposal by April 10.

Bullitt went back to Paris on March 25, elated that the U.S. had a unique opportunity to make peace with Russia, and turned himself eagerly to writing a report for the consideration of Wilson, Lloyd George, and the conference participants. In it he noted that Russia was in deep economic trouble, mostly because of the Allies' land and sea blockade; that the social order was being restored and the turmoil of the revolution was over; and that the Bolshevik government was stable and had widespread support from the Russian people. Most of all, he wrote, he was struck by the fervor the Bolsheviks brought to their cause, citing as characteristic the remark of one young Russian: "I am ready to give another year of starvation to our revolution." His traveling companions were in agreement, so much so that they were elated on their return,

Steffens making the well-known statement, "I have been over into the future, and it works."

The mission to Russia was an outstanding achievement on Bullitt's part — and yet it was a complete bust. Lloyd George and Wilson would not agree to meet the conditions by the April 10 deadline; worse, they barely looked at the plan. Lloyd George pleaded politics — domestic feeling in the U.K. against the Bolsheviks and Lenin made it impossible for him to consider Russia's terms. Wilson was similarly encumbered, burdened also by Washington's insistence that he ensure the U.S. would void overseas entanglements by convincing the peace conference to incorporate the Monroe Doctrine in the League of Nations Covenant — in the face of the absolute refusal of the Paris leaders to give him any such concession. He also became seriously ill in early April, perhaps with influenza, perhaps with the first of his strokes. Bullitt did not give up easily. He argued until the eleventh hour for the U.S. and Great Britain to draw up what was essentially a preapproved peace proposal, but the April 10 deadline came and went.

Bullitt was personally anguished by this inaction, but equally distressed by its political implications. His distress turned to horror when he read the treaty that finally emerged from the Versailles conference two months later. Bullitt felt that it showed no understanding of events in Russia, made unfair decisions regarding such areas as the Tyrol, Hungary, and Shantung, and, by abandoning the principle of freedom of the seas, made new international skirmishes certain, skirmishes that the League of Nations would lack the power to prevent. On May 17 he submitted his letter of resignation to Secretary of State Robert Lansing and wrote a passionate letter to Wilson himself, outlining his objections to the terms of the treaty and to the League of Nations. He wrote bitterly, but from the heart: "I am sorry that you did not fight our fight to the finish, and that you had so little faith in the millions of men, like myself, in every nation who had faith in you."

Wilson, whom he had once so admired, he now counted as an enemy. When the Senate Committee on Foreign Relations, under the Republican Henry Cabot Lodge, called a series of hearings on the treaty, Bullitt, away on a fishing trip in the Maine wilderness, was served with a subpoena to appear before the senators. With considerable trepidation — he knew it would finish his political career — he agreed to testify, believing it was the only way to stop the treaty and the world it would create. He told all, producing documents the president himself had declined to produce, recreating intimate policy debates — including ones that indicated Lansing's opposition to the League of Nations — and he presented his own ignored plan for peace. The general effect was exactly what Wilson's enemy Lodge had sought: the impression that the peace conference had been a sadly disorganized, strife-ridden affair.

Bullitt's testimony was extremely effective: he was credited for almost single-handedly causing the defeat of the treaty and the subsequent resignation of Secretary Lansing. He was, of course, vilified for the same reason. His ready cooperation before the Senate gave rise to an impression that he was a man who could not be trusted with secrets. The press attacked him for his Bolshevik sympathies. In this new light, his mission to Russia seemed a self-aggrandizing and foolish gesture. Bullitt himself appeared arrogant and guided by emotions.

The diplomat George F. Kennan, looking back over Bullitt's early career, made an incisive comment:

> I see Bill Bullitt, in retrospect, as a member of that remarkable group of Americans, born just before the turn of this century (it included such people as Cole Porter, Ernest Hemingway, John Reed, and Jim Forrestal — many of them his friends) for whom the First World War was the great electrifying experience of life. They were a striking generation, full of talent and exuberance, determined . . . to make life come alive. The mark they made on American culture will be there when many other marks have faded. But in most of them there seems to have been a touch of the fate, if not the person, of the Great Gatsby. . . . They knew achievement more often than they knew fulfillment; and their ends . . . tended to be frustrating, disappointed, and sometimes tragic.

"Tragic" may be too strong a word to use in connection with the debacle of Bullitt's Russian mission and its aftermath. But his frustration and disappointment were profound. He retreated totally. He may have hoped to reenter politics one day, but now that was the furthest thing from his mind. He intended to rest: to read, write, and travel. His immediate plans, he said, with characteristic drama, were to go to some exotic retreat and "lie on the sand and watch the world go to hell."

❖   ❖   ❖

Louise Bryant first met Bill Bullitt shortly after her return from Russia in 1921. He had, indeed, retired for a year or two and then, with Ernesta, bought and restored a farm in Ashfield, Massachusetts. But his marriage was in trouble. He had never really recovered from the death of a newborn infant in 1917, and was almost obsessed with fathering a child. Ernesta's sister believed that the marriage had always been difficult, writing, in her family memoir, "My sister's early ambition to marry a man who would let her argue with him did not materialize. With [Bill] I think no woman, beautiful or ugly, could have held her own." Bill asked her for a divorce, which she would not grant him until 1923, three years after they separated. He moved to New York (though he always listed his permanent address as Rittenhouse Square) and took a job as managing editor of the Paramount–Famous Players–Lasky Corporation, a job that involved editing film scripts and managing the office, which was situated in New York City for its proximity to Long Island, where many silent films were then being shot.

Bill was never very serious about the job, though once again, with the movie empire flexing its young muscles, it put him at the center of where things were happening. He made many friends in the film world, most notably Charlie Chaplin, with whom he did his share of womanizing.

It was in his capacity as a Paramount executive that he met Louise. She approached him with *Ten Days That Shook the World*, hoping to see it made into a film. Evidently nothing came of the project, but Bill was clearly quite smitten. The earliest evidence of their involvement is a note dated September 19, 1921, addressed to "Miss Bryant," asking her to accompany him to the theater. His chase was on, though it would take him almost two years to win her.

What did Louise Bryant see in Bill Bullitt? At first, it seems, not much — beyond a pleasant dinner companion and a man in a position to help her. Jack Reed, so much admired by Bullitt, had never particularly liked him. He had written to Louise in 1919 about the mission to Russia, saying, "And did you see that President Wilson has sent Lincoln Steffens, Bill Bullitt and two or three of that sort on a destroyer to investigate the Soviets?" What he meant by "that sort" is not clear — it may have been in reference to their privileged, establishment backgrounds, their status as mainstream journalists, or their support of Wilson, whom Reed and other committed Socialists mistrusted — but the caustic nature of the remark is self-evident. Yet Bullitt had been a valuable contact in the State Department in 1918, when Jack's papers had been confiscated on his return from the revolution; he seems to have been instrumental in getting them released.

Certainly Bill's politics, both before and after the peace mission, were in line with Louise's — though she and Jack may have had reservations because of his great wealth. Louise would write proudly in her 1922 profile of Lenin that "while John Reed was as near to his heart as was ever any Russian," Lenin also "considers William C. Bullitt a man of honor" — perhaps a nod of encouragement to her suitor. With his retreat from the world of public affairs, Bullitt seemed to be turning his back on a life of propriety and convention. He would never exactly be bohemian, but he was iconoclastic enough to do what he pleased and defy the expectations of both his tightly constructed social class and the status quo in general, a quality Louise would have fully appreciated. Then too there was the mood they found each other in following her tragedy and his disillusionment. Louise had written Andrew Dasburg after Jack's death that "The only way to endure [life] is to become utterly reckless and live each day as if no dawn would come," which is not so very different from Bill's announcement that he intended to lie on the sand and watch the world go to hell.

Kennan had compared Bill Bullitt to Jack Reed, and he was not alone in drawing such comparisons. Both were well educated, enormously talented, idealistic young men with conviction. Both were handsome men possessed of charisma so powerful that it affected every human exchange they experienced. Bullitt's admiration for Jack was clearly intense, and he seems to have felt a curious identification with him. Jack's death only further elevated his place in Bill's psyche, a great man becoming a kind of superman. Bullitt himself would probably admit that her previous marriage certainly was a factor in his initial attraction to Louise.

Moreover, Bullitt was indisputably the most charming of men. As George Kennan recalled, "His was outstandingly a buoyant disposition. He resolutely refused to permit the life around him to degenerate into dullness and dreariness. All of [those around him] were the beneficiaries of this blitheness of spirit, this insistence that life be at all times animated and interesting and moving ahead." This energy, also an element of Jack Reed's disposition, greatly appealed to Louise, herself restless and always ready for excitement.

Bullitt was an emotional man, not always entirely rational. Indeed, as the debacle with Wilson suggests, Bullitt's faults were as excessive as his good qualities. Arrogance he possessed in great measure, as well as a sense of entitlement that went hand in hand with a belief in a leveling democracy. He was an impatient man who, when he decided on a course of action, could not be swayed from it. He did not take advice well. The historian Kenneth Davis described him this way: "Ardent, charming, brilliant, highly emotional, a romantic idealist of conspiratorial temper for whom everything was purest white or deepest black (from first to last he had an excessively vivid sense of plot and counterplot going on all around him), he had several characteristics of the spoiled rich boy who won't play if he can't make the rules."

Volatile, dramatic, eminently respectable but determined to play by no one's rules but his own, Bill Bullitt naturally appealed to Louise Bryant. The journey out from the frontier of her early days had been, for Louise, a personal adventure, and her marriage to Jack had been an adventure on the world stage. Life with Bill promised adventure on an equally grand, if different, scale. Life with Bill would not — would never be — dull.

14

Bill in Pursuit

Years later, when her marriage to Bill Bullitt was breaking up, Louise would write a brief history of their relationship for her old admirer Frank Walsh, to whom she was appealing for aid in her divorce. "[A]fter Jack died," she wrote,

> I was alone and without family. I had a half-brother in California who had been gassed and blinded in the war and that was my only close connection. I met Bill and he was just getting out of his first marriage. I used to see him often in New York and he was rather in love with me. . . . It really was not my intention to marry anyone. I never thought whether he was rich or poor. To this day I do not know what his income is but I suppose he is very rich. I had (I don't know why) a number of offers of marriage. . . . I was interested in Bill because he suddenly went quite to pieces, and I need someone to mother.

Though Louise wrote this when she was ill and in rather desperate straits, and in order to present her side of the story, there is no reason to question its accuracy. Louise presents herself as alone in the world, as she no doubt felt she was. She evidently had lost touch with her mother and stepfather, who were still alive, though her mother would die in 1924 — a passage that went unmarked by Louise in her personal correspondence. Her sister, Barbara — now an Alaska resident — and her brother, Louis, seem also to have dropped out of her life. The life of her half brother Floyd, a Republican, Rhodes scholar, and graduate of Stanford University Law School, was following a distinctly upward trajectory. Floyd joined Standard Oil as an executive at around this time, in 1922; perhaps he wished to distance himself from his radical sister — a desire other family members may have shared. Not so William, the half brother Louise had so vigorously defended when he passed through the Village in uniform in 1917. He was indeed blinded and gassed in the war: his occupation, on his death certificate, would be given as "disabled war veteran." Although Louise would seldom mention him either, he was the one to whom she would turn when in trouble.

That Louise was not seeking to marry anyone seems also to have been true: Bill would pursue her for two years before he persuaded her to live with him, and she would not marry him for over three years — and then only when she was pregnant. The offers of marriage may or may not have any basis in reality. Louise was fond of referring to marriage proposals; many women of her time considered it the female prerogative, yet another feminine achievement. And perhaps Enver Pasha or, more prosaically, Frank Walsh, may have spoken of marriage to her. But Louise's point was that she was living a busy, successful, independent life when Bill came into it, and that she had her fair share of admirers.

Her statement about Bill's money is straightforward in a similar way. Nobody, over the course of Bullitt's lifetime, could ever determine the extent of his wealth. Yet, as Louise wrote, it was clear that he was very rich. He evidently did not provide Louise with any details, but he didn't need to: the family background was there, his Paramount salary was clearly nominal, and he never wanted for cash — ready or otherwise. His global pursuit of Louise alone would have settled this point.

Yet Louise's reference to Bill's money cannot simply be passed over. It would be the one feature of her marriage most commented on by friends and other observers, and until her death (and long after) it would damn her in most left circles. In choosing to live with and marry Bill Bullitt, Louise would cut herself off from her radical past.

Louise may not have foreseen this at the time — or perhaps she simply did not care. She seems to have been singularly indifferent to whether her general demeanor and behavior conformed to societal — or bohemian — notions of what was proper. She had disdained as hypocritical, for instance, the objections of Village women to her fine Russian clothes, clothes she had in fact bought for very little. In general, she had never had any patience with what would in the 1990s be termed "politically correct." Perhaps because of her working-class origins, she dismissed such gestures as hollow and even counterproductive. One's convictions and actions were what mattered, not the trappings of radicalism. She had a degree of perverse stubbornness; if her embroidered boots were criticized, she might trot out her Russian sables.

She may, then, have expected Bill's wealth not to be an issue with her radical friends — or have dared them to say so if it was. As she had discovered on her visits to the U.S. in 1921 and 1922, her friends had by and large dispersed, either going abroad or turning inward. Few were active any more in radical politics. As they aged, they seemed to become more interested in raising families and achieving material comfort. Floyd Dell married and bought a house in Croton, and Andrew Dasburg had gone off to Santa Fe, for example. The narcissistic 1920s had distracted them, and many devoted more time to internal backstabbing and infighting than they did to active political work. Louise had no reason to think that marrying a rich man was any more a betrayal than were the changes so many of her friends were making in the postwar period. If it were said that she betrayed the cause somehow — as, throughout the decade and after, it would be — she would certainly have chalked it up to the same kind of petty jealousy and hypocrisy she had experienced ever since she came east in 1916.

But, of course, she played right into the hands of her detractors when she married the privileged and monied Bullitt. For it was said, inevitably, that she did so for the money. And the possibility must be entertained. There is no question that her financial situation was precarious at times. Indeed, her ferocious activity in 1921 and 1922 for the wire services must have been at least in part due to her need to repay her debts and Jack's and carve out a viable financial existence for herself. As a top Hearst reporter she was paid handsomely, but only as long as she kept busy. This required constant activity: scanning the world for newsworthy situations, pitching ideas for assignments, and traveling continually — not to mention the actual interviewing, research, and writing. It is possible that she was simply tired, and the idea of having her material welfare provided for so that she could work when she wished — for she was sure she wanted to keep working — was extremely attractive.

But Louise would probably have resented such rationalizations. She liked fine clothes, travel, comfortable living quarters, good food and wine; luxury had become her ever since the days when she bred Persian cats in the elegant home she shared with Paul Trullinger. She was vain, to be sure. But was it really weakness to want to live well?

Moreover, Louise's history and the times in which she was living must be considered in this context. Her origins were humble, and she had struggled to climb out of the working class. She was used to making moves to better her situation, from marrying the Portland dentist to leaving him. Her alliance with Jack Reed was extraordinary by any standards. Though it seems at odds with her feminism, Louise cannot be faulted for participating in a reigning ideology that assessed a woman's worth according to her husband's. In such a context, she had made two fine marriages. Her third marriage, to Bill Bullitt, would be, to most of the world, a strikingly brilliant match. Bill was a remarkable man, possessed of a global vision. He and Louise were both disillusioned — deeply so — with history's failure to play out as they had hoped. Yet Louise almost certainly believed that Bill would soon be ready to pick up where he had left off, and that she would be able to continue with her career.

But Louise's stated reason for marrying Bill in her letter to Frank Walsh — that he "suddenly went quite to pieces, and I need someone to mother" — must be considered as well. Louise had a strong maternal streak. She had taken O'Neill in hand when he was struggling with alcohol. She was often at her best when Jack was ill and needed her. She adopted those in radical circles who seemed out of place and adrift, most notably the Irish nationalist Jim Larkin. Hers was a generous spirit, and she found it difficult to say no, a quality that got her into considerable trouble.

That Bill was "going to pieces" at the time may well have been reason enough for her to gravitate toward him: she needed direction, and constitutionally looked for it in other people who needed her help. She perceived Bill Bullitt as needy at the time, and she responded instinctually.

It is noteworthy that Bill, like Jack, was younger than Louise — in Bill's case, by six years. Against the inconvenience of lying about her age — Bill believed her to be twenty-nine when they were married, though she was in fact thirty-eight, and she did not enlighten him on the subject — was set the undeniable fact that she had an edge in experience over him. Though, as her lying about it suggests, aging was a curse for a woman so vital and beautiful, Louise may have felt satisfaction, perhaps unconsciously so, in having the upper hand in this way. It fitted her image of herself as a mother figure. Then, too, with a younger man she could imagine herself younger. What she does not mention is the possibility that she may simply have fallen in love with him.

He followed her around Europe like a puppy. Her assignments would take her to Rome, Paris, Athens, and Constantinople, and Bill was at her side throughout, sometimes talking her into brief pauses for rest and, one presumes, lovemaking. He was trying to extricate himself from his marriage to Ernesta all the while, hoping as well to convince Louise to give up her career and settle down as his wife. For the first year or so, it seems, she merely suffered his presence. Her identity as a Hearst correspondent was what had defined her in the period following Jack's death, and she saw no reason to alter that. With time, that would begin to change, and the focus of her life shifted to Bill and his problems. But in 1922 she was dedicated to her career, and Bill was an afterthought.

Yet her career was undergoing a transformation, just as surely as was the course of world news. With the diminishment of Lenin's powers — he would die in 1924 — and the ascendancy of Stalin, doors in the Soviet Union were closed to Louise. Many people she admired were now out of favor there, and the vision she had shared with Jack of the revolution was becoming increasingly cloudy. Although she would do fine work in Europe interviewing important figures, this wasn't what she had aspired to in her years with Jack. She had covered history as it happened, and now she was merely reporting or commenting on the doings of the newsworthy. Her profession inevitably came to seem less compelling, and she would increasingly save her enthusiasm for the arts, acting as a patron to such young writers as Claude McKay. This sphere simply seemed more interesting in a decade of conservatism in the West and inward-turning in Russia; it was a decade of news rather than history, and Louise much preferred working on a larger scale.

Yet one of the greatest coups of Louise's journalistic career, one that other journalists would remember as typifying her skills as a foreign correspondent, closed out 1922. She became the first reporter to obtain an "exclusive interview" with Benito Mussolini, the new strongman who had just come to power after his 1922 March on Rome. This description was somewhat misleading. The Hearst chain wanted a byline story from Mussolini and had been unable to get one. Louise hung about Rome and Milan for a month, pestering the new premier and winning his trust until he agreed to do the piece — a self-serving, bombastic bit of ominous rhetoric that appeared in the Hearst papers in the third week of January 1923.

It speaks to Louise's energy as a reporter and her considerable charm that she was able to get the distant dictator to write the article. But her real achievement was in the research and interviewing she did in the course of persuading him, which culminated in a feature story appearing the week after the Mussolini "exclusive" that stood out in insightfulness from other accounts of the day.

Finding Mussolini at first elusive — she later said that he laughed when she tried to reach him, delivering the message, "Women should write about blue skies" — she went to Milan for background on his family, and there elicited some fascinating details that many, more mainstream (and male) reporters missed. In particular, she found evidence of the stormy family life that would punctuate Mussolini's reign and, in the end, contribute to his downfall. She haunted the offices of *Il Popolo d'Italia*, the Milan newspaper run by Mussolini's brother, only to be repeatedly refused information about the dictator's family or their address. She finally found Madame Mussolini in a village market with a basket over her arm, which was interesting in itself. "Madame Mussolini has never been to Rome. She has not seen her husband since he rose to the Premiership," Louise would write, providing a nice insight into the character of the dictator — and that of the Italian people. She questioned the concierge at the family home as to whether reporters often visited. "No," the concierge returned. "You are the first. Madame Mussolini cannot receive her old time friends because they are all Socialists." Louise listened for more, and the concierge, "red in the face with embarrassment," burst forth, "If she were here now she would talk to you anyway. Benito Mussolini could say whatever he wanted to." Louise clearly reveled in this evidence of domestic insubordination and what it might symbolize for Italy.

In fact, while she was perspicacious in analyzing Mussolini's program and its chances for success in Italy, Louise concentrated in her feature on Mussolini's views on women. She pressed him so hard at one point that, as she later wrote, she almost undermined all the credibility she had gained with him by referring to the political rights of women. Flushing with anger, Mussolini demanded a pencil from his secretary and wrote out the following, in English, on a scrap of brown paper, "I am not a feminist because I believe women must think only of beauty and the home, and should not concern herself with politics," signing it with a flourish. Louise could not resist adding, "I often wonder about those auxiliary legions of women Fascisti. They must annoy Mussolini greatly."

Many radicals, including her old friend Lincoln Steffens, against their better judgment, showed some admiration for Mussolini, given that no one knew what exactly were his plans; they knew only that, while virulently anti-Communist, he was willing to use some elements of Socialist policy to achieve his vision of a "healthy" society. Louise found herself admiring Mussolini's energy, the fact that he pulled no punches, and his utter disregard for convention. She especially praised this independence, describing how the dictator had been thrown out of an opera for going without the proper coat; on another occasion, he had been asked to leave a play for laughing uproariously when the work being staged was a tragedy. Mussolini was basically an adventurer, and that, more than his ideology, was the source of his appeal in Italy — and to Louise. Like Enver Pasha, in fact, he was part of a new breed who dominated the stage in war-ravaged Europe, whom Louise saw, in part, as the only really interesting figures on the increasingly prosaic foreign scene.

Energy and defiance of convention were the objects of Louise's un-qualified admiration in general. Yet she obviously took pride in her frankness about the man, and in her resolve to paint a clear picture. She would never cease to be proud of this professional quality, saying later in her life, "I wrote as fairly about Mussolini as I did about Lenin whatever were my personal feelings." She knew this left her open to the gibes of detractors: "As one critic has said, I would probably have said that Nero was rather charming to meet socially in spite of the fact that he burned Rome." And she added, with a touch of defiance, "Perhaps I might have if I had lived in that time."

The piece on Mussolini concluded with an indelible image of the dictator, an image that stands as one of the most vivid of the first Fascist dictator:

> I will always think of Mussolini as one of the oddest characters in history, and I will remember him as I last saw him in the great white and gold foyer of the Grand Hotel, under a huge crystal candelabra slouching wearily into a graceful Louis XV ivory and enameled chair.
>
> His pale, heavy-boned face showed signs of sleeplessness. His strong body was bulging over the sides of the seat; his legs were spread wide over the pale, rose-colored velvet carpet. There was a little cup of black coffee, absurdly delicate, beside his gnarled work-warped hand.

❊   ❊   ❊

Louise's second book, *Mirrors of Moscow,* her collection of profiles of key political and cultural figures in the Soviet Union of the early 1920s, appeared in the U.S. in February 1923. The reviews were almost uniformly favorable — though some, as she had come to expect, were slightly condescending. The reviewer for the *New York World* called it "a book of interest and value," adding, "Its author has the golden gift of terseness and a pretty taste in similes." Katherine Angell, writing for *The Nation,* concluded, "The book is journalism at its best and something more." But, given her championship of involved yet unbiased reporting, Louise would have been most proud of the *New York Times* review, which praised its combination of advocacy and objectivity: "Miss Bryant is strongly pro-Bolshevik in her sympathies, yet she manages somehow not to let this bias interfere too much with the objectivity of her observations. . . . It is in the personal touches that she excels, and in these she 'lets herself go' completely, without relying for her effects on any admiration which she may feel for the personages with whom she deals." The left press, such as it was at the time, took no notice of the book.

Yet Louise and Bill would barely have had time to pause to read reviews. For the backdrop to Louise's professional success was considerable emotional turmoil. Their life together, so recently begun, would be marked in 1923 by separations and quarrels, nervous collapses, and legal entanglements — as well as considerable joy, as the couple were by all accounts very much in love. Bill wanted to marry Louise in the worst way, but Ernesta was being most uncooperative about a divorce. Louise was willing to live "as any artist would under such circumstances," as she wrote a friend, "but Bill is held back by . . . restrictions which are incomprehensible to me." They kept up their frantic traveling pace, but now they followed Ernesta in America and across the Continent, as Bill tried to make her see reason and consent to a divorce.

The spring of 1923 found them back in New York City, staying at the Hotel Brevoort, a suitably marginal establishment, situated as it was on Fifth Avenue yet in close proximity to the Washington Square arch. The hotel dining room had seen countless heated arguments and frivolity among notable bohemians and radicals over the last decade; it would be the favored place to stay for Louise and Bill while in New York over the years to come. Ernesta was at the Bullitt country house in Ashfield, Massachusetts, and Bill made at least two train trips to talk to her. He also made a two-day trip to Philadelphia to consult with his brother, Orville, and family friend Francis Biddle, who would later become a U.S. attorney general.

In the meantime Louise happily renewed her friendship with the sculptor John Storrs, who by a great coincidence was staying at the Brevoort as well. Louise had met John and Marguerite Storrs in Paris in 1917 and taken an instant liking to them. But, while they had corresponded sketchily over the intervening years, they were worlds apart in their activities. The Storrses were quite wealthy, maintaining a residence in Paris and a magnificent chateau on the Loire near Orléans. "John was a sensitive fine artist, she a patient hostess who spoke wonderful French," wrote a Paris friend. Entertaining at their chateau, they "mixed artistry with Boston aristocracy."

Because of the terms of John's inheritance dictating that he spend six months of the year in the U.S. (a circumstance that weighed heavily on the couple and their young daughter), he was back in New York. John was delighted to come upon Louise at the Brevoort and took an instant liking to Bill. He reported his discovery happily to Marguerite. Evidently she had reservations about the newly single Louise, for John wrote her in mid-February reassuring her that Louise was "like a sister" to him. Bill was wonderful, he said, and the two seemed crazy about each other. She must not worry about Louise, he said. "You need have no fears of her falling in love with me. Although she may have loved a number of men I don't think she ever has more than one at a time. Anyhow for me she is just a sweet girl."

John Storrs had breakfast nearly every day with Louise, and lunch with her and Bill when Bill was free. When John was called to Boston on family business, Bill rode up on the train with him as far as Springfield, where he got off to see Ernesta in Ashfield. With John, Louise made the rounds of galleries where his work was being shown, renewing her acquaintances with old artist friends like Bill and Marguerite Zorach. In fact, Louise's new attachment to the Storrses marked a change in her life. In the 1920s she would travel in artistic circles rather than among the old radicals, many of whom now shunned her. Her new friends found nothing to object to in Bill's wealth. Those who had known her before found her, as Storrs did, unchanged, still high-spirited and charming. For Louise's part, she could still consider herself a bohemian, an outsider, despite Bill's money.

Yet she and Bill were operating amidst considerable tension, as Ernesta still would not agree to a divorce. "She is a vacuum and will hold 'legality' over us like an axe," Louise wrote Marguerite. Ernesta's weapon was her knowledge that Louise and Bill were lovers, and she pressed the advantage fully. When Ernesta sailed for Europe, Louise and Bill set out to follow — though they had to travel by different liners, Bill setting off on February 23. In Bill's absence, waiting to depart, Louise collapsed under the strain. John Storrs visited her in the hospital on March 6. "She has just tired herself out trying to get everything done," John wrote his wife. "There was no stopping her." No doubt there was more to it than that. Perhaps she had lost the energy for romantic entanglements such as the ones with Jack and Gene O'Neill, or perhaps the drama of a high society divorce was more than she reckoned, but in any event without Bill there it was simply too much.

Louise sailed on board the *Majestic* in mid-March, and Bill met her at Cherbourg. Ernesta had decamped for Italy, having withdrawn a tentative consent to the divorce. Bill was close to nervous collapse. "So much unhappiness has come to us," Louise wrote Marguerite. "Bill is really ill and in despair."

When the Hearst chain dispatched Louise to Italy to interview the colorful Italian war hero Gabriele D'Annunzio, she jumped at the chance for some distraction from the divorce drama. By early April, Louise and Bill were ensconced at D'Annunzio's estate, surrounded by walled gardens in the Italian Alps, and Louise could report to Marguerite that "Things are better with us."

A soldier whose oratory had convinced Italy to join the Allies against

Germany and Austria-Hungary, D'Annunzio was an outlaw figure not
unlike Enver Pasha. He had drawn the attention of the world when he
captured the formerly Austrian island of Fiume in 1919 and there established his own short-lived republic, which, for reasons only D'Annunzio
understood, combined anarchist and proto-Fascist elements. It was in
large part his intervention that was responsible for Italy eventually
gaining sovereignty over Fiume, despite British and French determination to give the island to the new kingdom of Yugoslavia. A great
eccentric, D'Annunzio was known to wear lace underwear, mink-col-
lared robes — and, sometimes, the brown habit of a monk. A talented
poet as well, he was a self-styled mystic who built a soundproof thinking
room in his Lake Garda retreat and was said to use cocaine. Photographs depict a short, ugly man, but women nonetheless considered him
very attractive. He had lived for nine years with the celebrated actress
Eleonora Duse.

Louise too was drawn to this strange man, a dandy who owned a
hundred suits, kept a stable of greyhounds, and drenched himself in
Acqua Nunzia, a perfume he had made himself from an old recipe used
by nuns. Of course, any iconoclast appealed to Louise, but especially one
who at once defied convention and commanded world respect. She may
indeed have had some romantic involvement with D'Annunzio in 1921
or early 1922, as she spoke of him as a great friend long before she
officially interviewed him. Perhaps, like Enver Pasha, he had offered
one of the non-American proposals of marriage she told Frank Walsh
she had received before taking up with Bill. Evidently what drew her
were his charismatic personality and his energy, qualities she had admired in the Turkish adventurer and in Mussolini. Like Bill, he had
withdrawn from politics, and was now indulging in the equivalent of
lying on the sand and watching the world go to hell. Any political
leanings he might have were sympathetic to Fascism, but his eccentric-
ity was such that he could not conceivably be of much use to the more
purposeful Mussolini.

In the first of her two feature stories on the man she called the
"warrior poet," Louise wrote little about his political activities (though
the article was called "D'Annunzio Can Find No Menace in Turk
Revival") and instead described the parties at Lake Garda following the
publication of his book *Adventure without Adventure.*

"During the festivities a sensation was created by the arrival of Mr.

William Christian Bullitt of Philadelphia," she wrote, in the kind of statement whose meaning is difficult to decipher. D'Annunzio, she wrote, had rushed forward, embraced him, and took his own *arditi* celebration medal — an honor conferred on him by the black-shirted shock troops — off his lapel and pinned it on Bill's, kissing him, and exclaiming, "I decorate you for high moral courage at Paris, when no one dared speak against Woodrow Wilson." Though D'Annunzio no doubt did so decorate Bill, it was a curious, slightly irrelevant detail. Perhaps Louise was announcing her own approval of Bill's actions at the Paris peace conference and was anxious to let her readers know that, while he was out of the policy-making picture at home, he still had the admiration of world leaders, however renegade.

Yet an ominous note had crept into her reportage. Why refer to Bill as "Mr. William Christian Bullitt of Philadelphia," a pompous form of address, with its emphasis on social background, a factor she once would have scorned? Why the emphasis on parties over politics? Why the attention given to ceremonial decoration? For that matter, why the mention of her lover in the first place?

15

The Cloud General Prevails

*B*ill Bullitt never did anything by halves. When Louise was sent to Constantinople by the INS to cover the emergence of the new Turkish republic, and Bill, in her words, "came along," he made sure their Constantinople experience would be unforgettable. He rented a veritable palace on the Bosporus, a villa attached to a magnificent kiosk built by Kyöprülü Hüsseïn Pasha in the sixteenth century. The so-called golden room, the salon of the kiosk, extended out over the waters of the Bosporus, with dramatic views on three sides. The wooden walls were elaborately carved; above them rose a frieze of painted panels of flowers in blue jars, and in the center of the floor was a marble fountain. The room had been named for its ceiling — called by a turn-of-the-century traveler "the most precious thing of its kind in all Constantinople, if not the world" — a filigreed and ornate rose and gold dome that reflected the shimmering light of the Bosporus.

Its glory was faded, the kiosk nearly decrepit, which only added to the enchantment of the setting. "The fountain is still," continued the same observer, "the precious marquetry has been picked out of the doors, the woodwork cracks and sags, the blue jars and the flowers grow more ghostly, the gold of the ceiling grows dimmer every day." Yet, "the golden room has a charm that it can never have had when the afternoon sun first shimmered into it."

Louise may well have appreciated the faded luxury, but she was on assignment, and took a room in which to work in the modern Hotel Tokatlian, located in downtown Constantinople. Ernest Hemingway, also a correspondent covering Turkey at the time, remembers Louise working the same beat; he often saw her in the cafés. She was projecting a series of articles that could, like her Russian stories, be collected in a book, and was out on the streets of Constantinople gathering material. Her subject was the rise of Mustafa Kemal Pasha, later known as Atatürk, and his efforts to drag Turkey into the twentieth century by transforming the shrunken, defeated Ottoman Empire into a secular, modern state. Kemal's nationalist movement had only benefited from Turkey's loss in the war, and, having chosen Ankara as his base to galvanize Anatolian efforts in the Turkish War of Independence, moved the capital there in 1923. With some European recognition, Kemal sought to consolidate the new republic at the Lausanne conference, held over the months of November 1922 to July 1923. The sultanate was abolished in the fall of 1922, and in July 1923 Turkey would be declared a republic. Kemal was elected its first president in October.

No admirer of the new strongman, Louise believed that the recognition the Treaty of Lausanne gave the new republic would goad Kemal into starting new wars. She sensed a dictatorial tendency: "Kemal, ruling his party with an iron grip . . . recently declared Turkey to be a Turkish 'republic' with himself as President as well as head of the [Grand National] Assembly. Since there is not a government in Europe so completely controlled by one man the label of 'republic' is an absurdity."

While some Western journalists believed Kemal's secular bent would help the cause of the liberation of Turkish women, Louise's impression was quite the opposite. She reported on a suffrage meeting held in Constantinople, which sent a request to Ankara that women be allowed to vote in the elections two years away. From the new capital came a sharp reply: women were ordered not to attend political meetings but to "serve the state by looking after their own and orphan children."

Louise went off to Ankara in July, when the new republic was declared. For what seems to have been the first time ever she complained about the conditions under which she had to work, writing Marguerite Storrs that her ten days there were enough for a lifetime. The picture she painted sounded grim indeed: malaria had struck the rude outpost; her quarters were infested with bedbugs, mosquitoes, and flies; there were no sanitary arrangements, no electric lights or bathtubs for three hundred miles. Ankara, she wrote, was a mud village — "as primitive as China."

Conditions in Constantinople were not much better, though she could at least retreat to the villa on the Bosporus. Hemingway provided a vivid picture of the city in 1923 in an article published in the *Toronto Star*. The city left the overwhelming impression of dust, he wrote, which was almost ankle-deep — except when it rained, and Constantinople became a sea of mud. "There are no traffic rules and motor cars, street cars, horse cabs and porters with enormous loads on their backs all jam up together. There are only two main streets and the others are alleys. The main streets are not much better than alleys." There were 168 national holidays, he complained, remarking that every smart resident wanted a job in a bank. But the nightlife was wonderful: nobody dined until after nine, and smells of roasting sausages, potatoes, and chestnuts stirred the warm night air.

"Bill is more calm," Louise was able to write Marguerite shortly after they arrived there. He had discovered a new ambition and was writing a novel. *It's Not Done* was shaping up to be an acidly satirical portrait of old Philadelphia society, with thinly veiled Wanamakers and Wideners and other scions of Rittenhouse Square. The hero is John Corsey, a class-bound Philadelphia aristocrat who works as a newspaperman. He falls in love with the sculptor Nina Michaud, a character closely modeled on Louise, but marries Mildred, the socially proper woman his mother has chosen for him, who bears a distinct resemblance to Ernesta. Mildred is frigid, and an unhappy John is impotent. At the novel's end he rediscovers Nina, who has borne him an illegitimate son, a Communist rebel hero clearly based on Jack Reed. When John learns of the young man, he asks Nina to marry him, and she dismisses him airily; the suggestion, to her, is absurd.

It seems clear Bill was writing with the express purpose of settling some old grievances, as well as intentionally shocking his native Philadelphia. By contemporary standards, *It's Not Done* was racy as well, containing frank sexual discussions and steamy love scenes between John and Nina. When it was published in 1926 it became the talk of old Philadelphia — though Bill's brother made a valiant attempt to buy up every copy in town. It was a financial success as well, selling more than 150,000 copies and going into twenty-four printings.

Reviews were mixed, but almost every reviewer admired the sheer energy of the narrative. A typical review read: "Unusual talent is necessary to write a book that is so good at the same time that it is so bad. Mr. Bullitt stumbles into every pitfall ever laid for the unwary novelist, but he goes sprawling with such fine abandon, leaps up so blithely, and rushes on so obviously unhurt that the spectacle is rather magnificent." The *New York Herald Tribune*, while admitting that the words "literary value" would not be used in connection with the book, described it as "a triumph of audacity" and a "tour de force."

Yet Bullitt would not try his hand at writing fiction again; when a childhood friend, George Biddle, sensing his restlessness, suggested that he write another novel, Bill said simply, "Why should I?" Having done it once, he had proved he could, and he saw no need to so exert himself again.

The book was dedicated to Louise. Like the novel's hero, who finds himself writing fiction when he once again takes up a sexually fulfilling relationship with the unconventional Nina, Bill found that his relationship with Louise gave him the freedom he needed to undertake such a project. With her encouragement, the book took shape quickly in 1923; letters to the Storrses give updates throughout the year on Bill's progress. Louise was reporting, Bill writing; they were very much in love. Bill's Turkish neighbors nicknamed him Bulut Pasha, or Cloud General. In late July the Cloud General and his lover and muse learned that they were going to have a child, and their lives seemed full indeed.

Bill Bullitt "was crazy for a child," wrote a friend of Lincoln Steffens to Steffens's sister. The death of his infant son had shaken his marriage to Ernesta — and was reflected in his novel in the damage caused by the loss of a child to the marriage of the hero and to his conventional life. At the age of thirty-seven, Louise had had considerable difficulty getting pregnant, as she confided to Marguerite Storrs. On her return from Ankara in July, she took to her bed, thinking that the unhealthy conditions there had made her ill. When Bill and Louise learned that her symptoms were due to pregnancy, they were elated but cautious. Her doctors feared complications. Bill did not want her to travel. And he was protective in other, more curious ways, refusing, for example, to let Louise read aloud from Joyce's *Ulysses*, lest it influence the unborn baby.

"It was here," Louise later wrote in a letter to her old lawyer friend Frank Walsh, that "Bill began to make me lose myself as a person working as an artist or journalist or whatever you might call me. He wanted me to stop doing newspaper work and when I was asked to go down to some little Balkan town where trouble was stirring, he persuaded me to give up my work." She persuaded him to allow her to complete one more assignment on the conditions that he accompany her and that on her return she would cable the INS her resignation.

Wracked by war with Turkey, Greece nearly went to war with Italy in August over Italy's bombardment of Corfu. The country had long been divided between royalists and republicans, and at the time of Louise and Bill's trip in September 1923, the antiroyalists, under General Nikolaos Plastiras, were in the ascendancy. It was an extremely complex and potentially dangerous political situation. It was the kind of assignment to which Louise was accustomed and the kind of situation in which she thrived. Again, she scored a coup. King Constantine, who had enjoyed two embattled reigns as the country's ruler and had been deposed finally in 1922 and had fled to Palermo, had a policy of never giving interviews. But Louise, staying in the Villa Igea in a room just above his, noted that he was accustomed to taking long walks on the beach in the very early morning hours and began to take long walks herself — and got her interview. Back in Athens, she got an interview as well with Constantine's son and successor, George II (though, by the time it appeared, the king had been exiled).

At this point, Louise told Frank Walsh, "I sent a cablegram to my papers saying, 'My newspaper career is finished.'" Although she placed the blame for this move squarely on Bill, it is at least as likely that she acquiesced fairly readily to his request. For the time being she was very taken up with beginning a family. Although she chose to represent it differently, it was not at the time an altogether dramatic decision; she may indeed have intended to take up her work again after the child was born. Yet Bill asked that she make the formal gesture, and it was more fateful than she may have imagined.

Back in Constantinople, they made plans to move to Paris, where they could live in material comfort, as soon as Bill completed his novel. They were also very, very nervous about Bill's divorce, as both wanted to get married now with as little delay as possible. Ernesta had come to terms, but delays still cropped up. Louise and Bill thought the divorce would come through in October, but then it was pushed back to November 1.

In the meantime, Louise wrote Marguerite exuberantly about her plans for the future: "We are so excited and happy over everything." She was longing to get to Paris, where she could live and write and "really learn French." She outlined for Marguerite the accommodations she wanted, perhaps hoping her friend could help find them. She wanted an apartment with at least six rooms, furnished, with steam heat and an elevator, near the Luxembourg Gardens, and she and Bill could pay $300 a month for a six-month lease. She wanted to have a happy winter, she said, and to entertain a great deal. Though she made a passing reference to writing, she did not mention her resignation from the news bureau.

By the time Bill and Louise returned from Athens, Bill was able to report that "Louise is very well; indeed, we are very happy and everything connected with my affairs has worked out perfectly." In October, with the first draft of his novel completed, they left Constantinople for Paris, taking rooms in a hotel while they looked for a place to live. They also had a great deal to do prior to their marriage, for the French required a multitude of documents. They had not only to gather the usual birth certificates and the like (and Louise, of course, had none because of the San Francisco fire), but also to produce an acceptable copy of Jack's death certificate. Because Russia's Bolshevik government was not recognized by France, his Soviet death certificate had to be specially approved. All of this had to be done under wraps, for Bill (and possibly Louise as well) was most concerned about the timing of the divorce, their marriage, and the birth of the child, which was due in February. They were married on December 10, 1923, in Paris, in the utmost secrecy. The marriage would not be announced in the New York papers until the following July, when it was reported that Louise Bryant had married William C. Bullitt "a year and a half ago," in Rome.

The quarters Bill found in Paris rivaled the Constantinople kiosk in luxury. They leased a house in the avenue des Princes which belonged to the British writer Elinor Glyn, who had made her fortune turning out novels that were then considered quite scandalous. The most notorious was the 1907 *Three Weeks*, based on the 1903 murder of Queen Draga of Serbia, in which the heroine pays for her lapse from virtue with her life.

Glyn had decorated the house extravagantly. Bill, who had excellent taste in such matters, described it as "perfect for its type, Louis XV — Elsie De Wolfe, soft gray curtains, mauve taffeta curtains, green walls, curtained glass doors." The mauve and violet bedroom, however, bordered on the outrageous: it was dominated by an enormous canopied bed over which hung (somewhat perplexingly, given the canopy) a mirrored ceiling. Guests shown the room were gratifyingly scandalized, and Louise and Bill treated it as a great joke.

Despite the baby's imminent arrival, Bill and Louise took up an active, even flamboyant social life immediately after their marriage. They entertained dozens of visitors in their fashionable home and staged at least one ambitious party. Their closest friends during this period were the Storrses — John Storrs's diary for 1924 shows almost daily visits to or outings with the Bullitts — and Clive Weed, a cartoonist with artistic aspirations whose wife had taken up with another man, leaving him somewhat adrift and dependent on the Bullitts. A steady stream of friends and acquaintances passed through the avenue des Princes establishment. Almost all remembered how elegantly dressed and hospitable they found Louise: she had discovered high fashion, though for the time she was limited to maternity dresses designed by a dressmaker Marguerite had recommended.

The Bullitts would become noted for taking up talented young artists and musicians in Paris and introducing them to their elevated social circles. Their favorite of the moment — though in fact they would champion him for several years — was the avant-garde American composer George Antheil. Not yet thirty, Antheil was a boyish figure with a blond fringe of hair who dressed, according to one observer, "drolly," often in oversize clothes. Since his arrival in Paris in June 1923 he and his wife, Böske, had taken rooms over the bookshop of the literary patron Sylvia Beach. In his autobiography, the aspiring novelist and composer Bravig Imbs described how George was "caught up in a whirl of receptions and teas and parties" given by "the American society in Paris, fragile and frivolous," and remembered a grand reception given him at the home of Bill Bullitt (who Imbs described as "a hearty, charming and slightly silly gentleman"). The journalist Sisley Huddleston remembered the same occasion in the Bullitts' "much-mirrored" residence. Imbs described how Louise, "dressed in a gown of white fringe," greeted them graciously and immediately befriended his companion ("in three minutes [they] had discovered mutual friends and in five were talking chiffons"). Also among those present at the reception, where Antheil's "Quartet" was played, were the hostess Natalie Barney and Sylvia Beach.

But Louise was preoccupied with the impending birth of her child. She sought advice from Marguerite, who had also had a difficult pregnancy. And she turned to an old friend, Lincoln Steffens, now living in Paris. Steffens had, of course, traveled to Moscow with Bill as part of the abortive peace mission. While he had made his reputation in muckraking journalism, a milieu in which he was the mentor and friend of Jack Reed, he was also, at least by the 1920s, something of an establishment figure. Never a Marxist ideologue, he marched to his own drummer, and thus may have had none of the sort of pecking-order prejudices Louise's Village friends had about Bill. As such, he was comfortable in Louise's world as well as Bill's, and a friend from the past for both. He became that much closer a friend to them as a couple. They would grow still closer when, that summer, Steffens found his companion, Ella Winters, pregnant. He turned to Bill, who, with his experience regarding the timing of pregnancies and marriages, gave him some good advice. Steffens and his new wife celebrated their wedding in August 1924 with a breakfast with the Bullitts and the sculptor Jo Davidson and his wife. Steffens was determinedly loyal in keeping the secret of Bill and Louise's actual marriage date, telling his sister, in February 1924, that they had been married for a year, when in fact they had been married just over two months.

As Louise's due date approached, she wanted Steffens to be there for the birth, perhaps because he was her closest tie to Jack and her old life, or perhaps because she unconsciously viewed him as a kind of father figure, or at least a family member. Steffens was in London, however; as he later wrote his sister, "Louise kept writing that I must come home; she couldn't have the baby without me, and Billy wanted me there too."

She summoned other friends as well. Clive Weed called just as Louise was beginning labor — she had decided to have the baby at home — as did George Biddle, now a painter living in Paris. When Louise's pains began in the early afternoon of Sunday, February 24, Bill summoned Steffens, who lingered for several hours, but the baby did not arrive until just before midnight that evening. It was a girl.

Steffens left the fullest account of the child's birth, in a letter to his sister Laura — and a curious account it is. Bill and Louise both wanted a boy, he said, and told him that if it was a girl, Steffens could keep it. When the baby was born, Bill called his hotel to say "it was not merely a girl; it was a terrible, dominant female. It came out kicking Louise, it made a mad, bawling face at Billy, grabbed the doctor's instrument and threw it on the floor."

Whether Louise shared Bill's strange admixture of distance and cynicism is not clear. He seems to have been determined to present the birth of his daughter in a jaded, bored, and even callous fashion — perhaps to conceal his considerable pride, perhaps to distance himself should the baby, like his first, not thrive. According to Steffens, Bill's response to what he thought was the newborn's personality was even stranger: "I shall have nothing to do with it," Steffens remembered Bill saying to him, evidently taking seriously the conceit that, since it was a girl, the baby belonged to Steffens. "I am afraid of it," Steffens remembered Bill saying. "All I ask of you, as parent, is to keep it off the streets. But I doubt that you can do even that. It will do whatever it wants to do. I can't give it to you because it isn't mine. The baby belongs to itself. Even Louise feels that it is an utter stranger, self-reliant, aggressive, cold." The baby, Steffens added, almost as an afterthought, was "a pretty child . . . handsomer than any new-born baby I have seen." The Bullitts named her Anne.

If Bill's reactions, as reported by Steffens, seem to have crass overtones, he may have calculated them to seem so. Bill might have felt it would not do to show too much emotion at the birth of a child. And he was clearly proud in describing Anne as self-reliant and belonging utterly to herself. There is no question that, with Anne's birth, both Bill and Louise became loving, even doting parents. Hazel Hunkins-Hallinan, Louise's friend from suffrage days, remembered receiving a letter from Louise, describing "the ecstasy of motherhood," a letter "filled with emotion and love and exhilaration." Of course, as was common among the very rich, care of the child would largely be relegated to servants, with the parents reasonably free to continue living as they wished.

"At first [Bill] was all for a big family. Then he would not have any children except one," Louise wrote in her 1930 letter to Frank Walsh about her marriage, implying that Bill's attitude was a blow to the new mother. Yet it is just as likely that, since Louise was thirty-eight and had

had a hard pregnancy, it would have been considered difficult and even possibly dangerous for her to have another child. But both parents had affection in abundance for Anne, and soon they were talking about taking on another.

While in Constantinople they had become interested in an eight-year-old Turkish boy of royal descent named Refik Ismaili Bey. The son of an Adrianople hereditary grand vizier who was killed by Bulgarian patriots at the end of the Balkan Wars of 1912 and 1913, Refik was imprisoned as a baby with his mother by the Bulgars. Mother and child were later released and allowed to return to Constantinople, penniless. Refik was looked after by other members of the fallen Ottoman dynasty in Constantinople, but Louise and Bill felt that he needed a proper education and a real home.

Refik, known, unaccountably, as B.C., visited the Bullitts for an extended period in 1924 and became part of their family in late 1925. John Storrs's diary for 1924 records dining at Bill and Louise's with a Turkish "royal family" on March 10, just weeks after Anne's birth; most likely Refik was in this party, and was invited to stay with the Bullitts. By August they were thinking of asking him to join their family. "Our little Turk loves us so much," Louise wrote John Storrs in the early summer, "that I don't think we will send him away."

Louise had gone, seemingly overnight, from being unencumbered and independent to a married woman with a family and an active, even frenetic, social life. Managing such an existence soon became a full-time affair. Louise inherited her first servant, a Basque maid named Hortense de Jean, from Elinor Glyn. Later two more Basques joined the household: another maid, Louise, and a cook named Alfred. A nanny from Belfast, Mary Morgan, was hired — "the best kind of nanny," remembers Louise's daughter, one with voluminous dark blue costumes that reached the ground. There was also an Albanian butler, Philippe, whom one observer remembered as "a spectacle," dressed in an Albanian costume of light blue silk covered over with designs braided in silver. When, on a visit to the Bullitts, the journalist Vincent Sheean noticed Philippe carrying out a tray of cocktails, he asked Bill whether he did not mix his own. "Certainly not," Bill replied, "I'd as soon think of cooking my own dinner." In the spring the entire establishment — including a West Highland terrier named Pie Pie and a number of parrots, which flew free in Louise's bathroom — moved to larger quar-

ters at 10 rue Desbordes-Valmore, an elegant house set back from the
street and fronted by a lovely garden.

Visitors to the Bullitts during this period remembered, mostly,
Louise reclining on a sofa dressed in beautiful gowns; her favorite
designer was the current Paris rave Paul Poiret. Her old Portland friend
Sara Bard Field, at last married to C. E. S. Wood, came to call — and
thoroughly disapproved. "After Jack Reed," she later commented, "to go
to something so superficial, very rich and very society — I couldn't
believe it of Louise." Indeed, the record of Bill and Louise's whereabouts in 1924 and 1925 suggests a very strenuous social life. John Storrs
saw them almost daily, and John and Marguerite had them as frequent
guests at their chateau on the Loire.

Throughout the spring of 1924 Louise posed for a bust John was
modeling; at one point the work grew so demanding that he moved in
with the Bullitts for a week. In the end, though, Bill and Louise, "but
especially Bill," as John wrote Marguerite, did not like the completed
head. "Louise was very nice about it," he continued, "[and] said they
would rather keep our friendship than say they like it and then feel there
was an insincerity between us." Still, Storrs continued to rework the
head over the next year.

While Louise modeled, was fitted for gowns, and ran the household,
Bill similarly lived the life of a man of leisure. The Auteuil racetrack
was only a ten-minute walk away, and attending the races absorbed
them both, Bill especially. A favorite companion was the newspaperman
Harold Stearns, who wrote a column covering the races for the *Chicago
Tribune* under the name Peter Pickem. Unlike Stearns, Bill was interested in the horses mainly, the gambling being secondary, and was
particularly good at evaluating jumpers. After the races, Bill brought
friends at the track home — especially for Sunday lunch. Sunday lunch
at the Bullitts became something of a Paris institution in some circles, in
fact. George Antheil described one such affair, remarking that the Bullitts "seemed very happy together. They would reverently take us into a
little nursery in the back of their house to pick up the covers over a little
bed and show us their baby daughter." The Antheils could occasionally
get the Bullitts over to their apartment for a reciprocating dinner, "but
they accepted only rarely. For which we couldn't really blame them —
they were so popular."

George Biddle remembered this time as Bill and Louise's "happy period," each of them "as content as two such people, each liking to be the center of attention, could be. Louise was at her peak — captivating, and an able journalist, and Bill seemed loving." But troubles were inevitably brewing. Bill's novel was accepted and due out in 1926 from Harcourt Brace, and the ex-diplomat was restless. He was showing signs, too, of the nervous troubles he had suffered during the divorce from Ernesta. Although he could well afford it, Bill was never entirely comfortable with a life of rich idleness. Harold Stearns offered a trenchant analysis of Bill's restlessness:

> Bill was intelligent, friendly, rich — yet sometimes he made me uncomfortable, and I think it was what used to be called a curious 'inferiority complex.' I mean, Bill envied what he couldn't have been, even had he tried, for he had too much money — and something he would have despised really had he been forced to be it — that is, a Bohemian. He envied newspaper men, 'free lance' writers, irresponsible artists, talented musicians, sometimes (I think rather childishly) even Casanova-like amorous sure-fire heroes — and the truth is, he would have been bored to death, had he been forced, consistently, to be any one of these things.

Of course, this restlessness, this desire to be "Bohemian," was part of what had made John Reed such a fascinating figure to Bill, and what later drew him to Louise. But as Stearns's remark illustrates, that attraction contained the seeds of its opposite.

Louise, too, was beginning to grow restless. "I live a useless life," she told a visitor to the Elinor Glyn house. Much of the time in the beginning of her marriage to Bill she had to spend simply learning how to be rich — and it was a daunting task. With the implicit example of the gracious and cultivated Ernesta before her (who, as a divorcée, was on her way to becoming a preeminent interior decorator), Louise had to master running a household: the management of servants, the ordering of food and planning of menus, house decoration, flower arrangement, keeping a social calendar. She had to learn how to navigate the world of high fashion. She cultivated her manners, learning to affect the tone of the idle rich. She studied her husband to learn what things a person of her station was supposed to deem important and what not so. If, in the process, she temporarily lost sight of her own values, her own sense of what was important, her own self, it must be remembered that her useless life was keeping her very busy.

16

Parties and Problems

D id Louise mind her cosseted and pampered new (and, as she said, useless) life? Did this woman who once bought and set free all the game birds in the Constantinople market and who allowed her parrots to fly free in her Paris home, see herself as little more than a bird in a gilded cage? Seemingly overnight, she had turned her attention from causes to clothes, from politics to parties. It seems safe to say that in her few quiet moments she may have wondered at the new direction her life had taken. But it is also undeniable that her demeanor, her value system, and even perhaps her character took on a different coloration in the early years of her association with Bill Bullitt. She became arch, cynical, and even affected. Her speaking style changed: in numerous letters, for instance, she wrote of behavior that was "chic" or decidedly "not chic"; though this particular idiom was fashionable at the time, it is difficult to imagine the woman who had been at the barricades in revolutionary Russia judging by these standards. Less superficially, her concern for those without her privileges seems to have temporarily evaporated; now she spoke airily of "servant problems." Perhaps in deference to Bill's studied indifference to world events during the 1920s, she showed little interest in what was going on outside of her small sphere.

Of course, it is likely that this new bearing was only a mask, that underneath she was still the same restless, bohemian soul, passionately concerned with social justice and genuinely egalitarian in her worldview.

Fundamental changes in character are rare indeed. And Louise would insist later that she had never compromised in her marriage to Bill, that she always struggled against being "made into a Bourgeois," as she would later put it. And as the marriage to Bill broke down, Louise gave up the trappings of wealth with ease, as well as any affectations she may have picked up along the way.

In that sense, the change in her demeanor might best be understood as self-protection: she lived in the world of the very rich, and she must behave as if she belonged there. But this leads to another inescapable conclusion: she wanted to belong there. Whatever her motives in marrying Bill, there is no question that she initially liked the comforts and luxuries of her new life. Indeed, she embraced them, and it was arguably natural that she would come to behave as if she were accustomed and entitled to them.

Set against this, however, are the other probable motives she brought to the match. Her early years in the West and Portland were marked by a desperation to seek a wider stage, to escape the confines, first of a lower-class and then a middle-class existence. Life with Jack brought no such material relief, but it offered its own, more substantial rewards, and Louise came into her own. But, more relevantly, life with Jack was almost a perpetual trauma — privately, in the sense that issues of free love agonized them both, and more generally, in the sense that separations were constant and Jack's health precarious and that both were constantly in danger of being arrested. She felt agony during his last journey to Russia, with the months in a Finnish jail and the false report of his death. Their brief joy at their reunion in a very uncertain climate quickly gave way to Jack's horrifying illness, delirium, and death. Undone by grief, Louise had buried herself in her work, enjoying the prestige of a successful international correspondent while crisscrossing the world at an exhausting pace. She may have felt that she wanted and deserved a respite. She was open to experience, and the world of the rich was exciting in a quite different and far more comfortable way than the other worlds she had inhabited. If her brief sojourn into that world was, at least in the beginning, enjoyable, it is not hard to understand why.

Louise's old lover Andrew Dasburg, after an elaborate dinner with Louise and Bill in the late 1920s, was struck by the contrast between the elegant, detached Louise and the passionate rebel he had once known.

His friendship with Louise was over; this would be the last time he would see her. Louise's life with Bill — a round of parties, cynicism, and formality — seemed completely foreign to him, and he could attribute it only to a kind of randomness in the universe. "I couldn't escape the feeling," he commented about the evening, "that as well as I had known her, the wife of William C. Bullitt was a complete mystery to me. It was not only the scene itself, the three of us together and she so calm, as if it were the most natural thing in the world, [that] was unreal, but that all that had happened was — somehow beyond reason, as though all of us were pawns in a game of chess. As if what happened was beyond her wishes, if she had any, and beyond mine — as if control had left us somewhere along the way."

Though Dasburg's analysis was insightful, it is important to note that such randomness, such seeming meaninglessness, characterized the lives of many rich American expatriates in the 1920s. Bill and Louise were hardly atypical in partying through the decade. Educated and talented Americans were pouring into Paris in droves, fleeing the cultural sterility of America, now undergoing three straight Republican administrations. They were drawn as well by the downward spiral of the franc — the dollar was at 26.76 francs when the decade opened — and by the low price of passage over, about $80. In Paris, liquor flowed freely, while Prohibition was in force at home; indeed, as the poet William Carlos Williams wrote, "Whisky was to the imagination of Paris of that time as milk was to a baby." The expatriates congregated in the afternoons on the *terrasses* of the Café du Dôme and the Café Rotonde, at the intersection of the boulevard Raspail and the boulevard du Montparnasse, and stayed there far into the nights, piling up saucers.

Paris in the 1920s was also, of course, home to a great flowering of art and literature — both in French and English — a movement in which Bill and Louise could see themselves. Bill's novel, *It's Not Done,* debunked Philadelphia society in the tradition of Sinclair Lewis's hugely popular *Main Street;* closer to home, Bill saw himself as a contemporary of the Paris residents Sherwood Anderson and F. Scott Fitzgerald. The novel, of course, was a popular success, but it enjoyed no lasting critical renown, and, by the time it was published in 1926, Bill had grown bored with fiction.

He still thought, however, that in 1920s Paris he might be an artist of some kind or other; he just had not yet found his métier. As had Louise, who turned to writing poetry and, perhaps under John Storrs's tutelage, to sculpture. For the rest of her life she would travel with a mound of wet clay covered in a Turkish towel, ready to be shaped when the mood struck her. When the baby was old enough, she gave her lessons in sculpting and drawing.

Her last journalistic effort had appeared in *The Nation* in August 1925. A piece called "A Turkish Divorce," it reported on the end of Kemal's marriage to his childless wife and was one of her most strongly feminist efforts. She not only deplored Kemal's cruelty but also celebrated the women leaders of Turkey — "brilliant women, superbly educated, tolerant and progressive," especially Halide Edib Hanoum, the women's movement's "brightest star," who "had fought through the war at Kemal's side."

Journalistically, after inauspicious beginnings the decade was proving to be an especially rich time; Paris itself enjoyed a journalistic renaissance. Colonel McCormick launched the Paris edition of the *Chicago Tribune,* and jobs were available for reporters at the newly opened Reuters, Associated Press, and United Press desks, at the English-language *Paris Herald,* and even the Paris desk of the *Brooklyn Eagle.* Yet Louise was not part of it. This kind of journalistic work was far from the glamorous career of a foreign correspondent. Working on a Paris desk was a job, and she had no need of a job as such. It had been three years since she had sent off the fateful wire to the International News Service announcing her decision to end her career. A number of factors no doubt influenced her decision: her husband's strong feeling that she should not work, the demands of motherhood, and — perhaps paramount — her new position as the wife of a rich man. But it was a decision that she would come to regret very soon and that she would try valiantly to rescind.

Louise's sculpture has not survived, and the one example of her poetry from this period that has (a fragment about skyscrapers scribbled in a letter to the Storrses) suggests that it was decidedly mediocre. The only record we have of her playwriting is her description of a drama she was finishing in 1926; she said it contained "rough stuff," the last act being set in a Harlem café. But she needed the illusion of an artistic career in a way that Bill did not. It gave her a certain freedom — she kept her own studio — and made her feel that she was still an outsider at a time when she was, in reality, living a very establishment existence.

But as patrons and friends of artists, writers, and composers, Bill and Louise shone. Virtually every memoir of the twenties contains references to "evenings" at the Bullitts. Konrad Bercovici, an artist and chronicler of European gypsy life, wrote of "dining often" with Bill and Louise, whom he remembered as "beautiful, sparkling." At a musicale of Antheil's work staged at the Bullitts', Bercovici, who was no fan of Antheil, was seated next to an amused Louise, who enjoyed seeing him enraged.

The relationship between patron and artist has always been complicated. The patron can be truly generous, but in other cases resentful, unsure whether the artist is repaying the effort. The artist typically displays a range of emotion, running from gratitude to a sense of entitlement to resentment at dependence upon the patron. On the whole, however, Bill and Louise navigated this minefield with great success. Perhaps one of their most representative beneficiaries was the painter Marsden Hartley. Called by Alfred Kreymborg "the long lean eagle from the hills of Maine," Hartley's was an arresting presence. Probably homosexual, "Marsden was . . . a kind of grandpapa to us all, male and female alike," wrote William Carlos Williams. But to Bill and Louise, Hartley was abjectly dependent. When they were in Paris, he commonly took almost all his meals at their house; when they were in America, he was a frequent guest at their country home. Throughout the decade, his letters — most often to John Storrs — reveal how closely tied his fortunes were to theirs. He was almost frantic when he did not know their whereabouts. But in a telling remark to Storrs in the summer of 1927, he said wistfully that he hoped the Bullitts would return soon to Paris — for then he could at least have some sense of family.

The letters of Hartley, Storrs, and other painters whom Louise and Bill encouraged make it clear that the artists were made comfortable in the Bullitt household. Little Anne was probably one of the favorite children in Paris, with many unofficial artist godfathers (George Biddle was her official godfather — though Bill would later say George was so designated because his wife had just left him and he was brokenhearted). Artists paid tribute to her in the form of two small, child-sized chairs: one, by Marsden Hartley, painted in blue with red hearts and white flowers, was inscribed with her name; the other, bearing an embroidered seat, was designed by George Biddle and showed the baby Anne cradled in the Bosporus.

As for the more well-known artists and writers of the time, and especially the ones to whom Gertrude Stein referred when she said, "You are all a lost generation," Bill and Louise were, perhaps typically, closer to the hangers-on in the expatriate scene than to the principals. A representative example was Robert McAlmon, once thought to be a writer of great promise, but who now whiled away his days in cafés talking about writing. Having made a marriage of convenience to the writer Winifred Ellerman, known as Bryher, the daughter of shipping magnate Sir John Ellerman, McAlmon spent his money on the struggling Contact Press, which published his friends Ernest Hemingway and Gertrude Stein. It was easy to make fun of McAlmon, and he was openly mocked by his contemporaries (the newspaperman Morley Callaghan composed this ditty: "I'd rather live in Oregon / and pack salmon / Than live in Nice / And write like Robert McAlmon"), but he was nevertheless a highly valued and respected friend to many of them. He shared with the Bullitts their interest in Antheil, whom he supported for two years. He feted Louise and Bill in 1924 with a party on the Champs-Elysées, and they in turn gave him a big farewell dinner when he left Paris for a trip to the States. In fact, Louise's invitation to John Storrs suggests the desperate edge that was creeping into the Bullitts' socializing. She advised John that the dinner would probably move from the Bullitts' to dancing in Montmartre, and she admonished him to be prepared to be "wild." Louise wrote, "We think we need some sort of spree. Everyone is blue and serious and needs a shaking up — do you agree?" A postscript directed him: "And *dress.*"

Another representative friend was Kitty Cannell, an artist turned fashion writer, who was in Paris waiting out her divorce from her husband, Skipworth Cannell. She was, for a time, the girlfriend of Harold Loeb, and both would be viciously satirized in Hemingway's *The Sun Also Rises* as Robert Cohn and Frances Clyne. Kitty can be said to have returned the favor in a backhanded way by introducing Hemingway to a fashion editor for Paris *Vogue;* Pauline Pfeiffer in turn taught Hemingway's first wife, Hadley, how to dress — and, in an almost farcical turn of events, took Hadley's place as Hemingway's next wife.

Cannell was a link with Louise's past. She had been a Provincetown Player, and in fact had acted in Louise's play *The Game;* the two would become very close over the decade. Cannell remembered having dinner with Louise almost nightly for a time in 1926 when Bill was out of the city: "Almost every night I had dinner in the Bullitt home, and later she and I would go dancing in Montmartre with whatever attractive American was around." In the stormy period that lay ahead, Cannell would become one of Louise's staunchest defenders.

Cannell's alliance with Louise illuminates the plight of the expatriate wife in Paris in these years, which could be, as often as not, quite lonely. The wife who didn't work found herself alone in a strange land when the parties were over, and, like Louise, she sought out kindred souls. As a historian of the Left Bank has put it, traditional American expatriate culture — with the significant exception of the lesbian subculture — was by and large masculine:

> To the extent that Left Bank culture was dominated by men, the distinction between male authority and female subservience was precisely the convention that would not be put aside in this new environment. Expatriate women found themselves fighting in Paris the same kind of conventional attitudes toward women that were more strictly enforced back home. To a certain degree the Paris environment was perhaps more frustrating than that of Baltimore, for instance, because it promised a freedom that it could not entirely ensure.

This irony was surely not lost on Louise, and as the decade wore on she began to chafe at the limitations of the role of the expatriate life. Sometimes, it would take a benign form, like going out dancing with Kitty Cannell with whatever good-looking young men they could find; later, as the situation grew more intolerable, her actions would take more desperate form.

Just as Cannell passed through Hemingway's orbit, so too did the Bullitts. They were friends of Ford Madox Ford, the English writer and inveterate partygiver who ran *The Transatlantic Review*. Ford in many ways mentored Hemingway, a position that earned him considerable resentment from the younger writer, whose relationships with such father figures was marked by profound ambivalence. Some of this ambivalence may have colored his response to Bill Bullitt, but he found enough in Bill to dislike that he spoke of him with pure malevolence. Much of this hatred grew out of Hemingway's anti-Semitism, and from his overarching competitiveness. In a letter to Fitzgerald, concerning the people Hemingway was seeing in Paris, he wrote dismissively about "Bill Bullitt or Bull Billet a big Jew from Yale and fellow novel writer."

Yet Hemingway was a frequent tennis partner of Bill's and a regular companion at the racetrack; John Storrs's diary for 1924 indicates that the Hemingways moved in the same social circle. In years to come Louise was to figure in a well-known Hemingway anecdote, and she had a few stories of her own to tell that illustrated his much-vaunted masculine prowess.

Louise was the subject of an intense little exchange between Hemingway and the poet Archibald MacLeish, which suggests that Hemingway was considerably more ambivalent about Bill Bullitt's wife than he was about Bill himself. In fact, both he and MacLeish may well have had some strong feelings about her. MacLeish wrote Hemingway saying that he had been hearing claims from "Mrs. Bullitt" that inflamed his possessiveness about his own friendship with "Pappy." Louise, MacLeish wrote Ernest, said she knew "all about Pappy which I dare say he doesn't know himself. . . . I wont have more than every other person I meet knowing ALL about Pappy. It gets monotonous." Hemingway answered, with some heat, "As for Mrs. Bullet [sic] knowing all about me the bitch where in hell does she get that stuff. I went to their house once and refused many an invitation and didn't ask them to ours — and believe that is the best way to make half-kikes know all about you. I did know her when her hair was blonde but that was in Constantinople and besides the wench was surrounded by naval officers."

The tone of Hemingway's comment was certainly vicious, especially the hysterical reference to "half-kikes," extending to Louise his belief that Bill was Jewish. Yet Hemingway couldn't disguise that when he first met Louise in Constantinople he was immediately drawn to her. Blond was his favorite hair color, and the fact that it was dyed undoubtedly fanned his interest, given his near fetishism about dyed hair and sexuality. But surrounded as she was by other men, and men in uniform at that, he simply was not able to make any inroads — and she earned his contempt ever after for her frustrating inaccessibility. She became a bitch and a wench, and he pushed her out of his mind. Much of this was typical Hemingway. But Louise had a way of enthralling egotistical men, and then leaving them fulminating about her lack of response.

In the years 1924 and 1925, Louise and Bill traveled almost incessantly and changed residences several times. It is against this peripatetic background that the beginnings of their breakup, and the onset of Louise's decline, can best be understood. As Louise herself said later, "This story gets so involved."

They would travel between America and Europe many times, but a summer visit to the U.S. in 1925 was fairly typical. Louise wrote in detail many times to John and Marguerite Storrs during this trip, and her descriptions say a lot about her attitudes and behavior and the pattern of her life with Bill in America. Before settling in at Ashfield, she wrote, they spent several weeks in New York. She was feeling the strain of traveling with the baby and a retinue of servants, writing that New York with such an entourage was enough to put her in an early grave. In fact, keeping French servants in America was to become a particular trial, for the servants had six-month visas, and would each have to make a trek to Canada once during each American stay to reenter the U.S.

In New York, Louise and Bill took in all the latest plays, including "the new O'Neill play" — most likely *All God's Chillun Got Wings* — about which Louise was airily dismissive. "I could have wept [at the play] — so cheap — so much like all he hated, and once, ten years ago, strove to get away from and did for a while." In familiar egocentric fashion, her personal involvement with O'Neill clouded her critical judgment — for *All God's Chillun* could never reasonably be described, even by its detractors, as "cheap."

But Louise's new position in the world, it seems, had affected her opinions. With all the snobbishness of an expatriate American on a visit to the U.S., she wrote that they had also taken in Maxwell Anderson's *What Price Glory*. Though she found it "fine," she regretted Anderson's "appalling worship" of the "lowbrow," a worship she found particularly American and one she felt reached its apogee in American enthusiasm for the works of Sinclair Lewis: "If one spits and says 'gosh' and 'goddarn' the whole thing is a success at once." Of course, Louise was not alone in decrying her country's artists' discovery of the lowbrow — the terms "lowbrow" and "highbrow" had come into fashion in the 1920s. But with her working-class roots and her passion for justice, it is a bit strange that Louise did not welcome the fact that much American literature and art were moving in a socially realistic direction and attempting to reflect more truly ordinary life.

But the Louise who had wed Bill Bullitt was, after a year and a half of marriage, a changed person. She reported to the Storrses, for instance, that "strangely enough" she had enjoyed a visit to Rittenhouse Square, where Bill triumphantly presented her to Philadelphia society. Though their reaction is nowhere recorded, it is doubtful that many old Philadelphians would have received her without significant reservations. The mere fact that she was by birth Catholic would have influenced their welcome. But Louise noted only that she was feted at several dinner parties, that Philadelphia seemed a very "gay" place, and that such family members and friends as Orville Bullitt and Francis Biddle were lovely hosts. Still, it could not have been lost on her that Bullitt's fortune was based in part on his father's coal interests in the area, and that the Main Line was not so very far from the anthracite mines where her father, Hugh Mohan, had labored as a child.

Louise's letter describing her American visit closed with plans for her return. She refused to live in Boulogne, evidently referring to a house on the avenue Victor Hugo that Bill would later take despite her protests, but instead was "praying" for a place near the Luxembourg Gardens. She added a note to Marguerite at the end expressing two somewhat contradictory sentiments: first, that she hoped to begin writing and was "stimulated" by America to do so; second, that Marguerite should have come with her, for it would have been such fun to pass "the time having babies and learning to run Ford's automobiles."

In July 1925 Louise and Bill's "little Turkish boy" came to live with them — permanently, they believed. Newspapers noted the arrival of the "Turkish prince," reporting that Refik Bey would return with the Bullitts to Paris in November "after taking advantage of American surgical facilities to have his tonsils removed." Refik was fully accepted into the family. He would become Louise's fiercest protector: "His eyes shot fire when anyone looked at [Louise] too long," wrote Konrad Bercovici, who had to stop greeting Louise with a kiss for fear of those eyes. On grand occasions, Refik would act as Bill's doorman, wearing "the gorgeously tasseled costume of an Arnaut."

Family photos indicate that Refik was very much a regular schoolboy and a devoted big brother to Anne. While some observers remembered his elaborate Turkish dress, others emphasized his resemblance to an ordinary American boy. Thomas Chappell, the son of a Yale friend of Bill's, noted that on one visit to Ashfield Refik repeatedly begged him to play the children's card game slapjack. The boy attended the little public school in town for the months he was there.

The household at Ashfield in 1925 was, it seems, very happy. The setting was beautiful, atop a small mountain in the Berkshire foothills. Giant sugar maples shaded the south side of the house, where a very long driveway curved down the slope. Across it the land dropped; in the valley was a long meadow, a brook, and woods beyond that. On the west side of the house was an orchard — Bill had turned Apple Hill Farm, as it was known, into a going concern — and on the east a large hayfield and then more woods. The site was almost totally secluded, and Louise and Bill took full advantage of the fact, often spending the days naked; there was a dammed-up pond for skinny-dipping.

The original farmhouse, built around 1811, had been turned into a veritable showcase by Ernesta Bullitt in 1921; she wrote a witty article on the difficulties of country house renovation for *House and Garden*. An ell on the farmhouse, previously used as a cowshed, had become a dramatic two-storied drawing room; beyond it, the pigsty and horse stalls were now guest quarters, as was the hayloft above. The drawing room, with a balcony at one end and a fireplace in the middle of the west wall, was the focal point of the house; here the Bullitts entertained extensively. Frequent guests included Archibald MacLeish and his wife, who would settle on a nearby farm that Louise found for them, and the poet Edna St. Vincent Millay and her husband, Eugen Boissevain, who would drive over from their Berkshire farm to visit. Anne Bullitt would later remember being sent to Millay's guest room to ask what she wanted for breakfast; the poet replied, "Champagne on the lawn at dawn." It speaks to the atmosphere of elegance and romance that reigned on the estate that her request was not considered at all inappropriate.

Both Bill and Louise indulged their passion for pets to the fullest at Ashfield. Louise in particular was a great romantic about all animals. She and Bill added more dogs to their household, Louise a Doberman pinscher she named Captain, and Bill a German shepherd named Brenda; the two would later bear pups. Bill so loved Brenda that he had her head carved in a plaster pediment at one end of the drawing room. (He wanted Anne carved, naked, on the opposite pediment, but Anne's nanny — and a defiant Anne — vetoed the idea.)

They also had horses, Louise's named St. Bridget, and Bill's, St. Peter, and were very enthusiastic riders. Bill particularly loved jumpers; he often said that his fondness for jumping grew out of his impatience at being stopped by a fence. Louise, of course, had been an experienced rider since her days on Grandfather Say's ranch; Bill had had lessons for years as a boy and was an excellent judge of horses. It seems ironic that the beginning of Bill's troubles could be traced to his falling off his own horse, an event that would signal the disintegration of the marriage and the years of Louise's decline.

In the fall of 1926, with the Bullitt family back at Ashfield, Bill was a deeply troubled man. Everything had seemed — to outsiders — to have been going well that spring in Paris. Bill and Louise had moved to an apartment at 11 rue Las-Cases, "a house alone worth seeing, old and grand," wrote Lincoln Steffens to his son. "I guess Bullitt has been having some more aunts and uncles dying. He is rich, richer than ever, and their apartment is gorgeous, the lower floor of a house in a court with a picture garden in the rear."

The main criticism of Bill had always been his outsized pride. The art critic Bernard Berenson, who entertained Bill and Ernesta at the Villa I Tatti in 1922, found Bill "consumed with self-importance" ("but truthful in the main"). Hutchins Hapgood, who had known Louise in the Village and had visited Bill and Louise in Paris, found Bill "proud but haughty." Bill was not a large man, he later wrote, but "he struck me forcibly, as full of self-confidence and pride: like Theodore Roosevelt when Governor of New York as he descended from a train at Albany with his tall hat and Prince Albert coat; I felt in Bullitt the essence of physical and mental pride."

Others were struck by the disjuncture between Bill's deliberate effort to be bohemian and the extent to which he remained bound to the rigidities and affectations of Philadelphia Main Line society. As Vincent Sheean wrote, "I never knew anyone so conscious of social and economic privilege even while pretending to make fun of it." He seemed at war with himself; more probably, he was at war with some demons from his past, possibly his father in particular. His father had marked him out for the law, and immediately after his father's death, Bill renounced the profession. His father hated Europe, and in his will "expressed the hope" that his children not live abroad, a wish Bill flagrantly defied. In sending up Philadelphia society in his novel, and in marrying Louise, he cast himself as a rebel. Yet he remained deeply committed to propriety and convention and could be snobbish in the extreme. When he married Louise, for instance, he used the Moën spelling of her family name, rather than Mohan, and gave her middle name as Fiennes —

another name taken by the Say family, and a considerably more aristocratic one. Some might say that he repeated this pattern of ambivalence,
of submissiveness and insubordination, in his dealings with Woodrow
Wilson.

Moreover, he had an imperious manner, even with those he considered his equals: "He just would not abide anyone with anything less
than a first-rate mentality," wrote his cousin Orville Horwitz. A related aspect of his character was his violent changefulness, once again
prefigured by his fierce disillusionment with and rejection of Wilson: "If
he liked you, he thought you were God, and anything you did was
perfect," said his cousin. "[A]s soon as you did something that wasn't
perfect, he took it as a personal affront." In other words, he would often
turn totally against someone whom he'd earlier idolized, a characteristic
that would come into play as his marriage began to unravel.

The conflicting aspects of Bill's personality were not lost on Louise.
In her letter to Frank Walsh she would describe Bill's going "all to
pieces" in 1923 and needing "someone to mother" him, summoning her
in desperate telegrams and then not being there when she turned up.
Louise gave almost no further information about these episodes, but
at the very least they indicate that this smooth, urbane man of the
world was inwardly troubled. Leaving the eminently respectable Ernesta Drinker for the preeminently bohemian Louise Bryant had been
stressful, to be sure, but without further details his reaction to this
situation seems excessive; other, preexisting factors must have come
into play.

Bill had complained about his compulsions for some time, and by
1926 they were multiplying and precipitating some troubling incidents
in his daily life. He gave some examples: If he started out walking a
straight line, he felt that literally nothing, not even a chasm opening up,
could stop him, that whatever course he set for himself he had to carry
according to some prearranged plan. One time he was in the middle of
the street when he saw a truck bearing down on him at high speed; he
froze, and jumped out of the way only at the last second.

But most troubling to him, an accomplished horseman, was the time
he fell off St. Peter in the summer of 1926. "George, can you even
imagine my falling off my horse?" he said to George Biddle. He was
shocked that he could lose control in this manner — that he could not
remain, as it were, in the saddle.

Louise and Jack, center, in Petrograd in 1917, in the heart of the revolution

The Winter Palace in Petrograd, transformed almost overnight from the czar's residence to Bolshevik headquarters

Louise in Russian garb

Louise with Jack's coffin at the Labor Temple in Moscow, October 24, 1920

Above left: Louise's admirer Enver Pasha, 1920
Above right: Frank Walsh, labor lawyer and Louise's ardent suitor in the early 1920s
Right: The aristocratic William C. Bullitt, whom Louise would marry in 1924

Opposite page
Top left: The artist John Storrs. He and his wife, Marguerite, were Louise's closest friends during her years with Bullitt.
Top right: Lincoln Steffens, once a mentor of Jack Reed, became a close friend of Louise and Bill's during the 1920s.
Bottom: Louise as a rich man's wife

Louise acted as a mentor and patron of the young writer Claude McKay, even as she grew seriously ill.

The artist Gwen Le Gallienne, whom Bullitt named in his 1930 divorce suit against Louise

A mannish-looking Louise, circa 1930. She was suffering the ravages of Dercum's disease and the ailments that accompanied it.

Bullitt with Anne in 1933, after the divorce. Louise claimed she never saw her daughter again.

Anne Bullitt in 1934, age ten

There were other accidents that spring. "Bill broke a leg walking out a door and almost a head falling from a horse," Louise wrote, in her new, arch fashion, in a letter to Marguerite. Later, however, she would describe the events of that fall more seriously. In Ashfield, she wrote, Bill "developed the utmost of eccentricities. He would lie in bed for days and be afraid of anyone coming into the room. . . . I finally got him started abroad but he stayed about a week in the Brevoort Hotel [in New York City] refusing to get out of bed." Though there is no corroborating evidence for this, if Louise is to be believed — and there is no real reason she should not be — Bill was having a nervous breakdown.

Bill knew enough about psychology to know that some unconscious impulses were at work. "It dawned on me," he explained to Biddle, "I had *wanted* to fall off my horse. Fortunately I've read a great deal about psychoanalysis. I know all the theories. And I knew, George, that there was only one man for me to see: Freud." Psychologically shaky though he was, Bill had not lost any of his hubris. He would consult with no mere practitioner but only with the great man himself.

The Bullitts sailed back to France on board the *Paris,* arriving on November 13, and took rooms for themselves and their entourage at the Foyot, near the Luxembourg Gardens. Bill left at once for Vienna with Louise, leaving Anne and Refik in the servants' care. The story Bill later told about gaining access to Sigmund Freud may well have been an invention: he said a manservant, opening the door at Freud's house, said the doctor was ill and could see no one. Bill said, "Just give him my card and tell him Mr. Bullitt called." Freud must have been waiting at the top of the stairs, for he came running, saying, "You're not Mr. *William* Bullitt, are you? Mr. Bullitt of Philadelphia? I have been so interested in your work, I have wanted to know you."

There are reasons to believe that Freud *had* followed Bill's work with interest. The Austro-Hungarian Empire had been dismembered by the Treaty of Versailles, and the Viennese patriot bore Woodrow Wilson a special grudge. He may have followed the League of Nations Senate hearings closely and known of Bullitt's denunciations of the president. Then, too, as some Freud scholars have pointed out, he no doubt knew Bill was a very wealthy American, and during the 1920s Freud desperately needed money to support his *Verlag,* the publishing house devoted to disseminating his work and that of his followers. (Bill would, in fact, be very generous to Freud. It was he who provided the funds to get

Freud out of Europe during World War II.) In any event, he agreed to take Bill on as a patient, and the analysis lasted about a year, interrupted by visits to America.

Bill sent Louise back to Paris, where she found a house in the rue Montalivet, although she commuted frequently to Vienna. The dancer Mura Dehn recalled meeting Louise and Bill several times in Vienna, and being terribly impressed by Louise. She admired the "negligence" with which Louise wore her clothes, and thought she looked "as if she were born to elegance. . . . I quite fell in love with her, she was so free, so lighthearted, so beautiful. Unforgettable. . . . To me she seemed half bird, half tiger. There was a glamour about them both — he so very good-looking, she with that shining quality."

Yet Dehn also sensed that Bullitt's charming exterior was a mask that covered an almost palpable anxiety. She remembered her mother giving a dinner party at which there was a receptacle of paper napkins — then a new product — at each place setting. Bill compulsively pulled out napkin after napkin, wiping his brow and then wadding them up, until he was surrounded by a small pile of them. This detail, minor as it was, stayed with Dehn.

Another occasion, reported by Louise in her letter to Frank Walsh but corroborated by other sources, was more ominous. Louise came to Vienna and found Bill barricaded in his room at the Hotel Imperial, his furniture blocking the door. He screamed at her to get away, and it was hours before she could get him to open the door, after summoning friends and the hotel staff to help. It was the first of many embarrassing and painful scenes.

But it would be Louise, not Bill, who would star in most of these scenes. By the end of 1927 the most florid of Bill's symptoms — the compulsions, the nervous collapses — had abated, and Bill could be said to be well. The next three years would be very trying for him, but he would survive. His character flaws stayed with him, though a kinder way to put it would be to say that he remained an extremely eccentric man. And, for the thirty-seven years of life that remained to him after his divorce from Louise in 1930, he seems to have been, outwardly at least, a singularly happy man, with a remarkable appetite for experience.

In 1936, Bill denied categorically having been in treatment with Freud, and his family still denies it. It seems a curious thing to want to conceal;

for a wealthy, internationally oriented American to consult Freud or some other well-known analyst was almost *de rigueur* in the early part of this century. On one level, psychoanalysis was a great luxury, and did not even necessarily imply serious mental problems. Bill said that he was not treated by Freud but that he studied with him, and it is true that he did go on to study with the doctor. In the late 1920s he had begun work on a manuscript about Versailles, to which Freud wanted to contribute a chapter, and later he and Freud would collaborate on a psychobiographical study of Woodrow Wilson (though Freud's part in the actual manuscript that resulted, *Thomas Woodrow Wilson: A Psychological Study,* has been hotly debated). It is possible, and would have been characteristic, that Bill very quickly turned the analysis into an intellectual discussion and that that was how he remembered it and presented it to others.

The family has insisted that it was Louise, not Bill, whom Freud treated. Some evidence for this is to be found in a rather charming anecdote about Anne Bullitt that Lincoln Steffens passed on in a letter to his son: "I saw a dandy Irish girl for you today. Ann [sic] Bullitt is her name. She is about two years old now, talks a lot in two languages and says jolly things; 'My mama is my friend,' she said one day, and when someone asked her if her papa wasn't also her friend, she answered, 'Oh no, he is God.' Her mama repeated that to Freud one day, and he was delighted. 'That child is articulate,' he said. 'I have a theory that many children think that. Yours is the first to actually say it.'" It is possible that Louise told Freud of the child's comment on a social occasion — for it was not uncommon for Freud to socialize with his patients and their families. But at least two others have said that Louise saw Freud once or twice as part of Bill's analysis. In any case, the reports of friends that Bill, not Louise, was Freud's patient are too numerous to ignore, and Anna Freud herself verified the fact.

How the rumor surfaced that Louise consulted Freud is not hard to guess, however. For by 1927, when Bill was deep in his analysis, Louise was very ill, and almost overnight began acting bizarrely. Unlike Bill, who soon sprang back from his trouble with his usual buoyancy, Louise did not recover. While her husband lay on Freud's couch, by now engaging the great man in talk of Woodrow Wilson's perfidy, Louise was beginning her long, tragic decline.

17

The Inroads of Illness

*I*n June 1926, Louise first mentioned being ill in a letter to the
poet Claude McKay, whose stories she was reading and circulating among editors and agents in New York. She wrote that she
had been unable to finish his stories, saying she was "so sorry — but I
have been ill — in bed" and a week later wrote that she was still laid up.
While bouts of mysterious illness had long plagued Louise, this episode
seemed different. In retrospect, her collapse in New York in 1923 seemed
to her to have signaled the onset of her new trouble.

Apart from a general malaise and periodic "collapses," the disease
first appeared as a terrible and persistent pain in her thigh. To her horror,
the thigh turned lumpy and disfigured. In later months, other parts of
her body were affected; her jaw grew swollen and disfigured, and her
arms became lumpy as well. A photo attached to a 1929 application for a
passport shows a mannish-looking woman with a doughy, uneven face.
Many believed she had some form of elephantiasis, for she did not seem
to be gaining weight in a natural way. Still, in the early stages of the
disease, the only thing she could think to do to recover her appearance
was to starve herself. At various times she would get her weight close to
one hundred pounds, but the lumpiness and disfigurement would not be
dieted away.

Nor would the pain, which was overwhelming, and which the doctors
could not initially account for. Whether because of the pain or the

disease itself, she began to suffer mental confusion. Her daughter remembers Louise waking up Bill in the middle of the night, saying, "Bill, I'm changing. Something horrible is happening to me" and admonishing him to find someone to take care of Anne.

Though at first it seemed unrelated, she also began to drink heavily. Though before her marriage to Bill she had been a rather strict teetotaler, she and Bill participated fully in the general, and rather desperate, merriment of the 1920s, which included prodigious drinking. Both seemed to handle it well, but for Louise that had begun to change. Stories about her outrageous behavior when drinking began to surface, often in connection with general impressions that the marriage was souring. About his friend Bill, the journalist William Shirer wrote, "The old restlessness returned and with it a good deal of drinking and cutting up." The daughter of family friend Konrad Bercovici remembered an occasion at the American embassy when Bill struck an inebriated Louise in the face; Refik went for Bill in his adopted mother's defense. A Croton resident remembered a party given by George Biddle, who had bought a house there with his new wife in 1925, at which there was a great deal of drinking; Louise, she said, saw Bill dancing with another woman, and grabbed a pair of shears and threatened her.

These stories abound, many of which need to be taken with a grain of salt, factoring in the possible motives of the tellers. Bill Bullitt's own stories, given in his divorce testimony in 1930, are no exception. He was hardly a disinterested party. Yet his were recounted with a chilling specificity, down to exact dates — he seems to have kept a diary of his marriage's deterioration — that lends them a certain horrific credence.

He stated that his wife's heavy drinking began in 1926 and 1927. He described an incident at a 1927 party in New York City given by Theatre Guild founder Lawrence Langner, a party that, he added self-importantly, was of great moment to him because he had written a play he wanted to discuss with the guild. A musician began to play for the company. Louise was talking loudly to her neighbor, and would not stop even when asked to do so by the hostess. Finally, according to Bill, she "stood up and called out that it was an insult to intelligent people to have a pianist interrupt their conversation" and stalked out of the house in a rage, leaving an embarrassed Bill behind.

Bill was exasperated by his wife's behavior, but he remained patient for a long time. He was still very much in love with her, and seems to have understood that she was indeed changing, in ways that were perhaps beyond her control, that "something horrible" *was* happening to her. But he dropped his fundamentally sympathetic attitude when it did not serve his purposes. In his divorce testimony, for instance, he would say nothing of Louise's underlying illness, instead telling story after story of her drinking. Even then, however, he said that the hostility and irritability she showed when she was drinking "were not natural to her. . . . When she was not drinking she was always an extraordinarily charming and distinguished person."

He consulted scores of experts about her case, but they had seen nothing of the kind before. Almost defeated, he sent Louise to London in March 1928, staying home at the family's new quarters at 44 avenue Victor Hugo with Refik and Anne. In London, her illness would at last be diagnosed.

A rather hair-raising record exists of Louise's stay in London, a cross between a last will and testament and a suicide note. Begun on the back of a bill from the Hotel Metropole (a bill that mercilessly recounts "spirits consumption"), the note begins, "Please burn all my papers. And all Jacks personal papers. And love and love to Anne & Bis [shorthand for B.C., or Refik] and you. Louise." On the same note she identified herself and advised whoever found the document to contact "Mr. William C. Bullitt."

Another note attached to this one, seemingly written in a hurried, overwrought state, appears to be a request for her possessions, written by a woman clearly intending to go her own way, and who also intends to keep only those things that she brought to the marriage. If it also seems that Louise was inordinately fond of her possessions, it should be noted that those possessions sound remarkable indeed:

All my clothes — including my shoes, boots, evening slippers. Also all my embroideries and baubles that Jack and I got in Russia and the ikons and the Turkish things. Also, all the things I put in that black box (that included the Bokhara robes, etc.) I want all that [illegible] and other glass in the window of my room. I want my lamps, my pewter — I want the Early American rugs I bought and my Spanish shawls and my tortoise shell combs and my tortoise shell sets. I want the round silver 'slave' mirror and all the books I left in my little study. I demand [crossed out, replaced by "want"] those overstuffed chairs I had made for me (from the money I made myself) [parenthetical material added later] and all the books in my bedroom all the embroideries and linen that I bought.

Another, barely legible, note, read, "I must work very quietly. I cannot ask you to work with me any more. I know you for what you are. I have to — unhappily — take what I have. [Illegible] will leave you one day when she knows — Louise."

Louise was clearly in desperate straits — writing perhaps late at night, drunk, in the Hotel Metropole. From her turmoil emerge some salient points: she still loved Bill and her family, but felt she could no longer live with him because of some betrayal, perhaps with another woman. She was determined to regain her independence, and to work. But she doubted her ability to carry on. What she had learned from the doctors in London was that her ailment did have a name — it was adiposis dolorosa, or Dercum's disease — and that it was progressive and incurable. The mystery of Louise's condition took on a new, quite horrible reality.

Adiposis dolorosa was first identified, ironically enough, in Philadelphia, by Dr. Francis X. Dercum, who found it in three patients in the Blockley Hospital in 1892. A decidedly strange malady, it was — and is — extremely rare, or rarely diagnosed. It typically occurs in menopausal women between thirty-five and fifty years old, and almost never in men. A contemporary description calls it "a rare condition characterized by painful lipomas [fatty deposits] usually on the extremities." (Louise once said she was "ill of some curious sort of chalky deposits under my skin.") Even today, there is no treatment for the disease, though liposuction, or removal of the fatty deposits, can provide some relief from pain — without checking the course of the disease. No such procedure was known in the 1920s, of course.

The etiology of Dercum's disease is still not known. To complicate the picture, mental confusion is another symptom — or sequela — of the disease. "The psychic changes are varied, consisting chiefly of irritability alternating with depression," a 1922 medical text says. "Failure of memory and apathy are often noted, and occasionally there is dementia." Most accounts also include alcoholism or drug abuse or addiction as a feature of the disease, though it is not clear whether the relationship is organic or whether the patient turns to such substances for pain relief.

A complicated disease with a degree of mental involvement, and incurable. A somatic disease with possibly psychosomatic components, or at least ones that could not be quantified or verified. As such, Dercum's disease was, and is, open to all kinds of interpretations, including the following passage from a recent journal article that manages to question the pain the presenting patient says she feels, to malign her for alcohol or drug abuse, to suspect her of "faking it," and to locate a window of opportunity for the plastic surgery profession:

> The clinical picture of adiposis dolorosa makes a lasting impression on the examining physician. The patient is typically an obese, asthenic woman who appears to have a low pain threshold. She has an unusual distribution of fatty tumors, and her complaint of pain in these tumors seems out of proportion to physical findings. Alcoholism, emotional instability, and depression are common, and narcotic pain medicine is frequently requested. The patient is easily dismissed as a malingerer after a brief examination. However, liposuctioning of the painful fatty tumors appears to be both practical and effective. While adiposis dolorosa is an unusual disease, it is one that plastic surgeons can recognize and treat.

One gets the distinct impression that someone afflicted with Dercum's disease is now — and most likely was in Louise's time — rather a bother to the physician. Typically obese (though Louise was not), menopausal (and thus, given the prevailing sexist assumptions about menopause, a medical vexation), miserable (the adjective "dolorosa" refers to the fact that the patient often came to the office weeping), and complaining of pain the doctor could not make sense of, a sufferer was hardly an attractive patient, much less a challenge — or even a human being whose woes might be alleviated.

This, in fact, may be the most salient point. Though the disease is not fatal, nothing (short of liposuction, which was not available to Louise) can be done for the Dercum's disease sufferer. Even the most compassionate doctors may have been frustrated by such a case. Unfortunately, frustration could easily change to contempt — especially if the patient asked for narcotics, a request most doctors would regard as confirmation of their own powerlessness, and a symptom of what the physician might feel was an accompanying moral degeneracy.

The role of alcoholism in the disease would have further complicated doctors' reactions to Louise's condition. Long before the days of the medical model of alcoholism, experts considered drinking to excess a failure of will, a sign of moral weakness or even depravity. A woman who drank was particularly stigmatized, for a woman drinker given to outlandish behavior did not conform to prevailing beliefs about woman's proper demeanor and place. A drinking woman, especially if she were menopausal, was considered almost an abomination of nature. And, of course, Louise was diagnosed before the days of Alcoholics Anonymous or any other effective treatment for alcoholism; the drinker of her day was shunted off to sanatoriums or left to die on the street.

Beyond the pain, the mental confusion, the effects of heavy drinking (which, of course, would have intensified mental confusion and general despair), and the probable indifference or contempt of her doctors, the Dercum's sufferer had to contend with societal ignorance about the disease. It was simply so hard to explain. The patient's changed body shape alone made it embarrassing to discuss. To try to explain the connection between fatty deposits under the skin and mental confusion and alcoholism was, again, humiliating, and difficult if not impossible — especially since the connection was baffling, though undeniable, even to physicians. Not surprisingly, Louise seems to have told, after Bill, only one person about the disease. Those closest to her knew nothing of it, though many guessed, because of her appearance, that she had a disease. Others merely dismissed her as a drunk.

Louise and Bill visited many doctors before they got a diagnosis, and they continued to do so, hoping to alleviate her pain and, later, to control her drinking. But Bill's first reaction, typically, was to consult the source — Dr. Dercum himself. Reached by telephone, Dercum did not even need to see Louise; he simply responded, "Pray that she die as soon as possible."

Louise and Bill did what they could to carry on, and indeed there would be many good times in the two years after her 1928 diagnosis — though there would be much misery as well. Both were working; by 1928 they had focused on playwriting, and their plays came very close to being produced in New York (though none of this work survives, Bill's best hope was apparently about Woodrow Wilson, an unlikely subject). Louise kept up her sculpting and story-writing as well. As her condition grew worse, she felt correspondingly compelled to emphasize that she was hard at work. She sent a letter to John Storrs in 1929 when she was staying at Foyot's, "looking for a governess and *working*" — Louise's emphasis. In another letter she directed John, "Tell [Marguerite] the little story marks a new epoch in my existence since I began to write again." For his part, Bill had left aside his long manuscript on Versailles and returned, to Vienna, in 1929, to begin his work with Freud on Woodrow Wilson. He took Anne along with him, enrolling her in the first grade at Die Schwartzfelt Schule, and Louise resumed the pattern she had established in 1926 of going to Vienna for weekends and holidays.

Otherwise, they resumed their outwardly shining existence, entertaining expansively, spending late nights on café *terrasses,* enjoying family life with Anne and Refik. Mura Dehn ran into Louise in 1928 at the Montparnasse *gare* and found Louise talking excitedly about her hopes to return to journalism: "She looked beautiful," said Dehn. "She sparkled when she talked. . . . She gave me the feeling of a bird in flight." A friend saw them standing there chatting animatedly, and later told Dehn, "You two looked as if you had the world in your pockets."

Despite Louise's illness, the Bullitts' social life continued to be relentless. Vincent Sheean, known as Jimmie, had become a constant companion; interestingly, because he was a journalist, he had more in common with Louise than with Bill. One expatriate friend remembered seeing Louise and Bill often at the Dôme and the Coupole with Jimmie Sheean, Scott and Zelda Fitzgerald, and a woman artist with one arm, who sounds very much like Louise's old friend from her Portland days, Cas Baer. As an artist, she might well have turned up in Paris in the 1920s — and, if it were indeed she, may have been a great comfort to Louise. There is little other evidence that Louise and Bill spent much time with the Fitzgeralds, though it was quite natural that their paths would cross. Louise and Zelda, both with artistic ambitions, talented husbands, and young daughters, would have found a lot in common. Although they would likely not have discussed it or even recognized it at the time, both too were on the edge of madness and tragic decline.

Ernest Hemingway's life intersected Louise and Bill's as well in these seemingly happy years. Louise was, through Kitty Cannell, a friend of

Hemingway's second wife, Pauline, although she and Bill remained partisans of his first wife, Hadley. One night they were in the Trois et As Bar in Montparnasse with Hadley and Robert McAlmon when Ernest and Pauline walked in. Hemingway, who had converted to Catholicism to marry Pauline, was trying to convince Hadley that their marriage had not been valid because it was not performed by a priest. She coolly informed him that if it were true, their child, Bumby, belonged entirely to her, and went and rejoined her party. It was the first Bill, Louise, and McAlmon had heard of Ernest's conversion.

There were other, jollier occasions with Hemingway, who, strangely enough, felt compelled to challenge the young adolescent Refik to feats of masculine prowess. With his somewhat rough-and-ready background in Turkey, Refik was more than equal to such challenges. One night in a café, Hemingway was bragging about his knife-throwing abilities. Louise quietly murmured that she bet her Turkish charge could hold his own in this sport. In fact, she said, he could pin an object, such as a hand, to a door at twenty paces. Hemingway immediately ordered some knives from the kitchen, handed them to Refik, and stood against a door with his arm outstretched, fingers apart. The boy neatly landed the knives in the gaps between Hemingway's fingers.

On another occasion, Hemingway was with the Bullitts on the way to a ball; passing a shooting gallery, he announced that he would teach Refik how to shoot. The boy, who had learned in Ashfield, said nothing — and proceeded to outshoot Hemingway. Later that evening, back at the Bullitts', Hemingway was moved to hold his hand in the fire, "until the burning flesh smelled," remembered Louise's daughter. What is most interesting about Hemingway's friendly socializing with Bill and Louise is that the writer who characterized Bill as a "half-kike" had become sufficiently comfortable with them to be included in events that involved the children.

Louise and Bill kept up the pace in America as well. When they were in New York City, they often entertained theater and literary people. Ford Madox Ford was a regular guest, as was his agent William Aspenwall Bradley and his wife, Jenny, who maintained a celebrated salon on the Ile St.-Louis while in Paris. Lawrence Langner never mentioned the scene Bill said Louise made in the Langners' home, writing in his memoir instead of parties the couple attended that were frequented by such guests as the writers Fannie Hurst and Rebecca West, the publisher Horace Liveright, Algonquin denizens F.P.A. and Heywood Broun, Scott and Zelda Fitzgerald, and the critic Joseph Wood Krutch and his French wife, Marcelle.

Ashfield was mostly an idyllic retreat, and Louise's time there with Anne and Refik was happy. Bill put in asparagus beds; Louise had her mother's square Steinway piano shipped to her from California and installed it in the great hall. Life was pleasantly rustic; there was no electricity (Bill would not install it until the 1940s, to the discomfort of the resident caretakers, the Hartwells, because he did not want the poles and wires to mar the view), and candles and kerosene were bought at the general store. Still, when Bill and Louise entertained, which was often, the evenings were lavish, and liquor — despite Prohibition — flowed freely.

The Biddles were frequent guests at the farm, as of course was Marsden Hartley, who found it a peaceful refuge. In a 1928 letter to a sculptor friend, he talked of finishing a number of paintings there, and described a particularly magical evening on the terrace with Bill and Louise watching the Fourth of July fireworks over Greenfield, the nearest town, and, still later, watching the fireflies and the big red moon rise, talking far into the night about sculpture and painting.

During these years, when Louise was balancing an active social life with the encroachments of her disease and sporadically trying to write herself, she undertook what seems at first a rather curious project: supporting the career of the young Jamaican-born American writer Claude McKay. It was a sustained, vigorous effort, lasting over a period of many years, one that clearly took a great deal of dedication and energy on her part, even in intervals when she had very little of either.

At first, McKay must have represented to her a tie with the past. As coeditor, with Max Eastman, of *The Liberator,* McKay was a somewhat doctrinaire leftist, extremely sympathetic to Bolshevik Russia. He met Louise in about 1921 in New York, when he was reading with great enthusiasm the articles that would become *Mirrors of Moscow*. He first saw her just after Reed's death, he later wrote in his memoir *A Long Way from Home*, at the Village gathering place Romany Marie's, where she was surrounded by a group of young men: "At that time she was a pretty woman with unforgettably beautiful eyebrows. She had sent *The Liberator* a pathetic poem about her sorrow, and we had published it. I told her the poem had moved me more than anything that was written about John Reed's death."

McKay next saw Louise at Max Eastman's, where he told her that Jack had once extended him an invitation to a Comintern meeting in Moscow. They talked about the distinction between proletarian art and bourgeois artistic standards. Louise dismissed any distinction between proletarian and bourgeois art, saying she believed there was only good art and bad art. Interestingly, even before she took up with Bullitt, McKay saw her as quite bourgeois herself — though, perhaps, he conceded, only on the surface: "Externally her tastes were bourgeois enough. She liked luxurious surroundings and elegant and expensive clothes and looked splendid in them. But," he added, "her fine tastes had not softened her rebel spirit."

On the same occasion, she intervened in an argument McKay was having with Eastman over the direction of his writing: citing the success of his 1922 collection *Harlem Shadows,* Eastman wanted him to continue to write poetry, while McKay was inspired to write straightforward, raw prose about Harlem. Louise sided with McKay, saying that Jack Reed had early on written such prose "with no radical propaganda in them," and encouraged McKay "just write plain tales." Literary history would, of course, prove Louise correct, as McKay rose to prominence with his plain tales of Harlem life; indeed, Louise was prescient in her early recognition of and support for the reinvigorating influence of the new black renaissance.

McKay was known as the enfant terrible of the Harlem Renaissance — for his Communist sympathies, his insistence on painting an unvarnished view of African-American life, and perhaps because of his homosexuality. He was also a restless spirit, and the 1920s saw him traveling first to Russia and later in London, Berlin, Marseilles, and Morocco. In 1925 he fell gravely ill with pneumonia in Paris; he had been posing nude in chilly artists' studios to eke out a meager existence and his health had finally succumbed. A mutual friend, the illustrator Clive Weed, told Louise that McKay was in Paris and very ill.

Louise sent a doctor around immediately and, when McKay had recovered, went to see him herself. She packed him off to the south of France for his health, along with a check big enough for him to write and live simply for three months. She also resumed her role as mentor: "Remember our conversation in New York," she told him, "and don't try to force your stories with propaganda. If you write a good story, that will be the biggest propaganda."

McKay gave her manuscripts of several stories he had completed as well as early chapters from his new novel, *Home to Harlem*, about a black soldier returning from the war, and Louise took them to New York when she and Bill made their summer trip to America. She wrote enthusiastically that the Boni brothers, now the firm Boni and Liveright, wanted very much to publish *Home to Harlem*, though they were less enthusiastic about the stories, and that she had convinced Ford Madox Ford to write an introduction. (The introduction did not appear.) She was confident of her success, she wrote — for the first thing O'Neill had had published was a story she had convinced the editor Waldo Frank to take for *Seven Arts*.

Nothing came of these early developments, however, and by the next summer Louise had made, to McKay's dismay and irritation, little progress. She and Bill were editing his stories, she wrote, and Bob McAlmon had read them as well. She was having McKay's stories typed, she wrote, though her work had been delayed by a bout of illness. McKay, working as a manservant in Marseilles, grew testy and impatient. Louise sent him a thousand francs to tide him over.

That September, Louise, in America again, began to work actively to promote McKay's work, and even offered, in a sign of real commitment, to give him Jack's old typewriter. She was now scornful about Boni and Liveright, noting that they had told Bill his book would sell only three hundred copies. She now recommended Harcourt, as they had just had a great success with Bill's novel. Over the winter of 1926 to 1927, Louise arranged for William Aspenwall Bradley to represent McKay, and Bradley promptly went to see his client in Antibes, thereafter doling out small sums of money to keep the young writer going.

Toward the end of 1927 Louise wrote McKay that she was contacting Eugene Saxton, an editor at Harper and Brothers whom she had known for years, and in a subsequent letter she reported that Harper had agreed to an advance on *Home to Harlem* based on the portion of the manuscript she had shown them.

Harper did, indeed, take *Home to Harlem*, which it published to much critical acclaim in 1928; there were even rumors, she told him, that it would get Harper's $10,000 prize. McKay dedicated the book simply, "To my friend Louise Bryant."

Louise was proud of this triumph, which in some ways again situated her in a vital progressive movement of the sort that so energized her in her earlier, Village days. With enthusiasm, she turned her attention to McKay's next work, which would be published as *Banjo* in 1929. She felt the manuscript was "a lovely idea," but she wrote to McKay cryptically, "you simply haven't written it." Somewhat condescendingly, she admonished him, "Claude, Jack Reed often wrote a story as many as seventeen times!" But, she added, "[I]n order to do this one must not be rushed," and she understood that he did not have this luxury. She instructed him to be cheerful and keep her informed of his progress, and over the next several months she sent him small sums at regular intervals.

By 1928, Louise was no longer reading McKay's manuscripts but instead writing to critics and making sure his book was in the stores. She wrote to him regularly — but now her letters referred frequently to her illness or other troubles.

Her relationship with McKay was important to Louise; representing a link to the exciting cultural landscape she had left behind when she chose Europe over America after Jack's death and the breakup of the old Village crowd, and then married Bill. Other than Bill, McKay was the one person she told directly about the diagnosis of Dercum's disease, writing him after seeing the London doctors in March 1928. Her tone was almost arch, though she admitted to being shaken:

> I have been quite ill again and I went to London to see some specialists. They looked me over solemnly and then told me I had something called Dercum's disease and that it was incurable! All the happiness I got out of it was flying. I went both ways in a little plane and that was exciting. I am really pretty depressed because I have been almost continuously ill for about five years. Too ill to work. I am trying to do a novel now and I sit here hour after hour at that. I can tell you all this because I know how ill you have been yourself.

She next wrote in April from the sanatorium of a Dr. F. Dengler in Baden-Baden, a place she would visit frequently over the next years. She had been there for two weeks, she wrote, and had lost so much weight that her clothes looked "absurd" — though she felt better. But she did not stay long enough to significantly improve her condition, as she wrote McKay, after what was a rocky summer in Ashfield. Writing just before leaving America, she said that she was going straight to Baden-

Baden on her arrival in Europe, and that this time she intended to stay until she did improve. "I had a dreadful summer. . . . full of collapses. . . . I get thinner and thinner but I weigh 104 so I'm still visible." Her novel was going slowly, she told him — in fact, most of it was still in her head. She asked him to write her at Baden-Baden: "It's a lovely place. I walk for hours in the Black Forest. It is right in the heart of it, you know. I can't stand the sick people at the sanitarium but it's a fine regime for me. I got impatient and left too soon before. But imagine — it was spring. I thought of the Bois and the Champs Elysees and all the happy springs I'd ever known." She would not write again until another spring, the spring of 1930, when she again talked of having been very ill. She spoke with naked honesty about her condition, and her drinking: "So many sad things happened to me this year. I tried to forget it by drinking too much and that only makes me ill."

And 1930 would be a year of sad things indeed: Bill would divorce her amidst great scandal and she would lose custody of her child. McKay would know little of this. He mentioned her only briefly in his memoir *A Long Way from Home,* and recounted a last meeting with her around 1930. He wasn't particularly kind to her in this account — according to him, she had deteriorated terribly. But he did remark, perhaps remembering her generosity to him over the years, on "the overflow of pity pouring out of her impulsive Irish heart."

Louise Falls in Love, A Marriage Ends

The summer of 1928, which Louise described to Claude McKay as "a dreadful summer, full of collapses," was a turning point in Louise's marriage. Though there were pleasant intervals in Ashfield, when Bill and Louise went riding, or skinny-dipping, or sat on the terrace late at night watching the fireflies and the moon rise, Louise was drinking heavily and acting very strangely.

Bill's divorce testimony two years later, while clearly biased, is the best account of the events that followed; in many cases, it can be corroborated in Louise's letters and the accounts of others. According to that testimony, there was a miserable scene in June, when he and Louise attended the Harvard-Yale regatta in Connecticut at the invitation of the Yale Regatta Committee chairman. Bill was particularly starchy in describing this incident, pointing out that Louise was "on the Committee boat, an exhibition for thousands of people, many of whom we knew."

Louise, he said, staggered on board drunk when the varsity race, the main event, began, and would have fallen overboard had Bill not caught her. In what would become a common response to Bill's attempts to restrain her, she insisted on her right to behave as she pleased, however outrageously. She said that "she had a right to fall overboard if she wanted to, that I was trying to restrict her liberty," Bill testified. Though her remark might be dismissed as the pompous statement of a florid drunk, she was evidently trying to retain her dignity, as well as to insist that she had control over her actions when, in fact, any such control was beginning to elude her. Later, back at the hotel, she called him a "miserable bourgeois" who "could not appreciate an artist like herself, and could not appreciate her thoughts or anything she felt about life."

A corroborating account sheds a different light on the matter while confirming its particulars. The son of the committee chairman was Thomas Chappell, who had, with his parents, visited the Bullitts often in Ashfield, and who had a special fondness for Louise. He remembered that he found Louise, sober, alone on the deck, "clutching a stanchion," with Bill nowhere in sight. She told him miserably that she knew no one else on the boat.

Chappell's story reminds us that, however enthusiastically Louise may have appeared to take to her role as the wife of a rich man, at times she found it very lonely and cheerless. With their artist friends, she could hold her own, given her bohemian background and her own artistic leanings; even with the idle rich she could shine, discussing Paris gowns and servant problems. But in a group of upper-middle-class Yale graduates, for example, she would have felt out of place in a way she decidedly did not enjoy. Bill may have been of little help to her in such situations, and not only because he feared she might drink to excess. However beautiful she was, however charming, she was not entirely presentable in some of the circles he moved in — certainly not in the way his first wife, Ernesta, had been. In Ashfield, the townspeople had revered Ernesta as a gracious lady of the manor, but the bohemian Louise was quite another story. Instead she felt like an outsider on almost a daily basis. Over the years she came to accept this difference and even assert it, accusing Bill of trying to remake her into something she was not. In this light, her accusation that Bill was trying to "restrict her liberty" was really an insistence that she was her own person, and not someone he could make over into his desired image.

Merrill Field, who worked at the Bullitt farm from 1923 to 1928, remembers that Bill left Louise alone on the estate for long periods that summer. She passed the time gardening — something of a spurious activity on a working farm — but, more often than not, she drank. She took to hanging around a farmhouse on the property in which the farm's manager, Harold Hartwell, lived with his family. She often made passes at the hired help, Field said, who were impressed by her beauty but were intimidated by her advances.

Bill, in his divorce testimony, painted a devastating picture of the summer of 1928. Louise drank all day, usually gin or brandy and sometimes rum, but mostly gin. She would fall asleep throughout the day only to wake up and begin again. And she ruined one of Bill's favorite rituals. Every Sunday he would cook dinner over an open fire on the hill by the house; it was an event Anne especially loved. But on every single Sunday that summer, with only one exception, according to Bill, Louise had to be helped down the hill, staggering and unable to walk by herself.

Louise's own description of the summer being "full of collapses" indicates that drinking may have been only part of the problem, and she referred in a letter to Claude McKay at the time to being "too feeble to carry out anything" — suggesting that she was indeed physically ill much of the time. Yet she also learned to drive that summer, taking lessons from a man named Wayland Brown down in Conway, which gave rise to local rumors that she was having a romance with him. She was very proud of her new skill, writing McKay that she hoped to get a little sports car when she returned to France. "I get so damn restless," she wrote, "[and] I find it's not tiring at all to dash around in a car." She loved new experiences, she loved speed, and dashing around in her own car represented freedom.

Bill thought it imperative to get her back to Europe, where she could see her doctors. The voyage over was difficult. At one point, Bill would testify, they were sitting in the smoking room with six other people when they sighted another ship. The passengers rushed to the windows, and behind their backs Louise downed the dregs of their drinks. Bill said it was painful for him to see her this way, but a defiant Louise said it was her right to drink if she wanted to. On their arrival in France he packed her immediately off to Baden-Baden, but she returned after only a week, drunk again. Within two months, on November 15, she moved, alone, into the Hotel Ansonia. Bill claimed she never spent another night under his roof unless she was ill and needed nursing, or wanted to "sleep off a drunk," in which case she would later slip out between midnight and two in the morning. (It was an exaggeration to say she never stayed under the same roof with him, though when in Paris she did usually sleep elsewhere for the next year or so.)

The misery continued. Bill described Louise's behavior on a January evening in 1929, when she embarrassed him at a dinner given by the Duke and Duchess de Richelieu. She was unpardonably rude to the duchess, he said, and let the duke "paw" her in a most disgusting manner. (He did not pass judgment on the duke.) When they left, they argued on the sidewalk. Bill said her actions had been "really shocking. She said," Bill went on, "I was just a horrible petty bourgeois who was trying to turn her into a respectable bourgeois wife, which she did not intend to be." She also reiterated her right to do as she pleased, telling Bill, "she would go on drinking as she wished." The statement had the slightly ridiculous and undeniably pitiful overtones of a remark made by someone who could not control her drinking and needed to rationalize it. But by this time it had become a kind of battle cry for her right to misbehave or otherwise act however she wanted, regardless of decorum. Her whole life with Bill had come to represent, it seemed, just so much hypocrisy.

At this point in his testimony, Bill backtracked to January 1928 to explain another element that had crept into Louise's behavior, hastening the dissolution of the marriage. Louise, it seemed, was asserting her independence in other realms as well, and in ways that were more than Bill could stand. She had, he said, become involved with another woman.

Paris in the 1920s had a lively lesbian subculture that reached far beyond 27 rue de Fleurus, the well-known ménage of Gertrude Stein and Alice B. Toklas. Indeed, Stein's example shows just how widespread an influence lesbians had on Parisian literary, artistic, and social life. American lesbians gravitated to Paris, often finding French lovers, often other Americans. Sylvia Beach, the owner of the expatriates' favorite bookstore, Shakespeare & Company, and a patron of James Joyce and other artists, lived openly with Adrienne Monnier, who ran a French-language bookshop across the street. Janet Flanner, whose "Letter from Paris" became a regular feature of *The New Yorker,* lived with Solita Solano. The writer Djuna Barnes had a tortured relationship with Thelma Wood, who would become a character in Barnes's 1936 novel about alternative sexualities, *Nightwood.* Margaret Anderson and Jane Heap ran the influential *Little Review* together — though Anderson was involved with the eccentric performer Georgette Leblanc. Perhaps the central figure in lesbian Paris was the American writer Natalie Barney, an open advocate of promiscuity and hostess to a celebrated salon at her home on the rue Jacob, where homages to Sappho were reenacted before the Temple à l'Amitié in her garden.

Homosexuality was everywhere in Paris in the 1920s. It could be encountered by readers of Proust's two-volume *Sodome et Gomorrhe* (1921 and 1922); in the salons of Stein and Barney; among the American expatriates who frequented the cafés of the Left Bank; and, for fun and titillation or genuine interest, in the underworld of homosexual bars around the rue de Lappe. Gay culture was considered by straight sophisticates as exotic and different, and going "slumming" in the gay world was a new treat for the jaded and bored.

Kitty Cannell, who described herself as "a great friend" of the lesbian community in Paris, introduced Louise to such "low spots" as the Bal Bullier, where Trilby could be seen dancing and where the crowd would watch homosexual Argentine playboys tango. These evenings occurred, for the most part, when Bill was in Vienna in 1926, but later Bill would join them on these jaunts.

Heterosexual tourists could of course write off their interest as simple curiosity or, even more flattering to themselves, evidence of open-mindedness. But for Louise and Bill, according to Cannell, it became something more. Cannell rented an apartment in Passy to a well-known lesbian named Peggy Marquis, a chocolate heiress who, Cannell thought, had her cap set for Bill despite her sexual orientation. Marquis, said Cannell, was "happy to oblige" Bill in introducing Louise to lesbians.

This curious story raises more questions than it answers. Why did Bill want his wife to meet lesbians? Did the idea originate with him, and, if so, what kind of sexual ambivalence or prurience informed it? It is just as likely that the idea originated with Louise, and is perhaps a little easier to understand — though Bill's acquiescence (and even eagerness, as Cannell's account suggests) remains mysterious. And Cannell told her story later, after the divorce; as Louise's passionate defender, she may have wished to assign some of the "blame" to Bill.

Louise may have been sexually curious, or even genuinely attracted to women. It is impossible to know. Her more abstract but deeply held belief in sexual freedom and experimentation may have been at play as well, however. Most likely, she saw lesbianism as another kind of bohemian strategy, a way that people found of living in the margins of culture and in opposition to it. The heyday of radical politics had passed, and her favorite cause, suffrage, was now moot. The lesbian subculture may have seemed the only counterculture game in town, and Louise may have determined to shed her image as a bourgeois wife and become again an outsider.

Even though lesbians thrived in 1920s Paris, there was still prejudice against them. Theories of sexual inversion — the idea that a lesbian was a man trapped in a woman's body — were rampant, and were internalized by such writers as Radclyffe Hall, whose celebrated novel *The Well of Loneliness,* appeared in 1928, the year when Louise first began to turn up in lesbian circles. Books like Hall's at once reinforced popular feelings about lesbianism, while having a liberating effect in their frankness. Lesbians were a marginalized, misunderstood, oppressed group of the sort with whom Louise had always identified. Many Paris lesbians were in fact sexually quite conservative, many couples recreating heterosexual patterns in their alliances and participating in gender stereotyping by cross-dressing and the like. But they were deeply feminist for the most part, in the most basic fashion: they were not married to men, not allied with them (except in artistic encouragement and interchange with them, as in the case of Beach, Anderson, and Stein), and they did not play a subservient role to them. Louise, who had resisted defining herself in terms of men despite her string of male lovers and husbands, was chafing under Bill's thumb. She was likely to envy the spectacle of a life lived free of men.

Of course, her visits to Peggy Marquis's Passy apartment and her slumming in the rue de Lappe may have just been a lark. But the fact remains that when 1928 began, another person had come between Louise and Bill. The person was a woman, and Louise was in love.

Bill dated Louise's involvement with Gwen Le Gallienne to a party in January 1928 given by a host whose name he did not mention. Robert McAlmon, himself bisexual, brought them there. At the door, Louise and Bill met Gwen and her then lover, Yvette Ledoux. Bill said he immediately sized up the gathering, realizing that the party was divided into couples, "men talking to men and women talking to women." He told Louise that it was clearly "a party of homosexuals" and demanded that she go home with him at once.

Louise refused to leave, saying she was "amused by the antics of the people there." She pointed to Gwen and Yvette, and repeated some gossip she had picked up about them: "Look at Le Gallienne, she is wild with jealousy because another woman is talking to Ledoux. Gwen and Ledoux have been lovers for three years and Gwen is now frantic because she is getting tired of her."

Bill left the party alone, and at about five in the morning Louise returned to the avenue Victor Hugo apartment, with McAlmon, Gwen, and Yvette in tow. "They were all quite drunk," said Bill. "They had got some champagne from the cellar and I had really a very unpleasant half hour, because their conversation was pretty disgusting in every possible way."

Louise's involvement with Gwen Le Gallienne began over Gwen's relationship with Yvette Ledoux, which was indeed disintegrating. Gwen was an American-born sculptor of some talent. She was the stepdaughter of Richard Le Gallienne, a writer and general literary hanger-on, a friend of Oscar Wilde, the founder, with William Butler Yeats and Arthur Symons, of the Rhymers' Club, and a contributor to *The Yellow Book* — very much, that is, a product of the decadent British 1890s. His daughter by his second marriage was the noted actress Eva Le Gallienne; Gwen was his third wife's daughter. He maintained a studio at 7 rue Servandoni, where Gwen lived sometimes too.

Not much is known about Gwen beyond her family connections, which one observer felt she traded on, being something of "a climber." But her presence in the lesbian community is well documented. Jimmie Charters, a bartender at Hemingway's favorite watering hole, the Dingo, and a fixture on the Montparnasse scene, remembered Gwen as "a great friend" of the photographer Berenice Abbott. She and Abbott were once carried off in a police raid on one of the homosexual bars in the rue de Lappe. Gwen was an attractive, coltish-looking young woman and drew the attentions, at one point in the 1920s, of Djuna Barnes, pegged by many as a predator among lesbians. At one point, says Barnes's biographer, a committee was actually formed, with Ford Madox Ford as its "chairman," to protect Gwen from Djuna's supposed advances.

In 1928, Gwen was heartbroken over Yvette Ledoux's waning interest; Yvette had begun to take up with men. Others tried to help. Kitty Cannell said that she once saved Gwen from committing suicide when Yvette disappeared with two men. It was probably Kitty who interested

Louise in Gwen's plight. Bill said later that Louise was trying to rescue Gwen from "a terrible depression."

Obviously Gwen's situation aroused Louise's protective instincts. Just as Bill had done earlier in the decade, Gwen was going all to pieces. In a muddled way, Louise tried to comfort the young woman. When Gwen asked her for money, without specifying what it was for, Louise was probably relieved and eager to help; she was, after all, naturally generous and money was not a problem. According to Bill, she asked him for the sum, telling him it was for her disabled half brother William in California. In fact, Gwen needed the money because Yvette wanted to have an abortion. For reasons that are not clear, Louise stayed up two nights tending Yvette after the procedure, which she naturally resented. Presumably Gwen had absented herself in what must have been great misery; the abortion would mark the end of her relationship with Yvette, though not her grief.

Bill, at this point, saw the handwriting on the wall. When Louise asked him to take Gwen to lunch, saying that Gwen was worried she had made a bad impression on him, he ignored this colossal understatement and agreed. After what must have been an uncomfortable meal, Gwen took him back to her studio and showed him her paintings, which he admired. He found her, according to his testimony, "very intelligent and clever, but frankly and openly homosexual." Yet he did not believe his wife was sexually involved with Gwen. Indeed, he seems to have been more concerned with appearances than with what was actually going on, for when he returned from lunch he simply demanded that Louise stop seeing "so notorious a pervert."

Louise refused, and disappeared with Gwen, in what would be the beginning of a not-so-merry chase throughout 1928 and 1929. She and Gwen took the Bullitts' car, along with the chauffeur, to Switzerland and from there to the Riviera; Bill decided this would be a good time for him to take a vacation and arranged to meet Louise there, but she failed to turn up with the car at the appointed time and place. When he finally found her, with Gwen, they all drove together to Nice, where the women took a room next to him and kept him awake all night, he testified, with "drunken talk," and disappeared, like vampires, every day. In despair, Bill went off alone to Cap-Martin for two weeks and then returned to Paris to find the servants, Anne, and Refik in tears: Louise had fired the governess and gone off with Gwen again.

No doubt Bill hoped that the summer of 1928 in Ashfield would at least remove Louise from Gwen's physical presence. But that was the "dreadful summer, full of collapses" she described to Claude McKay, a disaster in every way, for her health and her marriage. On the Bullitts' return, when Bill shipped Louise off to Baden-Baden, she secretly arranged for Gwen to meet her there, confiding this fact to Bill later. The winter of 1928 to 1929 was full of triangular scenes. In his divorce testimony Bill described a typical one, when he issued an ultimatum, perhaps with the object of showing that Louise's behavior was threatening his family and that he, as man of the house, sought to put a stop to it. Bringing Anne along for a visit with her mother, he called for Louise at the Hôtel de l'Université, where she was staying, and received word from the front desk that she was ill and to pass the message on to Anne. Furious, Bill pushed his way past the hotel clerks to Louise's room, where Gwen answered the door. He rushed in and found Louise on the bed; according to his testimony, she was "sleeping off a drunk." Bill took Gwen aside and angrily forbade her to see Louise again. "You will not break up my family!" he shouted. He arranged to have Louise stay with friends, but she never showed, once again disappearing with Gwen.

Bill took Anne and went down to Villerville in Normandy, where he rented a house and left word with the servants at the avenue Victor Hugo establishment as to where he could be reached. Louise, who had again gone to Baden-Baden, finally did join him, and Bill kept a close eye on her drinking, but she slipped away to Paris more than once. He put her under the care of a Dr. Gyelin, who decided that she had an "epileptoid condition," and prescribed an "epileptoid starvation cure," allowing her nothing but coffee for five days. Louise gave her own version of this period in her letter to Frank Walsh, saying that she was confined to rooms on the top floor and that Bill never came up to see her. Bill remembered visiting her frequently from Paris, where he found her bedridden and semiconscious. According to Bill, as soon as the treatment was over she began to drink again. He went up to Paris, he said, to get tickets to the U.S., resolving to get Louise out of Europe, and when he came back to Normandy, found Gwen there with her. According to Louise, she emerged from her starvation cure severely weakened, and fell down a flight of stairs to the beach, striking her head in the process. "Bill said that I must have been drunk," she wrote laconically.

In March 1929, after this debacle, Bill took her and Anne — Refik, in the confusion, had been sent to school in Switzerland — to Juan-les-Pins, where, he was later to report, she drank almost nothing, and he saw some hope for their marriage. Back in Paris she seemed more settled, spending time sculpting in her studio. When she asked Bill's permission to take Anne to the studio with her, he agreed, but insisted she not drink when "the baby" was with her alone. But, Bill said, "she broke her word," and he found her with Anne in a restaurant, drinking with Gwen. He brought her home forcibly and kept her confined to the house for two hours, refusing to give her a drink. She pleaded to leave, and eventually he allowed her to go, dropping her off at Le Gallienne's studio in the rue Servandoni.

There were many more scenes and dramas that spring, but between his outbursts of anger and her rebellions, Bill remained patient and Louise somewhat docile. It was with great relief that he convinced Louise to make the usual trip, with the whole entourage, to America, and they sailed for Quebec — presumably because of technicalities concerning the servants' visas — on August 28. In a departure from their usual routine, Bill stayed in the same cabin with her to see that she had nothing to drink, so the trip was actually uneventful and quite pleasant.

The mood continued when they reached Ashfield and settled in there. Bill made sure there was no liquor on the premises, and without anything to drink, he said, Louise "began to return to her own charming personality." They talked over the events of the previous months "in a tranquil mood," continued Bill, and they were able to talk calmly about the exact nature of Louise's involvement with Gwen. According to Bill, Louise said "she had a strong feeling for the Le Gallienne girl; that she had a feeling of absolute peace with her, and the only way she could sleep was in the Le Gallienne girl's arms; and had done so." Most men would take this as an unequivocal statement of love, but not Bill. "[S]he said their emotional relationship had gone no further, which I believed at the time." Just one month after Bill and Louise left France, however, Bill would find his illusions shattered.

19

Divorce and Its Aftermath

*I*t all happened so very quickly that Louise quite literally did not see it coming — as Bill no doubt knew well. She was confused, ill, sometimes drunk. Before she fully understood what was going on, she had been divorced and had lost custody of her child. Bill had pulled off a coup fully as impressive as the most complex and demanding feat of diplomacy. Louise lost a game she had not even known she was playing, and lost devastatingly.

The chain of events began when Bill interrupted their summer in Ashfield with a trip to New York City, taking Louise with him. The Theatre Guild, he said, wanted changes in a play he was finishing up, which they were considering producing. Louise got drunk the very first day in New York, he said later in his deposition, and he took her immediately back to Ashfield, fearing that another embarrassing performance might jeopardize his attempts to break into the theater. He returned to New York alone.

On September 28, according to his divorce testimony, Bill was in his hotel room at the Plaza working on his play when Louise, having somehow made the journey from Ashfield, appeared at his door and "literally fell" into his room. He put her to bed and telephoned the doctor she had often seen in her early, happier days in New York, the

Village favorite Harry Lorber, who could be counted on to be discreet. While waiting for Lorber and watching Louise sleep, Bill thought to look through her handbag. There, he said, he found five old letters to Gwen, and two others written that very day.

Bill did not testify as to what the letters contained, but presumably they included evidence that the friendship between the two women had gone beyond the "emotional relationship" to which Louise had confessed a month before. He could barely register the knowledge when Louise created another scene. Dr. Lorber arrived, and Bill conferred with him in an adjoining room of his suite. They tried to reach a neurologist, Dr. Wechsler, recommended by Lorber, but as they were on the telephone, Louise drifted into the room naked. Lorber wrapped her in a blanket, and, when she was calm, they presented her with the alternatives: she could go into a sanatorium, or she could go somewhere quiet, free from temptation, until her condition improved. They would decide how to proceed from there.

Louise wanted nothing of sanatoriums, and could think of nowhere she could go. Finally she hit upon her half brother William, the disabled veteran in California, the only family member to whom she was close. With no further ado, Bill put her on the train. Nothing more is known about her visit, except that she was back in New York after a month.

During her absence Bill had evidently done a good deal of thinking and planning. When he met her at the train station, he took her to the Plaza and laid down his conditions. Louise later described the scene for Frank Walsh: "Anyway, Bill . . . said to me that either I was to have a 'splashing' divorce or I was to go into an 'institution' for two years. I don't know why but I suddenly revolted." She went to the telephone and called their friend Clive Weed, asking him to come get her. He did, and took her to the Brevoort, where, a week later, she took an overdose of sleeping pills. She was admitted to the Neurological Institute, in care of Drs. Lorber and Wechsler.

By now, Bill's plans were in motion. He had gone down to Philadelphia to arrange for a divorce, renting a big house to set up legal residence there. After she recovered from her suicide attempt, Louise joined him, either unsuspecting or perhaps feeling powerless to try to change the course of events. As Louise later put it, succinctly, "[W]e made a separation agreement. Bill told me the last thing in the world he wanted was a divorce. I said I would go abroad for awhile. I thought he would calm down but he had arranged for the divorce all along." She left for Europe on November 29 on board the *Paris,* going directly upon her arrival to the sanatorium at Baden-Baden and waiting for word from Bill. Though she did not know it, Bill would file for divorce exactly a week later, on December 24. The divorce would become final on March 24, 1930, while Louise was still abroad.

"You know how corrupt Philadelphia is," Louise wrote soon afterward to Frank Walsh, "and how easy it is to 'fix' things there. What a cradle of liberty!"

The Bullitt divorce case was, as they might have said in Bill's social circle, "highly irregular." He gave testimony, as was the custom in Pennsylvania when the divorce was not contested, before a master — in this case his old friend Francis Biddle. It is important to note that the divorce was not in fact contested, though Louise's lawyer, Arthur Garfield Hays, a friend of hers and Jack's from the Village days, was present at least part of the time — most likely to see that his client was protected in any alimony and custody issues that might arise.

Bill had mustered all the French servants to testify and arranged for their testimony to be translated. Bill himself testified for what must have been days, considering the litany of events he described — the scenes, reconciliations, mysterious disappearances, and the whole saga of Gwen Le Gallienne. But, if the divorce was not contested, why did he testify at such length, giving painful and intimate details of the deterioration of his marriage? Surely it would have sufficed to charge desertion — she had, after all, left the country. But instead he spilled everything, including Louise's wrenching declarations of independence.

Dear Duck,

I want to say to you only one thing — I have lived too long with unconventional people to be suddenly made into a Bourgeoise. This thought of mine will sound drunk — crazy — anything, but it is what people call "straight from the shoulder" in that country I happen to be born in — America. I want to *work!* And I *can* work. Anne is not a mediocre, she is a *person.* She will not mind if I do something during this little "passage" we call life which somehow matters to people. I have no neurosis. I am an artist who has gone back to work after a too long vacation. I will see you after some days. I am tired now — full of flu. Forgive any hurts I do to you.

Louise

Bill seems to have been gripped by an extraordinary confessional instinct, almost a compulsive need to tell all, no matter how unnecessary. Perhaps as well he felt a need to justify himself, to plead for sympathy before the people who really mattered to someone of his background: his Philadelphia peers. He was renouncing his bohemian past, and he had to make a clean breast of it to do so. In this light, it is also interesting that he chose Philadelphia as the venue for his divorce rather than, say, Reno. He did so in part because he knew he would get favorable treatment there, but perhaps also because it represented to him a return to his illustrious roots.

Also questionable are Bill's recitations of incidents that proved that theirs was still a loving relationship, in which both sides showed at times extraordinary patience and determination to straighten things out with each other — if only for the sake of the child.

The child, in fact, may have been the real issue in Bill's extensive, detailed testimony, for he very much wanted custody of Anne, and, as would become clear, to deny Louise any access to her. He seems to have wanted to convince the court that Anne's welfare was at stake in emphasizing Louise's drinking, her public scenes, and her relationship with Gwen. The tie with a known lesbian, times being what they were, would have been grounds enough alone for him to win custody.

Another remarkable aspect of Bill's testimony is that he made absolutely no mention of Louise's disease — despite the fact that it would have shed some light on her heavy drinking and bizarre behavior. Though he made much of her wanderings around Europe, he did not note that she was often on her way to and from Baden-Baden in search of some relief from her pain. He did not mention, for example, that the starvation diet prescribed by Dr. Gyelin at Villerville was a treatment for Dercum's disease. He instead left the distinct impression that this was an attempt to cure her of heavy drinking. Perhaps Bill's avoidance of the issue was insurance that Louise's case would be considered on the basis of her inappropriate behavior, no matter what its cause.

The unavoidable conclusion is that Bill cared less about the disease than he did about its manifestations — perhaps understandably, given their dire aspect. But why not mention it in the testimony, admitting that Dercum's disease often made its sufferers behave in these ways? Surely it would not have harmed his case, for the judge would probably have felt, as Bill did, that Louise's behavior, and not its underlying cause, was at issue.

Like Louise, Bill told almost no one about her illness, perhaps for the same reasons: embarrassment at having to explain her appearance, the difficulty of explaining the complexity of the condition, the awkwardness of acknowledging its horrifying symptoms, or its very incurability. If it was incurable but not fatal, why tell anyone? he may have felt. While his family believes that Bill sent Louise to consult with Freud about how to cope with her disease, evidence suggests otherwise. In a 1927 letter to Bill, Freud wrote that he was glad to hear Bill's (unspecified) good news, "except when you tell me news of trouble in your wife's health. I trust it will prove a passing one, as it is not in her nature to miss happiness by falling sick." Although this was written before Louise's diagnosis, Freud's wording, kind-hearted but somewhat offhand, suggests that Bill was his real interest, not Louise — appropriately so, since Bill was his patient. While attempts were quite conceivably made to get Louise to see Freud in the next year or two — and this is only speculation — they seem to have been unavailing.

It was undeniably in Bill's best interests to see that Louise was removed from his life. The kindest reading of the matter is that Bill simply had no choice: Louise's disease was progressive and incurable, and it had appalling and embarrassing symptoms. His marriage was threatening the social life to which he was accustomed, and in which he thrived: his connections with Yale alumni, with the Duke and Duchess de Richelieu, with the Theatre Guild in New York — all had fallen by the wayside. Any hopes he had for reentry into political life — and it was clear, by 1930, that he harbored such hopes — were thwarted if not dashed by Louise's strange, and career-threatening, antics. Perhaps most importantly, he wished to protect Anne. While he may indeed have judged Louise's behavior a poor example for a child, he no doubt did his best to shield Anne from seeing most of it; money made that possible. There was no question, however, that Louise sometimes behaved irresponsibly when Anne was in her care.

But was it entirely her behavior when drinking, or her relationships with people he considered unsavory, or her unreliability as a mother, that made it so imperative that he rid himself of Louise? Or was it her rejection of the role of a rich man's wife, which she had once taken up without objection, that so bothered him — her insistence that she not be made over as "a Bourgeoise?" That she "do something during this little 'passage' we call life?" That she insist on her own independent judgment, even when it came to rude behavior to a duchess? Her very independence, her bohemian exuberance and defiance of convention, were the qualities that had once attracted Bill to her; now he was reject-ing her for those very qualities. Perhaps it was parenthood coming to the fore, perhaps it was his restlessness with bored expatriate life, or perhaps it was his own patrician upbringing — about which his ambivalence, always strong, was becoming intolerable — but Bill could no longer bear Louise's determination to be a person in her own right, and to continue to work. Some saw in his rejection of Louise traces of the same pattern he had shown when he turned on Woodrow Wilson: the sub-jects of his hero-worship were inevitably toppled, and rejected utterly. As his brother Orville would later write, "He formed rapid and strong attachments and was bitterly disappointed when such acquaintances did not live up to the high standards which he expected of them. When this happened he would break the friendship with little compunction."

Where was Louise in all this, while her future was being decided? She was at Baden-Baden, although Bill said, unaccountably, that "the last he heard" she was in Algiers. She next surfaced after the decree was granted in Paris at a new studio at 84 rue d'Assas. Only through her accounts during that terrible, shell-shocked time can we piece together what happened in the interim — including the full nature of Bill's deceit.

According to Louise, she learned of the divorce only through word of mouth, perhaps through friends who saw the March 25 item in the New York papers, which said that "Mr. W. C. Bullitt" had obtained a divorce in common pleas court, citing "general indignities." Still not entirely sure what had hit her, she sent a series of letters to Frank Walsh.

She wrote him first from Dr. Dengler's Sanitarium in Baden-Baden, saying that "So many bad things happened in the U.S. that I couldn't get advice or say good-bye." She had had a heart attack (she seems to have clung to this explanation that she hoped would account for her dismay-ing collapses) but hoped a week or so in the Black Forest would do her good. "Now I am a vagabond again and will have to go back to work," she wrote. "That will be good for me."

After Walsh telegraphed her that he would do whatever he could to help, she wrote again from Paris, saying that she had never expected to turn to him, but that she didn't hesitate "now that I am in the deepest trouble of all my life." He may have heard, she wrote, that Bill had divorced her "behind closed doors" in Philadelphia, and she characterized the whole saga as a series of "frame-ups." There was "not the slightest grain of truth in what he accused me of," and, in any case, she said, evidently not yet fully aware of Bill's strategy, "I was abroad for my health." Indicating that she sensed the object of his actions, she closed by saying, "So he got Anne and I am alone in France (not very well) and rather tired of trying to make a new life." Though Bill had not yet barred her from seeing Anne, Louise evidently felt at this point that she had lost her.

From St. Brieux in Brittany Louise wrote to Walsh again, this time a very long, single-spaced typed letter giving her version of the marriage's history. It is an important document not only for the details she provides about her life with Bill, but also for the evidence it gives of her frame of mind at this time. In the midst of her anger and sense of betrayal, she could not help revealing a certain relief that the uncertainty and tension were over: "I have been wandering through Brittany for about three weeks and living in simple peasant inns and seeing simple people. It is like going up into the back country of Ireland. It restores one and, God knows, when I came down here I needed restoring! Why, Frank, I had forgotten how to laugh!"

She had not told anyone else what had happened to her, she wrote, "because I was trying to stand by Bill." In the face of what she had gone through, she invoked her sense of privacy, which she attributed to her ethnic background: "My idea of family is an Irish one. I don't know anything about 'divorce' or why people take their private emotions into court." In relating the hair-raising stories of her marriage, such as Bill's barricading himself into his hotel room in Vienna, she stressed that she wanted to keep the family together. But a recurrent theme had now crept into her description of what happened with Bill, which, in her account, included senseless, repeated beatings. "He appears so suave and rational that no one knows what it is like to live with him," she wrote. "Nevertheless, I would have stayed by without even thinking of anything, I suppose, except that [Bill's ill treatment] was my fate. But he had the idea of the divorce. I did not even know it was going to happen." After relating what she understood of the divorce, she conceded, "Through all this I feel that Bill has deeply cared for me but for some strange reason takes it out on me in these ways." She knew that Anne was still in the care of Nannie, the Irish nurse, and that helped, though she still missed her daughter terribly.

Evidence suggests that Bill brought Anne to France in the early months of 1930, and that a terrible scene took place around Easter. Louise, and perhaps Bill and Anne as well, must have joined Marguerite Storrs — John was in the U.S. — at the Storrses' summer place on the Loire, for she wrote Marguerite a strange, garbled letter from a hotel in the nearby town of Mer: "The devils are getting a hold of me and for fear of making a scene chez vous am flying to Paris. Will be 5 hrs. on the road without possibility of a drink and may come back in the same car tomorrow. Think I'm acting for the best anyway will be at the apartment in the morning — Telephone. Temprement [sic] is getting the best of me. Reason is dead —."

Whatever happened was enough to turn her old friends against her. John Storrs wrote Marguerite on May 5 from the U.S. that "with all you've gone through" she should certainly say no "to the Bullitt avalanche." And Bill wrote Marguerite a letter with decided tones of a smug conspiracy on June 15, when he and Anne were "safely back in America." He explained, "You were so very kind at Easter that I wanted to write to you constantly to thank you but silence was the better part of valor as long as we were in Europe." The latch string was always open for her and John at the Ashfield estate, he said in closing.

A July letter from Louise to Frank Walsh explained her version of the event and, most importantly, how she had finally and decidedly lost any chance for contact with Anne. Filling in the background, she explained again that she could not fight Bill because in spite of an "open suaveness," he really was "mentally deranged." Also, "He had my child." She had written, she said, to Arthur Garfield Hays for help, but thought he had probably been "taken in" by Bill: "I certainly was for so long."

Louise's version of how she lost visitation rights regarding Anne, though she was overwrought at the time, is a plausible explanation. When Bill was last in Paris (which would have been that spring) he claimed, she wrote Walsh, that she had tried to break into his apartment by force and steal his papers. "Imagine!" she snorted. "He had sent me a note saying I could see Anne at a place he keeps there if I went at 4 P.M." Louise went to the address — 46 rue de Ponthieu — and found the door open and strangers inside. She asked when Bill was due back and was told any minute. Abstracted, wondering where Anne was, she walked about the small apartment, idly lifting some papers off a table. Those present immediately snatched the papers from her hands, at which point she left. She learned not long after that the mysterious strangers were witnesses to prove that she had broken the separation agreement she had made with Bill the December before, when she thought there would be no divorce. By doing so she had lost any right to see Anne and, under the terms of that agreement (which Bill, to his credit, would modify), forfeited her right to alimony. In short, just as she had been tricked into a divorce, so too was she tricked into losing her child.

Louise fought back as valiantly as her weakened and confused condition and her limited material resources would allow, but letters to Frank Walsh, who was, after all, a labor lawyer with no experience in matrimonial cases, were not terribly effective. Her own lawyer, Hays, was evidently so powerless (he was not a divorce lawyer either) against the juggernaut Bill had mounted in the Philadelphia courts that she came to believe, as she wrote to Walsh, that Hays had been lured into Bill's camp. The whole chain of events, through Bill's devious strategy, had left her feeling powerless.

Objectively, she was powerless indeed. Bill had vast financial resources behind him, while she had none. In the spring of 1930, in the midst of her discovery of what had actually happened to her, she received word that her half brother William, whom she had visited in December, needed to have his legs amputated at the knees, and she sent him all the money she had. She was virtually friendless as well, most of their friends — Steffens, Hartley, the Storrses — having taken Bill's side (something she would have discovered only afterward), so that she had to turn to old, left-leaning friends from the days before her third marriage — who, however much they may have wanted to help, were not exactly experienced in or sympathetic to such matters.

Moreover, she knew just how difficult her case was. When her mind was clear, and not preoccupied by such notions as the right to drink herself to death if she wished, or to refuse to conform to societal norms, she could see that, in the eyes of an objective observer like a judge, her actions would be considered blameworthy — certainly enough to render her, in the conventional wisdom, an unfit mother. Though she would no doubt have bridled at the thought, she had evidently internalized, for example, widespread prejudice against same-sex relationships to such an extent that she never mentioned her relationship with Gwen to Walsh, Hays, or any of the others to whom she turned.

Even had she felt ready to stand by behavior that others might consider scandalous, there was the simple fact that it was her word against Bill's. She, with her bohemian background and her unconventional habits (including her drinking, which in sober moments, she acknowledged was a problem), her multiple marriages (one to a Communist), her lack of social standing or family to speak of, her compromised beauty, would not be the believable one. As she said so many times, Bill seemed so urbane and charming on the surface that no one would guess at the trickery — and, according to Louise, the cruelty — of which he was capable. Though theirs had been a rich and multicolored marital tapestry, with both sides guilty of betrayals and unkindnesses of smaller and lesser degrees, and throughout a thread of mutual love and compassion, by the time the ugly divorce played itself out, that no longer applied. Louise was, like so many women in her position, a victim of a man and a system possessed of more power than she could ever muster.

Sisley Huddleston provided in his memoirs of his Paris years a touching portrait of a woman and her troubled marriage, a woman who is almost unmistakably Louise:

> A certain girl of my acquaintance earned a cheerful living as a journalist. To be sure she could not afford luxuries, but she liked her work and the people it brought her into contact with, and was herself altogether likeable. Then she was courted by a rich man, and eventually she married him. They had a beautiful house in Paris where they entertained freely. Jewelry was lavished upon her, and her cheapest dress cost thousands of francs. Yet somehow she was not happy, and I remember one midnight, after the most dismal of parties, she unwound in desperation the swathing fold of her satin robe to make a skipping-rope in the drawing room.

Divorce followed, said Huddleston tersely.

It's a wonderful vignette of 1920s Paris, as Huddleston no doubt intended it to be. The ex-journalist's trick with her gown after a "dismal" party is itself a rather good metaphor for the closing out of the decade in Paris. Shaken by the 1929 stock market crash, the expatriate community was lining up in droves for federal emergency funds to return home. Outright cynicism had entirely replaced the rather dissipated boredom that had increasingly come to characterize the decade: "The snow of twenty-nine wasn't real snow," wrote F. Scott Fitzgerald. "If you didn't want it to be snow you just paid some money." Bill Bullitt, whose fortune was untouched by the crash, paid money and indulged in some fancy footwork to make the snow in his life go away; he left Paris, though not for good, and his life continued on its vigorous course.

Andrew Dasburg had compared Louise, Bill, and himself to pawns in a chess match, "as if control had left us somewhere along the way." The story of Bill and Louise's marriage certainly did have this romantic aspect: beautiful people, they had drifted together without obvious purpose or design, and for a time their lives were glittering and happy. Without purpose or design, they drifted apart.

But what happened to Bill and Louise's marriage was far more brutal, more purposeful, more frightening than Huddleston's vignette or Dasburg's analysis allows. As inevitable as the end of the marriage would seem in retrospect, there were no random fates at work in their story. Bill triumphed, though he carried his triumph, hollow as it was, secretly and perhaps in pain for the rest of his days. And Louise — well, it is tempting to end her meteoric story as Huddleston did, with the terse comment, "Divorce followed." But Louise would soldier on, and the fates that she had called on after Jack Reed died to "be kind to me and not make my life long" would not be so merciful. What she would make of her life in the years that remained to her would be attributable solely to her own refusal to fade away gracefully. Resigned she may have been; embittered by experience; even, sometimes, desirous of death; nevertheless, her rebel spirit was not one to go gently.

PART IV

The Downward Arc

20

Louise Learns to Fly

L ouise rallied in the summer of 1930, perhaps galvanized by the
finality of the miserable situation with Bill. She devoted her
energies to a project she had attempted, with varying degrees of
energy, throughout the 1920s: writing a book about Jack. Her last concerted effort had been in the summer of 1928 — the summer when, at
Ashfield, she had been subject to all kinds of collapses and had yet
summoned the energy to learn how to drive a car. That summer she had
enlisted Jack's mother in the project, evidently writing her that she was
putting her present marriage behind her to devote herself to her memories of Jack. Mrs. Reed wrote her back in June expressing her "sense of
outrage at the way Bill is behaving," and said, "I am glad you are going
to take back Jack's name." (There is no evidence Louise ever did.) Jack's
mother was filled with excitement at the prospect of such a book, and
looked forward to joining Louise in Paris to work on it. In the meantime, she was going through all of Jack's things, all jumbled together
and stored at her son Harry's house.

But Louise's life, in the wake of the summer of 1928, had become so
chaotic that no more came of this plan at the time. But at the end of
1929, just before she was packed off to her half brother in California, and
when the wheels of the divorce had, unbeknownst to her, been set in
motion, she had arranged for Mrs. Reed to deliver some materials to
Ashfield, where Louise's papers — commingled with some of Jack's

manuscripts and letters — were stored. During the horrible months when the divorce was going through and the gravity of what had happened began to sink in, she summoned the energy to see if she could retrieve the materials, as well as her personal effects. She knew it would be an uphill battle, writing Frank Walsh, "I am sure Bill will not want to give me any permissions to go and get them," and trying to track down Clarence Darrow, whom she knew personally, to help her in her efforts. This act would be the first in what would become a grueling saga: her efforts to have her papers and Jack's returned to her.

Louise was so narrowly focused on her goal that she could write of little else in letters to friends in the summer of 1930. Bill had promised to send the material — eight trunks' worth — but she did not know when or on what boat they would arrive, so she was forced to stay in Paris, which went very much against her grain, given the restlessness that had come to characterize her life since the diagnosis of Dercum's disease two years before. In the last letter she wrote to the Storrses, she explained, "I have to stay here in the studio to wait for what is sent," adding, "I never have news of Anne."

The papers would not arrive, in fact, for over two years — though Mrs. Reed sent the remainder of the material she had in October 1930. No letters from this period between Louise and Bill survive, but it seems clear that Bill was behaving somewhat inscrutably at the time — promising to send something and not doing so was fairly representative of his conduct. He may have been acting in what he felt were Louise's best interests; in the case of papers, for example, he may have believed she did not have the room to store eight trunks, the responsibility to take care of them, or the resources to use them for the project she planned. On the other hand, they were her property, and serving Jack's memory was becoming increasingly central to her continued existence. In this sense Bill's paternalistic attitude (that he knew best) and his unreliability (he never informed her of decisions he made) seem misguided if not hostile.

The same questions extend to his support of Louise. Though she believed that he had won the right to withhold alimony when she broke the separation agreement, it is extremely probable that he regularly sent her considerable amounts of money over the years. She commonly protested otherwise, which in the beginning concerned her friends greatly. Mrs. Reed, responding in August to a letter in which Louise pleaded poverty, wrote, "You write as if you have only what you earn — surely you were provided some after the divorce." Still, Mrs. Reed was concerned enough that she contacted Frank Walsh to see if he could determine whether Bill was sending Louise money. (She also inquired about the status of the eight trunks.) Frank Walsh had to reply that he wasn't sure.

Logic argues that Louise was receiving money from somewhere, as she had no paying work, and it seems unlikely that Bill, who, his daughter maintained, still felt much affection for Louise, despite his actions, would withhold money — especially since he had it to spare. At one point during these years, the Floyd Dells found themselves at a dinner party in Washington seated next to Francis Biddle, who had presided at Bill's divorce hearing. When they mentioned that they had heard that Louise was in bad shape financially, Biddle hotly denied it, saying that his law firm was in fact sending her the "substantial sum" Bill had settled on her. He did add that often the money was sent directly to Louise's concierge for rent because Bill was concerned as to how it might be spent. Louise had already fallen into a pattern of giving her money away, often to elusive characters who needed it for suspicious reasons. But once again, the attitude of Bill and his lawyers seems unnecessarily paternalistic, especially given the high priority Bill knew Louise would have placed on being treated as a responsible person. Most likely, Bill sent her money because he did not want it said that he was not providing for his ex-wife, and did not want a fresh scandal to arise if word were spread that she was in bad straits.

The question of Anne is more vexing. Louise had not always been an exemplary mother in the textbook sense. Like many of the very rich, she had often left the child's care entirely to servants. As Dercum's disease made its inroads, she was less able to care for Anne properly. Yet, perhaps because she tried to see her daughter only when she was at her best, Louise's relationship to Anne was extraordinarily close. Over sixty years later her daughter has only good memories of her mother, even from times when Louise was clearly in the grip of her illness. Once, Louise and the family were about to sail for America — Bill had taken the servants and all the trunks to the dock — when she suddenly de- cided there was a cathedral she wanted Anne to see. She took her daughter there and insisted that they stay until the light was exactly right; they watched together raptly as the sun went down, and when they finally got to the dock the ship had sailed and Bill was furious. Where Bill was the more traditional parent, seeing to Anne's education, giving her poems to memorize, and insisting that she speak French whenever possible, Louise was the one with the sense of play. The daughter of their friends Konrad and Naomi Bercovici remembers crossing the Atlantic with the young Bullitt family; Bill was nice enough, but Louise treated the children as equals, while seeing the world through their eyes and speaking their language.

When she lost custody of Anne, Louise believed she had lost her entirely, and described it that way over and over in letters to friends. She claimed she never was able to see her, and indeed she was not — on her terms, at least. Bill does seem to have allowed her occasional visits with Anne, but never when expected or at regular intervals, and only for the briefest of times, so that Louise's sense that her relationship with Anne had been severed when she lost custody was not entirely inaccurate. Anne, who was evidently effectively kept in the dark about her parents' problems, remembers that "nothing really changed" after 1930, but then she did not even learn that her parents had been divorced until after her father's death in 1967, when she went through his papers in the barn at Ashfield.

Bill made every effort to shelter Anne from knowledge of her parents' difficulties, including the fact that her custody was a battleground between them. While he obviously considered Louise a bad influence, he was also cementing the extremely close relationship he was forging with his daughter, ensuring her complete devotion to him. But the decision does not seem to have been solely Bill's. In the early stages of her disease, when Louise would wake Bill in the middle of the night to tell him that something terrible was happening to her, she always admonished him to see to it that Anne was taken care of. After the divorce, she went back and forth between desperately wanting to see Anne and feeling resigned that the course of her disease and the irregular and peripatetic life she led would have made it impossible for her to be Anne's sole caretaker. Indeed, she may have thought that Bill, with his wealth and position, could provide Anne not only with a stable upbringing but with all the advantages in life. Still, she wished Anne to be something more than "a mediocre," as she wrote in the letter Bill had read into the divorce record: "she is a *person*," she wrote insistently. It must have pained her deeply to know that Bill wanted Anne to lead a highly conventional life, bound by social proprieties and traditional sex roles — though she knew she had no hope of intervening.

What Louise wanted, and did not get, was regular news of Anne: it was to be her constant refrain over the next six years. She wanted an address where she could write her, she wanted to know how Anne was doing in school, she wanted to know where Bill was taking her. Yet Bill withheld all such information from her with chilling consistency. In letters to the most unlikely people — like Clarence Darrow — she begged help in learning news of Anne. In turn, she tried to send Anne news of herself. Until Bill put a stop to it, she had Wayland Brown, the Conway, Massachusetts, man whom she had befriended in 1928 when he taught her how to drive, relay messages to her daughter through Nannie. As late as 1935 she would write, "I can't follow [Anne] about so I have to wait, that's all. She isn't allowed to write to me and a letter sent to her would never reach her." The already wrenching separation between mother and child became all the more painful because Louise felt utterly cut off, dependent on Bill's whims or the occasional help of near strangers for the merest crumbs of information about her daughter's life.

While Louise had a photograph of Anne with her, and was ready to pour out the woes of a bereaved mother to anyone who would listen, she hardly lived the life of a Stella Dallas, forsaking all else for her daughter's welfare. She was too independent and too energetic to efface herself in that way; nor had she ever defined herself primarily as a mother. And in any case, she understood that it would have done no good. Moreover, she was trying to make a new life, to work, to take up the bohemian existence she had renounced so many years before for Bill, the only kind of existence that seemed meaningful to her now.

Whatever else can be said of Bill's financial support, he certainly did not set her up in style. The only home she could find that was affordable — in a city where the cost of living was very low — was little more than a garret. But her new studio, at 44 rue d'Assas, was a perfect — or perfectly eccentric — setting for her new life. Adjoining a nunnery, the studio was called by many a "cloister"; Louise, using a word that was almost constantly on her lips in these years, called it "absurd." A contemporary observer has left a remarkably evocative description; in the studio, he wrote,

> Candles afford the only light at night and dark shadows shiver on the walls and ceiling. From her window she can see the nuns walking in the garden; and sometimes at night, when the click of her typewriter ceases, Louise is in the habit of watching the shadows thrown from the candles while the nuns whisper in the garden below. The shadows fall on ikons, silken fans, bronze images, Japanese boxes and chunks of clay covered by Turkish towels. Also buckets of wood and pails of tin, for there is no running water in Louise's apartment.

No doubt it gave Louise, always sensitive to her living quarters, considerable satisfaction to be surrounded by such picturesque poverty, in a romantic garret reminiscent of her charming but humble Patchin Place mews apartment. But however picturesque, the lack of electricity and running water must have been a considerable inconvenience for a forty-six-year-old woman with a chronic illness; more importantly, one wonders about the psychological effect of living by candlelight, surrounded by precious artifacts from earlier, happier days, watching nuns move to and fro in the garden below. In a dark mood — when, for example, she was mourning her lost relationship with her daughter, or finding herself frustrated by her inability to carry through a project — the studio must have seemed little more than a prison.

Yet she was determined to project a rosier, more romantic image. In the summer of 1930, she had caught the attention of an American journalist with the improbable name of Wambly Bald. Once a proofreader for the Paris edition of the *Chicago Tribune*, Bald was recognized by the *Tribune*'s editor, Jules Franz, as an educated vagabond with a good eye for life on the streets; Franz gave him a weekly column in the newspaper, called "La Vie de Bohème," and an assignment to cover life in Montparnasse. Bald's column, which caught on immediately with the expatriate crowd, focused not on the famous artists and writers who frequented the Left Bank — though he duly noted their comings and goings — but on the life of the regulars of that world, the eccentric and the colorful, the geniuses and the madmen. He would become known as "the Left Bank's ubiquitous Boswell."

Louise became a regular feature in Bald's column, which was

launched in October 1929; indeed, the description of her studio is from an August 1930 Bald piece. He wrote about her so frequently and fondly that it seems he must have been somewhat enamored of her. And Louise welcomed the attention — as well as the opportunity to refashion the facts of her past life, the better to paint the picture she wanted of her new life. For all her troubles, she had an innate sense of dignity that forbade her to ask for pity; she wanted her troubles kept private. So, for example, in the first column Bald devoted to her, he reported the fact that her play, *The Game,* had been written when she was sixteen (she had been thirty); that she had been one of the original three directors of the Provincetown Players; and that she was working on two novels, one for Liveright and one for Harper Brothers. Bald got some things right: he described her coverage of Russia, Reed's death, Louise's exclusive with Mussolini. And he added some tantalizing touches: Louise had written a poem, he reported, called "The Myth of the Lady Unexplored," the first lines of which read, "And there was a round of absurdity / Called the earth." Also, he reported, she had taken up flying: "Three or four times a week, just before the sun comes up, we are accustomed to seeing this dark-eyed dynamo clad in a military blue mantle and a black beret, pacing nervously in front of the Dôme. She is waiting for the bus that takes her to Le Bourget field [where Lindbergh had landed in 1927]. For Louise loves to fly and we understand that she flies alone."

Bald's column would detail Louise's activities — invented, imagined, or quite real — for the next three years, but it seems worthwhile to pause and consider this particular detail: Louise had taken up flying. Jimmie Charters, the barman at the Dingo, mentions in his memoirs "Louise Bryant, who became so interested in aviation that she insisted on wearing the uniform of a French aviation officer at the Dôme." Nowhere else is her new interest mentioned. Yet it sheds fascinating light on Louise's state of mind and her hopes for a new life on her own again.

No doubt Louise was attracted to the still dangerous and unusual sport by her constitutional need for adventure; when she wrote to Claude McKay from London in 1928, after being diagnosed with Dercum's disease, she gave at least as much space to the excitement of her flight over from France as she did to her illness. Charles Lindbergh's solo flight across the Atlantic in 1927 had, of course, gripped the attention of the world, but it had been an epochal event for Americans in

Paris, who rushed to Le Bourget to welcome the hero from back home. And when Amelia Earhart became the first woman to cross the ocean by air a year later, she stirred Louise's imagination; something about this tall, boyish woman who physically resembled Lindbergh himself captivated her. Earhart was a woman of daring and a popular hero in an age when women's achievements were generally given second place — when they were considered sufficiently noteworthy to attract attention at all. Earhart was nothing less than a symbol of female emancipation, and flying seemed to Louise equally symbolic: it is hardly surprising that she took lessons with the object of solo flight.

In her quest, Louise suffered her share of mishaps, perhaps even more so than most because she had always been accident-prone. Bald reported in his column of October 14 that she had suffered a black eye and a small cut on the nose when her plane, setting down in the mud, jolted her against the dashboard. Yet she persevered. Beyond the clichés associated with solo flight, the physical stamina and mental acuity it demanded must also have represented a triumph over her illness. It was a statement of her own emancipation.

Louise made other such gestures in the months just after her divorce. Gwen had hurried to her side in Paris when she returned from Baden-Baden, and the two lived openly together through the rest of 1930. Louise's passport photo from November 1929 shows a boyish woman, dressed in a man's jacket and tie, her shining black hair worn short, straight, and slicked back from a part on the side. She looks happier and more attractive than she had in photos from prior years.

Gwen, whom he called "a girl of such poise that when she enters a room she appears to be stepping down from a cloud," was another favorite of Wambly Bald's, and his accounts of her doings in "La Vie de Bohème" suggest an altogether fitting companion for the new Louise. Bald introduced her in his September 16 column, directing the reader to watch "when she lopes with more than reasonable speed through Montparnasse traffic. Such speed has conviction; it presupposes an inner swagger, a remoteness, and above all, an indifference." This indifference, Bald explained, signaled that she was incapable of insincerity, simply not caring about social conventions. Her temperament, he wrote, "rests on chaos," her impulses were "fascinating." Her constant companion, Bald wrote, was a two-month-old Congo leopard, which, to Gwen's amusement, once swatted the columnist, drawing blood.

"I don't know what is meant by the 'real' Quarter or 'real' Montparnasse," Bald wrote, "but if there were such a spot, Gwen Le Gallienne would doubtless be sitting in the very center." He used the same language in describing Louise, writing that her studio "was a day and night club for everybody," frequented by the likes of Konrad Bercovici, Hemingway, and the financier Otto Kahn. A newspaper account would refer to her "famous cloister on the rue d'Assas," which "became a rendezvous for intellectuals of all kinds." She was, the piece went on, "a fixture of Left Bank American life in Paris." She was famous, wrote a Paris memoirist, "for the daring studio parties that she gave in the early hours of the morning."

Gwen and Louise, then, were reigning princesses in Montparnasse, and both openly enjoyed flaunting their relationship in the presence of the more conservative Right Bank American types — those with whom Bullitt was more likely to associate. No doubt word of their antics reached him in Philadelphia, and there ensued a long period in which Louise heard no news of Anne. Whether because of this, or because Gwen was a flighty sort at best, or because the disease grew worse, or because Louise began to drink heavily in response to all these factors, her happiness with Gwen was not to last. In fact, by the beginning of 1931 she suspected Gwen of trying to poison her. Her troubles had taken on a new form: paranoia. It would not be a passing phase.

Once again, what happened in late 1930 and 1931 can be pieced together only through the accounts of an eyewitness — and not the most reliable sort. Throughout the early months of 1931, both Frank Walsh and Mrs. Reed were besieged by letters from a certain Jean Ressing, residing at 7 impasse du Rouet, whom they would not be able to identify for some time. He was a Dutch journalist living in Paris and had met Louise in December 1929. He had evidently fallen in love with her, and set himself up straightaway as her protector.

Louise told him, at the outset, enough about her plight and about the sympathies of her U.S. friends that he became convinced that she needed not just a friend but a champion. Unfortunately, much of what she told him was born out of paranoia, a state of mind Ressing fell in with immediately. In his first letter, written to Mrs. Reed, he stated outright that Louise was *"empoissened,"* and had been for some time, even before she left for the U.S. in 1929. Gwen Le Gallienne, he asserted, had been giving her poison throughout the summer of 1930 and had stolen Louise's clothing and jewels while living off whatever money Louise had. Gwen was, moreover, writing letters asserting that they were lesbians — and was paid by Bill Bullitt to do so. Ressing was vague about what he wanted Louise's American friends to do, but said she must leave her studio, where she was unprotected, and move into a hotel. If Louise returned to the States, he said, she needed "an *Irish person*" to protect her there; there was no American she — or he — could trust.

His tales of Louise's woe and his recommendations for how she might be helped escalated in the series of letters he wrote Walsh and Mrs. Reed over the next few weeks: Montparnasse thieves had stolen Louise's most valuable belongings, and she needed a protector with a revolver; Louise had been attacked in her studio by an intruder; a fall in her studio had led to a two-week stay in the American Hospital; café proprietors tried repeatedly to poison her and she had to be warned not to let any glass or cup she was drinking from out of her sight; she was unable to walk without support and was often brought home by strangers; she had been attacked by the waiters at the Rotonde when a check of hers was stolen. Ressing was at his wit's end, he wrote; he carried with him a big stick but could not always be at her side to protect her. Finally he wrote that he was putting her on the U.S.-bound German steamer *Ballin* on April 24 with her last $300.

Frank Walsh and Mrs. Reed, understandably, did not know what to make of all this. Walsh wrote Mrs. Reed that Ressing seemed to him crazy or drunk; Ressing's letters, wrote Walsh, were written on the letterhead of the Dôme — "where drunken intellectuals congregate." As to Ressing's claim that Louise was destitute, Walsh said he had consulted Arthur Garfield Hays, who said he was "pretty sure" she was getting $300 a month from a trust fund set up by Bullitt.

But even setting aside the florid paranoia of Ressing's urgent letters, it is fair to conclude from them that Louise was in very serious trouble. Gwen and Louise had parted company in October, according to Ressing; by late December Bald was writing in his column that Gwen was traveling all over in the company of "a popular Russian woman,

Mariska Dietrich." Louise, whose penchant for giving away her possessions was becoming such a habit that it might almost be characterized as
a secondary symptom of her disease, may well have believed, in her hurt
at being deserted, that Gwen had stolen from her. She had, after all,
sacrificed a good deal for Gwen; it may even have seemed to her, at
times, that she had lost her child because of Gwen. Her claim that Bill
was paying Gwen to write letters about the nature of their relationship
was probably not true in its particulars, but as events would show, Bill
kept close tabs on her doings in the years after their divorce, often
employing underhanded means.

The question of poisoning can be easily dismissed. But there is, once
again, a grain of truth in Ressing's jumbled accounts. Louise's health was
obviously taking a severe downturn, one not entirely attributable to her
drinking. As early as January, before Ressing's wild letters, she wrote a
long but composed and probably sober letter to Walsh detailing her
problems. She had been "desperately ill," she wrote, having been hospitalized three times in the American Hospital in Neuilly-sur-Seine and
once in a French hospital — and this was before the hospitalization
Ressing spoke of in March. She was in financial trouble — the doctors'
bills kept her "hopping" — and she ate only one meal a day, which could
not have helped her weakened condition. Though she was not the
"borrowing kind," she asked Walsh if he or Clarence Darrow could raise
steamer fare for her to return to the U.S.: she had a 4.9 carat diamond
ring she wanted to pawn, and could get more money for it there. She
had been spending too much time cooped up in her studio, she said,
and was "very depressed."

Though the bit about the ring sounds irrational — why would anyone cross the ocean to sell a piece of jewelry? — the letter was more
upbeat than her description of her health would indicate. Between the
hospitalizations, she wrote, she had managed to do "quite a lot," including "crashing in aeroplanes" and traveling to Germany, Morocco, and
Brittany. She was looking forward to working for the newspapers again,
she said. She knew "the international questions" and wanted to return
home to make some newspaper connections ("and first to see my little
girl"). The letter closed on a wistful note: she had had four proposals of
marriage, she said (it's fair to say that at least one of these suitors can
be accounted for — her knight and protector Jean Ressing). "Oh, my
word!" she wrote in closing. "But I think I'll walk alone in the future."

21

The Harvard Men

I n late 1934, the past again intruded on Louise's efforts to carve out a new life. Some men at Harvard, it seemed, were going to write the book she had never been able to finish: a biography of John Reed. The prospect energized Louise, giving her life new purpose, and she threw herself into a concentrated effort to help them in the task, only to find that her involvement in this particular part of history was not of interest to them. It would be one of the most bitter disappointments of her life, perhaps even the ultimate betrayal.

The 1920s had been a decade of complacency and disillusionment with recent developments in the Soviet Union — Louise was not alone in her dismay as the Bolsheviks essayed a limited reintroduction of capitalism, then succumbed to Stalin's domination and embarked on an orgy of purges aimed at engineers and other educated groups. But in the 1930s, as the U.S. descended into economic collapse, many American radicals again turned to the ideals of the Russian Revolution, and the rolls of the Communist party in the U.S. swelled. Relevant here was the formation by *The New Masses,* in 1929, of the first John Reed Club, intended to foster a new revolutionary culture, and particularly proletarian art. Soon chapters of the club sprang up across the country, and Jack Reed emerged from the shadowy 1920s as a revolutionary hero for a new generation.

Far from surviving underground, as had the activism of the teens, this new radicalism permeated intellectual life in the early 1930s, extending into bastions of influence and power. At Harvard, Reed's alma mater, a John Reed Alumni Committee was formed with an eye to honoring the newly restored Communist hero. The man chosen by the committee to write Reed's biography was the Harvard graduate Granville Hicks, a 1920s liberal with Socialist leanings who had been galvanized by the Sacco and Vanzetti trial to take a closer look at radical politics. By 1931 he was a convert to Communism, which, like many others of the time, he carefully distinguished from the Communist party, which he would not join until 1935.

As the committee's formation suggests, the projected biography was planned out in deadly earnest. Beyond producing a rigorous work of scholarship about one of Harvard's own, Hicks and his colleagues wanted to cement the legend of this larger-than-life hero and to reclaim him as a guiding light for the new Communist movement. But they were stymied from the outset by a lack of access to Jack's papers — his letters, unpublished manuscripts, and the other masses of material so essential to the biographer. Hicks learned from Harry Reed that every-thing of Jack's that the family possessed had been sent to Louise in Paris in 1932. "That makes it all the more necessary to work as tactfully as possible on Louise Bryant," Hicks wrote Robert Hallowell, Jack's old classmate and artist friend, whom he had delegated to deal with Louise. "I must get that material if it's humanly possible." He planned out and mounted his strategy like a general deploying troops.

Bob Hallowell addressed Louise first, and on November 19 she sent off what she feared was "a bitter reply." She itemized the troubles she had had writing Jack's story herself: the noncooperation of Jack's friends, what she felt to be *New Masses* editor Mike Gold's perfidy in attempting a biography of Jack, and her difficulties getting an advance from a publisher. Then she got to the heart of the matter: "As for Mr. Hicks, however honest, straight, decent, he may be I do not see how in any way he could have known Jack's life earlier or later. I do not know if he ever met Jack." She catalogued the many aspects of Jack's life about which only she had concrete information. It was still her intention to write her own book, she declared. She devoted a whole page to those friends of Jack's who had treated him badly in his last days in America, when he was living way out on the radical fringe, singling out in particular

Harvard classmates Bobby Rogers, Dave Carb, and Robert Edmond Jones — all of whom Hicks and his committee had been counting on as key sources. She was determined to serve Jack's memory responsibly, she emphasized: "I mean to stand by Jack in his death as I did in his life. . . . Whatever I have to reproach myself for, I am sure I did not fail Jack."

That said, she closed the letter by hinting that she would cooperate if treated right: "I ask you to tell your friend, Mr. Hicks, to work with me and not be in a great hurry about such a book. At least he could send me a list of questions — so he might get a few things straight."

While she guarded Jack's papers and her own memories closely, Louise was obviously tantalized by the news of what the Harvard committee had in mind. It would bring *her* name, too, back before the general public. It would link her and Jack back up with the progressive left, after the long years as "Mrs. Bullitt." It would establish their place in history for a new generation. All this she wanted desperately in her lonely and impoverished exile.

Louise would learn, however, that Hicks and the committee were not much interested in any information or memories she might have. They wanted those papers. Louise offered to bring them over herself, saying she could not simply send them off unescorted, but evidently the committee did not want to deal with her presence or the issue of the money she said she would need to bring them. Louise's reputation as a decadent émigré queen preceded her, and they simply did not take her seriously as a source of information, much less a committed radical dedicated to Reed's memory. Indeed, they thought she might be an embarrassment. A certain gratuitous nastiness crept into the committee's efforts even at this early date. Corliss Lamont, in his capacity as secretary-treasurer of the committee, wrote a letter to Francis McClernon and Maurice Hindus, two Harvard graduates who he knew would be passing through Paris, asking them to do what they could. Hindus might have an in, wrote Lamont, because he had just been in Russia. "If necessary," he continued, "he might like to smoke a little opium with Louise if that is her favorite drug at present!"

Granville Hicks introduced himself formally to Louise in a January 21 letter, which he sent to Paris with John Stuart, who was to be his collaborator on the book. The letter is a masterpiece of tact, blatant flattery, and manipulation. Without overt condescension, he advanced the patronizing notion that there was room both for the book she was writing (which he clearly did not take seriously) and the book he had in mind; after all, hers would be a "personal account" (she had never given him any indication of this) while his would be a "more objective story." That said, he wrote that his book would be "incomplete" without her assistance, especially in countering the "slanders" of some of the men she had mentioned in her "bitter reply" to Bob Hallowell. If she would allow John Stuart to look at the papers in her possession — and make copies of them — "it will immensely enrich our account." In closing, he noted that she had mentioned that she had a lot of Jack's unpublished writings: why did she not bring out "a volume of his work"? He and Stuart would be "delighted" to help her secure a publisher for such a book.

With John Stuart breathing down her neck in Paris waiting to see the papers, she asked friends what she should do. She turned first to her Irish friends Jim Larkin and Jack Carney, making the impossible request that they come to Paris and help her with Stuart; Carney wrote her from Ireland that they could not, but made some kind remarks as to the sort of book he hoped for — he didn't want Jack "beatified," he said, but presented as the down-to-earth friend of the workers he was.

But by this time Louise was working with Stuart, whom she found, initially at least, that she liked. The committee, meanwhile, had been working overtime drumming up support for their project, and during Stuart's visit to Paris, she was barraged with letters from those she thought were her friends, like Arthur Garfield Hays, telling her to let Stuart bring the trunks of material back to America. Within a month she sent most of it to Harvard, reserving the intimate letters between her and Jack and her own papers.

Almost immediately she regretted her decision, perhaps intuiting that her usefulness to the committee was now over, and that she would have no further say in her husband's biography. On May 18 she sent Hays a long, rambling letter denouncing the Harvard men. She had spent over a month with Stuart going through the trunks in her studio, continuing to pay the utilities and rent on the place even though she had to live elsewhere for the interim. Though she did not say so openly, she implied that it had been a conflict of interest for him to advise her to turn over the papers, since he was her lawyer as well. She emphasized what would become a sticking point between her and the committee in the year to come: "I did not *give* the documents away. I *lent* them." Also, Stuart had promised to remain "in constant touch" with her and yet she had heard nothing from him. More importantly, "Of his promise to send me news of Anne — absolutely nothing."

After this indignant beginning, Louise's letter then lapsed into a long, disjointed account of being followed by detectives whom she believed had been hired by Bill. She believed they had been following her since she first returned from America in 1929. She went into great detail about their nefarious activities, which included bugging her hotel rooms, setting her up as a spy, threatening to kill her, and forcing her to jump from her hotel window, breaking her foot in three places.

Louise was obviously becoming increasingly paranoid. Yet despite her mental confusion, there was a certain degree of sense in her nonsense. Her elaborate fantasies of spies hired by Bill, for example, most likely did contain a grain of truth. Her ex-husband kept close tabs on her, not only through Paris friends, but also, possibly, through people he would have had to pay, for his friends would have been unwilling or unable to haunt the "low" circles in which Louise traveled. He watched carefully for any sign of lesbian activity, which Louise believed Gwen had been reporting to him. Even Kitty Cannell believed that Bill had his "spies" in the lesbian community, most notably Peggy Marquis, who Kitty still believed had designs on Bill. (Kitty also reported that Marquis, at a rowdy gathering, pushed Louise out of her studio window, breaking her foot in the process — possibly the source for Louise's jumbled account of that injury.)

Louise's feelings of persecution were undoubtedly fanned by the Harvard committee's conduct. She had essentially been tricked into giving up Jack's papers, whose true value she only fully recognized after she lost them. While the committee was outwardly treating her with deference, she must have sensed their underlying contempt. She had been used, and she knew it, and she saw evidence of other betrayals everywhere she looked.

She asked Hays to show the letter in which she described her fears of conspiracy to Lamont, but to let it go no further. It quickly found its way to Hicks, who duly catalogued it in his papers. Just nine days later, in a calmer sense of mind but convinced that any remnants of health were leaving her, Louise sent Hays a letter that she asked him to consider her last will and testament. She had, she said, about eight years ago made a will leaving everything to Bill; she supposed he had done the same, but that he had now changed it in Anne's favor. She did not have much, she wrote, but the papers she had withheld from Harvard and the personal effects in her studio, as well as her family photographs and books and manuscripts, she wanted eventually to go to Anne. She asked too that Bill be notified at her death so that he could provide her with a decent burial. In the meantime she was turning over all the remaining materials and letters in her studio to Hays's safekeeping; he could turn them over to the Harvard committee or to a man named H. D. Werner, who wanted to write a book about her (there is no other mention of this), "But in any case see that all these things are really returned to Anne," she wrote urgently.

At the end of the same month she sent a scribbled note addressed "to Corliss Lamont or John Stuart or Hicks." Though she was still showing traces of paranoia — she now referred to "the organization" that had set her up and made her jump from her window — she was now ready to state her wishes clearly, and to let the committee know her real griev-ances. Referring to the material still in her possession, she wrote, "Now my fear is not to lose the things I have left, which in many ways are as precious and maybe a little more clear than those [Stuart] took over." Clearly, she hoped mention of this cache would tantalize them and give her some leverage. She believed "the organization" was after the remain-ing papers, but now that she had shown them she did not fear death by jumping out of her window, they would never take them "unless I am not in this world." What happened after her death did not concern her: "I wanted Jack's story to be *clearly* written. I don't care what happens to mine. Most everyone seems to be making a mess of his. That is why I wrote to Art Hays my last will and testament and as soon as I can I'll send you a last letter to Anne (my daughter). So if chances are not in my favor some day she will know." She referred to John Stuart as "happy in his youth (and consciously male)" and stated unequivocally, "To me intelligence is not a matter of sex and age is not a crime," indicating that she clearly felt the committee was dismissing her because she was seen as just a bothersome old woman — most likely not far from the truth. The note closed with the plaintive query, "Why doesn't the Committee keep in touch with me?"

It is only fair to point out that most of Louise's communications with Hicks and the committee were not paranoid ravings but correctives of what she felt were inaccuracies of interpretations they alluded to in their letters to her. Some were more valuable than others. A typical sheaf of notes, written in a clear hand and mailed in the fall of 1935, contains little essays on such subjects as the mistaken notion that Jack ever served as American consul for Russia; on Louis Fraina, Jack's opponent during the divisive battles in the Socialist party in 1919; on the parts Jack had acted in the Provincetown Players' productions; on a speech she and Jack had given jointly at the Tremont Hotel in Boston. Though she sometimes had scores of her own to settle, her tone was respectful and helpful, if sometimes gently chiding.

Perhaps at the committee's urging — though probably not — Louise finally undertook a sort of memoir in late October. With the exception of her two books, it was the longest piece of writing she had ever produced, and in a sense the last "work" of her life. It was actually a transcription of remarks she made in a long conversation with a hired stenographer. Louise tried to give a straightforward account of her life, but she rambled and digressed; in her notes accompanying the transcription she complained that the stenographer kept interrupting her with questions — perhaps to keep her on track. It is a fascinating document and a compelling story, if one allows for the gaps, digressions, and abrupt changes of subject. The tone is very fresh and conversational, like that of an old veteran full of wonderful stories, which have been polished over the years and which the teller knows how to spin out to good effect. Louise knew how to rivet attention and to hold the stage, and the result could perhaps best be described as a performance. She begins with her childhood on Grandfather Say's ranch, discussing her upbringing, her years in Portland, meeting Jack, their earliest times together in New York, and the Provincetown summer when the Players were launched — this last in great detail. Then she digresses, with stories of the Russian Revolution and a few of her journalistic coups after Jack's death. She then returns to the story of her life with Jack — his hospitalization and the removal of his kidney and her own, simultaneous, mysterious illness; their life together in Croton; and her adventures in France during the painful separation of 1917. She tells about their first journey to Russia, after which she shifts gears again to begin a narrative about Jack's family background, later relating some miscellaneous anecdotes about their married life. The whole rambling thread breaks off abruptly after a long story about Jack's attempts to help out a young French dressmaker adrift in New York, whose care he gladly relinquished to

Louise when she turned out to be dishonest and a very bad dressmaker to boot.

Louise was thoroughly disgusted with the resulting document. She wrote to Hicks, "Looking over this mass of illiterate notes you will realize why I could not work with a stenographer of this type. She put things down in her own language not mine, "I said, he said" — every kind of street phrase without understanding for a moment what anything was all about . . . [L]ooking at [the notes] now I can scarcely believe that my eyes do not deceive me." Her concern, she said, was what might be useful to Hicks. Accordingly, she labored mightily over the notes, crossing out, for example, four pages about her own journalistic exploits. At one point she ripped out two pages entirely, which seem to have been devoted to Eugene O'Neill, writing in the margin that they were "of an intimate and unpublishable quality and no reference to any material you need." Indeed, she also scratched out and added words in nearly every sentence, improving the narrative flow and rendering the whole document less telegraphic. These are the emendations of a natural writer, one whose talent is still intact.

If Louise had begun the project to help Hicks with relevant material about Jack's life and their life together, her desire to tell her own story had obviously reasserted itself. But her experiences with Hicks and the Harvard men had been so demeaning and their priorities revealed so unflatteringly that she chose the route, in emending and bowdlerizing the "memoir," of self-effacement. Then, too, she must have realized midway that her life with Jack was only part of her story — and that her years alone as a thriving foreign correspondent and world traveler, not to mention her tumultuous marriage to Bullitt, its aftermath, her reexamination of her sexuality, and her illness, were of no interest to Jack Reed's biographer. So despite her editorial efforts, her narrative devolves into not very revealing anecdotes about her late husband before breaking off altogether. Yet she had started off strongly, with a sure knowledge that the minutest details of her strange childhood, for instance, were of implicit interest. Her life had been remarkable, and she knew it, but when she tried to tell her story for men who were only interested in resurrecting her second husband as a Communist hero, she lost heart. As it was, the Harvard men used nothing from the memoir she had worked so hard to compile.

As her life drew to a close, then — just over a month remained to her — her thoughts turned increasingly to Jack. Writing to her friend Art Young, the illustrator of the old *Masses,* she indicated that she had little time left on what in her late poem she had spoken of as this "round of absurdity / Called the earth." Like so many, Young had always been a little in love with Louise, and he referred to her as "this lovely daughter of a Fenian" in his autobiography, where he reproduced the last letter he received from her: "I suppose in the end life gets all of us. It nearly has got me now — getting myself and my friends out of jail — living under curious conditions — but never minding much. . . . Know always I send my love to you across the stars. If you get there before I do — or later — tell Jack Reed I love him."

In the summer of 1935, she had moved from her apartment in the rue Vavin (which she had taken after her eviction from her "cloister" for nonpayment of rent) to a rather seedy hotel in the rue de la Grande-Chaumière, the Hotel Liberia, which charged two dollars a night. She was found there on the landing, clutching a bottle of milk and a newspaper she had apparently picked up outside her door, at 4:30 P.M. on January 6, 1936, dead of a cerebral hemorrhage.

The saga of Louise Bryant and the Harvard men would have a curious and ultimately depressing coda. In a last letter to Hicks on December 2, Louise described how she had passed the anniversary of Jack's death. Some of what she wrote didn't make sense, like the description of a portent she believed referred to her upcoming birthday, and a mention of just returning from Turkestan "with a lot of first-hand info in my head." She promised she would send Hicks a note she had kept that had been written by Lenin, asking her to come to him at once and tell him what she had seen on her journey to the south of Russia. (This may have been a last joke on Hicks, for the penciled note, still at Harvard among Reed's papers and verified to be in Lenin's handwriting, was found years later to read, "Food tax.") The letter closed with a reminder that she had given the papers to the committee on the condition that they be returned to her daughter and that "one day they will tell my little girl, Anne, why."

The Harvard committee went on with business as usual, and Granville Hicks published *John Reed: The Making of a Revolutionary* in the same year as Louise's death. No effort was made to inform Anne that papers belonging to her were at Harvard, nor to tell her "why" — Louise's last request — nor to return them to her. This despite the fact that Louise had emphasized repeatedly that she was giving the materials to Harvard as a loan, not a gift, and that they were to revert to Anne. The letters, manuscripts, albums, clippings, family photographs, Jack's wallet and his address book — all stayed at Harvard as part of the Louise Bryant Collection. But that, too, would change. Just nine months after Louise's death, Corliss Lamont wrote a Harvard alumnus in answer to an inquiry, "There is no particular point in having the name of Louise Bryant connected with the material. And I think the title which you suggest, The John Reed Collection of Manuscripts and Documents, would be preferable." The John Reed Collection it became; Louise's name was effaced.

Postlude: Louise, Later

L ouise Bryant died penniless and alone, but her passing did not go unnoticed. Obituaries in Europe and the U.S. remembered this "pretty, sharp-witted" woman (*Time*), this "unusually competent journalist" (*New York Herald Tribune*), this "rebel woman of great charm and courage" (*The New Masses*), and noted her many accomplishments — her coverage of the Russian Revolution and her two fine books about it, her defiant testimony before the Overman Committee, her shining career as a Hearst correspondent. But hints of her decline were making their way into these accounts. *Time* noted that she was divorced for "personal indignities," adding, "Thereafter, in constant financial difficulties, she made her home in Paris." The *International Herald Tribune,* concentrating on her Paris years, noted that "she tried her hand at poetry, sculpture, composing, playwriting, and even aviation" and that she was "a fixture of Left Bank American life in Paris," her studio "a rendezvous for intellectuals of all kinds," but added, "She began to show the strain of her varied life and by degrees lost the true creative impulse."

These accounts were, of course, written by Louise's colleagues, who were paying tribute to her journalistic talents and achievements; she was a kindred soul, and they wrote respectfully of her decline and death. But many others would not be so kind. Somerset Maugham, whom Louise had known in Russia and who clearly followed her career with interest, portrayed her savagely in his 1943 novel, *The Razor's Edge,* as Sophie

Macdonald, an American expatriate who has lost her husband and child in a car wreck and now lives a sordid, underground sort of existence in Paris and Marseilles. A male defender of Sophie's sees the tragedy of her decline: "I suppose she didn't care what became of her and flung herself into the horrible degradation of drink and promiscuous copulation to get even with life that had treated her so cruelly. She'd lived in heaven and when she lost it she couldn't put up with the common earth of common men, and in despair plunged headlong into hell." But a woman friend is less sympathetic, and scoffs in response, "Sophie wallows in the gutter because she likes it. . . . Don't waste your pity on her; she's now at heart what she always was."

While portraits like Maugham's and the comments of acquaintances emphasized Louise's drinking and disgraceful behavior, the great majority of the postmortems damned her for becoming a hag. It is astonishing how many accounts of Louise in her later years stress her ruined looks. Even close friends like Kitty Cannell and Mura Dehn dwelled on her faded beauty rather than the other losses she had suffered. Louise had been a world-class beauty, and her looks had worked for her, not against her, throughout her career; the loss of them was indeed a tragedy. But the sense of accusation in all this — the references to her dirty hands, her disheveled clothes — remind us of another, uglier truth: women are blamed for losing their looks. Her disfiguring disease aside, Louise had aged: she was fifty when she died. In her case, too, because she had continued to be beautiful well into her forties and was able to lie so magnificently about her age — the obituaries reported her age as forty-one — it seemed that she became an old and unattractive woman before her time.

The sexism behind this kind of response barely needs comment. Louise was a woman of achievement who had led a rich and varied life, but observers of her in later years spoke not of what she had accomplished or the events to which she had borne witness, not even to regret how much had been lost when her energies failed her. Instead, they spoke of her compromised looks. She had become a visible reminder of decay and death. We find it hard to forgive our faded young.

But rumors about Louise — her waning beauty, her decline — had always threatened to eclipse the reality of her life. Granville Hicks, for instance, treated a woman he had never met with churlish disparagement. When one of Louise's biographers asked in 1977 why he had never responded to Louise's requests to be interviewed for his book on John Reed, or at least sent a questionnaire, he replied furiously, "Because she was always drunk!" Turning away, he murmured, "Or so I was told."

The example of Hicks, a doctrinaire leftist who may perhaps have viewed Louise dismissively because she did not continue to champion the Soviet Union in the 1920s, is representative in another way. Louise came in for the harshest treatment after her death from the left, which had always been guarded toward her but whose cause she had served so honestly and earnestly. Some rigorous party types used things she said, or that they attributed to her, to indicate that she was to blame for what they felt to be John Reed's disillusionment with Russia. Others, who felt differently about the Communist cause, gave her credit for this imagined act, but the result was the same: without much evidence to back them up, she was used by others to further their own predetermined conclusions.

Emma Goldman set the tone perfectly when she wrote to Alexander Berkman upon Louise's death: "The last time I saw her was at the Select when two drunken Corsicans carried her out of the café. What a horrible end. More and more I come to think it is criminal for young middle-class American or English girls to enter radical ranks. They go to pieces. And even when they do not reach the gutter, as Louise did, their lives are empty. . . . Of course, Louise was never a communist, she only slept with a communist." The mean-spiritedness of this is self-evident, as is the absurdity of Goldman's attempt to draw a condescending conclusion from Louise's case. Goldman initially became famous in the U.S. for her lectures introducing the drama of Shaw and Ibsen — who in plays like *Mrs. Warren's Profession* and *A Doll's House* portrayed the awakening liberations of middle-class women. She should have known better than to generalize in this way about class. Louise's origins, in fact, were as working-class as Emma's. One begins to wonder if it was precisely Louise's ability to move seemingly without effort *between* classes that rankled Goldman. In any case, it is dubious at best to imagine that young middle-class women lead empty lives because of their involvement with radical causes. The lives of women as diverse as Charlotte Perkins Gilman and Elizabeth Gurley Flynn — or even the life of Goldman herself — teach us that political commitment enriches rather than stifles. In Louise's case, the idea is even more absurd. Radicalism defined her, and working for women's rights and the Russian experiment gave her life meaning. The principles, loyalty, and sacrifice that radical work required remained with her long after she ceased to be actively caught up in politics.

Diminishing Louise's commitment by saying "she only slept with a communist" not only makes Goldman's argument double-back on itself and become contradictory, but it is a cheap shot, plain and simple. Goldman was not alone, however, in charging that Louise got as far as she did through her relations with men. Like the majority of her contemporaries, Louise — with the exception of her ill-fated interlude with Gwen — did not consider living without men an option; coming from, as John Reed said, "unfertilized soil," her only options were which men she would choose. But, while a connection with a talented man could, indeed, help a woman get a foot in the door, it did not guarantee success of the kind Louise achieved as a journalist and radical. Yet too many observers, beginning perhaps with the Provincetown woman who said, "Just because someone is sleeping with somebody is no reason we should do her play," have dismissed Louise as a footnote to male stories, defining her only in relation to the men in her life.

Commentators have attacked Louise in the same vein ever since. As recently as 1993 the radical historian Christine Stansell gave a paper titled "Louise Bryant Grows Old" at the eminent Berkshire Conference of Women Historians at Vassar College. Like Goldman, Stansell cast doubts on Louise's political commitment; what seems to have damned her the most in this Marxist historian's eyes was her marriage to the wealthy Bullitt. But along the way Stansell raised questions about the meaning of Louise's life, which she characterized as not terribly exciting, even pitiful. Louise Bryant, she claimed, dropped out of history as she aged; her life was, finally, not historically important. Along the way, Stansell faulted Louise for not guarding Reed's memory properly during the 1920s — but then criticized her for turning into a "professional widow" once Hicks began his biography. She saw Louise sinking into an alcoholic realm outside of history, nearly psychotic and ultimately pathetic — but did not mention the medical connection of this behavior to Dercum's disease. Finally, she looked to the cruelest trick that was played on Louise after her death: Corliss Lamont's casual decision to change the name of the papers she lent to Harvard, from the Louise Bryant Collection to the John Reed Collection. Far from deploring this dismissal of Louise's importance, Stansell asked whether he was right — and whether it mattered.

Of course it matters. Lamont did a serious disservice to history, effacing not just Louise's name but her very existence. Louise did not "drop out" of history — but her place has been obscured by a pattern of trivializing and minimizing that began when she appeared in New York as John Reed's girlfriend and has continued, it seems, ever since. Set in the turbulent Greenwich Village of the teens, Eugene O'Neill's Provincetown, Russia during the ten days that shook the world, Paris in the twenties, and the lesbian cafés of the Left Bank, Louise's life has obvious historical interest; in her long struggle to give every aspect of her life meaning she insisted that she was part of history. So why has she been so consistently denigrated over the years, by Goldman, by Hicks and Lamont, and so recently by Stansell? Ultimately they blame her, it seems, for becoming a victim — a designation that fits only in that triumph over an incurable disease and a devastating divorce eluded her. The irony is that each of these critics has victimized Louise all over again. To claim that Louise Bryant doesn't matter is a profound insult to this complicated and fascinating woman — and to history itself.

As women continue to struggle to break loose from the constraints of a male-dominated society, many continue to find the life of Louise Bryant inspiring and instructive. At the conference where Stansell delivered her paper, listeners were passionate in their defense of Louise Bryant, even those who had previously known little about her life. The conventions of scholarly discourse were simply done away with in the ensuing discussion. "I just want to say that I'm *for* Louise Bryant, and nothing you can say will change my mind," one woman stood up and stated indignantly, to wide applause.

For if Louise Bryant evoked a peculiarly negative response in some people, in many, many more her very name conjures up the image of a brave and committed — if in some ways tragic — heroine. Seemingly in direct proportion to the attempts of those who would diminish her accomplishments or erase her from history, Louise Bryant has had her staunch defenders. In fact, it is remarkable that of all the talented writers Louise knew, only Somerset Maugham used her dramatic downward trajectory as a subject. Bill Bullitt, who never remarried, would become the first U.S. ambassador to the Soviet Union and later ambassador to France, his star continuing to rise until he and FDR clashed in the kind of war of wills to which Bullitt was so relentlessly drawn; yet no acquaintance or friend would ever tell tales about his second wife. Louise traveled among the century's greatest movers and shakers, to borrow a term Mabel Dodge Luhan used for her memoirs, but, Maugham's and Goldman's slurs aside, most of them have shown a reticence that can only be characterized as noble about her decline. If Louise was, as one college classmate said, "like a shooting star," most observers saw only the bright arc of her ascendancy. The remarks of George Biddle — who well knew the vicissitudes of Louise's life — show how she was captured in the imagination at the height of that arc:

> Louise was a good deal like . . . La Passionara. Yes, she could take an audience by storm. It was her looks — her black hair, her high coloring, her white skin. And then, her emotion. No, that is not the word. She was no cold intellect — she was intuitive, she had a sense of her audience, and she could hold them.
>
> And, very typical of a person with that Irish charm, she was loyal, she was violent in her emotions; she was partisan. At her best, she was captivating, an able journalist, fierce in her loyalties — a straight shooter.

Diana Sheean, the wife of Vincent "Jimmie" Sheean, never met Louise but knew of her through her husband, and her response was typical of those who felt a strangely fierce fidelity toward her: "I don't know how precisely, but years ago, when I first met Jimmie and he spoke of Louise, this partisan feeling for her was awakened in me. I wish I knew just what it was he said that instantly made me feel so strongly for Louise and so subsequently outraged by misrepresentations of her." Louise, she said, needed someone to fight for her. Sheean invoked Shakespeare: "O God, Horatio, what a wounded name, / Things standing thus unknown, shall I leave behind me!"

Diane Keaton's spirited performance as Louise Bryant in Warren Beatty's 1981 film *Reds* undoubtedly helped to revive interest in the romantic, idealistic woman she played. In portraying Louise's appearance as a defiant witness before the Overman Committee, her zeal in pursuing a story (though the film exaggerates the journalistic help Jack gave her), her defiance of convention, her bravery in the face of Red-bashing, her sheer style, Keaton captures Bryant as a genuine twentieth-century heroine. The critic Elizabeth Hardwick has written that Louise died like a character out of Zola or Balzac, but suggested that the literary figure she most closely resembled was Sister Carrie, alone, at the end of Dreiser's novel, in her rocking chair. "Even [Louise's] journalism," writes Hardwick, "might remind one of the theatrical success of Carrie, some aspect of performance that is not art and yet a public definition." It is perhaps instructive that a film performance should have effectively given shape to Louise's life in a way she herself was unable to.

Of course, Bryant's life went far beyond the events portrayed in *Reds.* Her life went on; people's lives do that. The choices she later made, the men she loved, the causes she took up, these are subject to interpretation and debate. What remains clear is that she never lost her passion for life. This passion showed itself from her earliest days, running wild on her grandfather's ranch, and demanding, throughout her adolescence and young adulthood, an equal place in a masculine world. It showed itself in her life as a vagabond journalist in Russia and postwar Europe. Louise was always moving about, it seems, always a traveler. But it could also be said that the day she stepped off the train in New York City in 1916, she found her metaphorical home.

Bohemia once referred to a region in Europe, a place where, it seemed, no one lived but instead came from; Bohemians were gypsies, and gypsies lived freely in the margins of society, never settling in one place for long. With the rise of romanticism in France the word "Bohemia" came to denote the exotic underworld of struggling poets, writers, artists, and intellectuals. In America, Bohemia became a metaphorical place, as Greenwich Village became the New Bohemia and little bohemias were said to be popping up across the country: in Chicago, in San Francisco, in Boston. Over time, Bohemia became, as many have said, a state of mind. Yet there is still a territory we can call Bohemia, even if it cannot be seen or photographed: it is a territory of romance, risk, choice, commitment, and passion. Its terrain is fraught with perils, for those who choose to dwell there set themselves apart from the inhabitants of the earth while remaining, of course, among their number. As such they are open to all kinds of attack, some rational, some not, from those who choose more conventional lives. It is uncharted territory, where there are no rules or rulers, and in this anarchic, motley, exciting, and timeless land, Louise Bryant still lives as queen.

Acknowledgments
Notes
Selected Bibliography
Index

Acknowledgments

A number of individuals have been extremely generous in granting me interviews or guiding me to other sources. These include: Shari Benstock, Debbie Browne, Will Brownell, Norman S. Cohen, Joan Y. Dickinson, Leona Rust Egan, Merrill Field, Hugh Ford, Benjamin Franklin V, James Graham, Ann May Greene, Julia Van Haafeten, Robert Hamburger, Eric Homberger, David Hull, John Kerr, Philip Kruger, Carolyn Mohan, Peg Mowry, Jane Northshield, James Rentschler, John de St. Jorre, Peter Swales, Dick and Susan Todd, and Sarah Williams. Anne Bullitt very kindly spoke with me many times, though this is in no way an authorized biography. Karen Jastermsky, an independent scholar working on Louise Bryant, shared with me the fruits of her first-rate research on Louise, particularly Louise's uncollected writings. Her dedication to and enthusiasm for her work has been an inspiration as well as a considerable material aid.

In Portland, Oregon, I was fortunate to be taken under the wing of the extraordinary Gudrun Cable, a writer and artist and the proprietor of two legendary establishments, the Sylvia Beach Hotel in Newport, Oregon, and the Rimsky Korsakoffee House in Portland. Through Goody's generosity and hospitality, and with the help of *The Oregonian* book editor Paul Pintarich, I met many remarkable people who were instrumental in helping me learn more about Louise's years in Portland: Arthur Spencer, Brian Booth, Frances Dwayne McGill, Kina Armstrong, E. Kimbark MacColl, and Mary Rose. Janet Kreft joined me in geographical detective work and has been an enthusiastic and helpful friend over the course of this project.

A very unusual circumstance informed the course of my research. The Tamiment Institute Library at New York University, an extraordinary archive of labor and radical history, has seldom let me down when I am stymied by an elusive subject. When I paid a call there I learned that Louise's first biographer, the late Virginia Gardner, had willed all her papers to the collection, including nearly fifteen boxes of material relating to her research for her 1982 biography, *Friend and Lover: The Life of Louise Bryant*. Gardner worked on her project for over ten years, and the boxes contained treasures: transcripts of interviews with persons long dead, carefully collected clippings, and correspondence with relevant individuals, many of whom I was able to contact. The archivist Peter Filardo graciously allowed me access to this uncatalogued material, and I spent several weeks sifting through it. It seemed at first an odd way to do research — rather like reading someone's mail — but gradually it came to seem a natural result of the best kind of collaborative and generous scholarship. I do not agree with all of Gardner's conclusions — and, of course, I conducted independent research — but her gift was expressive of the best traditions of intellectual work.

Archivists and librarians at many other institutions offered invaluable help. They include: Denison Beach and Leslie A. Morris at the Houghton Library, Harvard University; Kenneth D. Craven at the Humanities Research Center Library, University of Texas; Fred Bauman and Charles J. Kelly at the Library of Congress; Ronald Bulatoff and Linda Wheeler at the Hoover Institution, Stanford University; Judy Throm at the Archives of American Art; Heather R. Munro and Saundra Taylor at the Lilly Library, Indiana University; Sara S. Hodson at the Huntington Library; Raymond Teichman at the Franklin Delano Roosevelt Library in Hyde Park; Mark Dimunation at Cornell University; Kenneth Heger at the National Archives, Civil Reference Branch; Janet West at Special Collections, Port Washington (New York) Public Library; Patricia Willis at the Beinecke Library, Yale University; Carolyn A. Davis at the George Arents Research Library, Syracuse University; Wayne Furman at the New York Public Library; and the staffs of the Harvard Theatre Collection and the Columbia University Rare Book and Manuscript Room. Those who assisted with photographs include Ellen Cordes at the Beinecke Library, Yale University; Allen Reuben at Culver Pictures; Allen Goodrich at the Hemingway Collection, JFK Library; Susan Marcotte at the Archives of American Art; and, especially, Debbie Goodsite at UPI/Bettman, who showed imagination and resourcefulness in ferreting out images.

Elaine Markson showed faith in this project in its earliest stages. Janet Silver, my editor, has shown critical enthusiasm, support, and intelligence throughout. To be edited by her is a gift. Wendy Holt has been capable and charming, and my manuscript editor, Jayne Yaffe, is at once exacting and inspired. My agent, Georges Borchardt, kindly commented on the entire manuscript.

All writers need computer gurus these days, but mine, John Goff and Jesse Nahan, have the added virtue of being very funny, and they carried the day in more ways than one. Among the friends who read or discussed parts of the manuscript with me and generally provided writerly support are Elayne Robertson Demby, Noël Riley Fitch, Jay Gertzman, Miriam Gurniak, Brendan Mernin, Mark SaFranko, James Waller, and, especially, Meryl Altman and Mary B. Campbell. Martin Hurwitz, Warren Johnson, Joe Markulin, and Mark Trottenberg were supportive throughout. Dick and Margery Dearborn read the entire manuscript more than once and provided excellent advice. I want especially to thank my neighbor and good friend, Sandy Schmidt, who at the end of many a long day provided advice and encouragement, amusing diversions, and good cheer. My greatest debt is expressed in the dedication to this book.

Notes

ABBREVIATIONS

Unless otherwise attributed, correspondence is in the John Reed Collection, Houghton Library, Harvard University, which is designated bMS Am 1091, by permission of the Houghton Library, Harvard University. Shelf marks for individual letters are given in parentheses. Those items not in this collection are fully designated.

LB: Louise Bryant
JR: John Reed
WB: William Bullitt

LB memoir: Louise Bryant's typed notes in the Granville Hicks Collection, Syracuse University Library, Department of Special Collections
NYPL: Rare Books and Manuscripts Division, New York Public Library, Astor, Lenox and Tilden Foundations (Francis P. Walsh papers)
AAA: Archives of American Art. References are given to microfilm reel numbers in the John Henry Bradley Storrs papers, 1847–1987; the Andrew Dasburg and Grace Mott Johnson papers, 1854–1969; and the Marsden Hartley papers, 1900–1967 (owned and microfilmed by the Beinecke Library, Yale University).

SRMR: Louise Bryant, *Six Red Months in Russia: An Observer's Account of Russia Before and During the Proletarian Dictatorship*
MoM: Louise Bryant, *Mirrors of Moscow*
TDTSW: John Reed, *Ten Days That Shook the World*
VG: Virginia Gardner, *Friend and Lover: The Life of Louise Bryant*

VG papers: Virginia Gardner papers in the Tamiment Institute Library, New York University

PRELUDE: PARIS, 1933

1   She is living: Wambly Bald, *On the Left Bank,* 22; Bald's column appeared on August 12, 1930.

5   The train thunders by: George F. Kennan to VG, March 25, 1977; quoted in VG, 286.
"She had no right": Dorothy Day, quoted in VG, 16.

I · CHILD OF THE WEST

9   "curious and sudden illnesses": LB memoir, 3.
Aaron Burr: LB to Corliss Lamont, November 4, 1935, Granville Hicks Collection, Syracuse University.
Oscar Wilde: Lawrence Langner, *The Magic Curtain,* 40. Neither claim is impossible.

10   She may have been German: Interview with Anne Bullitt, May 5, 1994.
At her marriage to John Reed: Marriage certificate of LB and JR, November 9, 1916, New York State Department of Health, no. 1292.
"with stock and goods": "James Say's Death and Funeral," *Lovelock* [Nevada] *Tribune,* January 8, 1906.
Mohan was a colorful: Rev. Msgr. Joseph M. Whalen of the Diocese of Allentown, Pennsylvania, to author, November 15, 1993. Information about the Charles Mohan family is from *Biography and Portrait Cyclopedia of Schuylkill County, Pennsylvania,* 689; and from an interview with Carolyn Mohan, April 6, 1993.

11   There he compiled: Hugh J. Mohan, E. H. Clough, and John P. Cosgrave, *Pen Pictures of Representative Men of Our Time.*
Mohan was thirty-two: VG to Marion Bryant, August 19, 1970, VG papers, Box 8.
After Louise's birth: "Louise Dolly Bryant Dies in Paris Closing Colorful Career that Won Her Fame," *Reno Evening Gazette,* January 19, 1936.

12   "the tough little town": See, for example, James W. Hulse, *The Nevada Adventure.*
"of drunken and improvident habits": Reno District Court records.
"Coming from one of those broken homes": LB memoir, 1.

13   "I *had* a father!": Ibid.
The idea behind the Truckee swing: Margaret Bome interview with L. Ferris Cunningham [n.d., 1970], VG papers, Box 8.
It was a considerable relief: LB memoir, 2.

14   "After a long deliberation": LB memoir, 1.

14   "It was a strange": Ibid., 2.

15   "Never forget": Ibid., 3.

Like other Wadsworth: Margaret Bome interview with Katherine M. Riegelhuth, August 18, 1970, VG papers, Box 8.

16   The University High School: Records from Registrar's Office, University of Nevada (Nevada State University), 16th, 17th, and 18th Annual Registers.

But a friend stressed: Margaret Bome interview with Millie H. Hamblet, February 25, 1971, VG papers, Box 8.

17   She remembered that she wore: LB memoir, 4.

2 · SURFACING

18   Her sister's husband: VG interview with Bertha Dorris Carpenter, July 27, 1970, VG papers, Box 8; Interview with Frances Dwane McGill, October 21, 1993.

She entered the university: Office of the Registrar, University of Oregon, to VG, January 22, 1970, VG papers, Box 8.

"She was a young woman": Julia Ruutila interview with Jacob Proebstel, June 3, [1970], VG papers, Box 8.

19   "floaty": Lucia Wilkins Moore interview with VG, August 21, 1970, VG papers, Box 9.

"our mystery girl": Julia Ruutila interview with Louise Gray, August 13, 1970, VG papers, Box 8; VG interview with Bertha Dorris Carpenter, July 27, 1970, VG papers, Box 8.

She came under the influence: Martin Schmitt, "Portrait of a Pioneer Radical," *Old Oregon* (January/February 1970), 19–23. Professor Howe backed down too, writing his sister that he was dropping Tolstoy and Ibsen from his syllabus for the next year and intended to keep a low profile.

20   "fast": Julia Ruutila interview with Lela Goddard Fenton, April 20, 1970, VG papers, Box 5.

Carl Washburne: Julia Ruutila interview with Claude B. Washburne, April 24, 1970, VG papers, Box 5.

The University of Oregon: Miriam Van Waters to VG, July 24, 1970, VG papers, Box 7.

21   "Louise Bryant interpreted": Ibid.

"It was why": Kathleen Ruutila to VG, November 8, 1972, VG papers, Box 9.

She had had an episode: VG interview with Bertha Dorris Carpenter, July 27, 1970, VG papers, Box 8.

Her brothers Floyd and Bill: Julia Ruutila interview with Claude B. Washburne, April 24, 1970, VG papers, Box 5.

21 She met with all: Julia Ruutila interview with Ray Woodruff Jenkins, July 17, 1970, VG papers, Box 5.

22 She was involved with another man: VG interview with Alice Bretherton Powell, June 9, 1970, VG papers, Box 8.

The most scandalous report: Kenneth W. Porter to Julia Ruutila, February 9, 1971, VG papers, Box 7.

Aside from San Francisco: E. Kimbark MacColl, *The Shaping of a City*, 492.

23 A friend asked her: Interview with Frances Dwane McGill, October 21, 1993; the friend in question was Frances Young. See also Arthur Spencer to VG, May 4, [1976], VG papers, Box 10; Spencer contends the window was in a church in Albany, another town outside Salem.

She had the independence: Julia Ruutila interview with Edward N. Weinbaum, December 2, 1970, VG papers, Box 7.

24 The Wold girls: VG to Arthur Spencer, June 3, 1976, VG papers, Box 10.

John H. Trullinger: See Agnes Field, *The Legacy of John Henry Trullinger*.

After a brief courtship: Marriage certificate filed December 16, 1909, Clackamas County Records, Book 13, 359.

They took up residence: Julia Ruutila interview with Ruth Bradley, May 2, 1970, VG papers, Box 5.

"She was not the sort": VG notes, VG papers, Box 10.

25 "humdinger": Undated letter from LB and Trullinger to Adele Trullinger and family, in the possession of Adele Trullinger. Evelyn Averbuck interview with Adele Trullinger, July 1, 1970, VG papers, Box 7.

Later she rented a studio: Interview with Arthur Spencer, December 3, 1993.

26 "very intelligent": Evelyn Averbuck interview with Adele Trullinger, June 1, 1970, VG papers, Box 8.

"She wore a long": Brownell Frasier, quoted in VG, 26.

"I thought, 'Oh, God'": Julia Ruutila interview with Marie Louise Feldenheimer, May 11, 1970, VG papers, Box 5.

Louise and Paul's social life: Interview with Kina Armstrong, October 10, 1993.

27 "We would have been called hippies": Julia Ruutila interview with Marguerite Dosch Campbell, August 27, 1970, VG papers, Box 5.

A Democrat, he was: Erskine Wood, "Life of Charles Erskine Scott Wood," 99.

"I opened the door": Evelyn Averbuck interview with Sara Bard Field Wood, March 26, 1970, VG papers, Box 8.

28 The issue of suffrage: On suffrage, see especially Eleanor Flexner, *Centuries of Struggle*.

"eight pretty maidens": *Portland Oregonian*, June 14, 1912.

"Oregon was extremely primitive": "Sara Bard Field: Poet and Suffragist," an oral history conducted 1959–1963, Regional Oral History Office, University of California, Berkeley (1963), 217. Courtesy of the Bancroft Library.

3 · ENTER JACK

30   In fact, she later claimed: LB memoir, 4.
     John Reed was not exactly: Robert A. Rosenstone, *Romantic Revolutionary*, 11.

31   "become tolerant": C. J. Reed, quoted in Rosenstone, 13.
     "A great deal of my boyhood": Ibid., 15.

32   "expression to the new social conscience": Ibid., 28.
     "the Harvard renaissance": JR, "The Harvard Renaissance," unpub. ms, 3.

33   "When Jack Reed came": Lincoln Steffens, "John Reed," *The Freeman*, (November 3, 1920): 181.
     "Steffens looked at me": JR, quoted in Rosenstone, 78.
     Professionally, Jack settled in: Rosenstone, 209–11.

34   "vagabond youths": Floyd Dell, *Love in Greenwich Village*, 34–35.

35   "Yet we are free": JR, "The Day in Bohemia, or Life Among the Artists," quoted in Rosenstone, 94.
     "bullets are not very terrifying": Ibid., 169.

36   "a woman who would later drive": Rosenstone, 177.
     "Bourgeois!" Hippolyte Havel, quoted in Parry, *Garrets and Pretenders*, 289.

37   "I always wanted somebody": LB memoir, 4.
     They were formally introduced: Interview with Goody Cable, October 10, 1993.

38   "It is a very difficult thing": LB memoir, 5.
     "Everyone [in Russia]": Barbara Gelb, *So Short a Time*, 55.
     With a strong, self-acknowledged: LB to Frank Walsh, May 17, 1930, NYPL.
     As the sides of the stove: LB to JR, December 29, 1915.

39   "passionately": Sara Bard Field, quoted in VG, 27–28. Sara Bard Field, however, was in New York City at the time, having completed a headline-making automobile tour of the country to raise support for suffrage; interview with Robert Hamburger, June 18, 1993.
     raise a little cash: She sold off goods from the Riverwood house which she felt belonged to her, including four French provincial gilt chairs she sold to a friend, Laurie Kerr. Interview with Arthur Spencer, December 30, 1993; the chairs are in the Jefferson Room in the Oregon State Historical Library.
     "This evening when I": LB to JR, December 29, 1915 (237).
     "Wonderful man": Ibid.

40   "This is to say, chiefly": JR to Sally Robinson, December 18, 1915.

"to make her way": Marguerite Campbell interview with Julia Ruutila, August 27, 1970, VG papers, Box 5.

4 · LOVE, FREE AND NOT SO FREE

43   "suspended between earth": LB, "From the Tower," *The Masses* (July 1916), 22; see LB to Sara Bard Field, [n.d.], Huntington Library.

"Poetry to Reed": Max Eastman, *Heroes I Have Known*, 213.

44   "for unorthodox women": Mabel Dodge Luhan, *Movers and Shakers*, 143. See also Judith Schwarz, *Radical Feminists of Heterodoxy;* Norman S. Cohen, letter to author, September 10, 1993, confirms LB's involvement with Heterodoxy.

"I began for the first time": LB memoir, 5.

"We had a habit": Ibid.

45   "clever with a certain": Luhan, 421.

"the people on *The Masses*": VG interview with Dorothy Day, March 20, 1972, VG papers, Box 8.

Louise put up a brave front: Interview with Robert Hamburger, June 18, 1993.

"terrible": LB to Sara Bard Field, June 12, 1916.

46   "though he looks pretty tired": LB, "Two Judges," *The Masses* (April 1916), 18.

"a sublime protest": LB, "The Poet's Revolution," *The Masses* (July 1916); reprinted as a pamphlet, a copy of which is in the JR Collection.

"[M]y little lover": JR to LB, February 10, 1916 (24).

She told one friend: VG, 19.

48   "It is such a queer little": LB to Sara Bard Field, June 12, 1916, C. E. S. Wood papers, Huntington Library.

When they arrived: LB memoir, 6.

"It was a strange year": Ibid., 8.

"Never any women": Ibid., 6.

Jack apparently found: William Zorach, *Art Is the Life,* 45.

Efforts to start: Helen Deutsch and Stella Hanau, *The Provincetown,* 3.

49   "The fishhouse was a hundred feet": Mary Heaton Vorse, *Time and the Town,* 118.

50   The first bill reprised: Robert Károly Sarlós, *Jig Cook and the Provincetown Players,* 21.

"his red-cheeked, freckled": Max Eastman, *Enjoyment of Living,* 566.

"hobo philosopher and mystic": Malcolm Cowley, *Exile's Return,* 199–200.

"was not left alone": Susan Glaspell, *The Road to the Temple,* 253–54.

51   "The sea has been good": Ibid., 254.

51   "We . . . turned": Zorach, 45–46.

52   She was required to pass out: LB memoir, 12.

      "Life was all of a piece": Glaspell, 258.

      Max Eastman believed: VG, 35.

53   Louise assuaged his guilt: Louis Sheaffer, *O'Neill*, 350.

      "Dark Eyes": LB, "Dark Eyes," *The Masses* (July 1917), 28. Legend has it that she passed him a note saying, "Dark eyes. What do you mean?" But this makes little sense, and the poem in effect asks this question more meaningfully.

      "Gene and I were working": LB to Corliss Lamont, November 4, 1935, bMs Am 1091.1 (8).

      "When that girl touches me": Eugene O'Neill, quoted in Sheaffer, 350.

      "Just because someone is sleeping": Sheaffer, 346.

      "When I saw Reed": Luhan, 483–84.

54   Hers is a bizarre story: LB to Corliss Lamont, November 4, 1935, bMs Am 1091.1 (8).

      "Jack asked him": Ibid.

      "Boyd was drunk": Ibid.

55   "a great woman": Agnes Boulton, *Part of a Long Story*, 105.

      "a little dove cottage": LB to JR, June 12, 1916 (242).

      Clever cat names: Eastman, 567.

56   "it has been so beautiful": LB to Sara Bard Field, June 12, 1916, C. E. S. Wood papers, Huntington Library.

      "My Rebels": Ibid., [n.d.].

57   Jack's kidney: Kitty Cannell to Robert Sarlós, [n.d.], Kitty Cannell papers, Lamont Theatre Collection, Harvard University.

5 · PLAYACTING AND A SEPARATION

58   "Here Pegasus was hitched": Sarlós, p. 69.

59   "quiet and peaceful": LB to JR, December 12, 1916 (260).

      To this end, they were married: Marriage certificate, New York State Dept. of Health, no. 1292.

      "I had a lump in my throat": LB to JR, [November 16, 1916] (249).

60   Marguerite and Bill Zorach: Zorach, 46.

      "the old faithfuls": LB to JR, November 14, 1916 (247).

      "Do write me right away": JR to LB, November 15, [1916] (41).

      "he put on another": LB to JR, November 14, 1916 (248).

      Lorber, a colorful Village: Hutchins Hapgood, *A Victorian in the Modern World*, 367.

61   "insides": LB to JR, December 7, 1916 (257).

      "But honey — it's awful": JR to LB [December 10, 1916] (54).

61 Word around the Village: Doris Alexander, *The Tempering of Eugene O'Neill,* 236; Sheaffer, 365–66.

62 "on the same floor": LB to Amos Pinchot, November 19, 1916, Amos Pinchot papers, Library of Congress.
"[B]e *sure* to let me know": LB to JR, December 12, 1916 (260).
"Oh honey heart": LB to JR, November 14, 1916 (248).
"terrible *scandal*": LB to JR, December 7, 1916 (257).
"Everyone else seems stupid": LB to JR, November 14, 1916 (248).

63 There was a beech tree: Interview with Mirel Bercovici, September 12, 1993.
"We were soon feeling": LB memoir, 21.

64 "We won't *ever* do that": LB to JR, November 14, 1916 (248).
"China is going to be": Ibid.
"He will hold the mirror up": *The Metropolitan,* quoted in Rosenstone, 262.
"Whose war is this?": JR, "Whose War," quoted in VG, 63.

65 "You can think anything you want": VG, 63–64. Floyd Sherman Bryant's daughter, Doris Griffith, would not discuss her father and his half sister.
"a serious talk": LB memoir, 21.
"thunderstruck": Ibid. There is no particular reason to doubt her account, which was written a decade after JR's death.
"Peach tree blooming": JR to LB, May 18, 1917 (60).

67 "as the heart beats": LB to JR, June 17, [1917] (263).
"My people are in no way": Ibid., June 9, 1917 (262).
"We'll take care": LB memoir, 22.

68 "the most exciting trip": LB, "Woman Tells Liner's Fight with U-Boat," *New York American,* sec. 52, p. 3.
"that people seldom find": LB to JR, [June 9, 1917] (262).

69 "Dearest of honies": JR to LB, [June 11, 1917] (61).
"When I say I've": Ibid., [June 27, 1916] (67).
Esther became an immediate friend: LB to JR, July 13, [1917] (274).

70 "When they used to come": LB memoir, 24.
"I just want my honey": LB to JR, July 8, 1917 (272).
"faithful and humble": Ibid., July 4, [1917] (270).
"O dearest, I *could* talk": Ibid., July 2, 1917 (269).

71 "Think about you and me": JR to LB, June 28, 1917 (68).
"I didn't, and couldn't": Ibid., July 5, 1917 (72).
"You see, my dearest": Ibid.
"four or five": Ibid.

72 "In other words": Ibid.
"Dearest," she began: LB to JR, July 17, 1917 (276).
"I must write anyway": JR to LB, July 15, 1917 (78).

73 "In thinking it over": JR, "Almost Thirty," quoted in Barbara Gelb, 111–12.

6 · AT THE BARRICADES

74   They were off to Russia: LB memoir, 25.

"dear people": LB to John and Marguerite Storrs, [August 17, 1917], AAA, Reel 1554.

75   "without even enough clothes": LB to Marguerite Storrs, August 20, 1917, AAA, Reel 1554.

76   "I had so planned": LB memoir, 25.

The world war: Sources consulted for Russian history include, among others, Alan Moorehead, *The Russian Revolution;* George F. Kennan, *Russia Leaves the War;* and Bertram D. Wolfe, *Three Who Made a Revolution.*

78   "From my elevation": *SRMR,* 19–20.

The atmosphere on board: LB memoir, 26.

79   "After we left Stockholm": *SRMR,* 20–21.

"great giants of men": Ibid., 21–23.

80   "dimly perceive": JR, quoted in Rosenstone, 284.

"But she wants": LB memoir, 27.

"Nobody believed": *SRMR,* 27.

"Out on the streets": Ibid., 37.

81   "marvelous audience": Ibid., 44.

"huge and hugely ugly": LB to John and Marguerite Storrs, AAA, Reel 1552.

"Petrograd looks as if ": *SRMR,* 39.

"Under dull gray skies": *TDTSW,* 11.

"The old town has changed": JR to Boardman Robinson, September 17, 1917.

"lay on a couch": *SRMR,* 117.

82   "no fixity of purpose": JR, "Red Russia — Kerensky," *The Liberator* (April 1918), 18–19.

"In the great white hall": Ibid., 48.

"Flashing out": Ibid., 67.

83   "Citizens! The provisional government": *SRMR,* 83–84.

"No more Government!": *TDTSW,* 74.

"We shall now proceed": *TDTSW,* 126.

84   "The Bolsheviks took Petrograd": LB, "Christmas in Petrograd 1917," [4], Granville Hicks Collection, Syracuse University.

"Do you think we'll ever": Albert Rhys Williams, *Journey into Revolution,* 41–42.

85   "Harvard Red!": Williams, 62.

86   "Weeks at a stretch": *SRMR,* 43–44.

87   "Of course we followed": Ibid., 83.

88   "It is fine to be here": LB memoir, [n.p.]

7 · THE COMRADES RETURN

89 "thousands of things": Granville Hicks, *John Reed,* 291.
91 "I think women are": *SRMR,* 169.
"much the same": Ibid., 169.
"I wish I could": Ibid., 169–70.
92 "works untiringly": Ibid., 129.
"On Kollontay's suggestion": Ibid., 133.
"as if she came": Ibid., 164.
93 "A hush fell": Ibid., 167.
94 "I am but a messenger": Ibid., x–xi.
95 "If one expects to find": Ibid., 267.
"I was present": Ibid., 273–74.
96 Doty described the trip: Madeleine Doty, "Women of the Future," *Good Housekeeping* (August 1918): 32–34.
97 "she and her husband": Robins, quoted in VG, 326.
"We have nothing to do": *SRMR,* 297.
"Seated at the table": *SRMR,* 299.
98 "Proletarians of the world": LB memoir, 34.
99 "that girl": Barbara and Arthur Gelb, *O'Neill,* 148–49. None of Louise's letters or writings document this curious episode; indeed, it is necessary to turn to the accounts of others simply to reconstruct what happened, most notably the report of Agnes Boulton, the young woman with whom O'Neill was living at the time and who would soon become his wife.
"Turn back the universe": Ibid., 365.
"She will come back": Boulton, 67.
100 "Louise wrote that she": Ibid., 113.
"She's crazy!": Ibid., 105.
"both escape and revenge": Ibid., 108.
101 "Her reply was quick": Ibid., 121–22.
"It's a most awful situation": LB to Upton Sinclair, March 9, 1918, Sinclair papers, Lilly Library, Indiana University.
102 "which is known to be a center": "Supplemental Memorandum re: Louise Bryant (Mrs. John Reed)," Department of State, Office of the Undersecretary, April 22, 1920.
"brought home the suffering": *New York Call,* quoted in VG, 132.
By April: LB to Upton Sinclair, June 12, [1919], Sinclair papers, Lilly Library, Indiana University.
103 "a writer of considerable": U.S. Military Intelligence Reports, Surveillance of Radicals in the U.S., September 4, 1918, Series 10058, Reel 33.
"well-known Bolshevik": Department of State, Office of the Counselor, September 5, 1918.

103   "It is hard for us": LB to John and Marguerite Storrs, May 9, 1918, AAA, Reel 1552.

104   "I started a big newspaper": JR, quoted in *The Autobiography of Lincoln Steffens*, vol. 2, 771.

8 · NEW DEVELOPMENTS AT HOME

107   "a reaction to Reed's": quoted in VG, 142.
       "John Reed started to": Ibid.

108   "the handsome, limping": Eastman, 525.
       But their paths crossed: Andrew Dasburg to Grace Johnson, November 17, 1916, AAA, Reel 2044.
       "We all hated the war": Andrew Dasburg, quoted in VG, 143.
       Once or twice they visited: Andrew Dasburg, unpublished manuscript, AAA, Reel 2050.

109   "Our relationship was so": VG notes in folder "In case Ms. Returned," VG papers, Box 5. Dasburg seems to have been a man of considerable stability and openness, perhaps attributable to psychoanalysis, in 1916 to 1917, with the eminent practitioner A. A. Brill.
       She had just finished reading: LB to John and Marguerite Storrs, December 14, 1918, AAA, Reel 1552.
       Number 1 Patchin Place: Orville Bullitt to VG, June 1, 1977; and Willard Trask to VG, May 1, 1977, VG papers, Box 8.

110   "disloyal, scurrilous": Rosenstone, 329.
       "Knit a Strait-Jacket": Ibid., 330.
       "was telling her his most": Floyd Dell, *Homecoming*, 327–28.

111   Once when Louise was off: This version is recounted in VG, 145–47. Dell said his wife, B. Marie, told him the story.

112   "fortunately, does not mitigate": *The Dial* (November 1930): 504.
       "fearlessly, without prejudice": *Pearson's* (December 1918): 90.
       The Socialist *New York Call: New York Call*, November 10, 1918, 10.
       "wealth of information": *The Nation* (November 6, 1918) 107:591.
       "Fortunate you": *The Liberator* (January 1919), 42–43.
       Upton Sinclair, the muckraking novelist: LB to Upton Sinclair, December 1, 1918, Sinclair papers, Lilly Library, Indiana University.

113   "a picture of flaming youth": Art Young, *On My Way*, 291.
       "plump, good-natured": *The Autobiography of William Carlos Williams*, 142.
       "a George Sand haircut": "Louise Bryant Lectures," *The Oregonian*, April 3, 1919.

114   "frivolous": VG, 141.
       "Cossack garb": VG interview with Susan Jenkins Brown, May 1972, VG papers, Box 8.
       "take her seriously": Emma Goldman, quoted in Winifred L. Frazier, *E.G. and E.G.O.*, 11.

115   "Louise was never a communist": Richard and Anna Marie Drinnon, eds., *Nowhere At Home*, 192.

"Yes, I'm really *Mrs.* Reed": LB to Upton Sinclair, March 9, 1918, Sinclair papers, Lilly Library, Indiana University.

But the double standard: See, for instance, Ellen Kay Trimberger, "Feminism, Men, and Modern Love: Greenwich Village, 1900–1925," in Ann Snitow, Christine Stansell, and Sharon Thompson, eds., *Powers of Desire: The Politics of Sexuality* (New York: Monthly Review Press, 1983), 131–52.

9 · A DEFIANT WITNESS SPEAKS

118   "and she is a very": "Bolsheviki Are Busy in the United States," *New York Times*, February 9, 1919, IV, p. 12.

"Miss Bryant appears": Ibid.

"Miss Bryant . . . Mrs. John Reed": Ibid.

119   "to begin an investigation": "Senate Orders Reds Here Investigated," *New York Times*, February 15, 1919, p. 1.

"several avowed agents": Testimony of Major E. Lowry Humes, quoted in Hicks, 330.

120   Clara Wold, her old: Clara Wold to LB, [n.d.] (1071b).

121   "At a time when most feminists": Rosalind Rosenberg, *Beyond Separate Spheres*, xiii.

"doing too little too late": Flexner, 307.

"The president is responsible": "Suffragists Burn Wilson in Effigy: Many Locked Up," *New York Times*, February 10, 1919, p. 1.

122   "Through the smoke": Ibid.

"Miss Louise Bryant": "Five Days in Jail for 25 Militants," *New York Times*, February 11, 1919, p. 3.

"There were no meals": Dorothy Day, *The Long Loneliness*, 74.

123   "the horrors of prison": LB to JR, [February 1919] (91).

"a person who has": Testimony from 65th U.S. Congress, 3d sess., Subcommittee of the Judiciary Committee, Bolshevik Propaganda Hearings, 465–561.

126   "When I . . . realized,": "Girl Author Visiting City Has Seen History in Making," *Seattle Union Record*, March 28, 1919.

Anna Louise Strong: "Louise Bryant Coming Here," *Seattle Union Record* [undated clipping at Hoover Institution].

127   But they found David Wallerstein: For Wallerstein's daughter's memories of this occasion (the Reeds stayed at the family's house), see Rose DeWolf, "John Reed, Louise Bryant Stayed at Her House," *Philadelphia Bulletin*, January 20, 1982, sec. C, p. 15.

"they are arresting Bolsheviks": Margaret Reed to JR, [March 11, 1919] (714).

127   "Like a prairie-fire": A. Mitchell Palmer, quoted in Curt Gentry, *J. Edgar Hoover*, 78–79.

128   Though she was technically: See, for example, Department of State, Office of the Undersecretary, "Supplemental Memorandum re: Louise Bryant (Mrs. John Reed)," April 22, 1920, which discusses the financing of LB's lecture tour.

        "I *do so want to visit*": LB to JR, March 12, [1919] (280).

129   "They gave me a grand": Ibid., [March 1919] (278).

        "a flock of newspaper men": LB to JR, March 13, 1919 (279).

        "Everyone is sneezing": Letter reproduced in LB memoir, 41.

        "not to worry": LB to Norman Matson, March 18, 1919.

130   "Anna Louise is belligerently": LB to JR, March 21, [1919] (280).

        "the roughest, finest": Ibid., March 24, [1919] (282).

        "I was going there": Ibid., March 29, [1919] (285).

        "So much for the return": March 31, [1919] (287).

        "has changed little": "Louise Bryant Lectures," *The Oregonian*, April 3, 1919.

131   "*much* relieved": LB to JR, April 4, [1919] (288).

        "an emissary of the Germans": Ibid., April 4, [1919] (288).

132   "My mother is absolutely": Ibid., April 6, [1919] (289).

        "not even a minute": Ibid. (290).

        C. E. S. Wood had finally left: Interview with Robert Hamburger, June 18, 1993.

        "quite immune": LB to JR, April 4, [1919], (288).

133   "The Mayor and the Chief": LB to Upton Sinclair, April 26, [1919], Sinclair papers, Lilly Library, Indiana University.

        "his old standby": Ibid.

        "I'm so glad yours is out": LB to JR, March 24, [1919] (282).

134   "full of enthusiasm": JR to LB, April 1, 1919 (101).

        "How hard it is to be away": LB to JR, March 23, [1919] (281).

135   "There was no military": *Tacoma Labor Advocate*, March 28, 1919, p. 1.

        "After what I've seen": LB, quoted in VG, 158–59.

10 · WORKING FOR A NEW WORLD

136   "Separations . . . are the cruelest": LB memoir, 42.

        "I had a sort of physical": LB to Upton Sinclair, June 12, [1919], Sinclair papers, Lilly Library, Indiana University.

        "like children who will": LB to Sara Bard Field, June 12, 1916, C. E. S. Wood papers, Huntington Library.

        "There is a sort of Colony": Clare Sheridan, *My American Diary*, 131.

        "It was as though": Ibid., 133.

137   "Welcome to the Mt. Airy": See Jane Northshield, "Mt. Airy Road," in Jane Northshield, ed., *History of Croton-on-Hudson, New York*, 147–57.

137   "I want sometime": LB to Sara Bard Field, C. E. S. Wood papers, Huntington Library.

   "until I have *one*": LB to John and Marguerite Storrs, January 14, 1918, AAA, Reel 1552.

138   "All the fruit-trees": LB, "Spring in Croton," quoted in LB memoir, 43.

   "stayed awake night": LB to Upton Sinclair, June 12, [1919], Sinclair papers, Lilly Library, Indiana University.

139   "Dearest lover": LB to JR, March 24, [1919] (282).

   "It cannot be said": Charles E. Russell, *New York Times*, April 27, 1919, Section 8, p. 1.

140   "Strewn all over": Benjamin Gitlow, *The Whole of Their Lives*, 32.

141   The couple's bank accounts: Rosenstone, 345.

   "about 15 jobs": LB to JR, [July 2, 1919] (294).

   "ride horseback": LB to Upton Sinclair, June 12, [1919], Sinclair papers, Lilly Library, Indiana University.

   "I have never taken a cent": LB to editor of *Soviet Russia*, July 19, [1919].

143   "He is not well": Ibid.

   "It may surprise you": Allen Churchill, *The Improper Bohemians*, 227–28.

144   "I wanted everything to be": LB to JR, August 20, 1919 (297).

145   "None better": Hicks, 365–66.

146   "We are the Russian": LB, "Out of the Sunset (Dedicated to British Diplomacy)," *Voice of Labor*, November 1, 1919, p. 4.

147   "The jails are filling": LB, *Voice of Labor*, November 15, 1919, p. 1.

   Another lead editorial: LB, *Voice of Labor*, December 15, 1919, p. 1.

   Deaths from these causes: Rosenstone, 362.

   In an interview: "Louise Bryant Prefers Reporting to Propaganda," *New York Call* clipping in Storrs papers, AAA, Reel 1552.

148   "the place where we": LB to John and Marguerite Storrs, March 15, 1920, AAA, Reel 1552.

   "frightfully mixed up": JR to LB, October 21, 1919 (107).

   "which has a large influence": Ibid.

149   "I fret and fume": Ibid., November 9, 1919 (109).

   And on April 16: Bainbridge Colby to LB, April 16, 1920 (973).

151   And he very likely: Rosenstone, 367.

   "You are a little confused": Emma Goldman, *Living My Life*, 740.

152   "and so am awake": JR to LB, May 13, 1920 (112).

   "temporarily returning": Ibid., June 7, 1920 (116).

II · A LAST SEPARATION

153   "Thinking and dreaming": JR, quoted in LB, "Last Days with John Reed: A Letter from Louise Bryant" in *The Liberator* (February 1921), 11–12.

   "Three ikons": LB, "Russian Memories," *The Dial* 68 (May 1920), 565–66.

154   A newspaper editor: Gilson Gardner to LB, May 5, 1920.

154   "wife of John Reed": "Memorandum re: Louise Bryant, Anne Mahon or
       Louise Bryant Reed," Department of State, Office of the Undersecretary,
       April 10, 1920.
       "political agitation": Ibid.
       "abuse . . . Consul-General": Department of State, Division of Foreign
       Intelligence, to Secretary of State, April 16, 1920.

155   "in the interest of": "Supplemental Memorandum re: Louise Bryant
       (Mrs. John Reed)," Department of State, Office of the Undersecretary,
       April 22, 1920.
       "*tovarisch* Bryant": LB to Bainbridge Colby, April 29, 1920.

156   "immediately upon your": Ibid.
       "the only organization": Ibid.
       "Jack is a poet": Ibid.

157   She spent a last, bittersweet weekend: See VG, 191–95.
       "where the officers go": LB to Andrew Dasburg, [n.d.] Dasburg papers,
       Syracuse University.
       "of good conduct": Ibid.

158   "I will go all the way": Ibid., August 12, 1920.
       "I am north of the": Ibid., [n.d.].
       "It is the most": Ibid., [n.d.].

159   "without giving the impression": Rosenstone, 377.

160   "I had made all": JR to LB, June 26, [1920] (120).

161   "We were terribly happy": LB memoir, 5.
       "White and slim my lover": JR, "Letter to Louise," quoted in LB mem-
       oir, 35.

162   "older and sadder": LB to Max Eastman, November 14, 1920.

163   "My dear little Honey": Ibid.
       Louise fought to be allowed: LB to Clarence Darrow, August 15, 1932,
       Lincoln Steffens papers, Columbia University.
       "He would have died days before": LB to Max Eastman, November 14,
       1920.
       "he fought so hard": LB to Margaret Reed, November 20, 1920, bMS Am
       1655 (98).

12 · TOWARD ANOTHER LIFE

164   "standing stiffly, their bayonets": LB to Max Eastman, November 14, 1920.
       Another observer noticed: Clare Sheridan, "Tchitcherin, Who Never
       Stops Work as Foreign Minister," *New York Times*, November 26, 1920, p. 1.

165   "On [the funeral] day": LB to Max Eastman, November 14, 1920.
       "Jack's illness and his death": LB to Andrew Dasburg, November 1920,
       Dasburg papers, Syracuse University.
       "That's why I'm still": LB to Clarence Darrow, August 15, 1932, Lincoln
       Steffens papers, Columbia University.

166 "[F]or myself — my life": LB to Margaret Reed, October 20, 1920, bMS Am 1655 (98).

"loved Jack greatly": Ibid.

"But I have been": LB to Max Eastman, November 14, 1920.

167 "everyone has written of": Theodore Draper, *The Roots of American Communism*, 293.

"I will give the story": Gitlow, 33–36.

"There are so many": Max Eastman, *Love and Revolution*, 249–50.

There was no doubt: See Rosenstone, 379n. For the best discussion of this controversy, see Draper and VG, "Appendix I," 301–306.

168 "said with a slight sneer" VG interview with Dorothy Day, February 24, 1978, VG papers, Box 9.

169 "What shall you do": LB to Andrew Dasburg, [November 1920], Andrew Dasburg papers, Syracuse University.

"I make Moscow": Ibid.

"The only way to endure it": LB to Margaret Reed, October 20, 1920, bMS Am 1655 (98).

"Faster and faster": LB, "Aftermath," *The Liberator* (November 1921); rpt. in *Current Opinion* (July 1922), 150.

170 "12020 exlouise bryant": Cable dispatch, Frank Mason papers, Hoover Institution.

"a ramshackle affair": Ralph Mahoney to VG, March 3, 1979, VG papers, Box 7.

"The plain truth is that": LB, "Tchitcherin 'Oddest Politician in the World,'" *New York American*, August 27, 1921, p. 2.

171 "only fighting ive seen": Cable dispatch, March 12, 1921, Frank Mason papers, Hoover Institution.

"I am glad there is": *MoM*, 11.

"The trains running out": LB, "Strangers Like Old Friends on Russian Trains," *New York American*, September 3, 1921, p. 3.

172 "clear down to the": Ibid.

"The present fine crop": LB, "Lenin Restores Sacred Koran to Samarkand," *New York American*, August 26, 1921, p. 3.

173 Their friendship was cemented: Interview with Anne Bullitt, October 5, 1994.

"No man I ever": *MoM*, 149.

"and not all with Americans": See, for example, LB to Frank Walsh, May 17, 1930, NYPL.

Some years later: Interview with Anne Bullitt, July 16, 1994; the "secret password" is in her possession. Louise included in her profile a curious detail about "an American girl" that provides another complicated piece to the puzzle. Enver saw that the Bolsheviks in central Asia were attempting to reestablish dominion over them, and revolts broke out against the pro-Soviet regimes in the region. In late 1921, just after his acquaintance with Louise, Enver changed his stripes yet again. He joined the Basmachi in Bukhara in their revolt against the Soviet regime. One account of his death that circulated in Moscow, which Louise reported in her profile, said that he died with the letters of an American woman next to his heart. This detail, along with the news of his death, was false, Louise reported (though he would be killed in Turkestan the following year by the Red Army).

174   "Jack, you are quiet": LB, quoted in Eastman, *Love and Revolution*, 224–25.
      "I could never bear": LB to Margaret Reed, October 20, 1920, bMS Am 1655 (98).

175   On April 30, a U.S.: Gray to Secretary of State, April 30, 1921. All documents relating to LB's return from Russia were obtained from the Department of State under the Freedom of Information Act.
      There was no response: Arthur Garfield Hays to Secretary of State, May 17, 1921.
      "full affidavit showing": Charles Evans Hughes, Department of State, to American consul, Riga, May 25, 1921.
      "she left United States": Hurley to Secretary of State, June 9, 1921.
      "I think that the Secretary": P. Adams, Internal memorandum, June 13, 1921, Department of State.
      "A refusal at this time": Ibid.
      "Louise Bryant Reed sailed": Gray to Secretary of State Hughes, July 13, 1921.

176   "Informed Mr. Hoover": P. Adams, quoted in VG, 220.
      The subtenant there: Mr. Diamond to LB, October 14, 1922, NYPL.
      "The houses have no": Sheridan, 129–30.
      "to be a sort of phonograph": *San Francisco Examiner*, August 17, 1921.

177   "were more virulent": LB, "Emma Goldman Wants to Get out of Russia," *New York American*, August 22, 1921, p. 2.
      "Remember that these are": LB, "Soviets Proud of Full Rights Women Enjoy," *New York American*, September 12, 1921, p. 2.
      "Few now can imagine": Max Eastman, quoted in Daniel Aaron, *Writers on the Left*, 100.

178   "The splendid stand": *New York Call*, October 18, 1921, p. 4.
      "Today Russia is being": "Special Report," October 22, 1921, FBI files.
      First she applied: LB to Worthington Hollyday, October 28, 1921.
      She appealed to Jack's: Lincoln Steffens to LB, February 18, 1922 (1061).
      Louise gave up: Anne Bursch to LB, May 26, 1922 (970).

179   "Mrs. John Reed": Mary Stuart to LB, January 9, 1922 (967).
      "It has been terrible": LB to Fred Bursch, February 13, 1922, bMS Am 1655 (96).
      "Get out!": Harold Stearns, quoted in Hugh Ford, *Four Lives in Paris*, 85.
      "A strange, brittle, cerebral": Van Wyck Brooks, *Three Essays on America*, 211.

179   "was one idea that": Cowley, 74.

180   "Of course when Jack died": LB to Anne Bursch, March 23, 1922, bMS Am 1655 (97).

         "Am down here in D.C.": Ibid.

         "surely there are other": Office of the Undersecretary of State Hurley to P. Adams, May 22, 1922.

181   "Miss Bryant has followed": Memo in re Passport Application of Miss Louise Bryant, Department of State, May 23, 1922.

         "that the reason": Ibid., May 24, 1922.

183   "There is always something": *MoM,* 67.

         "Madame Kalinin is an": Ibid., 107.

         "As champion of her sex": Ibid., 112.

184   "In his passing": "Frank Walsh Dies: Lawyer for Labor," *New York Times,* May 3, 1939.

185   "When are you coming": LB to Frank Walsh, June 20, 1922, NYPL.

         Louise cabled him: LB to Frank Walsh, September 18, 1922, and Frank Walsh to William Cosgrave, Desmond Fitzgerald, et al., September 20, 1922, NYPL.

186   On September 11: LB to John and Marguerite Storrs, September 11, 1922, AAA, Reel 1552.

         "I hope you had": Frank Walsh to LB, September 30, 1922, NYPL.

         "[S]ometime, maybe, you": Ibid.

13 · ENTER BULLITT

191   "I'm going to be": WB, quoted in Richard Billings and Will Brownell, *So Close to Greatness,* 50. The best sources on WB's life are Beatrice Farnsworth, *William C. Bullitt and the Soviet Union;* Orville Bullitt, ed., *For the President: Personal and Secret;* and Janet Flanner, "Mr. Ambassador — I" and "Mr. Ambassador — II." I also consulted E. V. Gulick's unpublished manuscript "Ambassador Bullitt and Ashfield," courtesy of the Ashfield (Massachusetts) Historical Society, along with Anne Bullitt's emendations and notes.

192   "Every Groton fellow": WB, quoted in Billings and Brownell, 20.

193   "No! . . . It isn't just": WB, Ibid., 36.

194   "a descriptive writer": quoted in Billings and Brownell, 50.

         "I have seen men catch their breath": Catherine Drinker Bowen, *Family Portraits,* 118–19.

195   "the sharpest of the American": Walter Lippmann, quoted in Billings and Brownell, 63.

         "editorials no one": WB, quoted in Farnsworth, 8.

197   "with as single": WB, quoted in Billings and Brownell, 68.

         "sick at heart": WB, quoted in Farnsworth, 25.

         "No machinery for peace": Ibid., 13.

198   "I am ready to give": WB, quoted in Farnsworth, 45.
199   "I have been over": Steffens, 799.
        "I am sorry that you": WB, quoted in Farnsworth, 56.
200   "I see Bill Bullitt": George F. Kennan, "Introduction," in Orville Bullitt, ed., xv–xvi.
        "lie on the sand": "On the Riviera Sands," *New York Times*, September 24, 1919, p. 16.
201   "My sister's early ambition": Bowen, 130.
        "And did you see that": JR to LB, March 21, [1919].
202   "while John Reed was": *MoM*, 10.
        "The only way to endure": LB to Andrew Dasburg, November 1920, Andrew Dasburg papers, Syracuse University.
        Kennan had compared: VG has referred to what she called Bill's "posthumous idealization" of Jack, and the phrase does not seem too strong. Many years later, on his next visit to Moscow, having divorced Louise, Bullitt's very first action would be to cut the yards of red tape necessary to view Reed's grave in the Kremlin wall. As Kennan reports, he stood before the grave with tears rolling down his face.
        "His was outstandingly": George F. Kennan, *Memoirs*, 79.
203   "Ardent, charming, brilliant": Kenneth S. Davis, review of *For the President: Personal and Secret* in *New York Times Book Review*, December 17, 1972, p. 4.

14 · BILL IN PURSUIT

204   "[A]fter Jack died": LB to Frank Walsh, May 17, 1930, NYPL.
        her mother would die: Death certificate, Louisa Bryant, May 9, 1924, State of California Department of Public Health, state index number 24–024659.
        The life of her half: "Floyd Bryant Dies; Ex-Defense Aide, 70," *New York Times*, April 11, 1965, p. 92. Bryant would become assistant secretary of defense in the Eisenhower administration.
205   "disabled war veteran": Death certificate, William Sheridan Bryant, March 29, 1944, State of California Department of Public Health, state index number 44–020062.
209   It speaks to Louise's energy: Benito Mussolini, "Mussolini's Own Story on How He Hopes to Save Italy," *New York American*, January 21, 1923, section 52, p. 1.
        "Women should write": Bald, 22. Bald's column was dated August 12, 1930. Louise's memory, or the report she gave Bald, may of course be suspect.
        "Madame Mussolini has never": LB, "Mussolini Relies upon Efficiency to Restore Italy," *New York American*, January 28, 1923, Section 52, p. 1.
210   "I am not a feminist": Ibid.

210   "I wrote as fairly about Mussolini": LB to Granville Hicks, November 5, 1935.

211   "I will always think": LB, "Mussolini Relies upon Efficiency to Restore Italy," *New York American*, January 28, 1923, section 52, p. 1.
"a book of interest": *New York World*, April 1, 1923, p. 8E.
"The book is journalism": Katherine Angell, *The Nation*, May 9, 1923, vol. 116, p. 548.
"Miss Bryant is strongly": *New York Times*, March 11, 1923, p. 23.
"as any artist would": LB to Marguerite Storrs, [n.d.], AAA, Reel 1553.

212   "John was a sensitive fine": Grace Moore, *You're Only Human Once*, 26.
"like a sister": John Storrs to Marguerite Storrs, [n.d.], AAA, Reel 1553.

213   "She is a vacuum": LB to Marguerite Storrs, [n.d.], AAA, Reel 1553.
In Bill's absence: John Storrs diary, AAA, Reel 1548.
"She has just tired": John Storrs to Marguerite Storrs, [n.d.], AAA, Reel 1552.
"So much unhappiness": LB to Marguerite Storrs, [n.d.], AAA, Reel 1553.
"Things are better": Ibid., April 10, 1923, AAA, Reel 1552.

214   "During the festivities": LB, "D'Annunzio Can Find No Menace in Turkish Revival," *New York American*, April 15, 1923; her subsequent article, "Secret of D'Annunzio's Hermit Light," appeared in the same paper on July 15.

15 · THE CLOUD GENERAL PREVAILS

216   "came along": LB to Frank Walsh, May 17, 1930, NYPL.
"the most precious thing": H. G. Dwight, *Constantinople Old and New*, 251.
"The fountain is still": Ibid., 254.

217   "Kemal, ruling his party": LB, "LB Reveals Kemal Pasha's Iron Rule," *New York American*, March 9, 1924, section 52, p. 1.
"serve the state by": LB, "Much-Heralded Emancipation of Turkish Women Is Only a Myth," *New York American*, section 52, p. 3.

218   "as primitive as China": LB to Marguerite Storrs, [n.d.], AAA, Reel 1553.
"There are no traffic": Ernest Hemingway, "Old Constan," *By-Line*, 47–49; the article appeared in the *Toronto Star* on October 23, 1923.
"Bill is more calm": LB to Marguerite Storrs, [n.d.], AAA, Reel 1553.

219   "Unusual talent is necessary": *Saturday Review of Literature*, May 1, 1926, p. 754.
"literary value": *New York Herald Tribune*, Book Section, April 18, 1926, p. 4.
"Why should I?": WB, quoted in VG, 247.
"was crazy for a child": Gussie Nobbes, quoted in Billings and Brownell, 111.

219   At the age of thirty-seven: LB to Marguerite Storrs, [n.d.], AAA, Reel
        1553.
        Bill did not want her: Ella Winters, quoted in VG, 246.
        "It was here": LB to Frank Walsh, May 17, 1930, Frank Walsh papers,
        NYPL.
220   Back in Athens: LB, "The Most Unhappy King in the World Was
        George of Greece, Now in Exile," *New York American*, December 23, 1923,
        sec. 52, p. 1; see LB memoir, 15–17.
        "I sent a cablegram": LB to Frank Walsh, May 17, 1930, NYPL.
221   "We are so excited": LB to Marguerite Storrs, [n.d.], AAA, Reel 1553.
        She wanted an apartment: Ibid., July 27, 1923.
        "Louise is very well": WB to Marguerite Storrs, September 18, 1923,
        AAA, Reel 1555.
        They also had a great deal: LB to Marguerite Storrs, [n.d.], AAA, Reel
        1553.
        "a year and a half": "Louise Bryant Wed to W. C. Bullitt," *New York
        American*, July 23, 1924.
        "perfect for its type": WB, quoted in VG, 246.
222   "drolly": Maurice Sachs, *The Decade of Illusion*, 35–36.
        "caught up in a whirl": Bravig Imbs, *Confessions of Another Young Man*, 96.
        "much-mirrored": Sisley Huddleston, *Back to Montparnasse*, 86.
        "dressed in a gown": Imbs, 103–104.
223   They would grow still closer: Justin Kaplan, *Lincoln Steffens*, 277.
        "Louise kept writing that": Lincoln Steffens to Laura Steffens, Ella Win-
        ters and Granville Hicks, eds., *The Letters of Lincoln Steffens*, 638.
224   "it was not merely": Ibid.
        "I shall have nothing": Ibid.
        "the ecstasy of motherhood": VG, 247.
        "At first [Bill] was all": LB to Frank Walsh, May 17, 1930, NYPL.
225   While in Constantinople: "Young Turkish Prince Here for Long Visit,"
        New York Times, August 7, 1925, p. 17.
        "royal family": John Storrs diary entry, March 10, 1924, AAA, Reel 1548.
        "Our little Turk": LB to John Storrs, [n.d.], AAA, Reel 1551.
        "the best kind of nanny": Interview with Anne Bullitt, October 5, 1994.
        "a spectacle": Thomas N. Chappell to VG, [n.d.], VG papers, Box 7.
        "Certainly not": WB, quoted in VG, 249.
        10 rue Desbordes-Valmore: Arlen Hansen, *Expatriate Paris*, 35.
226   "After Jack Reed": Sara Bard Field Wood, quoted in VG, 246.
        "but especially Bill": John Storrs to Marguerite Storrs, July 18, 1924, AAA,
        Reel 1553.
        "seemed very happy": George Antheil, *Bad Boy of Music*, 175.
        "happy period": George Biddle, quoted in VG, 245–46.
227   "Bill was intelligent": Harold Stearns, *The Street I Know*, 326.
        "I live a useless life": LB, quoted in VG, 246.

16 · PARTIES AND PROBLEMS

228   "servant problems": Thomas N. Chappell to VG, [n.d.], VG papers, Box 9.

229   "made into a Bourgeois": LB, quoted in VG, 273.

230   "I couldn't escape the feeling": Andrew Dasburg, quoted in VG, 263.

They were drawn as well: William Wiser, *The Crazy Years,* 29.

"Whisky was to the imagination": Williams, 194.

231   "brilliant women, superbly": LB, "A Turkish Divorce," *The Nation,* vol. 121, pp. 231–32.

one example of her poetry: LB to John and Marguerite Storrs, [n.d.], AAA, Reel 1553.

232   "dining often": Konrad Bercovici, *It's the Gypsy in Me,* 227.

"the long lean eagle": Gorham Munson, *The Awakening Twenties,* 34.

"Marsden was . . . a kind of grandpapa": Williams, 164.

But in a telling remark: Marsden Hartley to John Storrs, [n.d.], AAA, Reel 1552.

Artists paid tribute: Interview with Anne Bullitt, January 31, 1994. Biddle's chair probably stayed in Anne's room, for Bill and Louise, of course, didn't encourage discussion of where or when the child was conceived.

233   "I'd rather live in Oregon": Morley Callaghan, *That Summer in Paris,* 82.

"wild. . . . We think": LB to John Storrs, [n.d.], AAA, Reel 1552.

Another representative friend: Wiser, 70.

234   "Almost every night": Kitty Cannell, quoted in VG, 256.

"To the extent that": Shari Benstock, *Women of the Left Bank,* 189.

"Bill Bullitt or Bull Billet": Carlos Baker, ed., *Ernest Hemingway,* 268; the letter is dated July 27, 1927.

235   frequent tennis partner: Kenneth Lynn, *Hemingway,* 238.

"Mrs. Bullitt . . . Pappy": Archibald MacLeish, quoted in Reynolds, *Hemingway,* 137.

236   "This story gets so involved": LB to Frank Walsh, May 17, 1930, NYPL.

"the new O'Neill play": LB to John and Marguerite Storrs, May 26, 1925, AAA, Reel 1552.

"fine . . . appalling worship": Ibid.

"strangely enough": Ibid.

237   "praying . . . stimulated": Ibid.

"little Turkish boy": "Young Turkish Prince Here for Long Visit," *New York Times,* August 7, 1925, p. 17.

"His eyes shot fire": Bercovici, 227.

Refik repeatedly begged: Thomas N. Chappell to VG, [n.d.], VG papers, Box 9.

238   Louise and Bill took full advantage: Interview with Peg Mowry, May 24, 1993.

she wrote a witty article: Ernesta Drinker Bullitt, "The Country House a Ford Built," *House and Garden* (March 1925), pp. 72–73.

238   "Champagne on the lawn": Interview with Anne Bullitt, July 16, 1994.
Bill particularly loved jumpers: Interview with Peg Mowry, May 24, 1993.

239   "a house alone worth seeing": Steffens, *Letters,* vol. 2, p. 747.
"consumed with self-importance": Ernest Samuels, *Bernard Berenson,* 267.
"proud and haughty": Hapgood, 494–95.
"I never knew anyone": Vincent Sheean to VG, April 13, [1973], Kitty
Cannell papers, Lamont Theatre Collection, Harvard University.
"expressed the hope": Orville Bullitt, 159.

240   "He just would not abide": Orville Horwitz, quoted in Billings and
Brownell, 321.
He gave some examples: VG, "It Was Certainly Mr. William Bullitt,"
unpublished ms. based on an interview with Mura Dehn, AAA, Reel
2054.
"George, can you even *imagine*": WB, quoted in VG, 248.

241   "Bill broke a leg": LB to Marguerite Storrs, October 12, [1926], AAA,
Reel 1551.
"developed the utmost": LB to Frank Walsh, May 17, 1930, NYPL.
"It dawned on me": WB, quoted in VG, 248.
"Just give him my card": This is what George Biddle remembered WB
telling him; see VG, 248.
he no doubt knew: Interview with John Kerr, October 20, 1993; interview
with Peter Swales, November 15, 1993.

242   "negligence . . . as if she": Mura Dehn, quoted in VG, 255.
Yet Dehn also sensed: See VG, 254.
Another occasion: LB to Frank Walsh, May 17, 1930, NYPL; George
Biddle corroborated the story; see VG, 255.
In 1936, Bill denied: Flanner, "Mr. Ambassador — II," *New Yorker* (December 17, 1936), 25.

243   In the late 1920s: Interview with Will Brownell, August 30, 1993.
though Freud's part in: for the fullest discussion of this controversy, see
Peter Gay, *Freud,* 553–62 and 775–76.
"I saw a dandy Irish girl": Steffens, *Letters,* vol. 2, p. 745.
But at least two others: Vincent Sheean was one; see VG, 253. The Freud
scholar Peter Lambda was another; see Peter Lambda to VG, February 25,
1973, in Kitty Cannell papers, Lamont Theatre Collection, Harvard University.
Anna Freud herself: Anna Freud to VG, March 27, 1973, Andrew Dasburg
papers, AAA, Reel 2049.

17 · THE INROADS OF ILLNESS

244   "so sorry": LB to Claude McKay, June 11, [1926], James Weldon Johnson
Collection, Beinecke Library, Yale University.
the disease first appeared: Interview with Anne Bullitt, July 16, 1994.

244   Many believed: As did Floyd Dell, for instance; see VG, 259.

245   "Bill, I'm changing": Interview with Anne Bullitt, May 5, 1994.

"The old restlessness": William Shirer, *Twentieth Century Journey*, vol. 1, *The Start: 1904–1930*, 446.

The daughter of family friend: Interview with Mirel Bercovici, September 2, 1993.

A Croton resident: See VG, 262.

"stood up and called": VG typed notes on WB's divorce testimony, VG papers, Box 11. VG was given access to a copy of WB's divorce testimony by an unknown source, possibly Orville Bullitt.

246   "were not natural to her": Ibid.

"Please burn all my": [Drafts of notes to William C. Bullitt?, n.p., n.d.], (1423).

"All my clothes": Ibid.

247   "a rare condition": J. L. Held, J. A. Andrew, S. R. Kohn, "Surgical amelioration of Dercum's disease: a report and review," *Journal of Dermatologic Surgery and Oncology* (December 1989), p. 1294.

"ill of some curious sort": LB to Frank Walsh, May 17, 1930, NYPL.

"The psychic changes are varied": Wilder Tileston, "Obesity," in Llewllys F. Barker, ed., *Endocrinology and Metabolism*, 40.

248   "The clinical picture": A. J. DeFranzo, J. H. Hall, Jr., and S. M. Herring, "Adiposis dolorosa (Dercum's disease): liposuction as an effective form of treatment," *Journal of Plastic Reconstructive Surgery* (September 1990), p. 289.

249   "Pray that she die": Interview with Anne Bullitt, October 5, 1994.

they had focused on playwriting: Charles Ashleigh wrote to LB, for example, on January 28, 1927, saying he was interested in staging her play; Sigmund Freud to WB, April 17, 1927 (copy in the collection of the Ashfield [Mass.] Historical Society), mentions WB's play about Wilson.

250   "looking for a governess": LB to John Storrs, [n.d.], AAA, Reel 1552.

"Tell [Marguerite]": Ibid., Reel 1551.

"She looked beautiful": Mura Dehn, quoted in VG, 269.

251   One night they were: Robert McAlmon and Kay Boyle, *Being Geniuses Together*, 307; see also Gioia Diliberto, *Hadley*, 251.

One night in a café: See Denis Brian, *The True Gen*, 70. Morley Callaghan related this story, which he said LB told him.

"until the burning flesh": Interview with Anne Bullitt, October 5, 1994.

Lawrence Langner never mentioned: Langner, 197–98.

252   Bill put in asparagus beds: Interview with Peg Mowry, May 24, 1993; interview with Merrill Field, April 24, 1993.

In a 1928 letter: Marsden Hartley to Gaston LaChaise, July 14, 1928, AAA, Hartley papers, Reel x3.

"At that time she": Claude McKay, *A Long Way from Home* 253–54.

253   "Externally her tastes": Ibid., 254.

253   "with no radical": Ibid.

        McKay was known as the enfant terrible: Robert Bone, *The Negro Novel in America*, 67.

        "Remember our conversation": McKay, 254.

254   She wrote enthusiastically: LB to Claude McKay, December 18, 1925, James Weldon Johnson Collection, Beinecke Library, Yale University.

        That September, Louise: Ibid., September 26, 1926.

        She was now scornful: Ibid., May 18, [1926].

        Over the winter: Ibid., January 4, 1927; William Aspenwall Bradley to Claude McKay, October 30, 1927, and November 30, 1927, James Weldon Johnson Collection, Beinecke Library, Yale University.

        Toward the end of 1927: LB to Claude McKay, December 2, 1927, James Weldon Johnson Collection, Beinecke Library, Yale University.

255   "a lovely idea": Ibid.

        "I have been quite ill": Ibid., [March 21, 1928].

        "absurd": Ibid., April 16, [1928].

256   "I had a dreadful summer": Ibid., September 15, [1928].

        "So many sad things happened": Ibid., May 11, 1930.

        "the overflow of pity": McKay, 11.

18 · LOUISE FALLS IN LOVE, A MARRIAGE ENDS

257   "on the Committee boat": VG notes on WB's divorce testimony, VG papers, Box 11.

        "she had a right": Ibid.

258   "clutching a stanchion": Thomas N. Chappell to VG, [n.d.], VG papers, Box 10.

        Merrill Field: Interview with Merrill Field, April 24, 1993.

259   Louise drank all day: VG notes on WB's divorce testimony, VG papers, Box 5.

        "too feeble to carry out": LB to Claude McKay, September 15, [1928], James Weldon Johnson Collection, Beinecke Library, Yale University.

        Yet she also learned to drive: Interview with Merrill Field, Aprill 24, 1993.

        "I get so damn restless": LB to Claude McKay, September 15, [1928], James Weldon Johnson Collection, Beinecke Library, Yale University.

        "sleep off a drunk": VG notes on WB's divorce testimony, VG papers, Box 5.

260   "paw . . . really shocking": Ibid., Box 11.

261   Homosexuality was everywhere: Lynn, 320.

        "a great friend": VG interview with Kitty Cannell, February 18, 1973, VG papers, Box 5.

        "happy to oblige": Ibid.

262   "men talking to men": VG notes on WB's divorce testimony, VG papers, Box 11.

262 "amused by the antics": Ibid.

263 "a climber": VG interview with Berenice Abbott, [n.d.], VG papers, Box 8.

"a great friend": Jimmie Charters, *This Must Be the Place*, 216.

She and Abbott: Andrew Field, *Djuna*, 133.

"chairman": Field, 154.

264 "a terrible depression": VG interview with Kitty Cannell, February 18, 1973, VG papers, Box 11.

"very intelligent and clever": VG notes on WB's divorce testimony, VG papers, Box 11.

"drunken talk": Ibid.

265 "sleeping off a drunk": Ibid.

"epileptoid condition": Ibid.

"Bill said that I must": LB to Frank Walsh, May 17, 1930, NYPL.

266 "the baby . . . she broke": VG notes on WB's divorce testimony, VG papers, Box 11.

"began to return": Ibid.

19 · DIVORCE AND ITS AFTERMATH

267 "literally fell": VG notes on WB's divorce testimony, VG papers, Box 5.

268 "Anyway, Bill . . . said": LB to Frank Walsh, May 17, 1930, NYPL.

"[W]e made a separation": Ibid.

269 "You know how corrupt": Ibid.

"Dear Duck": LB, quoted in VG, 273.

271 While his family believes: Interview with Anne Bullitt, October 5, 1994.

"except when you tell": Sigmund Freud to WB, April 17, 1921, copy in possession of the Ashfield (Mass.) Historical Society.

272 "He formed rapid": Orville Bullitt, xl–xli.

"the last he heard": VG notes on BB's divorce testimony, VG papers, Box 11.

"general indignities": "Mr. W. C. Bullitt Gets Decree," *New York Times*, March 25, 1930, p. 60.

"So many bad things": LB to Frank Walsh, April 10, 1930, NYPL.

273 "now that I am in": Ibid., April 22, 1930.

"I have been wandering": Ibid., May 17, 1930.

"because I was trying": Ibid.

274 "The devils are getting": LB to Marguerite Storrs, [n.d.], AAA, Reel 1551.

"with all you've gone": John Storrs to Marguerite Storrs, [n.d.], AAA, Reel 1553.

"safely back in America": WB to Marguerite Storrs, June 15, 1930, AAA, Reel 1553.

"open suaveness": LB to Frank Walsh, July 12, 1930, NYPL.

275 "Imagine!" Ibid.

276   "A certain girl of my acquaintance": Huddleston, 56.

277   "The snow of twenty-nine": F. Scott Fitzgerald, "Babylon Revisited," in
        Babylon Revisited and Other Stories, 229.
        "as if control had left": Andrew Dasburg, quoted in VG, 263.
        "be kind to me": LB to Margaret Reed, October 20, 1920, bMS Am 1655
        (98).

        20 · LOUISE LEARNS TO FLY

281   "sense of outrage": Margaret Reed to LB, June 19, [1929] (1049).
282   "I am sure Bill": LB to Frank Walsh, May 17, 1930, NYPL.
        "I have to stay here": LB to John and Marguerite Storrs, July 20, 1930,
        AAA, Reel 1552.
283   "You write as if": Margaret Reed to LB, August 1, [1930].
        Still, Mrs. Reed was: Margaret Reed to Frank Walsh, August 1, [1930],
        NYPL.
        Frank Walsh had to reply: Frank Walsh to Margaret Reed, August 25,
        1930, NYPL.
        "substantial sum": Francis Biddle, quoted in VG, 287.
        Once, Louise and the family: Interview with Anne Bullitt, January 31,
        1994.
284   The daughter of their friends: Interview with Mirel Bercovici, September
        2, 1993.
        "nothing really changed": Interview with Anne Bullitt, January 31, 1994.
285   Until Bill put a stop to it: Jean Ressing to Frank Walsh, March 8, 1931,
        NYPL.
        "I can't follow [Anne] about": LB to John Stuart, September 2, 1935, bMS
        Am 1091.1 (11).
286   "Candles afford the only light": Bald, 22; column of August 12, 1930.
        "the Left Bank's ubiquitous Boswell": Benjamin Franklin V, "Introduc-
        tion," in Bald, xiii.
287   So, for example, in the first: Bald, 21–22; column of August 12, 1930.
        "Louise Bryant, who became": Charters, 153.
288   And when Amelia Earhart: Katherine A. Brick, "Amelia Earhart," *Nota-
        ble American Women 1607–1950,* vol. 1 (Cambridge. Mass.: Harvard Uni-
        versity Press, 1971), pp. 538–41.
        Bald reported in his column: Bald, 35; column of October 14, 1930.
        "a girl of such poise": Ibid., 102; column of March 29, 1932.
        "when she lopes": Ibid., 28–30, column of September 16, 1930.
289   "I don't know what is meant": Ibid.
        "was a day and night": Ibid., 96; column of February 9, 1932.
        "famous cloister on the rue": "Louise Bryant, American Writer, Dies in
        Paris Hospital": *International Herald Tribune,* January 10, 1936.

289   "for the daring studio": Samuel Putnam, *Paris Was Our Mistress,* 87.

290   *"empoissened"*: Jean Ressing to Margaret Reed, February 23, 1931, NYPL.
Montparnasse thieves: Jean Ressing to Frank Walsh, March 3, 1931,
NYPL; see also February 23, March 8, March 9, and March 27.
Finally he wrote: Ibid., March 27, 1931. NYPL.
"where drunken intellectuals": Frank Walsh to Margaret Reed, April 14,
1931, NYPL.
"a popular Russian woman": Bald, 45; column of December 30, 1930.

291   "desperately ill": LB to Frank Walsh, January 26, 1931, NYPL.
"quite a lot": Ibid.

21 · THE HARVARD MEN

293   "That makes it all": Granville Hicks, quoted in VG, 287, from a letter in
Corliss Lamont's papers. VG, who served as Lamont's secretary, had
access to his papers.
"a bitter reply": LB to Robert Hallowell, November 19, 1934, Granville
Hicks Collection, Syracuse University.

294   "I ask you to tell": Ibid.
"If necessary . . . he might": Corliss Lamont to Francis McClernon and
Maurice Hindus, November 27, 1934, VG papers, Box 8.

295   "personal account": Granville Hicks to LB, January 21, 1935, Granville
Hicks Collection, Syracuse University.
"beatified": Jack Carney to LB, March 1, 1935 (972).
"I did not *give*": LB to Arthur Garfield Hays, May 18, 1935, Granville
Hicks Collection, Syracuse University.

296   "spies": VG interview with Kitty Cannell, February 18, 1973, VG papers,
Box 5.

297   "But in any case": LB to Arthur Garfield Hays, [May 27, 1935], bMS Am
1091.1 (4).
"the organization": LB to "Corliss Lamont, or John Stuart or Hicks,"
March 30, 1935, Granville Hicks Collection, Syracuse University.

299   "Looking over this mass": LB to Granville Hicks, November 5, 1935,
Granville Hicks Collection, Syracuse University.

300   "this lovely daughter": Art Young, *Art Young,* 389.
"with a lot of first-hand": LB to Granville Hicks, December 2, 1935,
Granville Hicks Collection, Syracuse University.
"Food tax": See VG, "John Reed and Lenin: Some Insights Based on Ms.
Collection at Harvard," *Science and Society* (Fall 1967), 388–403, and the
correction of VG's translation in the following issue.

301   "There is no particular point": Corliss Lamont to Walter B. Briggs,
September 30, 1936, VG papers, Box 8.

POSTLUDE: LOUISE, LATER

302   "pretty, sharp-witted": *Time,* January 20, 1936, p. 59.
       "unusually competent journalist": *New York Herald,* January 10, 1936, p. 19.
       "rebel woman of great charm": *The New Masses,* January 21, 1936, p. 4.
303   "I suppose she didn't care": Somerset Maugham, *The Razor's Edge,* 214.
304   "Because she was always": See VG, 289.
       "The last time I saw her": Richard and Anna Maria Drinnon, 292.
305   "unfertilized soil": JR to Sally Robinson, December 18, 1915.
307   "like a shooting star": VG interview with Alice Bretherton Powell, June 9,
       1970, VG papers, Box 8.
       "Louise was a good deal": VG interview with George Biddle, October 1,
       1969, VG papers, Box 10.
       "I don't know how precisely": Diana Sheean, quoted in VG, 298.
308   "Even [Louise's] journalism": Elizabeth Hardwick, "A Bunch of Reds," in
       Bartleby in Manhattan and Other Essays, 112–13.

Selected Bibliography

Aaron, Daniel. *Writers on the Left.* New York: Harcourt, Brace and World, 1961.

Alexander, Doris. *The Tempering of Eugene O'Neill.* New York: Harcourt, Brace and World, 1962.

Anderson, Margaret. *My Thirty Years War.* New York: Covici-Friede, 1930.

Antheil, George. *Bad Boy of Music.* Garden City, N.Y.: Doubleday, 1945.

Baker, Carlos, editor. *Ernest Hemingway: Selected Letters, 1917–1961.* London: Granada, 1981.

Bald, Wambly. *On the Left Bank: 1929–1933.* Edited by Benjamin Franklin V. Athens: Ohio University Press, 1987.

Baskin, Alex. *John Reed: The Early Days in Greenwich Village.* New York: Archives of Social History, 1990.

Benstock, Shari. *Women of the Left Bank: Paris, 1900–1940.* Austin: University of Texas Press, 1986.

Bercovici, Konrad. *It's the Gypsy in Me.* New York: Prentice-Hall, 1941.

Biddle, George. *An American Artist's Story.* Boston: Little, Brown, 1939.

Billings, Richard, and Will Brownell. *So Close to Greatness: A Biography of William C. Bullitt.* New York: Macmillan, 1987.

Biography and Portrait Cyclopedia of Schuylkill County, Pennsylvania. New York: Wiley, 1983.

Bogard, Travis, and Jackson R. Bryer, editors. *Selected Letters of Eugene O'Neill.* New Haven: Yale University Press, 1988.

Bone, Robert. *The Negro Novel in America.* New Haven: Yale University Press, 1958.

Boulton, Agnes. *Part of a Long Story: Eugene O'Neill as a Young Man in Love.* London: Peter Davies, 1958.

Bowen, Catherine Drinker. *Family Portrait.* Boston: Little, Brown, 1970.

Boyce, Neith. *Intimate Warriors: Portraits of a Modern Marriage, 1899–1944.* Edited by Ellen Kay Trimberger. New York: Feminist Press, 1991.

Brian, Denis. *The True Gen: An Intimate Portrait of Ernest Hemingway by Those Who Knew Him.* New York: Dell, 1988.

Brooks, Van Wyck. *Days of the Phoenix.* New York: E. P. Dutton, 1957.

———. *Three Essays on America.* New York: E. P. Dutton, 1934.

Bryant, Louise. *Mirrors of Moscow.* New York: Thomas Seltzer, 1923.

———. *Six Red Months in Russia: An Observer's Account of Russia Before and During the Proletarian Dictatorship.* New York: George H. Doran, 1918.

Bullitt, Ernesta Drinker. "The Country House a Ford Built." *House and Garden* (March 1925): 72–73.

Bullitt, Orville H., editor. *For the President: Personal and Secret; Correspondence between Franklin D. Roosevelt and William C. Bullitt.* Boston: Houghton Mifflin, 1972.

Bullitt, William C. *It's Not Done.* New York: Harcourt Brace, 1926.

Callaghan, Morley. *That Summer in Paris: Memories of Tangled Friendships with Hemingway, Fitzgerald, and Some Others.* New York: Coward-McCann, 1963.

Charters, Jimmie. *This Must Be the Place: Memoirs of Montparnasse.* As told to Morrill Cody. Edited by Hugh Ford. 1937; rpt. New York: Collier, 1989.

Chisholm, Anne. *Nancy Cunard.* New York: Knopf, 1979.

Churchill, Allen. *The Improper Bohemians: A Re-Creation of Greenwich Village in Its Heyday.* New York: E. P. Dutton, 1959.

Cowley, Malcolm. *Exile's Return: A Literary Saga of the 1920s.* New York: Viking, 1951.

Crosby, Caresse. *The Passionate Years.* New York: Dial Press, 1953.

Cunard, Nancy. *These Were the Hours.* Carbondale: Southern Illinois University Press, 1969.

Davidson, Jo. *Between Sittings: An Informal Autobiography.* New York: Dial Press, 1951.

Day, Dorothy. *The Long Loneliness: The Autobiography of Dorothy Day.* 1952; rpt. Garden City, N.Y.: Doubleday, 1961.

DeFranzo, A. J., J. H. Hall, Jr., and S. M. Herring. "Adiposis Dolorosa (Dercum's disease): liposuction as an effective form of treatment." *Journal of Plastic Reconstructive Surgery.* (September 1990): 289–92.

Dell, Floyd. *Homecoming: An Autobiography.* New York: Farrar and Rinehart, 1933.

———. *Love in Greenwich Village.* New York: George H. Doran, 1924.

Diliberto, Gioia. *Hadley.* New York: Ticknor & Fields, 1992.

Deutsch, Helen, and Stella Hanau. *The Provincetown: A Story of the Theatre.* New York: Farrar and Rinehart, 1931.

Donaldson, Scott. *Archibald MacLeish: An American Life.* Boston: Houghton Mifflin, 1992.

Draper, Theodore. *The Roots of American Communism.* New York: Viking, 1957.

Drinnon, Richard. *Rebel in Paradise: A Biography of Emma Goldman.* 1961; rpt. Chicago: University of Chicago Press, 1982.

————, and Anna Maria Drinnon, editors. *Nowhere At Home: Letters from Exile of Emma Goldman and Alexander Berkman.* New York: Schocken Books, 1975.

Dwight, H. G. *Constantinople Old and New.* New York: Charles Scribner's Sons, 1915.

Eastman, Max. *Enjoyment of Living.* New York: Harper and Brothers, 1948.

————. *Heroes I Have Known.* New York: Simon and Schuster, 1942.

————. *Love and Revolution: My Journey through an Epoch.* New York: Random House, 1964.

Faderman, Lillian. *Surpassing the Love of Men: Romantic Friendship and Love Between Women from the Renaissance to the Present.* New York: William Morrow, 1981.

Farnsworth, Beatrice. *William C. Bullitt and the Soviet Union.* Bloomington: Indiana University Press, 1967.

Field, Agnes. *The Legacy of John Henry Trullinger.* Astoria, Oreg.: Clatsop Historical Society, 1989.

Field, Andrew. *Djuna: The Formidable Miss Barnes.* Austin: University of Texas Press, 1985.

Fitch, Noël Riley. *Sylvia Beach and the Lost Generation: A History of Literary Paris in the Twenties and Thirties.* New York: W. W. Norton, 1983.

Fitzgerald, F. Scott. *Babylon Revisited and Other Stories.* New York: Charles Scribner's Sons, 1971.

Flanner, Janet. "Mr. Ambassador" and "Mr. Ambassador — II." *The New Yorker.* December 10 and 17, 1938; 30–33 and 22–27.

Flexner, Eleanor. *Centuries of Struggle: The Women's Rights Movement in the United States.* 1959; rpt. New York: Atheneum, 1973.

Flynn, Elizabeth Gurley. *I Speak for Myself: The Autobiography of "The Rebel Girl."* New York: Masses and Mainstream, 1955.

Ford, Ford Madox. *It Was the Nightingale.* 1934; rpt. New York: Ecco Press, 1961.

Ford, Hugh. *Four Lives in Paris.* San Francisco: North Point Press, 1987.

————. *The Left Bank Revisited: Selections from the Paris Tribune 1917–1934.* University Park: Pennsylvania State University Press, 1972.

Frank, Waldo. *Time Exposures.* New York: Boni and Liveright, 1926.

Frazier, Winifred L. *E.G. and E.G.O.: Emma Goldman and The Iceman Cometh.* Gainesville: University Presses of Florida, 1974.

Freeman, Joseph. *An American Testament: A Narrative of Rebels and Romantics.* New York: Farrar and Rinehart, 1936.

Friede, Donald. *The Mechanical Angel.* New York: Knopf, 1948.

Freud, Sigmund, and William C. Bullitt. *Thomas Woodrow Wilson, Twenty-eighth President of the United States: A Psychological Study.* Boston: Houghton Mifflin, 1967.

Gardner, Virginia. *Friend and Lover: The Life of Louise Bryant.* New York: Horizon Press, 1982.

Gay, Peter. *Freud: A Life for Our Time.* New York: Norton, 1988.

Gelb, Barbara. *So Short a Time: A Biography of John Reed and Louise Bryant.* 1973; rpt. New York: Berkeley Books, 1981.

————, and Arthur Gelb. *O'Neill.* 1962; rpt. New York: Dell, 1964.

Gentry, Curt. *J. Edgar Hoover: The Man and His Secrets.* New York: W. W. Norton, 1991.

Gitlow, Benjamin. *The Whole of Their Lives: Communism in America — A Personal History and Intimate Portrayal of Its Leaders.* New York: Charles Scribner's Sons, 1948.

Glaspell, Susan. *The Road to the Temple.* New York: Frederick A. Stokes, 1927.

Glassco, John. *Memories of Montparnasse.* New York: Oxford University Press, 1970.

Goldman, Emma. *Living My Life.* 1931; rpt. Garden City, N.Y.: Garden City Publishing, 1934.

Guggenheim, Margaret (Peggy). *Out of This Century.* New York: Dial Press, 1946.

Hamnett, Nina. *Laughing Torso: Reminiscences.* New York: Long and Smith, 1932.

Hansen, Arlen. *Expatriate Paris: A Cultural and Literary Guide to Paris of the 1920s.* New York: Arcade, 1990.

Hapgood, Hutchins. *A Victorian in the Modern World.* New York: Harcourt Brace, 1939.

Hardwick, Elizabeth. "A Bunch of Reds." In *Bartleby in Manhattan and Other Essays.* New York: Random House, 1983.

Held, J. L., J. A. Andrew, and S. R. Kohn. "Surgical amelioration of Dercum's disease: a report and review." *Journal of Dermatologic Surgery and Oncology.* (December 1989): 1294–96.

Heller, Adele, and Lois Rudnick, editors. *1915: The Cultural Moment.* New Brunswick, N.J.: Rutgers University Press, 1991.

Hemingway, Ernest. "Old Constan." In *By-Line: Ernest Hemingway,* edited by William White, 1967; rpt. New York: Bantam, 1970.

Hicks, Granville. *John Reed: The Making of a Revolutionary.* New York: Macmillan, 1936.

Huddleston, Sisley. *Back to Montparnasse: Glimpses of Broadway in Bohemia.* Philadelphia: J. P. Lippincott, 1931.

Hulme, Kathryn C. *Undiscovered Country: A Spiritual Adventure.* Boston: Little Brown, 1966.

Hulse, James W. *The Nevada Adventure: A History.* Reno: University of Nevada Press, 1978.

Imbs, Bravig. *Confessions of Another Young Man.* New York: Henkle-Yewdale, 1936.

Jolas, Eugene. *I Have Seen Monsters and Angels.* Paris: Transition Press, 1938.

Jones, Margaret C. *Heretics and Hellraisers: Women Contributors to* The Masses, *1911–1917.* Austin: University of Texas Press, 1993.

Josephson, Matthew. *Life Among the Surrealists.* New York: Holt, Rinehart and Winston, 1962.

Kaplan, Justin. *Lincoln Steffens: A Biography.* New York: Simon and Schuster, 1974.

Kennan, George F. *Memoirs: 1925–1950.* Boston: Little, Brown, 1967.

———. *Russia Leaves the War.* 1956; rpt. New York: Atheneum, 1967.

Kluver, Billy, and Julie Martin. *Kiki's Paris.* New York: Harry N. Abrams, 1989.

Kohner, Frederick. *Kiki of Montparnasse.* London: Cassell, 1968.

Lanery, Al. *Paris Herald: The Incredible Newspaper.* New York: Appleton-Century, 1947.

Langner, Lawrence. *The Magic Curtain: The Story of a Life in Two Fields, Theatre and Invention.* New York: E. P. Dutton, 1951.

Le Gallienne, Richard. *From a Paris Scrapbook.* New York: Ives Washburn, 1939.

Lewis, Bernard. *The Emergence of Modern Turkey.* 1961; rpt. Oxford: Oxford University Press, 1972.

Lueders, Edward. *Carl Van Vechten and the Twenties.* Albuquerque: University of New Mexico Press, 1955.

Luhan, Mabel Dodge. *Movers and Shakers.* 1936; rpt. Albuquerque: University of New Mexico Press, 1985.

Lukacs, John. *Philadelphia: Patricians and Philistines, 1900–1950.* New York: Farrar, Straus and Giroux, 1981.

Lynn, Kenneth. *Hemingway.* New York: Simon and Schuster, 1987.

McAlmon, Robert, and Kay Boyle. *Being Geniuses Together: 1920–1930.* San Francisco: North Point Press, 1984.

———. *Robert E. McAlmon and the Lost Generation: A Self-Portrait.* Edited by Robert E. Knoll. Lincoln: University of Nebraska Press, 1962.

MacColl, E. Kimbark. *The Shaping of a City: Business and Politics in Portland, Oregon, 1895–1915.* Portland: Georgian Press, 1976.

McKay, Claude. *A Long Way from Home.* 1937; rpt. New York: Harcourt, Brace and World, 1970.

Madison, Charles A. *Critics and Crusaders: A Century of American Protest.* 1949; rpt. New York: Frederick Ungar, 1959.

Maugham, Somerset. *The Razor's Edge.* Garden City, N.Y.: Doubleday, 1943.

Mohan, Hugh J., E. H. Clough, and John P. Cosgrave. *Pen Pictures of Some Representative Men of Our Time.* Sacramento, Calif.: H. A. Weaver's Valley Press, 1880.

Monroe, Harriet. *A Poet's Life: Seventy Years in a Changing World.* New York: Macmillan, 1938.

Moore, Grace. *You're Only Human Once.* Garden City, N.Y.: Doubleday, 1944.

Moorehead, Alan. *The Russian Revolution.* New York: Harper and Brothers, 1958.

Morton, Brian T. *Americans in Paris: An Anecdotal Street Guide.* Ann Arbor, Mich.: Olivia and Hill, 1984.

Munson, Gorham. *The Awakening Twenties: A Memoir-History of a Literary Period.* Baton Rouge: Louisiana State University Press, 1985.

Northshield, Jane, editor. *History of Croton-on-Hudson, New York.* Croton-on-Hudson Bicentennial Committee, 1976.

O'Neill, William, editor. *Echoes of Revolt:* The Masses *1911–1917.* Chicago: Quadrangle Books, 1966.

————. *The Last Romantic: A Life of Max Eastman.* New York: Oxford University Press, 1978.

Parry, Albert. *Garrets and Pretenders: A History of Bohemianism in America.* 1933; rpt. New York: Dover, 1960.

Poiret, Paul. *King of Fashion: The Autobiography of Paul Poiret.* Translated by Stephen Haden Guest. Philadelphia: J. P. Lippincott, 1931.

The Provincetown Plays. 1st series. New York: Frank Shay, 1916.

Putnam, Samuel. *Paris Was Our Mistress: Memories of a Lost and Found Generation.* 1947; rpt. Carbondale: Southern Illinois University Press, 1970.

Rascoe, Burton. *Before I Forget.* Garden City, N.Y.: Doubleday, Doran, 1937.

————. *We Were Interrupted.* Garden City, N.Y.: Doubleday, 1947.

Reed, John. *Ten Days That Shook the World.* 1919; rpt. New York: Modern Library, 1935.

Reynolds, Michael. *Hemingway: The American Homecoming.* Cambridge, Mass.: Basil Blackwell, 1992.

Rodker, John. *Memories of Other Fronts.* London: Putnam, 1932.

Root, Waverley. *The Paris Edition 1927–1934.* San Francisco: North Point Press, 1989.

Rosenberg, Rosalind. *Beyond Separate Spheres: Intellectual Roots of Modern Feminism.* New Haven: Yale University Press, 1982.

Rosenstone, Robert A. *Romantic Revolutionary: A Biography of John Reed.* Cambridge, Mass.: Harvard University Press, 1990.

Rudnick, Lois Palken. *Mabel Dodge Luhan: New Woman, New Worlds.* Albuquerque: University of New Mexico Press, 1984.

Sachs, Maurice. *The Decade of Illusion, Paris 1918–1928.* New York: Knopf, 1933.

Samuels, Ernest. *Bernard Berenson: The Making of a Legend.* Cambridge, Mass.: Harvard University Press, 1987.

Sarlós, Robert Károly. *Jig Cook and the Provincetown Players: Theatre in Ferment.* Amherst: University of Massachusetts Press, 1982.

Schmitt, Martin. "Portrait of a Pioneer Radical." *Old Oregon.* (January/February 1970): 19–23.

Schwarz, Judith. *Radical Feminists of Heterodoxy: Greenwich Village 1912–1940.* New Lebanon, N.H.: New Victoria Publishers, 1982.

Scudder, Janet. *Modeling My Life.* New York: Harcourt Brace, 1925.

Sheaffer, Louis. *O'Neill: Son and Playwright.* Boston: Little, Brown, 1968.

Sheean, Vincent. *Personal History.* 1934; rpt. Boston: Houghton Mifflin, 1969.

Sheridan, Clare. *My American Diary.* New York: Boni and Liveright, 1922.

Shirer, William. *Twentieth Century Journey: A Memoir of a Life and the Times.* 1976; rpt. New York: Bantam, 1985.

Simonson, Lee. *Minor Prophecies.* New York: Harcourt Brace, 1927.

Slocombe, George. *The Tumult and the Shouting.* New York: Macmillan, 1936.

————. *Paris in Profile.* Boston: Houghton Mifflin, 1929.

Sochen, June. *The New Woman: Feminism in Greenwich Village, 1910–1920.* Chicago: Quadrangle Books, 1972.

Stearns, Harold E. *The Street I Know.* New York: Lee Furman, 1935.

Steffens, Lincoln. *The Autobiography of Lincoln Steffens,* vol. 2. New York: Harcourt Brace, 1931.

Strong, Anna Louise. *I Change Worlds: The Remaking of an American.* New York: Henry Holt, 1935.

Thayer, Charles W. *Bears in the Caviar.* Philadelphia: J. P. Lippincott, 1951.

Tileston, Wilder. "Obesity." *Endocrinology and Metabolism,* edited by Llewellys F. Barker, 29–50. New York: D. Appleton, 1922.

Trimberger, Ellen Kay. "Feminism, Men, and Modern Love: Greenwich Village, 1900–1925." In *Powers of Desire: The Politics of Sexuality,* 131–52, edited by Ann Snitow, Christine Stansell, and Sharon Thompson. New York: Monthly Review Press, 1983.

U.S. Congress, Senate, Subcommittee of the Committee on the Judiciary. *German Propaganda and the Brewing and Liquor Industries and Bolshevik Propaganda: Hearings and Report.* 66th Cong., 1st sess. Washington: Government Printing Office, 1919.

Vorse, Mary Heaton. *Time and the Town: A Provincetown Chronicle.* New York: Dial Press, 1942.

Watson, Steven. *Strange Bedfellows: The First American Avant-Garde.* New York: Abbeville Press, 1991.

Wertheim, Arthur Frank. *The NY Little Renaissance: Iconoclasm, Modernism, and Nationalism in American Culture.* New York: New York University Press, 1976.

Wickes, George. *The Amazon of Letters: The Life and Loves of Natalie Barney.* New York: G. P. Putnam's Sons, 1976.

Williams, Albert Rhys. *Journey into Revolution: Petrograd, 1917–1918.* Chicago: Quadrangle Books, 1969.

Williams, William Carlos. *The Autobiography of William Carlos Williams.* New York: Random House, 1951.

Wilson, Robert Forrest. *Paris on Parade.* Indianapolis: Bobbs Merrill, 1924.

Winnick, R. H., editor. *Letters of Archibald MacLeish.* Boston: Houghton Mifflin, 1983.

Winter, Ella, and Granville Hicks, editors. *The Letters of Lincoln Steffens.* New York: Harcourt Brace, 1938.

Wiser, William. *The Crazy Years: Paris in the Twenties.* 1983; rpt. New York: Thames and Hudson, 1990.

Wolfe, Bertram D. *Three Who Made a Revolution.* 1948; rpt. New York: Dell, 1964.

Wood, Clement. *Greenwich Village Blues.* New York: H. Harrison, 1926.

Wood, Erskine. "Life of Charles Erskine Scott Wood." N.p., 1978.

Young, Art. *Art Young: His Life and Times.* New York: Sheridan House, 1959.

———. *On My Way.* New York: Horace Liveright, 1928.

Zorach, William. *Art Is the Life: The Autobiography of William Zorach.* Cleveland: World Publishing, 1961.

Index